AFTER VALKYRIE

AFTER VALKYRIE
Military and Civilian Consequences of the Attempt to Assassinate Hitler

Don Allen Gregory

McFarland & Company, Inc., Publishers
Jefferson, North Carolina

ISBN (print) 978-1-4766-7152-9
ISBN (ebook) 978-1-4766-3447-0

LIBRARY OF CONGRESS CATALOGUING DATA ARE AVAILABLE

BRITISH LIBRARY CATALOGUING DATA ARE AVAILABLE

© 2019 Don Allen Gregory. All rights reserved

No part of this book may be reproduced or transmitted in any form or by any means, electronic or mechanical, including photocopying or recording, or by any information storage and retrieval system, without permission in writing from the publisher.

Front cover: image of hangman's noose © 2019 lekcej/iStock

Printed in the United States of America

McFarland & Company, Inc., Publishers
Box 611, Jefferson, North Carolina 28640
www.mcfarlandpub.com

For Samantha and Scout,
meine liebsten Töchter

Table of Contents

Preface	1
1. The Beginning of the End	7
2. Prehistory: Assassination Attempts and Resistance Groups	21
3. Investigations and Deceptions	48
4. Courts and Judges	66
5. Trials by Any Other Name	77
6. Suicides, Attempted Suicides and Unexplained Deaths	157
7. Survivors	167
8. The Beginning: A Germany Without Hitler or an Officer Corps	203
9. Epilogue and an Outsider's Observations	215
Appendix A: German Titles and Military Ranks	225
Appendix B: Prisoners Transferred from Dachau	226
Appendix C: Erika Canaris' Letter to General William Donovan	231
Appendix D: The Morgenthau Plan	234
Appendix E: The Marshall Speech	238
Bibliography	241
Index	245

"Life is hard for many, but it is hardest if you are unhappy and have no faith. Have faith!"—Adolf Hitler, Nürnberg, September 12, 1936

"While the bombs are falling like that all around the building, I cannot help thinking of God, his judgement, his hand stretched out and his anger not turned away (Isa. 5:25 and 9.11–10.4), and of my own unpreparedness."—Pastor Dietrich Bonhoeffer, Tegel Prison, Berlin, January 29–30, 1944

Preface

Just 284 days after July 20, 1944, when a group of conspirators tried and failed to assassinate Adolf Hitler, the earthly lives of the Third Reich and Hitler himself both came to an abrupt end. The assassination attempt was scene two of the final act of the play that had been running in Europe since January 30, 1933. Scene one had taken place on the beaches of Normandy just six weeks earlier, and scene three would be set in a defeated Germany.

If Stalingrad was the global military turning point in the war for Germany, then July 20 was surely the domestic equivalent. Hitler had promised a classless military and civilian Fatherland even before he became chancellor, and he was about to fulfill that promise. He had been covertly destroying the historic officer class in Germany long before Stalingrad with an "incessant stream of demotions and humiliations" (Speer 489), but the assassination attempt gave him the opportunity to accelerate the purge while also including the nobility and civilian leaders who opposed him. Hitler had despised them all from the beginning, but they were needed in the early years. It was now time to eliminate the lot, in much the same way that he had decimated the SA (Sturmabteilung; the "Brownshirts") leadership a decade earlier. Hitler had his own National Socialist officer corps as replacements, and its members were political as well as military soldiers. They would follow his every order without question.

The newspaper *Die Nachtausgabe*, published by Dr. Robert Ley, leader of the German Labor Front (Deutsche Arbeitsfront; DAF), "was used to feed Hitler's hatred and confirm his fears. A few weeks after the July bomb plot it had screamed hatred of the nobility, the Prussians and the high-born generals who lacked the common-sense, earthy values that Ley parroted back at Hitler on every possible occasion" (quoted in Thomas 84). However, before the assassination conspiracy was discovered to run so deep within the officer class, the opinion was manifestly different: "As early as 24 July, Martin Bormann had warned all Gauleiters that Hitler was anxious that comments about the coup should not degenerate into an all-out attack on the officer corps. Emphasis should be on the assassination attempt as a lone gesture, not on a wide-ranging conspiracy" (Vassiltchikov 218). That authorized position from the chancellery would soon change.

The failed assassination attempt is necessarily the beginning of the present account, with Hitler's survival marking the end of the organized resistance movement in Germany and the visible beginning of the end of the German officer class as well. These stories cannot be separated. The occupation of Germany after the war completed the destruction, when starvation became the great equalizer for all Germans, from the nobility to the defeated foot soldiers and their families—a classless society indeed.

Since the end of the war, no effort has been spared in documenting the events leading up to the assassination attempt and the attempt itself, but less consideration has been given to the aftermath that resulted in arrests, trials, and executions of German civilian and religious leaders, members of the nobility, and military officers. The prosecutions continued right up until Germany's formal surrender, with repercussions of those prosecutions sporadically arising decades afterward.

The publicized fate of prominent members of the officer corps after July 20 had served as a clear warning to those remaining. Despite the Nazi government's specific evidence being a closely guarded secret at the time, the broader investigation of the coup attempt was widely known to be the Gestapo's highest priority even as the Russians approached Berlin. Abundant information is available today on the most famous officer conspirator, Colonel Claus von Stauffenberg, and his summary demise after he was identified, so only a brief account of his role is given in this volume. This story is not about him; by no means did he act alone, and by no means was his death the end of the story. Nor is this particularly a story about the history of the German officer corps or the nobility of the time; there is no shortage of books on either topic. The failed assassination attempt was in reality the beginning of a very different tale, with a cast of thousands, featuring its own heroes and villains. It is the story of the disappearance of Germany's officer class and, for a time, its nobility and civilian leadership, all of which has become Hitler's lesser-known legacy.

> Nothing better illustrates the gangster quality of German political life under the Nazis than the kind of widespread revenge Hitler set in motion after July 20, a large part of it directed at the leadership of the Army, which was the only institution left with enough prestige and power to oppose him [Korda 508].

In researching topics for this account, a significant number of discrepancies were found in the telling and retelling of certain stories, which initially seemed rather peculiar since this is relatively recent history and some of those involved wrote their stories soon after the events occurred. As has often been said, however, much of this history is an intentionally tangled web—tangled during the war by those who desired to conceal their involvement in the resistance, and then tangled after the war by those who wished to enlarge it. There is considerable evidence to support this assessment. Nonetheless, it is possible today to reliably reconstruct and connect important events and related biographies of the principal characters, coherently piecing together the post–July 20 history. Bits of this twisted story are usually relegated to the last pages of the last chapter of books written fifty or more years ago.

There is an old maxim, quoted by Winston Churchill (although it certainly did not originate with him), that history is written by the victors, but it seems that after World War II the vanquished did a lot of writing as well, and no small amount of it was self-serving. At least one member of the resistance, who turned author after the war, confesses the premise up front:

> In any case the historian must not wait until the legend is established. He must seek to shape the historical picture of our times even if he runs the risk of becoming subconsciously involved in the political struggle he describes, of re-opening wounds that have barely healed, and of raising against him angry protests from more than one side, for he cannot escape speaking from a political and moral viewpoint and confessing where he stands [Ritter 8].

History also evolves. Some stories get retold and inflated, while others are rarely told and diminish with time. Were the conspirators traitors or heroes? Literally, they were traitors, and some admitted as much, in many instances confessing to treason against the legally elected government even before they were arrested. The general public and the rank-and-file military largely agreed with this assessment at the time and, indeed, for decades after the war. German courts ruled that widows of the conspirators were to be denied pension benefits available to every other war widow (*Newsweek*, August 6, 2014), while some former members of the resistance were excluded from serving in the postwar military because of their acts of treason (von Gersdorff 210). However, history is the final judge, and it is apparent that history has cast its temporal vote toward classifying these men as heroes. If German president Joachim Gauck's 2014 seventieth-anniversary commemoration of the assassination attempt is any indication, the conspirators' status is secure (at least for the present generation). Perhaps there is something yet to be learned, however, by looking at the one-time traitors as mortal men with their own individual reasons for wanting to outlive Hitler.

Just who were these would-be assassins and their networks of resistance supporters; where did they come from, and what happened to them after July 20? Some of them were fearless and dedicated to their causes, while others were not; many were even members of the Nazi party (the *Nationalsozialistische Deutsche Arbeiterpartei*; the National Socialist German Workers' Party). Others "had previously participated in the war of racial extermination, or had at least approved of it for quite a time and in some cases had actively promoted it" (Mommsen 250). Some with streets and buildings named for them today could easily have been tried for war crimes had they survived. Indeed, many were solid supporters of Hitler until the war started going badly for Germany. Sir John Wheeler-Bennett, who could turn a phrase like a sharp knife, put it very succinctly more than fifty years ago in describing the number and quality of those in the resistance: "It must, however, be emphasized and reiterated that 'those who held their heads above the crowd' were pitifully few ... even when all these are taken together and full due is paid to them for their courage, the number is small beyond belief in a nation of eighty million." He goes on to say, about those who would plan in detail but never act, "The Führer and his regime were clearly not to be conjured away by moral influence" (Wheeler-Bennett 389). Wehrmacht Captain Hermann Kaiser, one of the conspirators, wrote similarly in his diary on February 20, 1943, regarding the generals who were hesitant to commit, "One is ready to act when he is ordered to do so; another is ready to give orders when action has been taken" (quoted in Zeller 424).

The internet has proved to be a great source of information, as well as misinformation, where anyone can write anything with little or no validation. However, some of the more academic websites and those managed by reputable groups are genuinely credentialed and stand out as flowers among the weeds. Much use has been made of these sources in writing this story, and they are cited when appropriate, along with some of the references they include. Initial sources for many of the short biographies were website for the following groups: the German Resistance Memorial Center, the Jewish Virtual Library, the World War II Database, the Knight's Cross index (provided at www.das-ritterkreuz.de), and the Deutsches Historisches Museum. Often they were the major sources for some of the less well-known characters, and their use is indicated when appropriate. Particularly useful was the German website *Allgemeine Deutsche Biographie & Neue Deutsche Biographie*, which contains digitized pages from the Duncker & Humblot (Berlin) published book of the same name. A point was made of checking any website's references in important matters involving the principal characters and that often led to primary sources.

Other (sometimes) revealing stories are contained in long-out-of-print books that, even with the internet, are difficult to find (or pay for), and a few of them are excerpted here. It was soon discovered in reading the history that some of the currently accepted accounts that often superficially reference these older books are not verifiable with any certainty—which is unfortunately standard for much of the recorded history of the Third Reich. A few of the stories that were found to have dubious pedigrees, obvious bias, or important mistakes are identified in this book, with the discrepancies noted and corrected when possible. (Some are interesting reading in spite of their cavalier treatment of facts.) Websites that were found to be generally useful (and reliable) sources of information and additional references are likewise cited.

It is not possible in a single general interest book to detail the life stories of all the reported thousands of officers and civilians who were arrested or executed as a result of the July 20 assassination attempt, most of whom had nothing directly to do with these events. Therefore, a few have been chosen to represent the many: those from the military, the nobility, the political opposition, the church, and ordinary citizens (there were a few) who found themselves caught up in the investigations. Some are well known, while others will have their stories committed to paper here for the first time. As to the motives of individual conspirators, they are as varied as their circumstances. Some of those bent on ending Hitler's rule cited humanitarian concerns, particularly for the Jews, while others condemned his mismanagement of the war. As one modern historian observes, "Humanitarian concerns were probably mixed with much more pragmatic considerations, for even the best have morally confused motives" (Burleigh 711).

It has been said, disparagingly, that many writers of history simply read twenty books and then write the twenty-first based on what they have read. There were actually about twenty core books used in this investigation, but another two hundred sources had that one bit of information needed to complete a story. In the modern vernacular, the process of writing this book might be called "data mining." Several dozen books are required to finally satisfy one's curiosity about who the conspirators were, where they came from, what happened to them, and the immediate consequence of their actions. There is no single source (preferably in English) that provides this information. This book is meant to fill part of that void for those interested in the details. Nevertheless, this is history and, as such, important specifics should still be referenced, but some are so well known, even to casual readers, that including references for them would be superfluous. The decision regarding what should and should not be referenced was made after reading contemporary books on related topics, with any significant omissions that remain being my own. A list of references used is included and websites are given when cited in the text. The reader will also encounter a number of German words and titles. Often they are words that have become integrated into English over the years, such as *verboten* and *Feldmarschal* (field marshal); a glossary of conspicuous German titles is provided in Appendix A, which also includes military rank equivalents. German spellings are used throughout except when confusion might result, so the "ß" for "ss" and umlauts (¨) will be seen.

With a brief prehistory introduction, the events recounted here are the reconstructed stories of what happened in Germany *after* July 20 through the end of the war and immediately following, told through a number of brief (and often interconnected) biographical sketches and other reasonably verifiable written accounts. This is necessarily the story of the destruction of Germany's officer class, which had arguably existed since the reign of Frederick William I (1713–1740), more than two centuries before the Nazis came to power. The descendants of those Prussians figure prominently in the present account. These are also the stories of the survivors of the July 20 purge and those who prosecuted them, those who were never captured, those who committed suicide or died at the hands of their saviors, and those who were held in prisons and concentration camps until liberated after the war. The journey here necessarily begins with the end and ends with the beginning—the beginning of what would have been unimaginable before the war's end: a Germany without Hitler and a Germany without an officer class.

Special thanks are due Mr. Wilhelm R. Gehlen, my coauthor on three previous books—*Jungvolk, Two Soldiers, Two Lost Fronts,* and *Hitler's Home Front*—for help in some complicated translations, as well as guidance from one who lived through this period of German history. Lastly, this book would not have been possible (or, in any case, would not have been readable by anyone with an academic inclination) without the assistance of Sharlene D. Bruce, who managed to create an acceptable format for the manuscript and references.

1

The Beginning of the End

Late on the night of Thursday, July 20, 1944 (1:00 a.m. on July 21), every German near a radio, from the military to the nobility to the average Bürger on the street, would have heard the unmistakable voice of their Führer, Adolf Hitler. The rest of the world was listening as well (Shirer, *Rise and Fall*, 1069; Manvell and Fraenkel, *The Men Who Tried*, 155; and Manvell 132).

> My comrades, Men and Women of the German People:
> By now I do not know how many times an assassination has been planned and attempted against me. I speak to you today first in order that you should hear my voice and know that I am unhurt and well, and secondly, that you should know of a crime unparalleled in German history.
> A very small clique of ambitious, irresponsible and, at the same time, senseless and stupid officers concocted a plot to eliminate me, and with me, the staff of the High Command of the Wehrmacht.
> The bomb planted by Colonel Count Stauffenberg exploded two meters to the right of me. It seriously wounded a number of my true and loyal collaborators, one of whom has died. I myself am entirely unhurt, aside from some very minor scratches, bruises and burns. I regard this as a confirmation of the task imposed upon me by Providence.
> The conspirators have very much deceived themselves. The allegation by these usurpers that I am no longer alive is contradicted by this very moment in which I speak to you, my dear comrades. The circle of these usurpers is very small and has nothing in common with the spirit of the German Wehrmacht and, above all, none with the German people. It is a gang of criminal elements which will be destroyed without mercy.
> I therefore give orders now that no military authority is to obey orders from this crew of usurpers. I also order that it is everyone's duty to arrest, or, if they resist, to shoot at sight, anyone issuing or handling such orders.
> To create order, I have appointed Reichsminister [Heinrich] Himmler Commander of the Reserve Army. I am convinced that with the disappearance of this very small clique of traitors and conspirators, we are finally creating in the homeland the atmosphere which the fighters at the front need. It is unthinkable that at the front, hundreds of thousands, no, millions of good men, should be giving their all while a small gang of ambitious and miserable creatures here at home tries perpetually to sabotage them. This time we shall settle accounts with them in the manner to which we National Socialists are accustomed.
> Probably only a few can imagine what fate would have befallen Germany if the plot had succeeded. I thank Providence and my Creator, but not because He has preserved me. My life is solely devoted to worry, to working for my people. I thank Him, rather because He has made it possible for me to continue to shoulder these worries, and to pursue my work to the best of my abilities and according to my conscience.
> Once again I take this opportunity, my old comrades in arms, to greet you, joyful that I have once again been spared a fate which, while it held no terror for me personally, would have had

terrible consequences for the German People. I interpret this as a sign from Providence that I must continue my work, and therefore I shall continue it.

These words, spoken in just six minutes, were pure unspun Hitler, with a small group of German officers clearly to blame for the attempt on his life. The Reich propaganda minister, Dr. Joseph Goebbels, was not there at the time to write or edit what Hitler would say. Instead, he was in Berlin trying to manage the chaos of the day, and no doubt he and other high-ranking Nazis were pondering the "what ifs" this situation had raised: What if the assassination attempt had been successful? What if the military coup taking place prevailed and led to popular civilian uprisings? Who would speak for the National Socialists remaining? Surely not Himmler, and Hermann Göring was not nearly as popular as he once was—not since the incessant bombing by the British and the Americans began. Hamburg had been substantially destroyed a year before, with 50,000 people reportedly killed. By this time, almost everyone in Germany knew someone who had been killed or injured in an air raid. Goebbels was neither liked nor trusted, and the military would not tolerate him as commander of the armed forces. So, who would lead the National Socialist Party? It was a serious question that all high-ranking party members knew the answer to, though none wanted to admit it: without Adolf Hitler, there would be no National Socialist Party. There was no heir apparent—not even a deputy Führer, since Hitler had abolished the position after Rudolf Hess took off for Scotland on May 10, 1941.

Certainly Goebbels could have written a better speech than the one Hitler gave (as he would do later), but the words of Germany's Führer were very clear to all who heard his voice that night, and they set the stage for what would come in the following months. It was an unpronounced death sentence for the prominent members of the conspiracy—from Berlin to Vienna and Paris—and a warning to everyone else that Hitler was still very much in charge. He had survived, and with him the National Socialist Party, but the leader of the Greater German Reich had been shaken; he would never again speak in public to his people.

The above translation of Hitler's speech should be compared to the one provided below, which was no doubt hurriedly published by *The Guardian* on July 21, 1944 (www.theguardian.com/theguardian/1944/jul/21/fromthearchive). There are subtle, yet significant, differences in content that cannot be explained by ever-present variations in translation.

> In his broadcast speech this morning Hitler said:
>
> "For the third time an attempt on my life has been planned and carried out. If I speak to you to-day it is, first in order that you should hear my voice and that you should know that I myself am unhurt and well; second, in order that you should know about a crime unparalleled in German history. The claim made by the usurpers that I am no longer alive is being contradicted at this very moment now that I am speaking to you.
>
> "A very small clique of ambitious, irresponsible, and at the same time senseless and criminally stupid officers have formed a plot to eliminate me and with me, the German Wehrmacht command.
>
> "The bomb was placed by Colonel Graf von Stauffenberg. A number of collaborators very dear to me were very seriously injured. I myself sustained only some very minor scratches, bruises and burns.
>
> "The bombs exploded two metres to my right. One of those with me has died. I myself am completely unhurt.
>
> "I regard this as a confirmation of the task imposed on me by Providence to continue on the road of my life as I have done hitherto. For I may confess to the nation that since the days when

I moved into the Wilhelmstrasse I had only one thought—to dedicate my life ever since I realised that the war could no longer be postponed. I have lived for worry worry, work, and worry only.

"Suddenly at a moment when the German Army are engaged in a bitter struggle a small group emerged in Italy and in German[y] in the belief that they could repeat the 1918 stab in the back. But this time they have made a mistake.

"The circle of these conspirators is very small and has no connection with the German Wehrmacht, and above all none with the German people. It is a miniature group of criminal elements who will now be ruthlessly exterminated.

"I therefore now order that no military authority, no leader of any unit, no private in the field is to obey any orders emanating from these groups of usurpers.

"I also order that it is everyone's duty to arrest, or if they resist, to kill at sight anyone issuing or handing on such orders.

"I order that no civil authority is to accept orders from any official post usurped by these usurpers....

"I have therefore, to create order once and for all, nominated Reich Minister Himmler to be Commander-in-Chief of the Home Army. I have summoned Colonel General [Heinz] Guderian to join my General Staff and to replace the Chief of the General staff, who has been taken to hospital.

"Another proved Easter[n] Front commander has been called in by me to assist him. There has been no change in any other office in the Reich.

"Orders have been issued to all troops. These will be blindly executed in accordance with the obedience characteristic of the Wehrmacht....

"I am convinced that with the emergence of this quite tiny clique of traitors and destroyers there has at long last been created in our rear that atmosphere which the fighting front needs. For is it possible that out there hundreds of thousands and millions of brave men sacrifice their lives while at home a small, filthy ambitious, self-seeking group should seek to sow the seeds of despair?

"This time we shall get quits with them in the way that National Socialists are accustomed. I am convinced that every decent officer, every gallant soldier, will comprehend this at this hour.

"What fate would have been in store for Germany had this attempt on my life succeeded is too horrible to think of.

"Every German, therefore, quite irrespective of who he may be, has the duty ruthlessly to call to book these elements at once, either to arrest them promptly, or, if they should offer resistance of any kind, immediately to wipe them out.

"It has again been granted to me that I should escape a fate which would have been terrible, not for me but for the German police. They see in this again the pointing finger of Providence, that I must and will carry on with my work."

Hitler's speech was announced by the Berlin radio stations only ten minutes before he was on the air. He spoke slowly and haltingly at first. He sounded tired and seemed breathless. Towards the end he began shouting excitedly.

Reichsmarshal Göring spoke after Hitler (quoted in Zeller 342):

Comrades in the Luftwaffe, today an unbelievably squalid attempt to kill our Führer was made by one Colonel Count Stauffenberg, on orders from a miserable clique of ex-generals who had to be thrown out because of their poor and cowardly leadership. As if by miracle, the Führer was saved by omnipotent Providence. Now these criminal usurpers are trying to cause confusion among the troops by putting out false orders. Any officers or other ranks, and civilians too, who act on behalf of these criminals and approach you to win you over for their abominable schemes must be immediately apprehended and shot.

Wherever you yourselves are given the task of wiping out those traitors you must act ruthlessly. They are the same wretches that have been trying to betray and sabotage the front.

Any officers involved in this crime have forfeited their place among the people, and the Wehrmacht, their honor as soldiers, and have broken their oath of allegiance. Their destruction will give us new strength. The Luftwaffe will set its pledged loyalty and deep affection for the Führer against this treachery and will go all out for victory. Long live our Führer, on whom Almighty God has today bestowed his patent blessing!

Großadmiral Karl Dönitz was last to speak (quoted in Zeller 343):

> Men of the Navy, we are consumed with holy wrath and boundless fury at the criminal attempt on our Führer's life. But Providence has willed otherwise. It has protected and preserved the Führer for the German Fatherland in its fateful struggle.
>
> A small clique of mad generals, having nothing in common with our brave Army, instigated this murder in cowardly disloyalty, committing the most dastardly treachery against the Führer and the German people. For these criminals are nothing but the stooges of our enemies whom they serve with unprincipled, cowardly and false cleverness.
>
> In fact, they are utterly stupid. They think that by removing the Führer they can relieve us of the hard but inescapable struggle that fate has imposed on us, and in their blind and fearful stupidity they do not realize that their crime would plunge us into terrible chaos and deliver us, defenseless, to the enemy. We shall put a stop to the work of these criminals. The Navy, loyal to its oath, stands faithfully by the Führer, and remains unconditionally ready for battle. It will ruthlessly exterminate anyone that turns out to be a traitor. Long live our Führer, Adolf Hitler.

After the attempt on the Führer's life, more than seven thousand people were eventually arrested and as many as five thousand executed after being manhandled by Ernst Kaltenbrunner and his Gestapo or the SS, or else upon direct orders from Hitler or Reichsführer SS Heinrich Himmler (Eberle and Uhl 161). In the first few weeks after July 20, some six hundred people, in addition to those directly involved, were arrested. Operation Thunderstorm (Aktion Gitter), as it was called, began in mid–August and would result in more than five thousand arrests (Fest, *Plotting*, 295).

> There was no direct connection between the 20 July investigations and the mass arrests of 22 August 1944 when some 5,000 ex-parliamentary deputies and officials of the old political parties (including Konrad Adenauer and Kurt Schumacher) were taken into custody in a synchronized operation throughout the Reich and thrown into concentration camps; this had been planned long before by the Gestapo [Hoffmann, *The History*, 516].

A small number of those arrested were brought to trial charged with treason. Others died in prisons or concentration camps with or without trials, mostly with predetermined verdicts. The public had its own opinion of the goings-on and began to doubt the historic sworn loyalty of the officer class—with a little help from the Nazi propaganda machine. It was the second opportunity Hitler had to rid himself of those who threatened his authority. The "Night of the Long Knives" (Operation Hummingbird—*Kolibri* in German) had taken place ten years earlier, and the nonbelievers needed to be purged again. This purge, however, would be a holocaust compared to the first one, decimating the officer class, the nobility, and the ranks of Germany's prominent civilian leadership. There was little distinction made between the three groups, who were all distrusted by the Nazis. The officer class primarily came from the titled nobility, which had its roots in the military of the previous two centuries.

The investigation of the assassination attempt proceeded up to the very end of the war, with some of the conspirators being executed just days before Hitler took his own life. A few of the conspirators imprisoned in the camps while awaiting trial or serving their sentences survived; most did not. Some of those executed have gradually become almost mythical heroes in modern Germany, especially Claus von Stauffenberg. Today there are dozens, if not hundreds, of buildings, schools, train stations, and streets named for members of the conspiracy scattered throughout Germany and what was the Greater German Reich. Plaques and monuments can be found in almost every major German city that had a remote connection to the assassination attempt.

Top: Von Stauffenberg plaque at the house where he lived from 1943 to 1944 on Tristanstraße, Berlin. *Bottom:* Goerdeler plaque, Sybelstraße, Berlin-Charlottenburg.

Helmuth James Graf (count) von Moltke, one of the key civilian resistance leaders, wrote from prison in a letter to his wife that "'their task would now have to be to fabricate their own legend.' In this the conspirators, dead and alive, were successful. Der Juli 20, 1944 has become the alibi of a nation" (quoted in Koch 210). Future generations of Germans would point to the conspirators, once they had become martyrs, as proof that the whole country was not taken in by Hitler—that there were "good" Germans. There were other alibis as well. The SS was universally labeled a criminal organization by the Allies after the war, and surviving Germans with a public voice soon jumped on the bandwagon, attributing all the wartime atrocities committed to that evil Hitler invention, when earlier those same Germans were so very proud of their husbands and sons who were selected to serve in it. Nazi judges were often convenient scapegoats as well, blamed after the war for the imprisonment and execution of the "good" Germans and earning their own trials at Nürnberg; in reality, most of those judges were not allowed to resign and were routinely told in advance by their Nazi handlers what the verdicts would be in major trials. Then there is the all-encompassing "I was only following orders" alibi, which in fact was rarely (if ever) used as a serious defense—only as a statement of fact. It is a Western distortion of the faithfulness to the oath of loyalty that was sworn by every member of the German military, regardless of rank. Had the war ended differently, Allied military personnel would likely have been accused of using the same argument as justification for certain questionable actions taken during the conflict.

The conspiracy reached deep into the Third Reich and shook the roots of the most powerful in the National Socialist hierarchy. If Hitler could be assassinated (or nearly so), how safe could any of them be? This was one instance when Hitler surely did have the unwavering support of all those closest to him in positions of power, ranging from local party chiefs to his inner circle. If Hitler were killed and a coup resulted, their authority would surely be eliminated (and probably many of them as well). There was also a war going on that Germany was rapidly losing. Hitler used this failed attempt on his life as a pretext to remove anyone in the established military, civilian, or industrial complex of Germany who opposed him, regardless of whether they had anything directly to do with this (or any other) attempt. Hitler vocally blamed the officers for prior military defeats, and he saw this as his opportunity to rid the country of these defeatist traitors and replace them with true National Socialists. The attempted coup was to be the last time anyone openly challenged his authority. Hitler saw his survival as a sign that he was destined to live on and see the war come to a successful end. No one around Hitler who valued his life saw fit to disagree at the time.

The well-documented Operation Valkyrie (Walküre) was an official emergency plan developed by the Replacement (or Reserve) Armed Forces Office (Wehrersatzamt) and approved by Hitler himself. Excerpts from the plan are provided below. Hitler routinely approved the many modifications of the plan as they arose, and there is no indication of any major changes made by him. *Valkyrie* was also the code word used by the conspirators to set the coup in motion. The plan, as ratified by Hitler, was originally intended to be made operational if the recurrent disruptions caused by the Allied bombing of German cities led to a breakdown in communications and law and order, or (if it became necessary) to put down civil disturbances instigated by the millions of forced laborers from occupied countries then working in Germany. Both were very serious concerns late in the war. Unknown to Hitler, however, the very office assigned to create and oversee Operation Valkyrie was, by 1942, heavily populated by members of the resistance, chief among them General Friedrich Olbricht. He and his minions (notably von Stauffenberg) subtly modified the original Valkyrie plan many times so that it could be used to take control of German cities, disarm the SS, and arrest the Nazi party leadership after the assassination of Hitler. It was a very good plan; however, only General Friedrich Fromm (commander of the Reserve Army) or Hitler himself could put Operation Valkyrie into effect, so it seemed that Fromm had to be convinced to join the conspiracy or otherwise be removed in order for the plan to work. However, there was a third option, which the conspirators eventually employed: forging Fromm's name on the initial order. Fromm knew about the existence of intrigues against Hitler, but he never openly supported the conspirators; however, he did not report them up the chain of command—an omission that would eventually cost him his life.

There was never an actual named "Valkyrie Order." It was, as stated below, a "General Order to the Armed Forces of the State." *Valkyrie* had always been the code word for putting the emergency plan in motion, as well as the name of the overall operation, but the following statement is often referred to as the order itself. The first two specific orders listed are often called Valkyrie I and Valkyrie II, and there is disparity regarding which one was initially transmitted by the conspirators (Hoffmann, *The History*, 681). The order, as published by Wheeler-Bennett and presented here, seems to be an edited version of the teleprint message given elsewhere (Wheeler-Bennett 724; Hoffmann, *The History*, 755). Operational plans of the coup detailing precise assignments and timing surely existed but have not come to light; however, a draft version is available, and the rest can be construed from teletype messages sent by the conspirators from the Bendlerstrasse. The version of the teleprint message given in one published account does not have the first line given below, but it does appear in the version provided in another account (Zimmermann and Jacobsen 131–43; Hoffmann, *The History*, 755). The message from German Naval Headquarters to all officers, intercepted by decoders at Bletchley Park, certainly did have the beginning sentence in it, so it seems to have been a last-minute addition and may not have appeared in all messages sent (see *The Telegraph* [London], July 26, 2003). Hoffmann refers to the following as the message to instigate Valkyrie II (*Stauffenberg*, 269).

I. General Order to the Armed Forces of the State [Wheeler-Bennett 724; von Schlabrendorff, *Revolt*, 96]

   The Führer Adolf Hitler is dead.
   An irresponsible clique of party leaders, strangers to the front, has tried to exploit this situation and to stab the hard-struggling army in the back in order to snatch power for their own selfish ends. In this hour of supreme danger, the Reich Government, for the sake of preserving law and order, has proclaimed a state of military emergency and has entrusted to me both the supreme command of the armed forces and the executive power in the Reich. In this capacity I issue these orders:
   1. I transfer the executive power, with the right of delegation, to the territorial commanders; in the home territory, to the commander in chief of the home army, who has been promoted to commander in chief of the home front; in occupied territories, to the commanders in chief.
   2. To the holders of executive power are subordinated:
      a. all army units within their districts, and army officers, including the Waffen SS, the Reich Labor Service, and the Todt Organization;
      b. the entire civil service of the Reich, the whole security and public order police and police administration;

  c. all officials of branches (Gliederungen) of the NSDAP (National Socialists Workers Party) and associations belonging to it;
  d. lines of communication and supply.
3. The whole of the Waffen SS is to be incorporated immediately into the army.
4. The holders of executive power are responsible for the maintenance of order and public security. Any resistance to the military executive power is to be relentlessly suppressed.
5. In this hour of great peril to our country, close unity in the armed forces and the maintenance of discipline is a paramount necessity. I therefore charge all commanding officers in the army, the navy, and the air force, to give full support to the holders of executive power in the fulfillment of their important duties, and to secure compliance to their orders from all subordinates. To the German soldier, an historic task is entrusted. Whether Germany is to be saved will depend upon his energy and morale.

(Signed) [Erwin] Von Witzleben, Field Marshal
Commander in Chief of the Wehrmacht

  This simple document, which had been amended many times by Olbricht's office, was to be the spark to light the fuse to the bomb that was to blow up the Nazi regime. This is the so-called Valkyrie Order, but in reality it is merely the preamble. Field Marshal von Witzleben had no sanctioned authority to issue such a statement; however, his name was well known throughout the Wehrmacht, and an order from him would be taken seriously. The actual order, complete with Fromm's forged signature, continues (as outlined below) and gets much more interesting, with specific directions from the conspirators to all territorial military authorities, soldiers, and the German people. Unfortunately for the conspirators, not all of these orders were given, and those that were transmitted were soon followed by counter orders from Hitler and the armed forces high command, with the OKW (Oberkommando der Wehrmacht) declaring, "The Führer is alive! In perfect health! Reichsführer SS [Himmler] C in C Replacement Army; only his orders valid. Orders from General Fromm, Field Marshal von Witzleben and Colonel General [Erich] Hoepner not to be executed! Maintain contact with Gauleiter and Senior SS and Police Commander!" (quoted in Moorhouse 266). There were two other ancillary documents from the conspirators intended for release: one was a statement to the press, and the other contained the manuscript for a radio announcement. Neither was transmitted to the relevant conspirators who could have carried out these tasks. Eberhard Zeller states that the appeals to the nation and to the Wehrmacht generally quoted by Fabian von Schlabrendorff and others were earlier versions found together with some of Carl Goerdeler's papers at the Askanischer Hof, not at the Bendlerstrasse on July 20 (Zeller 204).

 II. General Order to Wehrkreis [Military District] Commanders:

  In virtue of the authority given me by the Commander in Chief of the armed forces, I invest the Commanding General with executive power in all military districts. The following immediate measures are to be taken:

Occupation of all transport and communication centers, all radio amplifiers, and broadcasting stations; all gasworks, power stations, and water works.

To be relieved of office forthwith and placed in secure military confinement: all Gauleiters, Reichstatthalters, Ministers, Provincial Governors, Police Presidents, all senior SS and Police Chiefs, Heads of the Gestapo, of the SS Administration, and of the Propaganda Bureau, and all Nazi District Leaders. Exceptions only by my command.

The concentration camps are to be seized at once, the camp commandants are to be arrested, the guards to be disarmed and confined to barracks. The political prisoners are to be instructed that they should, pending their liberation, abstain from demonstration or independent action.

If compliance by leaders of the Waffen SS appears doubtful, or if they appear unsuitable, they are to be taken into protective custody, and replaced by officers of the Army.

Valkyrie message with the first sentence declaring that Hitler is dead.

> To deal with all political questions arising from the state of emergency, I attach a political officer to every military district commander.
> The executive power must tolerate no arbitrary or revengeful acts. The people must be made aware of the difference from the wanton methods of their former rulers.
> (Signed) Fromm, Colonel-General [the signature was forged by the conspirators]
> (Signed) von Stauffenberg

There was also an appeal to the Wehrmacht, an appeal to the German people and even a statement for the press contained within the distributed order (Wheeler-Bennett 726; Pechel 305).

The German military and civilian resistance movement was all but powerless during the rise and peak of Hitler's popularity. With economic recovery and military successes, his public support was overwhelming. The resistance nevertheless had strong leaders, among them Dr. Carl Friedrich Goerdeler, a civilian and former mayor of Leipzig, whose pertinent talent was recruiting members to the resistance and then organizing them into loosely connected groups. The German nobility was represented in men like Ewald von Kleist-Schmenzin (not to be confused with Field Marshal Ewald von Kleist, although they were no doubt distant relatives) and his son Ewald Heinrich, as well as respected legal authorities and intellectuals like Johannes Popitz, Ulrich von Hassell, Professor Jens-Peter Jessen, and Dr. Paul Adolf Franz Lejeune-Jung. Resistance groups also attracted members like General Henning von Tresckow, the well-known lawyer Fabian von Schlabrendorff, and the military intelligence officer Major General Hans Oster. Even conservatives like Hans Bernd Gisevius (of the Gestapo) and union organizers like Julius Leber, who had virtually nothing in common with the military elite or the nobility, joined resistance groups. These were very different men with divergent politics and agendas, and there were multiple reasons why they joined the resistance, but they all shared one goal—removing the National Socialists from power. The various circles, however, did come to recognize Generaloberst Ludwig Beck as their shared leader—at least in military matters. The conspirators would plan for any opportunity to assassinate Hitler, even when it seemed that he could do no wrong on any front. In the east, the military resistance group led by von Tresckow attempted to assassinate Hitler in "Operation Spark," which failed only because the bomb planted in the airplane carrying him did not explode. The responsibility for the assassination would finally be shifted to von Stauffenberg and his many attempts, ending with the events of July 20.

Pottsdam's Infantry Regiment 9 deserves special mention in any history of the resistance because so many of the principal players served in this group during their careers. This regiment had a long history of being populated by the nobility and was (derogatorily) referred to as Graf Neun (Count Nine) or Infantry Regiment von Neun because of its distinctive Prussian ancestry. It had always been the core of Germany's officer class and one of the few regiments allowed to exist in the Reichswehr after World War I, primarily because of its history. Nineteen of the conspirators have been identified as coming from this regiment, more than from any other single regiment in the Wehrmacht. Many of the following names will be encountered numerous times in this book.

Lieutenant Colonel Hasso von Böhmer
Major Axel Freiherr von dem Bussche-Streithorst

Carl Goerdeler before Judge Freisler at the People's Court (Bundesarchiv, Bild 151–58-16 / photographer unknown, used with permission).

Captain Dr. Hans Fritzsche
Lieutenant Colonel Helmuth von Gottberg
Lieutenant Colonel Ludwig Freiherr von Hammerstein
Lieutenant Colonel Carl-Hans Graf von Hardenberg
Lieutenant General Paul von Hase
Lieutenant Ewald Heinrich von Kleist-Schmenzin
Colonel Hans Otfried von Linstow
Captain Friedrich Karl Klausing
Major Ferdinand Freiherr von Lünick
Major Herbert Meyer
Lieutenant Georg-Sigismund von Oppen
Major Kurt Freiherr von Plettenberg
Colonel Alexis Freiherr von Rönne
Lieutenant Fritz-Dietlof von der Schulenburg-Tressow
Lieutenant Colonel Gerd von Tresckow
Major General Henning von Tresckow
Lieutenant Colonel Hans-Alexander von Voß
Captain Achim Freiherr von Willisen

So, what were the motives of these desperate and disparate men of the officer class and civilian leadership of Germany? It should be borne in mind that "'Hitler's army' had many discrete niches, where traditional values lingered despite attempts to convert the military into political soldiers" (Burleigh 705). There seem to have been two broad groups among the conspirators: those who concentrated on how best to kill Hitler (including when and where and who would do it), and then there were those who were primarily interested in the political consequences (forming a new government and obtaining the support of the public, the military, and foreign leaders). Within these two large groups, there were at least four subgroups: those who had opposed Hitler from the beginning, particularly the way he had seized power and the way he governed; those who opposed the war, specifically on moral, religious or other grounds; those who did not oppose the war but opposed the way the war was being run; and those who morally opposed Hitler's treatment of the Jews and other people in conquered countries, notwithstanding the war itself.

> [The elite's] rebellion against the regime was inspired in each case by individual motives, among which the national interest played an important part. It is perfectly clear that, as a general rule, the Nazi persecution of the Jews was a minor factor in their decision to commit high treason. This is true even of those on the political left, among whom anti-semitic attitudes were only occasionally to be found. Furthermore, it was never the intention of the KDP [the German Communist party] or leftwing socialist resistance groups to involve Jews in their conspiracies and thus increase the risk of exposure by the Gestapo. Nevertheless, in communist underground propaganda, the importance of the persecution of the Jews should not be underestimated [Mommsen 254].

At trial, many of the conspirators would proclaim their moral objections to the Nazi regime, but this was also after they undoubtedly knew the consequences of their actions. Dr. Goerdeler, Dr. Berthold von Stauffenberg (Claus' brother), Julius Leber, Admiral Wilhelm Canaris, General Hans Oster, Adolf Reichwein, Count von Moltke, Count Peter Yorck von Wartenburg (often referred to simply as von Yorck), Johannes Popitz, Hans von Dohnanyi, Pastor Dietrich Bonhoeffer and many others cited the persecution of the Jews as their primary reason for participating in the coup. However, there were just as many valid reasons for *not* joining the resistance. By the time of von Stauffenberg's attempt, all military ranks had been subjected to intense propaganda to convince them that treason against Hitler, the head of state (*Hochverrat*), was synonymous with treason against the country (*Landesverrat*), and *that* action was something no German soldier could tolerate. Nevertheless, Hitler well knew that the traditional officer corps had a history of prioritizing loyalty to country over any political leader, and he surely anticipated that this loyalty would withstand any attempted indoctrination to the contrary.

The assassination attempt of July 20 was different—very different. This was not a lone idealist with questionable motives, and it wasn't so badly carried out that it could be labeled amateurish or the act of a madman. This time, well-known members of the officer corps were undeniably involved. Today it seems that almost everyone who was anyone in Berlin knew something was afoot long before von Stauffenberg acted. Private Reichspost and Feldpost (military) letters between individuals who were in no way connected to the coup indicate as much. The news, when it finally came on July 20, was a shock only to those who were not so well connected.

The rank-and-file military largely saw the attempt as a blatant act of treason during wartime—case closed. Ordinary Germans, who had already endured five long years of war, saw it as either a military act with political consequences or a political act with military consequences. Whichever was the case, they had other things just as important to worry about, and Hitler would take care of it. Hitler Youth leader Alfons Heck recalled his impression of the general sentiments of the time:

The Führer, his voice harsh with bitterness for the infamy committed by "a few traitorous officers," addressed the nation at one o'clock the following morning, and attributed his miraculous escape to providence. He alone could save Germany from the fury of her enemies. Millions of Germans shared his belief, even as their cities were being turned to rubble. There was widespread, often genuinely spontaneous condemnation of the plotters, with church services and demonstrations of thanksgiving held all over the country. I went to early mass in the morning, something I hadn't done since leaving home, and lit a candle for the Führer [Heck 104].

However, Marie Vassiltchikov disagreed with Heck's assessment, writing in her diary, "Public opinion, however, does not seem to be on the government's side. In the streets people appear pale and downhearted; they seem to scarcely dare look each other in the face" (Vassiltchikov 207). Her brother, George Vassiltchikov, writing in 1985 as a commentator in Marie's book, said that "SD (Sicherheitsdienst, Security Division of the SS) reports on the mood of the population (which came to light after the war and are surprisingly reliable) show that the attempted coup was, in fact, not well received either by the man in the street at home or the military at the front. Even the churches condemned it" (Vassiltchikov 207). Marie was in Berlin, the center of the conspiracy, as details were revealed daily, and her brother's comment came forty years later when much more was known about the events of July 20.

In any case, no amount of propaganda could cover up the reality of bombs falling on all the major German cities. The Greater German Reich was shrinking daily as invasions from the East and the West progressed. German mothers saw their teenage and pre-teen Jungvolk and Hitler Youth sons being trained and sent to cities far away to dig anti-tank ditches, while their daughters were assigned to hospitals and farms, and even their fathers were being drafted into Volkssturm (national militia) battalions. Their husbands and brothers were already on the front somewhere, and many of them had not been heard from in months. Food was becoming scarce and rations were being cut every time the women went to the markets to wait in long lines. The third (and final) call-up of Hitler Youth members for military service occurred not long after July 20. The boys, often no more than ten years old, were quickly trained to use anti-tank Panzerfausts (bazookas) and sent to the front lines. In truth, by this late stage of the war, there were far more important things for the average German citizen (and soldier) to worry about than the state of Hitler's health. The war was coming home to the Reich, and they were scared.

And what was the Allies' reaction to news of the July 20 insurrection? "Immediate Allied reactions to the failed coup were deeply negative. In fact, there was a startling confluence between the Allied attitude toward the resistance and that of Hitler and Goebbels" (von Hassell and MacRae 233). It seemed (publicly at

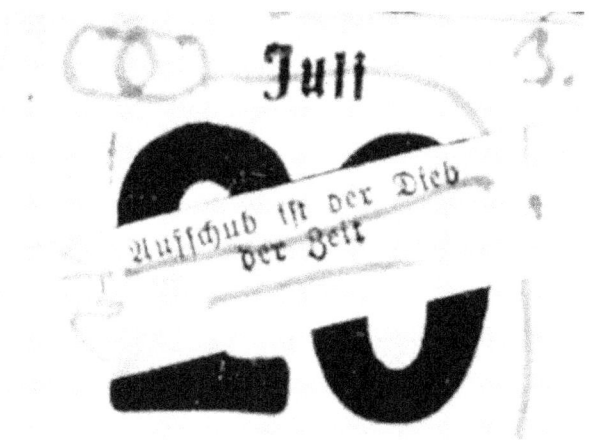

Translation: "Hesitation is the thief of time." This item was cut from a calendar and paperclipped to a letter dated June 6, 1944 (author owned).

least) that the Allies thought no better of the traitors than did the Nazis. The Americans and the British had serious misgivings about trusting the German resistance, if it really existed, and had no desire to support a coup that might result in another totalitarian state after Hitler. President Franklin D. Roosevelt particularly "did not want to support the 'vons' who were so heavily represented in the resistance. American boys were fighting and dying for democracy, not aristocracy" (quoted in von Hassell and MacRae 229). Most British and American newspapers reported the coup attempt as giving Hitler the opportunity to eliminate high-ranking military officers whom the Allies would otherwise be chasing down after the war anyway. There was no publicly declared Allied support for those who had directly participated in the revolt or others who had supported the resistance and were now being rounded up all over Europe.

> On July 26, 1944 a directive from OSS Morale Operations suggested that OSS posts in Europe "give the SS names of all German officers and Nazis known to you and state that they were involved in the putsch. This will have the effect ... of creating confusion in the SS, and liquidating the people denounced." This was entirely in accord with an earlier recommendation from Wheeler-Bennett. In a mid-1943 memorandum for Halifax, entitled: "On What to Do with Germany," Wheeler-Bennett offered his suggestion: the Allies should "stand outside" while the purges went on. "Total occupation ... should not be effected until a beneficial degree of liquidation has been achieved" [Hassell and MacRae 233–34, cited in the National Archives at College Park, MD, RG 226, Entry 134, Box 303; Meehan 402].

An article written by Dr. Robert Ley, which appeared in the *Angriff* on July 23, spelled out how the officer corps would be treated. He made it clear that "the regime had launched a campaign against the old military aristocracy." Ley described them as "degenerate to their very bones, blue-blooded to the point of idiocy, nauseatingly corrupt and cowardly like all nasty creatures; such is the aristocratic clique which the Jew has sicked on National Socialism. We must exterminate this filth, extirpate it root and branch. It is not enough simply to seize the offensive ... we must exterminate the entire breed" (quoted in Speer 498).

2

Prehistory: Assassination Attempts and Resistance Groups

The daylight hours of July 20, 1944, were unremarkable for most Germans, but over the coming night and the next few weeks, details of the assassination attempt spread throughout the highly filtered news media, either by radio or through newspapers. The general public had heard about some of the other earlier attempts and suspected there had been even more. They knew Claus von Stauffenberg was not the first person to try to kill Hitler. In fact, there were seventeen legitimate attempts before the war's end, and a few of them received widespread publicity, though usually not in the official press. Benito Mussolini seemed to think that Hitler himself had something to do with one attempt (Goerlitz 366). Perhaps Hitler's intent at the time was to draw attention to the fact that there was underground opposition to the Reich that needed to be eliminated, or perhaps the intent was to reassure (or warn) the German people that their leader was indeed well protected.

Hitler had attracted assassins before he was named chancellor and even more afterward. Just two months after he took office in 1933, a shipwright named Kurt Lutter planned to eliminate Hitler with a bomb. This attempt never materialized, but a legal investigation was called for in May of that year. There were some half dozen attempts planned by individuals and small groups in the first five years of Hitler's chancellorship alone, resulting in numerous arrests and some executions (Hoffmann, *The History*, 251–52). Late in the war, there was even a fantastic plan by the British to hypnotize the imprisoned Deputy Führer Rudolf Hess and send him back to Germany to kill Hitler (Moorhouse 220). During his interrogation at Nürnberg, Albert Speer was asked about assassination attempts other than the well-publicized one of July 20: "In that period [near the end of the war] it was remarkably easy to concoct a plot. You could accost almost anyone on the street. If you told him what the situation was, he would answer: 'It's sheer madness' and if he had the courage, he would offer his aid.... It was not so dangerous as it looks from here, for there were perhaps a few dozen irrational people; the other eighty million were extremely rational as soon as they realized what was involved" (Speer 651).

The first truly organized plot to get rid of Hitler did not involve assassination *per se*. It was a plan hatched among those trying to avert the invasion of Czechoslovakia in 1938. The instigators were two German officers—General Hans Oster and Admiral Wilhelm Canaris. The Abwehr (intelligence) chief had finally come on board with Oster's plans. Canaris had not believed Hitler was serious about going to war until he saw proof

(Parssinen 62). One version of the story involves a plan formulated by Canaris to kidnap Hitler and have him declared insane. This idea was presented to the group of conspirators on September 15. Canaris was to request an audience with Hitler and bring his adjutant, Captain Franz Maria Liedig, with him. Canaris would manufacture an illness at the last moment, and Liedig would then ask Hitler to meet two officers who had distinguished themselves at the front. These officers would manhandle Hitler out of the chancellery through a back door and drive him to a sanitarium run by the well-known psychiatrist Dr. Karl Bonhoeffer (the father of Dietrich and Klaus Bonhoeffer). If Hitler resisted (which would have been likely), he would be killed. Evidence had already been presented to Dr. Bonhoeffer by Hans von Dohnanyi (Dr. Bonhoeffer's son-in-law) detailing Hitler's mental condition, and he was willing to commit Hitler to his sanitarium (Lifton 86). Other versions of this story are not nearly as dramatic, but they all may be true, for at this time there were multiple plans by those who had the resources to see them through, such as General (later Field Marshal) Erwin von Witzleben and Lieutenant General (later Colonel General) Franz Halder. At one time there was even a proposal by Oster to assassinate Foreign Minister Joachim von Ribbentrop as well (Moorhouse 111). The announcement that Neville Chamberlain had agreed to meet with Hitler to discuss the Czechoslovakian question effectively put an end to the military coup idea for the time being (Galante and Silianoff 86).

The first attempt to kill Hitler that became general public knowledge was implemented by Johann Georg Elser, born January 4, 1903. He was an apprentice cabinetmaker of no particular merit who had worked in Switzerland for four years before returning to Germany in 1932 as an employee in his father's woodworking business. He explicitly condemned the National Socialist policy regarding trade unions and created a plan to kill Hitler with a time bomb—or so the story goes. The device was placed inside a hollowed-out portion of one of the wooden columns behind the podium in the Bürgerbräukeller in Munich where Hitler was to speak on November 8, 1939. The bomb was supposedly set to go off at 9:20 p.m. Hitler arrived at the beer cellar at about 8:00 p.m. and shortly afterward began speaking. A normal Hitler speech could last a few hours, but this time he cut his speech short and left the place at 9:12 p.m. A few minutes later the bomb exploded, killing eight people and wounding sixty-five others. Curiously, Eva Braun's father, himself a Nazi party member, though not an "Altenkampfer" (old fighter), was among the wounded (Duffy and Ricci 29). Seven of the eight killed were also Nazi party members. Elser was later arrested as he tried to cross the border into Switzerland at Konstanz.

Artur Nebe (who would years later figure large in the July 20 conspiracy) was put in charge of the investigation. Elser was held for questioning and later deposited at the Sachsenhausen concentration camp and eventually moved to the camp at Dachau, where, it is known, he was treated much better than the other prisoners. William L. Shirer reports that he and the other war correspondents always thought that Himmler had masterminded the bombing to get rid of "Nazi fry" and further states that Elser was promised 40,000 Reichsmarks and his freedom at the end of the war (Shirer, *End*, 177; Gun 100). Elser was held at Dachau until April 9, 1945, just two weeks before the end of the war, when he was executed by the SS.

So why did Hitler uncharacteristically shorten his speech that night, and why was Elser held so long and treated so well before being executed, and why was Eva Braun's father in the crowd? Perhaps Braun went to the Bürgerbräukeller hoping to have a word with his daughter's idol. This was the attempt that many have said Hitler knew about—and perhaps it was all staged. It is well known today that Eva's parents initially disapproved of their daughter's relationship with Hitler. Both had written letters to him early on asking for their daughter to be returned to her family. A final letter written by her father on September 7, 1933, was given to Hitler's photographer, Heinrich Hoffmann, for delivery to Hitler, but he instead gave it to Eva, who tore it up (Lambert 145). Another letter, written by Eva's mother in the same time period, might, however, have been read by Hitler (Gun 106).

In 1939, prior to the outbreak of World War II, German General Kurt von Hammerstein-Equord tried several times to bait Hitler into visiting his command post along the Siegfried Line near the Dutch border. He and his co-conspirator, retired general Ludwig Beck, and a small group of soldiers planned a fatal accident for Hitler during his inspection of the base. Exactly how this was to be explained as an accident is not known, but Hitler's death would probably have been blamed on enemy artillery. Hitler never accepted any of the invitations and soon forced the "politically unreliable" von Hammerstein-Equord to retire (von Schlabrendorff, *The Secret War*, 105). Beck's role in the larger conspiracy was just beginning, although he had already resigned as chief of the German General Staff over the planned attack on Czechoslovakia. However, Beck wasn't always in favor of doing away with everything Nazi related. When General Werner von Fritsch was forced to retire in February 1938 over a (false) accusation of homosexuality, his friends tried to solicit protests from the generals. When General Halder suggested military action against the Berlin Gestapo headquarters, "Beck cut him off angrily: 'Mutiny, revolution. Such words do not exist in the dictionary of a German officer!'" (quoted in Burleigh 682).

Another attempt, even if poorly planned, to assassinate Hitler was supposed to occur on July 27, 1940, in Paris. Fritz-Dietlof von der Schulenburg-Tressow (a long-time member of the Beck-led conspiracy and assistant to Wolf-Heinrich von Helldorf, president of the Berlin police) planned to shoot Hitler from the reviewing stand during a military parade arranged in Hitler's honor (Duffy and Ricci 117). This would have been quite a feat. Hitler, however, changed his plans without notice, which he often did, and secretly toured Paris beginning at 6:00 a.m. on the morning of July 23, visiting his choice of the city's architecturally significant buildings in the span of three hours, and then left the city altogether. The July 27 military parade was cancelled. This was to be Hitler's first and only visit to France after the occupation.

Field Marshal von Witzleben, a diehard opponent of the Nazis, had new plans of his own to assassinate Hitler. In May 1941, he attempted to lure Hitler back to Paris for a parade appearance scheduled for May 21, but the event was abruptly called off at the last minute. It's not known how well planned this operation really was. In any event, by this time Hitler's schedule was almost impossible to follow, and he would regularly change his travel plans without warning.

There were no other organized assassination attempts of note until 1943, when Germany's advances in Russia had already come to a standstill. By that time a sizeable conspiracy had been created in the officer corps by retired General Beck and Colonel (later Major General) Henning von Tresckow. Together they hatched several assassination plots against both Hitler and Heinrich Himmler, but all of them failed to materialize. One early plot to do away with Hitler involving the Beck conspirators was formulated at Army Group B Headquarters at Walki near Poltava in the Ukraine. Those directly involved were General (der Gebirgstruppe, mountain troops) Hubert Lanz, Beck's chief of staff; Major General Dr. Hans Speidel; and Colonel Hyazinth Graf von Strachwitz, the commanding officer of the Großdeutschland Tank Regiment. They planned to arrest Hitler on his anticipated visit to Army Group B on February 17, 1943, and use von Strachwitz's troops to restrain Hitler's SS detachment. Hitler, at the last minute, once again changed his mind and instead visited Field Marshal Erich von Manstein's forces, fighting further east in Zaporozhye (Saporoshe), where his death could easily have been officially attributed to a Russian tank attack. However, any actions at Zaporozhye would have required von Manstein's approval, which would have been problematic (Moorhouse 175).

Beck and his followers' plan to arrest Hitler was not a closely held secret, with much of the command of Army Group B aware of their intentions, but neither were there endless documents that could be used as proof against the plotters later. It is said that Field Marshal Erwin Rommel had been informed of this operation as well (Hoffmann, *The History*, 280). Lanz was soon relieved of his command of the Armeeabteilung (Army Detachment) that had been detailed to hold Kharkov against impossible odds. This was Lanz's only direct involvement with coups, although he certainly knew of the plans of the July 20 conspirators (Mazower 207). He survived the war, only to be charged with war crimes regarding offensives committed by those under his command during September 1943. It was revealed that on the island of Cephalonia, troops from Lanz's 22nd Gebirgstruppe based in Greece executed some five thousand Italian soldiers (Moorhouse 271). Lanz served three years of a twelve-year sentence and died in Munich in 1982.

In March 1943, three known attempts on Hitler's life were planned. Field Marshal Günther von Kluge, commander of Army Group Center on the Eastern Front, had finally managed to convince Hitler to visit his headquarters at Smolensk, where, he believed, they would have ample opportunity to kill him one way or another. Bombs, if required for the task, were brought to Smolensk by Abwehr General Lahousen-Viremont. The initial plan was simply to capture Hitler when his plane landed. This was to be the responsibility of Lieutenant Colonel Philipp von Boeselager and his men, but von Kluge refused to issue the order and von Boeselager would not recognize orders from anyone else (Havas 47–48). These plans were all part of "Operation Flasch" [Spark], which ended with an attempt to blow up Hitler's plane. On March 13, 1943, at the end of Hitler's visit to Schmolsk, von Tresckow loaded explosives onto Hitler's Condor plane concealed as a package that was reported to contain bottles of cognac. Von Tresckow asked Lieutenant Colonel Heinz Brandt, who was traveling with Hitler, to take the package along on the flight and deliver it to another officer, Hellmuth Stieff, at Hitler's headquarters in East Prussia. However, the bomb failed to detonate, Hitler arrived safely in East Prussia, and Brandt escaped being blown up—for a while. He would not be so lucky on July 20, losing a leg and dying the next day as a result of von Stauffenberg's attempt. Lieutenant Fabian von Schlabrendorff, another member of the plot, eventually retrieved the bomb and disposed of it (von Schlabrendorff, *They Almost Killed*, 60).

A few days later, on March 20, 1943, Colonel Rudolf-Christoph Freiherr von Gersdorff (sometimes incorrectly spelled Gertsdorff), General Kluge's chief of intelligence and a member of the von Tresckow conspiracy, attempted to kill Hitler at a display of Russian war trophies at the Zeughaus in Berlin. The bomb, carried by von Gersdorff, was to be detonated by an acid-activated time fuse while he stood close to Hitler in the exhibit hall, killing both of them. However, the timing wasn't right, and Hitler left the building before the fuse could be set. According to von Gersdorff, he immediately entered a toilet and ripped out the fuse (Fest, *Plotting*, 196).

In November 1943, twenty-five-year-old infantry captain Axel von dem Bussche-Streithorst agreed to blow up Hitler and himself with a hand grenade in Berlin while he demonstrated a new army winter uniform, which Hitler insisted on inspecting himself. The date for the event was set for November 23, but the uniforms were destroyed the day before during a British air raid and Bussche-Streithorst had to return to duty at the Eastern Front the following day. A few weeks later another "uniform" attempt was made. This time the volunteer was Ewald Heinrich von Kleist-Schmenzin, son of one of the high-ranking conspirators (Ewald von Kleist-Schmenzin). Another British air raid just before the scheduled demonstration forced its cancellation as well. A third "uniform display" attempt was planned for early July 1944, but that one was also a failure. Hitler was proving to be a hard man to kill.

In 1944, Army Group Center Reserve cavalry captain Eberhard von Breitenbuch, an aide to Field Marshals Erwin von Witzleben, Ernst Busch, and Günther von Kluge, approached Colonel von Stauffenberg and offered a very direct solution—to simply shoot Hitler at the next available opportunity. Von Breitenbuch was convinced that the war was lost and the only way to prevent the destruction of all Germany was for someone to kill Hitler—the sooner, the better. On March 11, 1944, he attended a conference at the Berghof on the Obersalzberg, accompanying Field Marshal Busch, with the intention of carrying out such a plan and, if necessary, forfeiting his own life in the process. His son Andreas, however, tells a somewhat different story today—that his father's goal was only to participate in the conspiracy and to convince Field Marshal von Kluge to join them (www.jewishvirtuallibrary.org/eberhard-von-breitenbuch). Regardless of the specifics, Hitler was aware of certain machinations and took precautions, ordering that none of the attendees' adjutants were to be admitted to the conference. Von Breitenbuch was turned away at the door. His involvement in the resistance never came to light, and he lived another thirty-five years after the end of the war.

The idea of simply shooting Hitler had been thought of by others as well. On January 25, 1944, Marie Vassiltchikov recorded in her diary a conversation she'd had with the famous Luftwaffe night fighter ace Heinrich von Sayn-Wittgenstein the previous year. He had just come from a meeting with Hitler a few days earlier, where he had received the Oak Leaves to his Knight's Cross (on September 22). His pistol had not been taken before he was admitted to the Führer's headquarters in East Prussia. "So that it might have been possible 'to bump him off' right then and there," she records von Sayn-Wittgenstein as having said (Vassiltchikov 140). Vassiltchikov's diary entry was made the day she learned that he had been killed in battle at Neuermark-Lübars.

Then there was the British plan to assassinate Hitler—one that did not involve hypnotizing his former deputy—called "Operation Foxley," which was instigated before July 20, but the feasibility study alone wasn't completed until November 1944. The idea was to somehow derail Hitler's train or poison its water supply, or for a sniper to shoot him at the Berghof. The plans have been evaluated by Roger Moorehouse, who concluded that "the SOE [Special Operations Executive] was not especially energetic in recruiting a sniper" (Moorehouse 220). It is not known whether any of the German conspirators knew of the British plans. Even at this late date in the war, the conspirators, both civilian and military, were not universally believed or trusted by members of the British government.

Von Stauffenberg ultimately concluded that he alone could assassinate Hitler, and he would have that opportunity on July 11, 1944, when he was ordered to attend a military conference at the Berghof. The plan was to do away with Hitler, Göring, and Himmler all at the same time. A time bomb was hidden inside his briefcase, and his accomplice, Captain Friedrich Klausing, was waiting in a getaway car. Inside the Berghof, von Stauffenberg soon learned that neither Göring nor Himmler were present. With a phone call, von Stauffenberg was instructed to abandon the plan and return to Berlin after the conference. His second opportunity occurred at Hitler's Wolf's Lair (Wolfsschanze) headquarters near Rastenburg, East Prussia. On July 15, 1944, he attended a briefing there with both Hitler and Göring present, but Himmler was not. The attempt was again called off.

As an interesting aside, one author contends that Eva Braun had also been a target of the conspirators—that on the July 11 attempt, von Stauffenberg "planned to kill Hitler, Göring, Himmler, Eva Braun and everybody else there." According to this source, von Stauffenberg intended "to place a bomb under the dining table between Hitler and Eva Braun" (quoted in Gun 215–16). It is unlikely that Eva Braun was ever a serious target, but she could have become collateral damage if this planned attempt at the Berghof had materialized.

Von Stauffenberg's final attempt occurred on July 20, 1944. By this time, a warrant had been issued for Goerdeler's arrest and he was on the run. Four days earlier, Hitler's demise had been planned during a meeting at Berthold von Stauffenberg's home at No. 8 Tristanstrasse, Wannsee. The decision was made that as long as Hitler was present, the attempt would go ahead. At noon on July 20, von Stauffenberg and Colonel General Friedrich Fromm arrived at Field Marshal Wilhelm Keitel's office at the Wolfsschanze for a briefing prior to being invited into the main conference already in progress. At 12:37 p.m., von Stauffenberg placed his briefcase containing the bomb under the map table; then he left the room on the pretext of making an urgent telephone call. The officer (the unfortunate Colonel Heinz Brandt) who took his place noticed the briefcase and, with his foot, pushed it farther under the table. At 12:42 p.m., the bomb exploded. The heavy oak table substantially shielded Hitler from the full destructive power of the explosion. At this time, von Stauffenberg was already in a car on his way out through the security gates. In the confusion after the explosion, he was able to leave Hitler's headquarters and fly to Berlin-Rangsdorf, where he joined his fellow conspirators Albrecht Ritter von Mertz von Quirnheim (often referred to simply as von Mertz) and General Friedrich Olbricht at the Bendlerstrasse to set the full coup in motion throughout Germany and beyond. General Eduard Wagner, the quartermaster general of the German Army, was the one who had insisted that Himmler be present at any assassination attempt, and he was responsible for providing the airplane that flew von Stauffenberg from Rastenburg back to Berlin after depositing the bomb. Wagner committed suicide by shooting himself on July 23 to avoid implicating others in the plot (Wheeler-Bennett 690). There were no contingency plans, so many of the others directly involved would choose the same fate rather than fall into the hands of the Gestapo.

In Berlin, the insurrection was rapidly shut down by SS soldiers of the Großdeutschland infantry division, under the command of Major Otto Ernst Remer, who had been ordered by General Paul von Hase, commandant of the city of Berlin, to arrest Minister Goebbels and occupy the Propaganda Ministry. Goebbels, however, convinced Remer that Hitler was very much alive and put through a phone call to him, having himself already spoken to his Reich press chief, Dr. Dietrich, at Rastenburg and received confirmation that Hitler was indeed alive (Speer 487). Remer recognized Hitler's voice on the phone and was ordered to put down the putsch, while at the same time receiving two immediate promotions to Oberst (colonel). Remer's actions effectively put an end to the larger military's role in the revolt, and in spite of Gisevius' contention that Remer committed suicide soon thereafter, he lived until October 4, 1994, and never renounced his actions of July 20 (Gisevius, *To the Bitter End*, 564, and *Valkyrie*, 200).

At 6:28 p.m. a radio broadcast from the Wolf's Lair reported for all to hear that Hitler definitely was alive and only slightly injured in the bomb blast. Later in the evening it became all too clear to the conspirators in the Bendlerblock that the coup would fail. Their command center was soon occupied by Remer's troops, ending the Berlin involvement in the day's events. That night, at 12:30 a.m., von Stauffenberg and co-conspirators Werner von Haeften, Olbricht and von Quirnheim were arrested, summarily tried by Colonel General Friedrich Fromm—a lukewarm supporter at best who betrayed them once he saw that the attempt was going badly—and shot and buried at the Matthäus Church in Berlin's Schöneberg district. A full report written on July 23 by First Lieutenant Rudolf Schlee, commander of the firing squad, survived the war (Zimmermann and Jacobsen 149). Himmler later ordered the bodies exhumed and burned and the ashes scattered. Beck was allowed to commit suicide, albeit with some help (Hoffmann, *The History*, 508).

Those, other than Hitler, present at the conference at the time of the explosion who were injured or killed were General Alfred Jodl (slightly injured), General Adolf Heusinger (severely burned), Luftwaffe General Gunther Korten (died of his wounds), Colonel Heinz Brandt (died of his wounds), Luftwaffe General Karl Bodenschatz (severely injured), General Rudolf Schmundt (died of his wounds), Lieutenant Colonel Heinrich Borgman (severely injured), General Walter Warlimont (concussion), and stenographer Heinrich Berger (killed). SS Hauptsturmführer Otto Gunsche, Rear Admiral Karl-Jesco Von Puttkamer, Naval Captain Heinz Assmann, General Walter Scherff, General Walther Buhle, Rear Admiral Hans-Erich Voss, Colonel Nikolaus Von Below, stenographer Heinz Buchholz, General Ernst John von Freyend (adjutant to Keitel), SS Lieutenant General Hermann Fegelein, Major Herbert Buchs (adjutant to Jodl), Lieutenant Colonel Heinz Weizenegger, counselor Dr. Franz Von Sonnleithner, and Field Marshal Wilhelm Keitel were also present but not injured (Wheeler-Bennett 639).

In a strange turn of events, one of those present in the conference room and injured during the blast would later be accused of being involved in the plot. General Adolf Heusinger was arrested by the Gestapo on July 23 at the insistence of Himmler and interrogated multiple times at the Prinz Albrecht Strasse Gestapo headquarters. He was able to answer questions without being intimidated, providing information he was sure they already had. Heusinger freely admitted to knowing most of the major players in the attempt, stating that he saw General Erich Fellgiebel (chief of the Signal Command and heavily involved in the plot) almost every day, but the Gestapo had no hard evidence linking Heusinger to July 20. He probably knew about the conspiracy, though certainly not about the final plans. He was released in September and summoned by Hitler to OKH (Oberkommando des Herres—the German army ground forces' high command) headquarters in Angerburg. Hitler told Heusinger that he was sorry that he had been dragged into the investigation and regretted that he had been mistreated (Galante and Silianoff 256 and 265). Heusinger survived the war and was interrogated by the U.S.

Army Intelligence, but never charged with any war crimes, and served as the first inspector general of the Bundeswehr. A short, and perceptibly biased, biography of General Heusinger covering his pre- and postwar career is given in *The Brown Book* (National Council 202).

The attempted assassination and coup of July 20, 1944, instigated the last major shift in the internal policy of the National Socialist government. What had previously been a tightly controlled citizenry became a true police state—and the state was paranoid, and the state was Adolf Hitler. He was soon convinced by the evidence that his enemies were well organized, that the conspiracy was widespread and that the officer corps was behind it. Goebbels' propaganda initially spouted just the opposite—that it was a small group of desperate officers who had carried out the attempt, which *was* Hitler's pronouncement immediately after the attempt. In a speech given by General Jodl, chief of the OKW operations staff, to his staff on July 24, he admitted that "the action spread farther than was indicated by the Führer in his speech. Persons who do not belong to the armed forces were also involved" (quoted in Zimmermann and Jacobsen 187). Reichsführer SS Himmler and the chief of the OKW, Wilhelm Keitel, met with Hitler at his headquarters at Rastenburg on July 30 to organize the investigation of others who might have been involved in the attempted coup. The first order of business was establishing a "Court of Honor" of army generals and field marshals to deal with removing the suspected traitors in the military from their positions. This was done so that they could be tried and sentenced by the civilian "People's Court" (the Volksgerichtshof, or VGH), thus avoiding a military court martial and trial where the outcome would not have been as certain. Kaltenbrunner had already prepared an initial report that concluded, "It cannot be concluded that security measures existing as a safeguard against such attempts broke down in this instance; for the possibility that a general staff officer summoned to a briefing session would lend himself to such a crime had not been reckoned with" (quoted in Zimmermann and Jacobsen 131).

It is obvious from the preceding short history and modern hindsight that there was never a "good" time to kill Hitler. At no point would the assassins have been seen as liberators, with the government of Germany just being handed over to the military or mostly unknown civilian leaders after the deed was done. Only six weeks before July 20 the Allies had invaded the continent at Normandy and were not being thrown back into the sea as Hitler had promised. The Russians were on the march toward Berlin, North Africa had been lost, and most of Italy was likewise lost. For ordinary Germans, it was no time to be thinking of politics. The survival of the country was in the balance, and Hitler still had enormous public support. In any event, there was no guarantee that the military forces would follow the orders of von Witzleben or Beck once the particulars of the assassination were revealed, and they could not have been contained for long. The general public would not have recognized many (if any) of the major conspirators. Certainly Göring and Himmler had more influence on people and events than any of the nobility or members of the officer corps involved in the coup, and both men would have to be placated—or assassinated—if a regime change were to be successful. These were the details that no doubt kept the planners in the conspiracy awake at night.

Hitler took his survival of July 20 as another example of divine Providence and went so far as to commission a special military decoration, the Wound Badge of July 20, 1944, which was awarded to those who were in the conference room at the time of the explosion. Every member of the Wehrmacht was also soon required to retake his loyalty oath. The Reichswehr had already sworn an oath of unconditional obedience to Hitler on the day Paul von Hindenburg died (August 2, 1934), replacing the oath previously made to "my people and my country" (Hoffmann, *The History*, 27). This change is significant in that previously only the SS had sworn allegiance exclusively to Hitler, but now the entire military came under the same obligation. On July 24, 1944, on Göring's order, the traditional military salute was officially replaced throughout the armed forces with the well-known raised right arm "Heil Hitler" (Galante and Silianoff 255).

The best known today of those executed on the night of July 20, 1944, Lieutenant Colonel Claus Philipp Maria Schenk Graf von Stauffenberg (born November 15, 1907), was the son of Alfred Schenk Graf von Stauffenberg, a nobleman and the last Oberhofmarshal (chief administrator of the royal court) of the Kingdom of Württemberg, and Caroline Schenk Gräfin (countess) von Stauffenberg (née Gräfin von Üxküll-Gyllenband—sometimes written Uexküll). He had older twin brothers, Berthold and Alexander. Claus was born at the Stauffenberg castle in Jettingen, located between Ulm and Augsburg in eastern Swabia, which was a part of greater Germany. Von Stauffenberg was one of the oldest and most distinguished names in the aristocratic Roman Catholic circles of southern Germany. However, Claus' maternal ancestors were Protestant and included several famous Prussians, with Field Marshal August von Gneisenau being the most recognizable. Claus married Magdalena Elisabeth Vera Lydia Herta Freiin (baroness) von Lerchenfeld (who was called Nina) on September 26, 1933 (*Allgemeine Deutsche Biographie*). They would have five children, the fifth being born shortly after Claus' death.

Claus von Stauffenberg joined the family's traditional Regiment 17 in Bamberg in 1926 and began his active military career with a commission as a second lieutenant in 1930. His regiment became part of the German 1st Light Division under General Erich Hoepner, who had been involved in planning a coup in September 1938, which largely fell apart after Hitler's Munich Agreement was signed by Germany, France, Britain, and Italy. Hitler's popularity was such that the conspirators had difficulty rationalizing the coup even to themselves, and certainly not to the typical German citizen. Indeed, Hoepner's 1st Light Division was one of the divisions that eventually occupied the Sudetenland as a result of the Munich Agreement. Von Stauffenberg did not oppose the occupation or the exploitation of Poland; however, he did not approve of the methods employed in the annexation of the Sudetenland and he strongly disapproved of the invasion of Prague and Czechoslovakia (Hoffmann, *The History*, 318). He generally described the Poles in a letter to his wife as "unbelievable rabble; a great many Jews and a lot of mixed race. A people that is only comfortable under the lash. The thousands of prisoners will serve our agriculture well" (*The Times* [London], January 15, 2009). This was an expression of the long-held belief among the German aristocracy that the eastern territories, particularly Poland, should be a German possession to do with as they saw fit and that it shouldn't really matter how they got hold of this territory. There is no reason to doubt that von Stauffenberg viewed the National Socialist treatment of Poland merely as a means to an end. "There are ways," von Stauffenberg is recorded as having said, "of inducing the citizens of a nation freely to accept the necessary differences of position, wealth, and prestige which occur in any society" (quoted in Zeller 195).

It is not surprising that von Stauffenberg, with his aristocratic breeding, never joined the National Socialist Party. He would likely have viewed politics in general as beneath his status, and besides, he was a Catholic and Hitler had quickly broken his 1933 Reichskonkordat agreement with the church. German Catholic bishops publicly protested the violation of this agreement, which, in 1937, led to a papal encyclical condemning the violations, as well as National Socialism's racist ideology in general. This action by the church is likely what formulated von Stauffenberg's views on the growing systematic ill treatment of Jews and the mounting suppression of religion, leading him to comment that the November 1938 Kristallnacht terrorist actions against the Jews by the Nazis had brought shame on Germany. At his trial, however, Berthold von Stauffenberg stated he was

> "a patron of the church in Lautlingen," that his family had ancient roots in the Catholic Church and that they had valued a Catholic education for the children. Speaking also for his brother he added: "We are not really what are called Catholic believers in the proper sense. We did not go to church very often, nor to confession. My brother and I feel that Christianity is unlikely to produce anything creative" [quoted in Zeller 448].

Von Stauffenberg's mother's brother, Nikolaus Graf von Üxküll, whom von Stauffenberg revered, had approached him even before the Polish invasion, asking him to join the established resistance movement against the Nazis, but it was only after the occupation of Poland that he seriously considered the idea. A creative approach was used by Peter Yorck von Wartenburg and Ulrich-Wilhelm Graf Schwerin von Schwanenfeld to enlist von Stauffenberg. They urged him to consider becoming the adjutant of Field Marshal Walther von Brauchitsch, the supreme commander of the Army, believing his influence might make von Stauffenberg receptive to the idea of participating in a coup against Hitler. However, von Stauffenberg's Prussian military training would not permit full involvement in such action, as it was still unthinkable for a person of his standing to participate in an *organized* coup against the legally elected government. In fact, "from expressions used by von Stauffenberg, many of his colleagues concluded that he welcomed and supported the Nazi regime; not until after 20 July did they wonder whether he had spoken from convictions or to camouflage his real ideas" (Hoffmann, *The History*, 316).

Von Stauffenberg was transferred to the OKH during the lull before the Battle of France (1939–1940). The mass executions of Jews, Poles, and Russians (after the invasion of 1941) added to what von Stauffenberg already perceived as poor military leadership—beginning with Hitler, who declared himself the supreme military commander in December 1941. General Hoepner and several other generals had their commands taken away with the implementation of this decree, which, for von Stauffenberg, was the last straw and convinced him in 1942 to contact resistance clutches within the Wehrmacht. He surely realized that this was the only collection of men with a viable hope of removing Hitler (Zimmermann and Jacobsen 222).

In the conquered regions of Russia, von Stauffenberg was involved with recruiting volunteers for the Ostlegion (the Wehrmacht foreign fighting force), which was managed by his office, while carefully refusing to enforce the Hitler-instigated Commissar Order, which Hitler withdrew a year later. Germany's Führer was at the height of his popularity in 1942 and could not publicly be criticized by anyone—certainly not by a member of the military. From this time on, the brothers Berthold and Claus von Stauffenberg maintained close contact with former military commanders, particularly Hoepner, and with the so-called Kreisau resistance circle, which allowed nonpolitical civilians and Social Democrats as members, the most prominent being Julius Leber (Steinbach and Tuchel

195). Von Stauffenberg and Leber were from opposite ends of German society and would have had nothing in common but for the conspiracy to remove Hitler.

Early in 1943, von Stauffenberg was promoted to lieutenant colonel of the General Staff and sent to North Africa to join Erwin Rommel's 10th Panzer Division. There, on April 7, while doing reconnaissance, looking for a new location for the command center, his vehicle was strafed by British fighter-bombers and he was severely wounded. He was immediately sent to a hospital in Carthage and subsequently spent three months in a hospital in Munich. He lost his left eye, his right hand, and the fourth and fifth fingers of his left hand. He was awarded the Wound Badge in Gold on April 14, 1943, and on May 8 he was awarded the German Cross in Gold for heroism in combat.

Von Stauffenberg was sent home to Schloss Lautlingen in southern Germany (one of several castles belonging to his family) to recuperate. By September, he had made up his mind to kill Hitler himself. One of the conspirators, Major General Henning von Tresckow, was in a position to have von Stauffenberg assigned as a staff officer to the headquarters of the Ersatzheer (literally, Replacement Army) in charge of training reinforcements for first line divisions at the front. His office would be located on the Bendlerstrasse in Berlin, in close proximity to others of the same mindset and the perfect location from which to coordinate a coup.

One of von Stauffenberg's new superiors was General Friedrich Olbricht, a longtime member of the military conspiracy. The Ersatzheer command was in an ideal position to stage a coup, and Olbricht knew it. One of the organization's responsibilities was ensuring that Operation Valkyrie was ready. This Hitler-approved invention of General Olbricht's was designed to place the Ersatzheer in control of the entire Reich in the event of an emergency. This was the perfect platform from which to launch the coup and remove the leadership of the Reich before the rest of the general military and the SS could react. The carefully planned assassination attempts that were to follow (particularly the Axel von dem Bussche-Streithorst attempt in November 1943), organized by von Stauffenberg, von Kleist-Schmenzin, von Gersdorff, von Breitenbuch, and others, failed primarily due to Hitler's unpredictable schedule. Changes in routes, times, and locations were made with little or no warning. The conspirators now planned to be ready whenever a target of opportunity presented itself. This meant having bombs and assassins always at the ready, which must have been a logistical nightmare.

In late 1943, von Stauffenberg composed a list of demands he intended to present (via the new German government they would create) to the Western Allies as conditions for Germany to agree to an immediate peace with them while Germany continued the war in the east. These demands would probably not have been taken seriously because they included Germany retaining its 1914 eastern borders, encompassing the Polish territories of Wielkopolska and Poznan. Other equally unlikely demands included Germany retaining Austria and the Sudetenland within its borders, while giving sovereignty to Alsace-Lorraine. The demands even included an *expansion* of the German border in the south to include Tyrol as far as Bolzano and Merano, which would never have been accepted by the Allies. According to this document, Germany would also not be occupied by the Allies and would not hand over anyone accused of war crimes; the argument being that Germany would try its own war criminals (Zimmermann and Jacobsen 95–96). The British government, however, was already somewhat tired of hearing tales from the German resistance, which never seemed to do anything but talk.

On June 6, 1944, the Allies landed in France and would soon be on the move toward

Germany. Von Stauffenberg (and most well-informed higher officers) had no doubt that the war was now lost and that his previous list of demands would not be taken seriously by the invaders, even if Hitler were dead. "When the Western Allied troops had finally landed, the only remaining question was how to shorten the catastrophe of a long drawn out war, with its countless and senseless sacrifices" (Zimmermann and Jacobsen 222). Only an immediate cease-fire could stop the unnecessary bloodshed and avoid irreparable damage to Germany's infrastructure. Von Stauffenberg was committed to carrying out the assassination himself, knowing that history could easily label him a traitor. "He had the noble impatience of those who are destined to die young" (Zeller 432). He is reported to have told a co-conspirator, von dem Bussche-Streithorst, that he intended to commit the very definition of high treason and that he would attempt it with all his might ("Gehen wir in medias res, ich betreibe mit allen mir zur Verfügung stehenden Mitteln den Hochverrat") in an attempt to rid the world of Hitler's regime (quoted in Fest, *Biographie*, 961, and *Hitler*, 703).

Von Stauffenberg personally had little hope that any of his assassination attempts would be successful, but von Tresckow convinced him to continue trying: "The assassination must be attempted, at any cost. Even should that fail, the attempt to seize power in the capital must be undertaken. We must prove to the world and to future generations that the men of the German resistance movement dared to take the decisive step and to hazard their lives upon it. Compared with this objective, nothing else matters" (quoted in von Schlabrendorff, *They Almost Killed*, 103).

Immediately after July 20, von Stauffenberg's wife and four children were taken into custody by the Gestapo. The children were all reasonably well treated and survived, being held in a special camp in Bad Sachsa, Lower Saxony, until near the end of the war, when they were moved by SS troops into the Alps. They were actually freed on April 30 by Wehrmacht troops who turned them over to American forces in northern Italy (Posner 172). Nina, who was pregnant when arrested, gave birth to the fifth von Stauffenberg child while in a former Nazi maternity center in Frankfurt. Wehrmacht troops also freed other members of the von Stauffenberg family in the operation ordered by Colonel General Heinrich von Vietinghoff, commander in chief of the southwest (Hoffmann, *The History*, 520; Henke 875).

One hundred thirty-nine specifically chosen prisoners from Dachau had been transferred on April 24, 1945, to Niederdorf/Hochpustertal, some 70 kilometers northeast of Bozen. The transport was guarded by SS men who had no idea whether they would be ordered to shoot the lot or release them. Colonel Bogislaw von Bonin, who was himself a prisoner in the group, managed to get a message sent to Captain Wichard von Alvensleben, commander of Wehrmacht headquarters in Bozen, informing him of what was taking place. With orders from von Vietinghoff, von Alvensleben and troops under his command left for Innsbruck to take possession of the prisoners from the SS men, who were no doubt all too anxious to be rid of them. On May 5 American forces arrived at Niederdorf and took charge of the prisoners without incident. In addition to the prominent prisoners, two inmates of the Dachau concentration camp—the cook (or circus clown, or both) Wilhelm Visintainer and the barber Paul Wauer—were in the transport (Manvell and Fraenkel, *The Men Who Tried*, 248; and *World Heritage*, article WHEBN 0020000711). A reasonably complete list of the prisoners is given in Appendix B.

It is a mystery to many why some of these prisoners were allowed to live, as it has often been stated that Nazi policy was to punish family members of those found guilty of crimes against the state. Evidence can be found, however, that *Sippenhaft* orders were not generally carried out but used as "more of an implied menace against the population" (Loeffel 3). It is true that family members were often arrested with much publicity, but then they were usually released soon after, and rarely was property confiscated (Koch 217). The exception was the treatment of families of soldiers captured by the Russians who joined the National Committee for a Free Germany (or the League of German Officers) for anti–Nazi propaganda purposes. For them, the menace was more than implied.

When it came to prosecuting the July 20 conspirators, there were annoying laws that prevented even Hitler from doing whatever he wanted right away. He could, and often did, have laws written or changed that allowed him to eventually have his way, but he was obligated to follow the laws in force at the time. In the case of the von Stauffenbergs and other important prisoners being held along with them, it is also likely that, at this late date, their guards and superior officers did not want to be responsible for the deaths of such prominent people with the war obviously lost. The Allies' well-publicized promise to prosecute war criminals no doubt left many German soldiers (particularly those in the SS) hesitant to carry out orders in these final days that would likely lead to their arrest after the war.

First Lieutenant Werner Karl von Haeften was born October 9, 1908, in Berlin to Major General Hans and Agnes (née von Brauchitsch) von Haeften. His siblings were an older brother, Hans Bernd, and a sister, Elisabeth. He studied law in Berlin, became a lawyer, and worked for a bank in Hamburg until the outbreak of World War II, when he voluntarily joined the German army, along with millions of other Germans of his age. In 1939, he became a first lieutenant in the reserves and took part in Operation Barbarossa, the invasion of Russia, where he was seriously wounded (Fest, *Plotting*, 387).

In 1943, von Haeften became adjutant to von Stauffenberg in the Ersatzheer headquarters after recovering from a serious wound suffered on the Eastern Front (Steinbach and Tuchel 80). He and his brother were committed supporters of the conspiracy; however, Hans Bernd was opposed to the assassination itself on religious grounds. This view was shared by many of those involved. Killing in battle is very different from premeditated murder. Werner Karl, however, had no qualms about killing Hitler himself and made that clear to Dietrich Bonhoeffer two months before Bonhoeffer was arrested (Manvell and Fraenkel, *The Men Who Tried*, 75).

On July 20, 1944, von Haeften flew with von Stauffenberg to the Wolf's Lair in Rastenburg. After the bomb meant to

Dietrich Bonhoeffer in London, 1939 (Bundesarchiv, Bild 146-1987-074-16 / photographer unknown, used with permission).

kill Hitler exploded, von Stauffenberg and von Haeften flew to Berlin to ignite the coup, which had not begun as planned due to conflicting information regarding whether Hitler had survived. Ultimately, von Haeften was arrested (along with von Stauffenberg and fellow conspirators Olbricht and von Quirnheim) and condemned to death by General Fromm. All four were shot after midnight in the courtyard of the Bendlerblock by a ten-man firing squad from the Großdeutschland Guard Battalion. In a final act of defiance, von Haeften threw his body in front of von Stauffenberg when the firing squad was ordered to shoot (Duffy and Ricci 189). Von Haeften's brother Hans Bernd was executed on August 15 at Plötzensee Prison.

General Friedrich Olbricht was born October 4, 1888, in Leisnig, Saxony. He was the son of a mathematics professor, Richard Olbricht, who was also the director of the Realschule (secondary school) in Bautzen, Germany. Friedrich Olbricht was married to Eva Koeppel and the couple would have two children, a son and a daughter. Olbricht successfully passed the Arbitur (university preparatory school exit examination) in 1907 and then accepted a commission as a Fähnrich (ensign) with Infantry Regiment 106 in Leipzig. He fought in World War I, was promoted to captain and chose to stay in the Treaty of Versailles–decimated military (the Reichswehr) after the war (Das-Ritterkreuz).

Olbricht was an early bellwether of the National Socialist Party's true objectives, all the way back to the Beer Hall Putsch of 1923. His countrymen in the opposition came to include Abwehr officer Hans Oster (whose chief was Admiral Canaris), General (later Field Marshal) Erwin von Witzleben, and General Georg Thomas. They were alarmed by the initial support the Nazis were attracting from a substantial portion of the military (no doubt due to the legendary General Erich Ludendorff's participation in Hitler's putsch). Nonetheless, they believed that as long as von Hindenburg withheld public endorsement of National Socialism, Hitler would not be allowed to get out of control.

Olbricht was assigned to the Reich Defense Ministry as leader of the Reichswehr's Foreign Armies Bureau in 1926. After the Night of the Long Knives raid, he was able to save several of those arrested from execution by finding or creating positions for them in the Abwehr, which was soon to be led by Canaris. He was appointed chief of staff of the 4th Army Corps stationed in Dresden in 1935, an assignment that lasted until 1938, when he was promoted to commander of the 24th Infantry Division (Zimmermann and Jacobsen 225). Olbricht has the distinction of being one of the few officers who supported General Werner von Fritsch, the commander in chief of the German armed forces who was accused of homosexuality in January 1938. After von Fritsch's resignation, it was discovered that the charges had been invented, based on the contrived testimony of a man whom some say was recruited by Himmler (Hoffmann, *The History*, 42). The tale had been concocted as part of Hitler's plan to gain control of the military—which he did.

Olbricht commanded the 24th Infantry Division during the invasion of Poland in 1939. He literally led the division, remaining at the front during battle, and was awarded the Knight's Cross of the Iron Cross on February 15, 1940, for bravery and leadership (Das-Ritterkreuz). Olbricht was soon promoted to general of the infantry and eventually appointed chief of the General Army Office (Allgemeines Heeresamt) in the OKH. He was ultimately made chief of the Armed Forces Office (Wehrersatzamt), a division of the OKW. During the winter of 1941–1942, he was tasked with assisting in the development of an emergency plan (the Valkyrie Plan), which he recognized straightaway as a promising foundation for a coup, and he began modifying the plan for that purpose. With his rank and position, he was able to work covertly with leaders of the resistance including

General Beck, Carl Goerdeler, and Major General von Tresckow, passing on information gained through his normal undertakings.

Olbricht and von Quirnheim initiated Operation Valkyrie on July 20, 1944, by mobilizing the Ersatzheer. Olbricht gave the initial order (Fest, *Plotting*, 394). When it became widely known that von Stauffenberg's briefcase bomb had failed to kill Hitler, the coup began to fall apart, and the Nazi leadership was able to regain control in Berlin within a few hours. Olbricht was arrested in the Bendlerstrasse at 9:00 p.m. by soldiers from the Berlin Großdeutschland Guard Battalion. Later that night, Colonel General Fromm hastily convened a court martial, which resulted in Olbricht, von Quirnheim, von Haeften and von Stauffenberg being taken outside to the courtyard and executed by firing squad. Von Stauffenberg is generally credited by history with being the martyr of July 20, but Olbricht had the foresight long before von Stauffenberg had the commitment.

Claus von Stauffenberg (left) and Albrecht von Mertz von Quirnheim (German Resistance Memorial Center, Berlin, used with permission).

Colonel Albrecht Ritter von Mertz von Quirnheim was born March 25, 1905, in Munich. His father was Hermann Ritter Mertz von Quirnheim, a captain on the Bavarian Military General Staff. The young von Quirnheim spent much of his privileged early years in the Bavarian capital. One of his childhood friends was Hans-Jürgen von Blumenthal, and he soon became friends with the brothers Werner Karl and Hans Bernd von Haeften. (Years later the four would be reunited in planning Hitler's demise.) After receiving his diploma, von Quirnheim joined the Reichswehr in 1923, and his friendship with Claus von Stauffenberg began in 1925 at the War Academy in Berlin (Steinbach and Tuchel 137). With the Polish invasion, von Quirnheim was appointed a staff officer in the General Staff's organizational division.

Von Quirnheim was initially a loyal supporter of National Socialism and requested a transfer to the SA after Hitler became chancellor (Fest, *Plotting*, 392). By 1941 he was in a position to know details of the sanctioned (or overlooked) abuse of civilians in Nazi-occupied Eastern Europe. In 1942 he was promoted to lieutenant colonel and then to chief of staff of the 24th Army Corps on the Eastern Front in support of the Stalingrad offensive. He served at the Führer's headquarters at Vinnitsa with von Stauffenberg until von Stauffenberg was transferred to North Africa (German Resistance Memorial Center). Von Quirnheim was promoted to colonel in 1943 and married Hilde Baier (Steinbach and Tuchel 137). His sister's husband, Wilhelm Dieckmann, formally introduced him to the organized resistance. In his new position, having replaced von Stauffenberg as chief of staff to General Olbright in Berlin, he was able to ensure the continuation of the conspirators' strategies against Hitler.

By September 1943 von Quirnheim was fully engaged in plots to assassinate Hitler. He, von Stauffenberg, and Olbricht all had a hand in creative changes made to Operation Valkyrie, gradually turning it into an outline for the coming coup. Immediately after von Stauffenberg's final attempt, von Quirnheim convinced General Olbricht to activate Operation Valkyrie in Fromm's name, even though they were not certain that Hitler was dead. It was von Quirnheim who took the orders for Operation Valkyrie out of the safe and, according to generally accepted history, either he or Olbricht forged Fromm's signature on the order. Von Schlabrendorff states that it was von Quirnheim who issued the order (*They Almost Killed*, 115). Von Quirnheim did indeed sign at least one (the second) mobilization order on July 20 and he did not forge Fromm's signature on this document. It is clearly signed *v. Mertz* (as in von Mertz von Quirnheim). Within hours, von Quirnheim, von Stauffenberg, Olbricht and Werner von Haeften were arrested and executed at the Bendlerblock. A few days later, von Quirnheim's parents and one of his sisters were arrested by the Gestapo and locked up. His brother-in-law Dieckmann died under mysterious circumstances in Lehrter Strasse detention on September 13, 1944 (Steinbach and Tuchel 44).

In telling this story, it is worth taking note of just how many of the principal members of the conspiracy were related. Several have already been mentioned: von Quirnheim and his brother-in-law, Wilhelm Dieckmann; von Tresckow and his relative, von Schlabrendorff (although Wheeler-Bennett says they were not related [514], Gisevius says they were [*To the Bitter End*, 252]); Werner von Haeften and his brother Hans Bernd (who were nephews of von Brauchitsch); and von Stauffenberg and his brother, Berthold. Many more will be added to this list. It is possible to construct a virtual family tree of conspirators involved in one plan or another for doing away with Hitler.

The second mobilization order pertaining to Valkyrie. This one, signed by Albrecht von Mertz von Quirnheim, does not have a forged signature of General Fromm. The signature is "v Mertz" (German Resistance Memorial Center, Berlin).

An updated and summarized list of some of the better-known assassination plots and attempts directed against Adolf Hitler, both before and during his time as Führer of Germany, has recently been compiled (see www.axishistory.com/index.php?id=2972). Some attempts were no more than initial plans, but there were several serious attempts made as well.

Then there is the strange and well-known "non-attempt" by Luftwaffe Oberstleutnant (Lieutenant Colonel) Horst von Riesen, who was forced in an emergency to drop his bombs near Rastenburg on July 20—an unfortunate day for such an emergency. He was arrested but released when it was proven that he had nothing to do with the assassination attempt.

Had the coup of July 20 succeeded, Goerdeler's grand vision of a post–Hitler cabinet (as of June 1944) was as follows (according to Wheeler-Bennett 623):

- Reichsverweser (Regent): General Ludwig Beck
- State Secretary to the Regent: Count Ulrich Schwerin von Schwanenfeld
- Chancellor: Carl Friedrich Goerdeler
- State Secretary to the Chancellor: Count Peter Yorck von Wartenburg
- Vice-Chancellor: Wilhelm Leuschner
- Deputy Vice-Chancellor: Jakob Kaiser
- Minister of War: General Friedrich Olbricht
- State Secretary to the Minister of War: Colonel Count Claus von Stauffenberg
- Commander in Chief of the Armed Forces: Field Marshal Erwin von Witzleben
- Commander in Chief of the Army: General Erich Hoepner
- Minister of the Interior: Julius Leber
- Minister of Economics: Dr. Paul Lejeune-Jung
- Minister of Finance: Ewald Loeser
- Minister of Justice: Joseph Wirmer
- Minister of Education: Eugen Bolz
- Minister of Agriculture: Andreas Hermes
- Minister of Reconstruction: Bernhard Letterhaus
- Minister of Information: Theodor Haubach

Fest states that the above list was never found, but a few pages later he refers to the list as if it had been (Fest, *Plotting*, 295 and 307). Almost every resistance circle created lists of potential cabinet members and constructed detailed organizational charts for the new government. These lists, once discovered by the Gestapo, served as the grounds for multiple arrests after July 20. The position of minister of foreign affairs would have gone to either Ulrich von Hassell (former ambassador to Italy) or Friedrich-Werner Graf von der Schulenburg-Tressow (former ambassador to the Soviet Union and often referred to simply as von der Schulenburg), depending on who signed an armistice with the new German government first—the Western Allies or the Soviet Union. At the time, it could have gone either way, as both armies were rapidly advancing toward Germany.

Other lists of people to lead the post–Hitler government were much more detailed and included particulars down to regional and local leaders (Hoffmann, *The History*,

367). Being on one of these lists ultimately became grounds for a charge of treason, and often a death sentence, whether or not the individual had anything at all to do with the events of July 20 or even knew his name was on such a list. The Gestapo had a great deal of information to work with immediately after the attempt—provided by the conspirators themselves. A list of reliable liaison officers had been compiled by von Stauffenberg, and it was discovered at the conspirators' headquarters in Bendlerstrasse on July 20. The historic officer corps was well represented. These men would be the effective commanding officers of the districts (Wehrkreise) until other arrangements could be made. In early 1943 Colonel General Beck demanded that the liaison officer list be created; it was completed later that year and delivered to Ulrich-Wilhelm Graf Schwerin von Schwanenfeld, Beck's representative. This list, like the previous one, was uncovered by the Gestapo at the conspirators' headquarters after the coup fell apart, and it conveniently provided the names of core military supporters of the putsch in Germany and occupied countries. The list was updated several times before the coup, and the version current as of July 20 survived the war (Hoffmann, *The History*, 349).

There was another long list of non-military political advisors to the Wehrkreis commanders (Hoffmann, *The History*, 357). The Gestapo used this list in subsequent arrests, which later led to trials in some cases, but being on that particular list was not an instant death sentence. Many of those so included argued successfully that they were not even aware that they had been named as advisors in a post–Hitler government. This was not a ruse; many of them had not been consulted and did not know of their pending appointment.

The Conspiracy Groups

Disparate groups of resistance-minded individuals began to coalesce soon after the Nazis came to power, and the number of groups and their membership grew after each Nazi-sanctioned crime or military reversal. Only a few of the well-known groups that were connected to July 20 are discussed here, but there were dozens of them. Some members of the major groups had their own circles within the larger organizations, so that it is often not possible to absolutely identify an individual as belonging to a single group. Other resistance groups that were not at all involved in the assassination attempt also existed. Perhaps the best known of these were the so-called Red Orchestra (Rote Kapelle), a Soviet-backed group of infiltrators from early in the Hitler regime, and the White Rose, a Munich University–based group whose most famous members were Sophie Scholl, Hans Scholl, Alex Schmorell, Willi Graf, Christoph Probst, and Kurt Huber (all executed by guillotine in 1943). There are also modern references to the Schwarze Kapelle (Black Orchestra) as the all-inclusive "Gestapo name for the informal group of aristocrats, senior officers, and diplomats in Germany who opposed Hitler and talked about bringing him down, but were unable to do so" (Dear and Foot 982). However, this designation is far too broad and not mentioned in period documents.

The conspirators did not receive much tangible encouragement from foreign leaders. They were either not believed at all or thought to be too weak, full of words instead of action. One of the members of the Oster conspiracy of 1938, who was never discovered, wrote, "This [German resistance] movement was not only not encouraged, but was indirectly opposed by Germany's enemies" (quoted in Parssinen vii). The fundamental opinions of foreign governments regarding Nazi Germany did not change substantially throughout the war, notwithstanding the existence of resistance groups. There were, however, individuals within the Allied governments who unofficially supported the resistance. In June 1942, two German pastors, Dr. Hans Schönfeld and Dietrich Bonhoeffer, met face to face with the bishop of Chichester (George Bell) in Stockholm in order to substantiate the existence of anti–Nazi groups in Germany. The bishop took this revelation seriously and wrote a detailed letter to Anthony Eden of the British Foreign Office informing him of what he had learned. In a reply to the bishop, Eden stated bluntly, "I have no doubt that it would be contrary to the interest of our nation to provide them [the pastors] with any answer whatever" (quoted in Zimmermann and Jacobsen 64). And that was that.

The so-called Freiburg Circle consisted of a group of anti–Nazi political science, economics, and history professors at Freiburg University, but its best-known members were Gerhard Ritter, Adolf Lampe, Erich Wolf, Walter Eucken, Franz Böhm, and Constantin von Dietze (Rothfels 99). Ritter was a long-time outspoken opponent of the Nazis, but he managed to survive the war (though just barely) and wrote an often-quoted book on the resistance. In 1938 Ritter gained local attention by being the only faculty member at Freiburg University to attend the funeral of Edmund Husserl, a professor there until his retirement in 1928. Husserl was born a Jew but converted to Christianity, and he was an outspoken critic of Nazi racial policies. Ritter's presence at the funeral was seen as a protest of the Nazi regime and was no doubt noted by the increasingly more powerful Gestapo arm of the party. The Kristallnacht pogrom against the Jews ultimately convinced Ritter that the resistance needed to organize much better if it was going to be the recognized opposition to Nazi policies. The result was the formation of the resistance circle initially composed of the Freiburg University professors listed above. Although Ritter was a confirmed member of the Confessing Church, the circle grew to include Lutherans, Catholics, and Calvinists who were all beginning to see Nazism as a threat to any denomination. Dietrich Bonhoeffer visited the university in the fall of 1942 and convinced a number of the faculty members to prepare and sign a declaration stating the position of the Confessing Church with regard to Europe's reconstruction after the war. Meetings with other resistance leaders, including Goerdeler, soon followed (Dulles 122).

The Freiburg Circle is best known for its widely circulated (among members of the resistance) memoranda during the war detailing discussions on a proposed structure of the German government after Hitler—another list of names that would prove useful to the Gestapo. The wording of some of these discussions was controversial at the time, and still is today, because of the "solution" to the Jewish problem being proposed. Ritter was probably the primary author of these documents, which rejected Nazi racial propaganda but also forbade German citizenship for Jews after the war. The memoranda also included projected restrictions on where Jews would be allowed to live and their relationships with Germans, banning marriage between Jews and Germans and sexual relations between Jews and German Christians (Friedlander 50). As can be imagined, these were points of contention with other, more liberal-minded resistance groups.

The Solf Circle was one of the original resistance groups and was organized by Johanna (Hanna) Solf and her daughter in 1936 after her husband's death. Johanna Solf was the widow of Dr. Wilhelm Solf, the imperial colonial secretary before World War I and later the ambassador to Japan under the Weimar Republic. Solf and her late husband were confirmed political independents who strongly opposed National Socialism policies.

The circle came to include ranking members of the Foreign Office, industrialists, academics, and statesmen. The group met regularly at the Solfs' residence in Berlin to discuss the war and coordinate relief for Jews and political enemies of the regime. Various members of the Solf Circle were also affiliated with the better-known Kreisau Circle. The prominent members of the Solf Circle included Countess Hannah von Bredow (a granddaughter of Otto von Bismarck); Count Albrecht von Bernstorff (a nephew of Count Johann von Bernstorff, who was the German ambassador to the United States during World War I); Father Friedrich Erxleben, a well-respected Jesuit priest; the historian Maximilian von Hagen; Nikolaus-Christoph von Halem, a businessman and proxy for Admiral Canaris; Richard Künzer, a lawyer in the Foreign Office; and Otto Kiep, a foreign policy advisor for the OKW and liaison officer to the Foreign Office (*The Sunday Herald* [Scotland], January 16, 2009; von Hassell and MacRae 195). Von Halem was arrested on February 22, 1942, after being denounced (under torture) by Josef Römer, a man he had paid to recruit someone to kill Hitler (von der Groeben 62, citing a People's Court document). Von Halem was sentenced to death on June 16, 1944, and executed on October 9, 1944, in Brandenburg-Görden. "The radiance and strength of his personality made him one of the most dangerous enemies of the regime" (Zimmermann and Jacobsen 255). Von Halem had nothing at all to do with the planning or execution of the coup attempt of July 20.

The Solf Circle was eventually infiltrated by a Gestapo agent named Paul Reckzeh (occasionally spelled Reckse), and on September 10, 1943, he collected enough information to effectively destroy the enclave. Several members of the circle met on that day at a birthday party given by Elisabeth von Thadden, the Protestant headmistress of a well-known school for girls in Wieblingen (and the contact between ex-chancellor Josef Wirth and General Halder) (Reitlinger 478). Guests at the party included Otto Kiep; Johanna Solf and her daughter, Countess Lagi Ballestrem-Solf; retired state secretary Arthur Zarden; and several others (Wheeler-Bennett 594).

Von Thadden had invited Reckzeh to the gathering, thinking he was a Swiss doctor (he was a doctor, though certainly not Swiss) working in Berlin. At the party, Reckzeh spoke up against the Nazis as a cover in order to encourage others to make comments that could be used against them. Countess Ballestreme-Solf stated, "Although the conversation at the tea was more guarded than usual because of his presence, everyone in that circle was so accustomed to speaking freely with the others that an outsider could easily pick up anti–Nazi statements" (quoted in Boehm 135). Kiep and Bernstorff were especially vocal and provided Reckzeh with all the information he needed. He would later testify in People's Court proceedings against Kiep and von Thadden. As a final ruse, Reckzeh offered to pass on written correspondence from members of the circle to their contacts in Switzerland and several of those at the party accepted his offer. Of course, these letters were immediately delivered to the Gestapo along with his report. The Gestapo, however, did not immediately act and arrest the lot, but the surveillance intensified.

The Solf resistance group was not without a spy network of its own, however. Unknown to Reckzeh, he was being watched and his true mission was soon discovered. Helmuth von Moltke, a member of the Kreisau Circle, quickly warned Kiep that he had been compromised. Kiep then informed the rest of the Solf Circle of the treachery. The information gained by Reckzeh was soon passed by the Gestapo to Reichsführer Himmler, who waited four months before acting, hoping to snare other members of the resistance.

On January 12, 1944, more than seventy people, including everyone who had been at the tea party as well as von Moltke, were arrested. The Solfs escaped to Bavaria but were caught there by the Gestapo and thrown into the Ravensbrück concentration camp. This operation was also the beginning of the end for the Abwehr's role in the resistance, as the connection of many of its members to the Solf Circle had been exposed (Hassell and MacRae 195).

Erich Vermehren, an established lawyer from Hamburg, and his wife, the former Countess Elisabeth von Plettenberg, were caught up in the operation as a result of their acquaintance with Kiep. Vermehren immediately arranged an escape by having himself transferred to the Abwehr office in Istanbul. He took his wife along with him, but they were both presently summoned to Berlin by the Gestapo to be questioned in connection with Kiep's case. The two of them, with the assistance of British MI6, managed to escape to Great Britain in February (von Klemperer 336). The British made certain that news of their "defection" was broadcast to the world. All this, combined with other revelations about the Abwehr, was too much for Hitler to tolerate, so on February 18, 1944, he ordered the Abwehr abolished, with its responsibilities to be taken over by the RSHA (Reichssicherheitshauptamt [the Reich Security Main Office]) under Kaltenbrunner and thus Himmler. This decision effectively eliminated most of Germany's military intelligence-gathering capabilities for the duration of the war. The competent officers remaining in the Abwehr immediately asked for and were granted transfers. Himmler preferred to employ more politically reliable people, and a number of Abwehr personnel preferred not to work for the SS in any event. The reorganization of the Abwehr was an ominous loss for the German war effort, but it also removed a valuable resource of information for the resistance movement.

Albrecht von Bernstorff, after his arrest, was first sent to Ravensbrück, where he was tortured by the Gestapo before being transferred to the Gestapo lockup at Prinz Albrecht Strasse. He was scheduled to stand trial in the People's Court, but an air raid on February 3, 1945, killed Judge Roland Freisler, which temporarily discontinued the trials. The Russians liberated the prison on April 25, but von Bernstorff, along with Richard Künzer, had already been executed by the SS on the night of April 23. The execution order may have come from the Nazi foreign minister, Joachim von Ribbentrop, but this is questionable (Hill 223). If this was the case, it is the only execution believed to have been directly ordered by him.

The Solf Circle members were tried and convicted in the People's Court, and most were eventually executed. Kiep was found to have connections to the July 20 plot, which condemned him to death automatically. He was executed in Plötzensee Prison on August 15, 1944. Elisabeth von Thadden was beheaded on September 8. (Like most of the rest of the world, Germans were hesitant to hang women regardless of their crimes.)

Johanna Solf and her daughter were thrown into Ravensbrück after their arrest, and sometime in December 1944 they were transferred to Moabit Lehrter Strasse Prison to await their trial in the People's Court. Allen Dulles writes that that "Frau Solf escaped through the intervention of the Japanese ambassador who declared that her execution would cause Germany to lose face in Japan" (Dulles 88). Her trial was subsequently delayed by Freisler until February 8. The Solf file was destroyed in the same bombing that killed Freisler, so the case was officially postponed again until April 27, by which time the Russians were already in Berlin (Wheeler-Bennett 595). These last two generally accepted facts (and historical records on the Solfs) are currently being researched by

Haftbuch (custody record book) from the Moabit Lehrter Strasse Prison. The last column gives the date on which the prisoner was either released or executed.

Eugen Solf, a grandson of Johanna Solf (see wais.stanford.edu/Germany/germany_ resistance.htm). Solf and her daughter were inexplicably released from Moabit on April 23 and survived the end of the war. By that time most of the remaining lower-level Nazi bureaucrats in the city were much more concerned for their own personal safety than following one last order that might soon land them in front of a war crimes tribunal.

After the war, Solf moved to England briefly, and her daughter was eventually reunited with her husband, Count Hubert Ballestrem, who was an officer in the Wehrmacht. Solf died on November 4, 1954, in Starnberg, Bavaria. Countess Lagi von Ballestrem-Solf died a year later on December 4, 1955, at the young age of 46 (Cook 1: 52).

The Kreisau Circle was so named (by the Gestapo) for the von Moltke family's Kreisau estate. The leaders of the circle included members of some of the best-known families in all of German nobility. Helmuth James von Moltke was the great-great nephew of the famous Field Marshal Helmuth Karl Bernhard von Moltke, who had led the Prussian army to victory over France in 1870. Peter Yorck von Wartenburg was a direct descendant of the Prussian field marshal (of the same name) of the Napoleonic era who negotiated with the Russians behind Napoleon's back, arranging the defection of the Prussian army from the French side in 1813 (Russell 8). "Goerdeler, Wilhelm Leuschner, and Jakob Kaiser were not members of this Kreisau Circle. At the risk of being condemned as too old and too reactionary, the three forbore to consider premature experiments. Goerdeler in particular was given short shrift by the 'youths'—an attitude which was to have a fateful effect upon the preparations for and the execution of the putsch of July 20" (Gisevius, *To the Bitter End*, 434).

Most members of the Kreisau Circle were conservatives from German nobility, but other intellectuals were included as well: two Jesuit priests and two Lutheran pastors, political conservatives, liberals, socialists, Communists, landowners, former trade-union leaders and diplomats (Steinbach and Tuchel 120). Through the circle, von Moltke met Augustinus Rösch, a Jesuit provincial priest, who introduced him to two other Jesuits— Alfred Delp and Lothar König. The Jesuits were the link between the Kreisau Circle and southern German resistors, including a group of monarchists led by Franz Sperr, with Dietrich Bonhoeffer (of the Freiburg Circle) being one of the group's contacts to members of the Abwehr. He was in prison at the time of the July 20 plot, having been arrested in 1943, but his resistance connections were soon discovered by the Gestapo. Major General Heinrich Graf zu Dohna-Schlobitten was a Confessing Church member who had left the military in 1919 for religious and ethical reasons, though he was recalled when the war with Poland began. He resigned again in 1943 but was executed on September 14 as a result of the July 20 plot and his connection to the Kreisau Circle.

All of the members of the Kreisau Circle were united in their core opposition to National Socialism, and many of their meetings were devoted to discussing the structure of the German government after Hitler. They were originally a nonviolent group, not planning the overthrow of the government by force, but they did what they could to inform the rest of the world about Nazi atrocities. Once their efforts in this area were uncovered, that alone was enough to put every known member of the circle under Gestapo surveillance. Eugen Gerstenmaier had this to say about the Kreisau Circle after the war:

> The Kreisau people busied themselves almost entirely with the political, cultural, economic and legal problems which a new German government would have to face after Hitler's departure. The military was not its field. The people of the Kreisau Circle were neither generals nor did they possess another order, their will to overcome the ideology of the total state, their goal to rebuild Germany in the spirit of Christianity and social justice and to coordinate it with a unified Europe [quoted in Zimmermann and Jacobsen 38].

Von Moltke was arrested on January 19, 1944, which caused the Kreisau Circle members to become much more concerned for their own lives; the group was effectively neutralized. Some of the members, including Adam von Trott zu Solz (often referred to simply as von Trott), contributed to the failed attempt of July 20 and were arrested soon afterward. First Lieutenant Peter Yorck von Wartenburg was also arrested even though he was not part of the coup itself. Von Moltke and Theodor Haubach were executed in Plötzensee Prison on January 25, 1945, along with eight other conspirators, including Nikolaus Groß, Hermann Kaiser, and former Württemberg state president Eugen Bolz.

The Wednesday Society predated the Nazi regime by some sixty years and until that time had nothing to do with political resistance.

History records the Wednesday Society (Mittwochs-Gesellschaft) as being a center of resistance to the National Socialist regime; however this is not corroborated by facts. Members of the Society represented all attitudes, from direct involvement in the July 20 conspiracy to active participation in wartime efforts and extermination programs.

The Mittwochs Gesellschaft für Wissenschaftliche Unterhaltung (the Wednesday Society for Scholarly Entertainment) was a kind of private academy, created in 1863 [January 19] as a discussion forum for prominent male representatives of the German elite (universities, military, industry, and politics). New members to fill vacancies, preferably Berlin residents, were accepted only with the approval of the Society. [The society was limited by its charter to 16 members.] The Society met about every fortnight in the home of one of the members, normally the evening's speaker, and attendance was expected. Minutes were archived, normally including the text of the lecture and brief notes on discussions.

The Gestapo reported on July 26, 1944 that the Society was "a center for [political] reaction" and on August 23 that "in fact, the Society appears increasingly to be a crystallizing nucleus [of resistance], where defeatist personalities hostile to National Socialism meet and reciprocally invigorate their attitudes." This report marked the end of the Society. It is often stated that the Society was a node of resistance, that membership *ipso facto* indicated association with non-conformists, and that new members were particularly chosen because of their critical view of the Nazis. This view of the Society is often quoted in the case of Werner Heisenberg, whose membership is supposed to add credibility to his post-war claims of covert resistance to the Nazis, but available evidence does not corroborate this. However, the Society may have served as an ostensibly neutral meeting opportunity for the few members who were indeed in the resistance network. A look at the list of members active in the period 1933–44 justifies doubting Heisenberg's conjecture. A majority of the members had, at least in 1933, greeted the new state as a promising resurrection of Germany. There were Society members who were closely aligned with National Socialist ideology and its implementation, and others who simply acquiesced to Nazi policies and discriminatory directives. There were other members who would not get involved in any pronounced dissidence, either because they regarded themselves as apolitical and had settled in to survive as best they could, or because they did not believe in the project. There were also members with exceptional courage and moral integrity, some of whom eventually made contact with the resistance group led by Carl Goerdeler and other key actors in the July 20 conspiracy; a few of them were even, at some stage, considered for a role in an interim government. However, it is doubtful whether, at the time of the crisis, these few members of the Society had any key roles either in planning the coup, or in the anticipated leadership. [The final meeting, the 1,056th, was held on July 26, 1944, with only 5 members participating (Zeller 404).]

Only four Society members are known to have been actively involved with resistance of any significance; including the July 20 attempt, and only three (Ludwig Beck, Johannes Popitz, and Ulrich von Hassell) were part of the core conspiracy. However, these three were all key players from 1938 onward. The Society cannot as a whole be described as a nucleus of resistance, which would at least have required absolute confidence between all members, some of whom were deeply involved with National Socialist policies. In popular history, the involvement of these members, by association, has determined the image of the Society, to an extent, because of their connection to the Goerdeler Circle. It is difficult to understand Heisenberg's acceptance of membership in the Society, as he probably was warned about the surveillance of some members by the SS. There is no objective evidence that Heisenberg was taken into confidence by the organized resistance or that he was considered an asset in that respect. He was not even interrogated following July 20. Only Ferdinand Sauerbruch was arrested, and he was released after some time, probably because of his important contacts to Reichsmarshal Göring [Excerpted from "A Note on the Wednesday Society and Some Related Topics," by Stephan Schwarz, Copenhagen; unpublished, used with permission of the author].

Other resistance circles of significance include the Cologne Circle and the concentrated circle around Goerdeler, although both eventually became superficially connected to the better-known groups discussed above. The Cologne Circle (Kölner Kreis), as the name implies, was based in the city of Cologne, which had for many years been a hotbed of political resistance in one form or another. As early as 1935, 232 Social Democrats were tried there as part of the Nazi mission to destroy all opposition parties (Hoffmann, *The History*, 22). On September 9, 1939, Colonel General Kurt von Hammerstein-Equord was appointed, for a short time, as commander of the loosely organized Army Detachment A, which had its headquarters in Cologne. He was an avowed enemy of Hitler and intended to invite the Führer to the area in order to capture him (Wheeler-Bennett 458). During the planning, von Hammerstein-Equord was in constant contact with members of the resistance in Berlin, particularly Fabian von Schlabrendorff. Hitler stayed away from the area, however, and on September 21, he retired von Hammerstein-Equord (for a second time), but the former officer remained active in the resistance through the Cologne Circle. Hitler, wary as always, did not make an official visit to the area until December 1939 (Hoffmann, *The History*, 114). When the resistance reconstituted itself after the war in Poland, and once again after the fiasco at Stalingrad, Cologne was always counted as one of the major cities (with officers, troops, and civilians) that could be relied upon for support when the time for action came.

Goerdeler, from Berlin, maintained constant contact with Nikolaus Groß and the KAB (Katholischen Arbeitnehmer Bewegung [Catholic Workers Movement]) in Cologne. Groß had become the unofficial spokesman for the Cologne group and liaison to the Christian trade unions, the Center Party, and the Catholic priest Alfred Delp. The Cologne Circle met at the Kettelerhaus, which was the KAB's headquarters in Cologne. Father Otto Müller tacitly led the circle and made the Kettelerhaus available for meetings. Müller himself was in contact with military opposition circles before the beginning of the war.

Goerdeler did not have universal support for his conservative-leaning ideas within the Cologne Circle, however. Father Delp promoted an alliance with the Kreisau Circle and wanted social reform to be the primary goal of any future government, which was a basic Kreisau tenet. When Joseph Joos was arrested by the Gestapo and Bernhard Letterhaus was drafted into the Wehrmacht, the Cologne Circle was left in shambles. Letterhaus had been the secretary of the Catholic Labor Movement in München-Gladbach before moving to Cologne, while Joos was a leader in the Christian socialist wing of the Center Party. Without these two men, the Cologne Circle drifted toward Goerdeler's politics, and communication between the two groups increased. Goerdeler's resistance group was based in Berlin and had useful connections with like-minded men in the military, particularly through the Abwehr; however, the ultra-conservative views of the group continued to be opposed by the more progressive Kreisaus.

> [The Goerdeler circle] drew many of its ideas from a reform movement dating from the Weimar period. Only thus can we explain the high proportion of senior civil servants in the resistance, as well as their intensive and persistent preoccupation with detailed plans for a new administrative organization to be introduced after Hitler's fall, even though it was very far from certain that Hitler would in fact be removed [Ritter 23].

Dr. Karl Strölin, the mayor of Stuttgart, was one of the elected politicians in the Cologne Circle, and he had an old friend he would draw toward the resistance: Field Marshal Erwin Rommel, who was informed of the assassination plans by Strölin in February 1944 on behalf of the Goerdeler group (Watson 169). Two months later, on April 14, General Hans Speidel (Rommel's chief of staff) represented his superior in a second meeting with Strölin at Freudenstadt in Württemberg (Majdalany 331). The field marshal was never persuaded to become an active participant in the plot, but the connection had been made. After the failure of the assassination attempt, the Gestapo arrested the remaining Cologne conspirators. Father Otto Müller, who was extremely ill at the time, was imprisoned in the hospital in Tegel Prison in Berlin. He died there on October 12, 1944.

In November 1941 there was a curious attempt made by the resistance to go through the American press to get their message to Washington politicians (Rothfels 133). Louis P. Lochner, who had supervised the Berlin office of the Associated Press for many years, was invited to meet "twelve to fifteen idealistic men." This group included representatives of the free trade unions, the Christian trade unions, the Confessing Church, the former Center Party, the Democratic Party, the Social Democrats and the German People's Party. There were also representatives of Admiral Canaris and General Beck in attendance. Lochner already knew a great deal about the situation in Germany: "Certainly more than Mr. William L. Shirer" (Rothfels 133). All those attending agreed that the United States would not be able to avoid entering the war soon, but none of them could have imagined that U.S. involvement would come a month later. The bombing of Pearl Harbor and the entrance of the United States into the war, for the most part, put an end to resistance representatives meeting directly with the American press.

3

Investigations and Deceptions

"Hitler lives." That was the news late on the night of July 20, 1944. It came as a shock to most citizens of the Reich to learn that there had been a serious attempt on their Führer's life—and in the middle of a war no less—and this time it had almost succeeded. This was obviously not a propaganda stunt. To the planners of the assassination, the news was a death knell. They had known when they joined the conspiracy that their lives would be forfeit should the attempt not succeed, and now that the assassination had failed, they would eventually be found out. These were not suicidal fanatics who sought martyrdom—they intended to survive, but there was no contingency plan if the assassination failed, and because of this, members of the conspiracy largely went their own ways immediately after July 20 and just waited for their arrests. Thousands of others who slept well, with clear consciences, would find themselves somehow accused of being connected to the plot in the coming months. Even a superficial connection to, or knowledge of, the conspiracy could result in a death sentence in the imminent trials.

It did not take Reichsführer SS Heinrich Himmler long to respond to Hitler's order for an investigation, with no time or expense to be spared. SS Obergruppenführer Dr. Ernst Kaltenbrunner, who had replaced SS Obergruppenführer Reinhard Heydrich as chief of the internal security branch when Heydrich was assassinated two years earlier, was designated by Himmler to oversee the investigation, called *Aktion Gitter* (Operation Thunderstorm). SS Obersturmbannführer (lieutenant colonel, and later promoted to Standartenführer and Gestapo commissioner) Walter Huppenkothen was ordered by Kaltenbrunner to lead the interrogations. Kaltenbrunner set about his work with enthusiasm and a desire to please the upper echelon of the party, at one time commanding as many as four hundred men during the investigation (Manvell 138). Kaltenbrunner, trained as a lawyer, did not have the flair and ambition of Heydrich, but he was much more methodical, knowing that his actions would be reviewed by the Reichsführer and always keeping in mind what had happened to his predecessor. He also knew that progress reports of his investigation would immediately reach Hitler, through Reichsleiter Martin Bormann, and eventually some version of the report would get to the public through official or unofficial routes.

Kaltenbrunner went where the evidence led him, and often where it did not, disregarding proper channels when it suited him. Reich Armaments Minister Albert Speer became aware of Kaltenbrunner's authority when he was questioned concerning a document discovered after July 20 that listed his name as a "possible" choice for armaments minister in a post–Hitler cabinet (Speer 500; Jacobsen 2: 1015). It was rumored that even

Himmler was on Kaltenbrunner's unwritten list of persons of interest. It is also known that Himmler went so far as to order Huppenkothen to investigate Reichsmarshal Göring's possible connection to resistance circles (Reitlinger 334). Marie Vassiltchikov wrote in her diary that Göring was "manifestly terrified of being somehow implicated in the recent events himself" (Vassiltchikov 225). In any case, once given his orders, Kaltenbrunner became for a time the most feared man in the Reich. In hindsight, the final destruction of the officer class, the nobility, and non–party affiliated civilian leadership was no doubt Hitler's intended by-product of the investigations.

Born in Ried im Innkreis (near Braunau), Austria (near Hitler's birthplace), on October 4, 1903, Kaltenbrunner was the son of Hugo Kaltenbrunner (a lawyer) and Therese Udwardy. He was educated at the State Realgymnasium in Linz, where Adolf Eichmann was one of his boyhood friends, and at Graz University. Kaltenbrunner received a law degree in 1926 (Wistrich 135). He soon took a trainee position in Linze-an-Danube and in 1928 continued his training in Salzburg. Kaltenbrunner joined the Nazi party in 1932 and shortly afterward became a member of the SS. He was a legal consultant for the SS VIII Abschnitt (division) in Austria and eventually became a Gauredner (representative) for the National Socialists. In 1933 he was appointed commander of SS Standarte (Regiment) 37 and later led the SS VIII Division. Kaltenbrunner was perceived as a threat by Austrian officials and, in January 1934, was briefly interned by the Engelbert Dollfuss government (with other National Socialists) at the Kaisersteinbruch concentration camp. Later that same year he was detained again on suspicion of treason related to the assassination of Dollfuss. This charge was soon dropped, but he was sentenced to six months in prison for conspiracy and his law license was revoked. Kaltenbrunner married Elisabeth Eder in 1934, and they had three children. He also fathered twins, born in 1945, with his long-time mistress Gisela Gräfin (Wolf) von Westarp. It is reported that all five of his children survived the war (*Berliner Zeitung*, April 23, 2005).

In 1935 Hitler made Kaltenbrunner the all-encompassing leader of the Austrian SS, and in this position he was instrumental in bringing about the inclusion of Austria into the Reich (the Anschluss) on March 12, 1938. For this action he was promoted by Hitler to SS Brigadeführer. Six months later, on September 11, he was promoted to the rank of SS Gruppenführer and that same year became a member of the Reichstag. On January 30, 1943, Kaltenbrunner was appointed chief of the RSHA and the SD. T he RSHA was made up of the Security Police (Sicherheitspolizei, or SiPo), the KriPo (Criminal Police), and the Gestapo (Geheimstadtpolizei [Secret State Police]). He replaced Reinhard Heydrich, who had been assassinated in June 1942, and held this position until the end of the war. After the death of Heydrich and Hitler's appointment of Kaltenbrunner as head of the RSHA, Himmler rightly believed that he had gained complete control of all Reich security. The events of July 20, however, must have made him more than a bit insecure in that knowledge. It is rarely mentioned that another of Kaltenbrunner's many positions, assumed after Heydrich's assassination, was president of the International Criminal Police Commission (ICPC), which evolved into today's Interpol.

After July 20, Kaltenbrunner had direct access to Hitler, albeit through Bormann in most cases, reporting directly to them more often than going through Himmler, which would have been the normal chain of command (and the correct one prior to July 20). Kaltenbrunner was responsible for directing the investigation of anyone involved, however remotely, in resistance organizations, and late in the war he would often authorize clandestine trials of those accused, frequently leading to their execution. These were the often-cited "hundreds of cases" that were not heard by the People's Court. Even in cases where the defendants were not given a death sentence in the People's Court system, once they were in the concentration camps, they were subject to having their sentences changed by Hitler or to trials by the Gestapo or SS, with execution being the most likely verdict. This is where the often-quoted "thousands perished after July 20" statement originates. These executions, needless to say, were not mentioned in newspapers and were, for the most part, only discovered after the war, if at all. An American correspondent was, however, told that "thousands, literally thousands of civilians were involved in the assassination plot" (quoted in Rothfels 97).

On December 9, 1944, Kaltenbrunner was awarded the Knight's Cross with Swords. He had already been awarded the Golden Party Badge and the Blood Order Badge, making him one of the most decorated members of the party without having ever led in battle during a war. Some of Kaltenbrunner's reports on the investigations after July 20 have been preserved and published, but only in German (Jacobsen, vols. 1 and 2). He was tried for multiple war crimes at Nürnberg and executed by the American hangman, John Chris Woods, on October 16, 1946.

Walter Schellenberg, Admiral Canaris' replacement after the Abwehr had been absorbed into the SD and then incorporated into the RSHA as Division VI, had this to say about Kaltenbrunner after the war:

> I know of no limitation placed on Kaltenbrunner's authority as Chief of the RSHA. He promptly entered upon the duties of the office and assumed direct charge of the office and control over the offices. He made it very clear in his official relations with all of us who were his Office Chiefs that he was the head of the office exercising full executive powers and deciding all matters of policy. He permitted us to issue directives within the organization in our own names pursuant to fixed policies established by him, but all important matters had to be submitted to him whether he signed them or we signed them. He was constantly informed of all matters of importance which went on in the entire organization [Jewish Virtual Library].

In fact, even before July 20, Kaltenbrunner had the authority to throw suspects and their relatives into concentration camps or to have them executed on the spot. He and his organizations were also responsible for capturing enemies of the state outside Germany proper. He ordered the roundup of dozens of suspects in Paris who were thought to be members of resistance groups, regardless of whether they had any involvement in the events of July 20. The destruction of evidence was the first item of business Kaltenbrunner had to deal with after the attempt, because by the time he was ordered to lead the investigation, four of the primary conspirators had already been executed and another had been allowed to commit suicide in an obvious attempt by others (who might otherwise be implicated) to cover their own tracks. Colonel General Friedrich Fromm was only the first of many who would try to avoid Kaltenbrunner's scrutiny.

Fromm was born in Berlin on October 8, 1888. He joined the German army when he came of age, and by the end of the First World War he had reached the rank of lieutenant. Fromm remained in the army (the Reichswehr) after the war, serving under General Ludwig Beck, the chief of the general staff. In 1937 he was made commander of the Ersatzheer, and during the Second World War he served as chief of armaments from 1939 to 1944 (Wistrich 69). He was an early supporter of the Nazis but later became cynical because of Hitler's micro-management in planning the war and refusal to countenance any criticism.

There is an interesting story related by Guderian, who brought Fromm along with him several times to his meetings with Hitler: "Fromm knew how to state a problem clearly; he had presence and diplomatic tact. After several conferences, in fact, his influence increased, but opposition appeared both from Field Marshal Keitel, who saw his position threatened, and from Dr. Goebbels, who tried to persuade Hitler that Fromm had a dangerous political record. Finally, Hitler clashed with Fromm over a question of reserve supplies. Curtly, Guderian was told never to bring Fromm with him again" (quoted in Speer 312). Fromm was a large, physically imposing officer—more than 6 feet, 5 inches tall—but he was continually pushed into the background by those close to Hitler, particularly Keitel.

> In the summer of 1943 the pressure on Olbricht, especially by Goerdeler and other civilian confederates became almost unbearable. At the same time his relations with Fromm grew increasingly tense. After Stauffenberg had joined Olbricht's office there began a rivalry for his services. In 1944, Fromm insisted on having "the toy" himself, as Stauffenberg put it, and to make him his own chief of staff. Before taking up his post, Stauffenberg had had a straight talk with Fromm and let him know what was in his mind. Fromm raised no objections and merely sought an assurance that his special friend Wilhelm Keitel would not be forgotten in the "clean out" [Zeller 211].

Fromm was suspected of being directly involved in the July 20 plot, but Kaltenbrunner was never able to uncover positive proof, perhaps because Fromm sufficiently covered his tracks by having von Stauffenberg, Olbricht, von Quirnheim, and von Haeften executed immediately after the failure of the coup (before they could talk) and allowing General Ludwig Beck to commit suicide. Reichsminister Speer, who was a friend of Fromm's, intended to prevent the executions, despite the certainty that doing so would raise suspicion of him; however, he arrived at the Bendlerstrasse too late (Speer 494). This apparent cover-up by Fromm did not go unnoticed by Dr. Goebbels, who was the first high-ranking party member to speak to him the night of July 20. He told Fromm, "You've been in a damned hurry to get your witnesses in the ground" (quoted in Lemons 483).

Fromm was arrested the day after the failed coup and dismissed from the military by a Hitler-instituted Court of Honor on September 14, but he was not brought before the People's Court until March 7, 1945. His accusers did not have enough evidence to connect him directly with the planning of the assassination attempt, so they charged him with not reporting the conspiracy soon enough. Fromm was found guilty, though not immediately executed. Dr. Goebbels remarked that "Colonel-General Fromm has been sentenced to death for cowardice in face of the enemy. He thoroughly deserves this sentence. Admittedly it could not be proved that he was actually involved in 20 July, but he did not take the measures which were his duty in order to prevent 20 July" (Goebbels 90). Speer recalled after the war:

> I heard, or rather had it hinted to me, that Hitler had ordered the execution of General Fromm. A few weeks before, Minister of Justice [Otto] Thierack had remarked to me, offhandedly and completely unmoved between two courses of a meal: "Fromm's going to lose his bonnet soon too." My efforts to speak up for Fromm that evening remained fruitless; Thierack was not in the least impressed. Consequently, a few days later I sent him a five page official letter in which I refuted most of the charges against Fromm, insofar as I knew what they were, and offered to appear before the People's Court as a witness for the defense. That was probably an unprecedented request on the part of a Reichsminister. Only three days later, on March 6, 1945, Thierack wrote me curtly that I would have to obtain permission from Hitler in order to testify. "The Führer has just informed me," Thierack continued, "that he has no intention of issuing exceptional permission

to you in the case of Fromm. I therefore will not include your statement in the records of the court." The executions also made me aware of the nature of the risk I was running [Speer 563].

Hitler wanted Fromm kept alive because he was certain that Fromm would lead investigators to others. Fromm was finally executed by firing squad on March 12, 1945, at Brandenburg an der Havel, just weeks before the end of the war (Hoffmann, *The History*, 528; Wistrich 69 gives the date as March 19). Hitler personally intervened and changed his method of execution from hanging, which was the prescribed sentence, to the more honorable firing squad.

The first conspiracies against Hitler and the subsequent cover-ups had occurred many years earlier, and some were only revealed during the July 20 investigation. Letters and diaries found by the Gestapo in the homes and offices of those arrested after July 20 identified some of those involved in the plots of 1938, 1939, and 1943. These discoveries led to the arrests of several high-ranking officers, including General Franz Halder, who managed to survive the late executions and finish the war in a concentration camp.

The longest-running and, without doubt, most widespread and successful deception was orchestrated by Admiral Wilhelm Canaris, the chief of the Abwehr. The grandiloquent plan hatched by Canaris (with Beck, von Witzleben, Hoepner, von Helldorf and others) to abduct Hitler in 1938 and have him secretly committed to a mental institution was only one of the strategies to come from this group. Unfortunately for those involved in the resistance, Canaris kept a diary (with multiple copies) and the most damaging parts of that diary were found—but, luckily, not until April 4, 1945. The war was coming to Berlin, and it was too late to arrest and execute everyone implicated who had thus far escaped the investigations. Canaris and his organization had (for years) concealed the identities of some of the conspirators in earlier assassination attempts.

Other diaries and writings of the conspirators led to a large number of arrests and executions; only the end of the war stopped the investigations. Most of those who ultimately avoided arrest made their way to the Americans and surrendered. Several eventually came to the United States and worked for the U.S. government, often with the only other choice being extradited to the Israelis for possible trial and execution. Other participants were never identified by the Gestapo and survived the war to later become well-known politicians (Kurt Waldheim being the perfect example). Konrad Adenauer, the first German chancellor after the war, had nothing to do with July 20 and had early on (1933) been forced from his position as mayor of Cologne; however, he was among those imprisoned after the failed coup attempt.

Canaris has been called the German "spy in chief" for good reason, as he was able to effectively run his organization while keeping others in the Hitler inner circle at arm's length. He was involved to some degree in almost every serious attempt (save the first) to get rid of Hitler. He was able to do this without attracting attention to himself or others in his organization because he performed his job to the satisfaction of his OKW superiors. In practice, he was aiding the conspirators while at the same time tracking them down.

> To deny that Canaris and Oster constituted the intellect and the sword-arm of the conspiracy in its early stages would be to deny truth. To underestimate the work done by many of the conspirators who were merely operating under Abwehr cover, such as Josef Müller, Dietrich Bonhoeffer, and [Rudolf] Count Marogna-Redwitz, the head of the office in Vienna, would be equally unjust. But to assume, as there is a certain proneness to suggest, that the Abwehr were "really on the Allied

side all the time" would be equally wide of the mark and equally unjust to men who, however inefficient they may have been as intelligence officers, were assuredly German patriots [Wheeler-Bennett 597].

Canaris was the most secretive member of the entire Nazi hierarchy, and he was able to hide his underlying plans for doing away with Hitler from all but a few of his closest collaborators in the resistance. He intentionally preferred to listen rather than talk when engaged in conversations with others, but he did keep detailed records of everything he was involved in. Perhaps secrecy was part of his personality, or maybe it came about because of his training, or it could be that he was wiser than those who spoke too freely. He was the ultimate secret keeper for those who opposed Hitler and firmly believed in the possibility of making a separate peace with each of the Allies. Canaris' spy network eventually reached around the world, and even Reichsführer SS Himmler, in his commanding position, was wary of the Abwehr chief's talent for information gathering.

Admiral Wilhelm Franz Canaris was born to a wealthy industrialist family on January 1, 1887, in Aplerbeck, near Dortmund, Germany. His father was a mining director in Westphalia. Canaris entered the German navy in 1905 at the age of 17, and in 1911 he was promoted to lieutenant (Wistrich 29). "Few personalities of our time have been the subject of so many legends, fables, and contradictory estimates" (Deutsch, *The Conspiracy*, 55).

Very early in the First World War, Canaris was on the German light cruiser *Dresden*, a participant in the South Atlantic Battle of the Falklands, which resulted in a British naval victory over the Imperial German Navy on December 8, 1914 (Zimmermann and Jacobsen 232). The British had sent a large force to track down and destroy the German cruiser squadron responsible for their defeat at the Battle of Coronel on November 1. Admiral Graf Maximilian von Spee commanded the German cadre of two armored cruisers (SMS *Scharnhorst* and SMS *Gneisenau*) and three light cruisers (the *Nürnberg*, the *Dresden* and the *Leipzig*) when they attempted to plunder the British supply base at Stanley in the Falkland Islands. Unknown to the Germans, a British squadron of two battle cruisers (HMS *Invincible* and HMS *Inflexible*), three armored cruisers (HMS *Carnarvon*, HMS *Cornwall* and HMS *Kent*), and two light cruisers (HMS *Bristol* and HMS *Glasgow*) had arrived at the port only the day before. The British were in pursuit of the five German ships as soon as they were sighted on December 8. Four of the five ships were sunk. The *Dresden* survived and escaped to the Pacific, but was finally trapped by British cruisers HMS *Glasgow* and HMS *Kent*, as well as the armored merchant cruiser *Orama*, off the Chilean coast and shelled into surrendering. During the ceasefire negotiations the ship was scuttled by its crew on March 15, 1915, to avoid capture (*Allgemeine Deutsche Biographie*; Manvell and Fraenkel, *The Canaris Conspiracy*, 252).

Canaris was held in an internment camp in Chile until he escaped in August 1915 and reached Germany in October 1915. He was then ordered to the intelligence branch of submarine operations in the Mediterranean, where he became an undercover agent working in Italy and Spain. By this time, the British knew very well who he was and sent their own agents to assassinate him. Avoiding that attempt, in 1917 he was made commander of a submarine himself and was highly decorated for his service in the Mediterranean, sinking eighteen British vessels. His success certainly did not go unnoticed by the British intelligence service, MI6. In 1919 Canaris married Erika Waag, and the couple had two daughters, Eva and Brigitte (Jörgensen 45).

Canaris joined the Freikorps and then the Reichsmarine after the war ended, took part in putting down the Kapp Putsch, and eventually became a part of Germany's secret submarine building program. He was promoted to captain in 1931 and was given the battleship *Schlesien* to command, but he felt that intelligence work was his real future. From 1930 to 1933 he made contact with various German military officers, politicians, and industrialists as well as undercover political assassins, preparing himself for a career change. By the time Hitler came to power, he was in a position to be of use to the Reich; in 1935 he was made chief of the Abwehr and later that year was promoted to rear admiral. Canaris spoke five foreign languages without accent, including English, which made him practically invisible wherever he traveled. During his career, Canaris was decorated with the Iron Cross First and Second Class, the German Cross in Silver, the Cross of Honor, and the Wehrmacht Twelve- and Twenty-Five-Year Service Ribbons (Mueller 25; Moorhouse 111).

Canaris created the German-backed spy organization in Spain in 1935–1936, and his language skills, along with his growing reputation, gained him access to Spain's dictator Francisco Franco. Undoubtedly, Canaris was also the mastermind behind Germany's decision to side with Franco during the Spanish Civil War. At this time Canaris was a strong supporter of Hitler, believing him to be the only hope of halting the rise of Communism in Europe. This opinion changed in a couple of years, and Canaris began to actively work against the Nazi regime and would do everything he could to sidetrack Hitler's plans for invading Czechoslovakia; later he went so far as to advise Franco to refuse permission for German forces to pass through Spain to capture Gibraltar. Large sums of money given to Franco and his generals by the British government probably also helped Franco make up his mind (Zimmermann and Jacobsen 235; *The Times* [London], October 15, 2008).

Canaris was involved in some of the earliest plans to assassinate Hitler in 1938 and 1939. He and Ewald von Kleist-Schmenzin hatched a very direct plan to simply kidnap Hitler and kill him before the launch of the Czechoslovakian invasion. Von Kleist-Schmenzin visited Great Britain secretly and met with politicians and MI6 to get a feel for how they would react to a replacement government. He carried with him an unambiguous promise from General Beck: "Bring me certain proof that England will fight if Czechoslovakia is attacked, and I will make an end of [Hitler's] regime" (quoted in L. Thompson 103). In these visits, the name "Canaris" was all too familiar to the British. Most German upper-echelon officers fully expected a war to result if Czechoslovakia was invaded, and generally British politicians and MI6 agreed that there was no other possible outcome. None of them took into account the lethargy of the British government and particularly the prime minister, Neville Chamberlain. The annexation of the Sudetenland was met with hardly a protest, and certainly not with threats of war. The Munich Agreement between Hitler and Chamberlain temporarily put to rest all fears of a war and gave Hitler what he wanted: a free hand in Czechoslovakia and time to build his forces. The immediate result was more far reaching than either man expected. Hitler became a true hero in Germany, and Chamberlain was seen as a peacemaker in Great Britain. Only Winston Churchill seemed to understand the Nazis' real aims, but few would listen to his doomsday predictions. One significant result of the Munich Agreement could not have been predicted by either Chamberlain or Hitler: the political maneuvers and Hitler's hero status essentially put an end to the plans of the resistance for the time being.

It is easy to blame Chamberlain for his "appeasement" of the Nazis, but in truth, if there had been no agreement, Hitler would still have insisted on invading Czechoslovakia, and Great Britain would not have been able to do much about it before the operation would have been a *fait accompli*. The British were not ready for war, mentally or materially, but without the Munich Agreement, the resistance might have unified and ended the war soon after it began—by eliminating Hitler. At the time of the Sudetenland Crisis, Germany was not prepared for war either, and even when the Munich Agreement was finalized a few months later, the Germans were still not totally prepared materially, though mentally the entire country was on a war high. Germany would likely have crushed the Czechs within a few weeks, with Hitler getting the victor's boost in popularity in any case—if he had survived the planned coup. There are, however, those who disagree with this view, among them William L. Shirer, who was in Berlin during the time of the Sudetenland Crisis and the Munich Agreement, and also in Nürnberg in 1945 when many of the secret documents of the Nazis were made public.

> Munich, then, was not a bluff, as most of us had believed. Hitler was ready to go to war and would have, had not Chamberlain and Daladier surrendered. Some may think this vindicates the bungling British Prime Minister. But I take the opposite view ... he only postponed the World War by eleven months. Had Germany started it in 1938, I think we are justified in concluding from these German documents themselves that it would not have lasted long, that Germany would have been easily and quickly beaten.... In the opinion of most of the German military experts themselves, the Third Reich was not powerful enough in 1938 to take on Britain, France, Russia, Czechoslovakia, and probably Poland at one time [Shirer, *End*, 311].

Shirer here assumes there would have been an immediate grand coalition of the countries mentioned to oppose Germany, which is a rather optimistic conjecture.

After the Munich Agreement on September 22, 1938, and the forced resignation of General Beck, the conspirators reorganized and approached General Franz Halder, Beck's replacement, to lead a broad military rebellion. A coup was planned to begin soon after the Allies' declaration of war in 1939, but before overt military operations commenced. In support of these intrigues, Canaris convinced Halder to establish an Abwehr office under the Oberquartiermeister IV (intelligence) division at the headquarters of the OKH at Zossen. This office was initially under the command of Oberstleutnant (Lieutenant Colonel) Helmuth Groscurth, the former chief of Abwehr Group II (sabotage intelligence). Groscurth's command had only four officers—Dr. Kurt Fiedler, Dr. Hasso von Etzdorf, Ernst von Weizsäcker, and Werner Schrader—and they were all firmly in the anti–Nazi camp. Canaris was explicit in his orders "that any officers transferred from Austrian intelligence to the Abwehr must be anti-Nazis. 'Bring me real Austrians,' he said, 'and not Ostmärker'" (quoted in Deutsch, *Hitler*, 374). The command's official task was to act as a liaison between Halder and Hans Oster at Abwehr headquarters in Berlin, but its undercover mission was to support the planned coup of anti–Nazi elements in the OKH.

In one of his many creative moves, Canaris invented the "Dutch War Scare" in January 1939 in an attempt to warn the British of events to come and potentially bring about a change in British policy toward Germany. It was a contrived leak of information indicating Germany's intent to invade the Netherlands in a month and then use the Dutch airfields to attack Great Britain. The fabricated information was taken seriously, and to Chamberlain's credit, he responded by sending ground troops to France the next month. Canaris' fiction turned out to be a forecast that would come true soon enough.

On September 22, 1939, Himmler appointed Obergruppenführer Reinhard Heydrich to be chief of the Reich Security Main Office (RSHA). Heydrich had been chief of the SD (Sicherheitsdienst) within the RSHA since 1932 and had served under Canaris as a naval officer. The two of them were also friends, making Canaris' appointment as Abwehr chief in 1935 almost assured. The Abwehr, however, reported directly to the OKW, not the RSHA, and its role was often seen as being in conflict with the SD. In outward appearance, Canaris' Abwehr cooperated fully with the RSHA at all levels, but this was a marriage in name only. He was swiftly expanding his spy network with the blessing of the OKW, which had an upcoming war to worry about. During this time, Canaris' agents maintained contact with the British MI6 even as war was becoming a certainty.

Soon after the war began in September 1939, Canaris visited the front in Poland and saw first-hand an example of the atrocities committed by Himmler's SS Einsatzgruppen in the burning of the Bedzin synagogue with two hundred Jews inside. He knew from his agents about other killings being committed in the region as well (World War II Database). Canaris recounted what he had seen to Field Marshal Wilhelm Keitel, warning him that the world would someday hold the entire German military responsible. Canaris was not a champion of the Jews by any means and believed that segregating them or exporting them to former German colonies in Africa and the Pacific would be fitting solutions to the Jewish problem (Mommsen 260). However, the blatant murder of the Polish Jews was intolerable. This became his motivation for reviving plans to rid the country of Hitler and the Nazis, but he had to continue cooperating with the SD if his plans were to remain secret. Canaris instructed his agents to collect information on war crimes being committed in Poland; he then passed this information on to Dr. Josef Müller, a leading Catholic member of the resistance, who passed it on to the Vatican in Rome. Canaris likewise sent Dietrich Bonhoeffer to Sweden to meet with Bishop Bell of Chichester to personally inform him of the massacres in Poland and convince him that there was a rising resistance movement in Germany. Canaris also began systematically leaking information to General Beck, Carl Goerdeler, and others who were creating their own plots against the regime.

Canaris was promoted to full admiral in January 1940 and soon began enlisting resistance-minded members of the Wehrmacht to serve in the Abwehr. He was also in contact with a British agent named Halina Szymanska, the wife of Polish colonel Antoni Szymanska, the last prewar Polish military attaché in Berlin. There are indications that Canaris' relationship with Halina may have been more than professional (N. West 136). Canaris soon appointed his long-time friend, Major General Hans Oster, to be his second in command at the Abwehr. Oster transformed resistance members into Abwehr agents and gave them just enough confidential information to make the ruse believable. Another Canaris friend, Major General Erwin Lahousen-Viremont, and civilian Catholic lawyer Hans von Dohnanyi would also figure prominently in the Abwehr resistance circle. Oster was soon made responsible for all the agency's military plans. He and Canaris were able to use the Abwehr itself to cover resistance missions, to aid Jews escaping from Germany, and to act as a liaison between the different resistance circles throughout the Reich.

Churchill became British prime minister in May 1940, thus changing everything. Canaris knew of Churchill's outspoken opposition to the Nazis long before the war, so he had reason to believe that British support of German resistance would now increase, but the official word from Churchill was that unconditional surrender would have to occur first. This news did not deter Canaris because he knew that Churchill couldn't say anything else, since unconditional surrender was the widely accepted British position before he became prime minister. However, on January 20, 1941, Churchill made it clear that his Foreign Office was to ignore any peace feelers from inside Germany: "Our attitude towards all such inquiries or suggestions should be absolute silence" (quoted in Vassiltchikov 190).

Just prior to Operation Barbarossa, the invasion of Russia, Canaris received and passed on detailed information to OKW regarding Russian troop strength and formations. It is speculated today that the information came from the British with Churchill's blessing—the same conclusion drawn by Heydrich and Himmler. They would file away that knowledge for future use against Canaris. At this time the British had no official agreement with Russia, and there were many in the government who believed the German invasion would counter the spread of Communism.

The first serious conflict between Canaris and Heydrich arose over a known British secret agent arrested by the Gestapo. Heydrich was by this time also the Reichsprotektor of Bohemia and Moravia, and the agent was a Czech named Paul Thümmel. Canaris demanded his release, saying he was an Abwehr agent, but Heydrich suspected Thümmel's true allegiance and that he was Canaris' contact with British MI6, which was indeed the case. Thümmel was set free, but Canaris himself had attracted additional suspicion. It would not be the last time he would intervene to rescue individuals detained by the Gestapo, claiming that they were arresting his agents. He personally had several MI6 contacts through Zurich, Spain, and the Vatican, and there is reason to believe that the assassination of Heydrich in 1942, with its organization credited to MI6, was carried out substantially to protect Canaris' position. The inscrutable Canaris delivered one of the eulogies at his friend's funeral (Wistrich 29).

After the defeat at Stalingrad in January 1943, Canaris had a plan in place to arrest the entire Nazi high command for crimes he knew about and could prove. Hitler would be judged insane and imprisoned for life. This was actually the revival of an Abwehr plan (discussed earlier) hatched before the war (Dulles 77). However, despite the defeat in Russia, Hitler's civilian popularity did not significantly decline and there was no guarantee that his arrest would be seen as anything other than high treason.

In March 1943 Canaris traveled to Smolensk in the company of conspirators on the staff of Army Group Center to plan Hitler's assassination. Later he also convinced Hitler that the Allies would not land on Anzio, presumably so the landing would have a better chance of success. In April 1943, Canaris met with George H. Earle, President Roosevelt's representative for the Balkans, then posted to Istanbul. He told Earle that a surrender of German forces to the Americans could be arranged—shades of 1918, except this time it would clearly be the military giving the "stab in the back." Earle immediately informed Washington, but a month later he was still waiting for a reply. Canaris met with General Stuart Menzies (chief of British intelligence) and William J. Donovan (head of the American Office of Strategic Services) at Santander, Spain, in the summer of 1943 and suggested another plan for ending the war immediately: Hitler would be eliminated by arrest or assassination in return for a cease-fire agreement in the West and permission to continue the war in the East. All three agreed on the plan, but it was dismissed out of hand by Roosevelt as unfeasible because of obligations to the Russians and his mistrust of the Germans' ability (or willingness) to go through with the plan.

The evidence that Canaris was working with the Allies against the Nazis soon became too persuasive to ignore; at the urging of Göring, Himmler appointed Oberkriegsgerichtsrat Dr. Manfred Roeder to investigate the Abwehr. Roeder had been responsible for exposing the Red Orchestra conspiracy group and had a reputation that earned him the nickname "the bloodhound" (Wheeler-Bennett 565). The investigation led to the arrest of Dietrich Bonhoeffer, Josef Müller and Hans von Dohnanyi in April 1943. Canaris was able to hang on to the Abwehr with the assistance of Oster, who wasted no time in destroying much of the incriminating evidence against those arrested, but time was running out. Hitler removed Canaris from the Abwehr in February 1944 and replaced him with Walter Schellenberg. Himmler finally got the Abwehr under his control when Hitler ordered it merged with the SD. Canaris was not thrown in jail, but he was put under house arrest, which prevented him from further involvement with the conspirators.

After July 20 Himmler was informed that one of the officers involved in the plot, Oberstleutnant Werner Schrader, had been responsible for keeping detailed records of meetings and various assassination plans. Kurt Kurstenhan, Schrader's driver, led the Gestapo to the files in Zossen. The documents described multiple attempts that had been planned, with some having been implemented unsuccessfully, and revealed multiple officers and civilians who had up to this point escaped attention. The files also included documents related to Josef Müller's negotiations with the British government through the Vatican, often referred to as the "X-Report," and parts of Canaris' diary (von Hassell and MacRae 254). This discovery led to hundreds of additional arrests and more investigations. Canaris himself was soon arrested, along with several others under his command. They were locked in cells in the basement of the Gestapo headquarters at Prinz Albrecht Strasse. Canaris was given special attention by being kept in solitary confinement, bound in chains, starved, and not allowed to sleep. He was fifty-eight years old and not a physically strong man. After being regularly tortured and interrogated, his health deteriorated rapidly. Oster, also tortured regularly, did his best to deflect the questions of the SS interrogators (Franz Sonderegger and Walter Huppenkothen) away from Canaris, but when he was questioned regarding the previously obtained statements of Alexander von Pfuhlstein and Friedrich Wilhelm Heinz that directly implicated Canaris, Oster was forced to talk (Mueller 245–46).

It is generally believed that Himmler kept Canaris alive because he planned to use him in a bargain with the British to end the war, with himself left as chancellor after Hitler was eliminated. Hitler wanted Canaris kept alive so that information could be extracted regarding others involved in the resistance. Canaris, however, thought well ahead of his interrogators and only told them things they already knew, and the Allies had no desire to negotiate with Himmler for anything, so neither plan came together, and Himmler finally received approval from Hitler to execute Canaris. On February 7, 1945, Canaris was transferred to the Flossenbürg concentration camp, where his ill treatment continued, as did the fruitless interrogations.

Huppenkothen and SS Judge Otto Thorbeck were sent by Himmler to Flossenbürg to try Canaris and the other resistance members held there. These SS officers held a trial for the prisoners as instructed, with Huppenkothen prosecuting, and on the morning of April 9, 1945, gallows were erected in the courtyard of the camp. Canaris, Bonhoeffer, Oster, Judge Advocate General Karl Sack, and Captain Ludwig Gehre were ordered to undress. They were then marched to the gallows past a line of SS men who mocked and cursed them. After being given a moment to pray, they were all hanged, and their bodies were left at the gallows (Manvell and Fraenkel, *The Canaris Conspiracy*, 225). On April 25 Flossenbürg was liberated by American troops, just two weeks after the hangings. A letter written by Canaris' wife in November 1945 to William Donovan (head of the

Office of Strategic Services) is included in Appendix C. This correspondence reveals, in a few paragraphs, Canaris' true character.

The former director of Danish military intelligence, Colonel Hans Mathiesen Lunding, was locked in the cell next to Canaris, and the two communicated via tapping on the wall. Just before he was led out to be executed, Canaris reported that he had been badly beaten and that this was probably the end for him. He also asked Lunding to contact his wife if he himself survived (Manvell and Fraenkel, *The Canaris Conspiracy*, 225).

After the war, Huppenkothen and Thorbeck stood trial three times, but they were never convicted of murder. The final ruling in 1956 was that the SS court had in fact been legal and that the Nazi regime had the right at the time to execute traitors (Ueberschär 308). This ruling, however, did not stand the test of time.

Hans Bernd Gisevius, one of the surviving conspirators, wrote about Canaris in 1947:

> In reality this small, frail, and somewhat timid man was a vibrating bundle of nerves. Extremely well read, oversensitive, "sicklied o'er with the pale cast of thought," Canaris was an outsider in every respect. In bearing and manner of work he was the most unmilitary of persons ... Canaris had a natural bent for leading his opponents astray. He could recite the Nazi verses so convincingly that even the greatest skeptics temporarily no longer dared to question the genuineness of his claims. As one of the leading Gestapo officials exclaimed in angry candor to one of the few survivors of the July 20 Putsch: "That Canaris fooled everyone, Heydrich, Himmler, Keitel, Ribbentrop, and even the Führer" [Gisevius, *To the Bitter End*, 444].

The Nürnberg trials revealed a great deal more about Canaris' efforts to stop executions by the SS in Russia and his having helped in saving the lives of hundreds, if not thousands, of Jews. From a German point of view at the time, he would also have been recognized as the most dangerous traitor of all those working against the Reich, deserving whatever punishment befell him. "From Kaltenbrunner's last reports to Hitler in the autumn of 1944 one can see how much the Gestapo was still in doubt which side Canaris really stood on" (Zimmermann and Jacobsen 236, citing von Schlabrendorff, *The Secret War*).

Lieutenant Colonel Werner Schrader was born on March 7, 1895, in Rottorf, Germany. At the outbreak of World War I, he enlisted in the Wehrmacht and served until the surrender and beyond. He left the military in 1920 as an Oberleutnant (first lieutenant). Schrader then taught school from 1924 to 1927 in Wolfenbüttel and was deeply involved with the Stahlhelm (literally, Steel Helmet, an organization of ex-military servicemen, founded in 1918 by Franz Seldte), eventually becoming the Landesführer (district leader) for the Brunswick area in 1927 (German Resistance Memorial Center). Schrader was an early antagonist of the National Socialists and, through his position in the Stahlhelm, regularly voiced his opposition. This made him an immediate target of the SA, which eventually succeeded in getting him arrested and thrown into a concentration camp. Schrader soon escaped from the camp and, as an officer, was able to reenter the Wehrmacht without inquiry, but his past began to catch up with him and he was certain he would be arrested again (Deutsch, *The Conspiracy*, 60–61). Admiral Canaris requested Schrader's transfer to the Abwehr in 1936, which relieved the immediate threat of arrest and gained Canaris a ready-made member of his nascent resistance group (Zeller 219). Schrader was posted to several intelligence organizations, including those based in Munich and Vienna, and by 1938 he was covertly collecting criminal evidence against the Nazis. In Munich and Vienna, he became acquainted with many who would later figure prominently in the resistance—notably, Lieutenant Colonel Helmuth Groscurth (Deutsch, *The Conspiracy*, 199).

Schrader was promoted to major in September 1940 and assigned to XVII Corps headquarters as an Abwehr officer. A year later he was reassigned to the Heerwesenabteilung (ground forces support battalion) in Zossen under the command of Oberst (Colonel) Albert Radke. Schrader eventually commanded a reserve battalion there and was promoted to Oberstleutnant (lieutenant colonel) in 1944. This assignment would be his last. In 1944 the entire detachment was transferred to Oberst Wessel Freytag von Loringhoven's Abwehr II.

Schrader's relevance to the present story is his role as caretaker of the files and papers of the Abwehr resistance circle, and specifically the files of Hans Oster and Hans von Dohnanyi that became evidence after July 20. Schrader had kept records since 1939, moving them several times for safekeeping. They included a detailed account of the 1938 and 1939 coup plans, complete with names of those involved, and detailed evidence of Nazi war crimes committed in Poland after the war began. Dietrich Bonhoeffer's father, Dr. Karl Bonhoeffer, had prepared a preliminary mental evaluation of Hitler in 1938 with information gathered by his son-in-law, von Dohnanyi, which was to be used as evidence against Hitler in a trial planned by the resistance after they kidnapped him. This documentation was also in Schrader's files, along with reports of Josef Müller's and Bonhoeffer's secret missions to the Vatican and Sweden (the X-Report among them). The accumulated files were kept in order to provide written evidence (after Hitler's demise) to the world that an active resistance had existed in Germany for some time and that it included both civilian and military personnel. Schrader was also custodian of Canaris' personal diary covering the years 1938–1942. Later diaries stayed in Canaris' possession except for small excerpts from 1943, which were locked in Schrader's safe at Zossen. The early diaries were more damaging in that they contained details of Canaris' involvement in previous conspiracies and his personal opinions of Hitler (Manvell and Fraenkel, *The Canaris Conspiracy*, 191 and 232).

The earliest files compiled and kept by Schrader were hidden at his mother's house at Groß Denkte and later at the farm belonging to his brother-in-law, Franz Kracke, also at Groß Denkte. These files were eventually combined with those of Oster and von Dohnanyi, and several of the files were even kept in Oster's office safe. Most of the files, with the exception of Canaris' diary, were moved in 1942 to the vault of the Preussiche Staatsbank in Berlin, where Oberst Friedrich Wilhelm Heinz's brother-in-law was the manager. The files were moved again a year later (after von Dohnanyi's arrest and Oster's dismissal) to a bunker at Camp Zeppelin in Zossen, where Schrader's office was located. After Schrader's suicide, his wife Cornelia burned all the remaining files that were at Groß Denkte.

Other responsibilities assigned to Schrader had him heavily involved in the procurement and safekeeping of explosives for the conspiracy, and according to SD reports submitted by Kaltenbrunner to Bormann, he was directly involved in the procurement and delivery of the explosive that von Stauffenberg used at the Wolfsschanze on July 20. However, several deliveries of explosive were made to the conspirators during this time period, so there is no way of knowing with certainty if Kaltenbrunner was right.

In June 1944 von Loringhoven became head of Abwehr II, and at the end of the month Schrader delivered explosive material and fuses to him, which were then passed on to von Stauffenberg. It is possible, then, that Kaltenbrunner was correct in his report that this was the explosive used on July 20. Earlier, on November 28, 1943, some of the explosives procured by General Stieff and kept by Schrader were buried under a watch-tower at Rastenburg by co-conspirators Major Joachim Kuhn and Lieutenant Albrecht von Hagen, but they were seen in the act by guards. These were explosives that were to have been used by Axel von dem Bussche-Streithorst for one of the uniform display attempts mentioned earlier (Fest, *Plotting*, 224). The guards promptly investigated and found the explosives, but they had not been close enough to identify those involved. An investigation was called for, and as luck would have it, Schrader, as an Abwehr officer, was put in charge of it (Zeller 264). Another story involves the unexpected detonation of explosives buried under a water tower at Rastenburg in late 1943, with Schrader handling the investigation (Duffy and Ricci 138). It is quite possible that these two stories are describing the same event with some important differences in details (see "Oberst i.G. Henning von Tresckow und die Staatsstreichpläne im Jahr 1943," *Vierteljahrshefte für Zeitgeschichte*, 55 [2007], 331–364).

Schrader is known to have visited Canaris several times after Canaris was relieved of command of the Abwehr in February 1944. Schrader also briefed Canaris' immediate successor, Colonel Georg-Alexander Hansen, on the SD's hostile takeover of the organization. In early July Schrader told Canaris what he knew of von Stauffenberg's plans, but it is unknown whether Schrader himself had been given specific details of the operation or whether Canaris was already aware of everything he was told.

On July 26, after von Stauffenberg's failed attempt, Schrader returned to Zossen to remove or destroy any compromising records stored there, but the heavily guarded Zossen complex was locked down soon after Schrader's arrival, probably because of the suicides of General Eduard Wagner and Oberst Wessel Freytag von Loringhoven that same day. Schrader had no opportunity to destroy the records. At 5:30 p.m. on July 28, Schrader shot and killed himself, leaving a note that said, "I will not go to prison; I will not let them torture me" (quoted in Hoffmann, *The History*, 516).

Werner Schrader was posthumously expelled from the army on August 4, 1944, by an Army Court of Honor, demanded by Hitler and chaired by General Field Marshal Gerd von Rundstedt (Zimmermann and Jacobsen 196). His wife and one of his sons, Werner Wolf Schrader, were also soon arrested. Werner Wolf was a member of the Abwehr, serving as a member of von Loringhoven's Abwehr II, and was stationed in Yugoslavia on July 20. He was never implicated in the conspiracy and survived the war (Manvell and Fraenkel, *The Canaris Conspiracy*, 191).

Kurt Kurstenhan was Schrader's driver and had been involved in several of the document transfers. He was a loyal member of the resistance dating back to Otto Strasser's anti–Hitler "Black Front." Kurstenhan was interrogated by Franz Sonderegger after Schrader's suicide and eventually gave up information on the 1943 transfer of documents to Zossen. Kurstenhan led Sonderegger to the safe in the Zossen bunker, and when it was cracked open, Sonderegger found the complete von Dohnanyi archive. This new evidence led to more intense interrogation of Canaris, who was already in custody, and to the implication of many others not yet connected to the conspiracy, including Generals Georg Thomas and Eduard Wagner, SS Gruppenführer Artur Nebe, and Field Marshal von Brauchitsch.

Canaris' Zossen diary for the years 1939–1943 was discovered on April 4, 1945, when General Walther Buhle moved his headquarters into another Zossen bunker that had earlier been used by the OKH. Buhle was one of those seriously wounded in the July 20 attempt, so he did not hesitate to turn the diary over to the SD. The diary soon made its way to Hitler, who immediately ordered the execution of Canaris and others of his group (forum.axishistory.com/viewtopic.php?f=5&t=111316&p=980237&hilit=+werner+schrader+).

Field Marshal Erwin Rommel was also accused of having knowledge of the July 20 plot and not passing it up the chain of command—the very same charge lodged against Fromm. According to Speidel, "Rommel made up his mind to do his part in ridding Germany of Hitler's rule" (quoted in Shirer, *The Rise and Fall*, 1042). Although Rommel was not visibly (or regularly) a part of any organized resistance movement, he was known to privately criticize the government and express his disillusionment with Hitler. There is no hard proof, however, that he actively participated in any assassination attempt, while there is evidence that he was in favor of arresting Hitler and putting him on trial (Speidel 74; Majdalany 332). As the Allies marched west after the Normandy invasion, Rommel took his life in his hands by writing a teletyped memo to Hitler on July 15 that could easily have been interpreted as an ultimatum regarding the desperate military situation in the west. When the message had been sent, he told Speidel, "I have given him his last chance. If he does not like it, we will act" (Speidel 111). The memo was sent just two days before Rommel was seriously wounded and almost killed in an air attack on his staff car. "Rommel was in fact eliminated in the very hour his army and his people could spare him least" (Speidel 112).

Rommel's fame in Germany—and indeed throughout the world—made his opinions on anything worrisome to those in the Nazi hierarchy. Goerdeler had gone so far as to list Rommel (almost certainly without his knowledge) among those to be brought into a post–Hitler government, naming him as a possible presidential candidate. After the July 20 attempt, Goerdeler's list found its way into the hands of the Gestapo, and, under torture, other members of the resistance revealed Rommel's knowledge of the coup. That was far too much to be forgiven, regardless of the field marshal's popularity. Information from Colonel Cäsar von Hofacker (a cousin of von Stauffenberg) obtained during his interrogation by the Gestapo implied (or the Gestapo twisted it to imply) that Rommel *may* have known about the July 20 plans and *may* have known about other attempts as well. Nazi party officials in France relayed to Berlin that when Rommel had been hospitalized there earlier in the year, he had disparaged party leaders and referred to crimes committed on their orders. After weighing all this damaging evidence, Hitler ordered Rommel's execution. An Army Court of Honor was then called for (where he could very well have been found innocent by his peers) to determine whether Rommel should be handed over to the People's Court for trial. Gerd von Rundstedt was a member of the Court of Honor, and in the past he had met with Rommel often enough to develop a trust in his judgment. He also understood the need to replace Hitler; however, by this time von Rundstedt had become dispirited regarding the resistance and saw its failure as inevitable. He did not advocate for Rommel's acquittal, and the Court of Honor's decision was a foregone conclusion without his support. Rommel was to be handed over to Judge Freisler's People's Court, where the verdict would almost certainly be guilty. Hitler would not have permitted a finding of innocent to stand in any event.

It would not be so simple, however, to try Rommel in the People's Court like the others. Rommel was very popular, and there would be a public outcry if he were dragged through the mud. Also, since he had often been publicly extolled by Hitler, it could not appear that Hitler had anything personally to do with Rommel's prosecution. A way was needed to dispose of Rommel without Hitler being connected to the deed. That duty was assigned to Field Marshal Keitel, who gave Wehrmacht generals Wilhelm Burgdorf and Ernst Maisel the task of approaching Rommel on October 14 and demanding his choice in the matter—committing suicide or facing the People's Court (Persico 411). Rommel made his decision and said his farewells to his wife and son, telling them he would be dead within a quarter hour. Rommel got into Burgdorf's car, driven by SS Oberscharführer Heinrich Doose, and rode with them and Maisel toward Ulm. Burgdorf had the car stopped along the way and ordered Maisel and Doose out of the car. They got out and walked away, leaving Rommel alone with Burgdorf. After a few minutes, Burgdorf called the two men back to the car. Rommel was already dead from the poison Burgdorf had brought along. Rommel's wife was subsequently informed that her husband had died from a brain hemorrhage (Manvell and Fraenkel, *The Men Who Tried*, 203).

It was initially reported by the news media that Rommel had either suffered a heart attack or died as a result of injuries he had received when his car was strafed earlier that year. However, there were widespread rumors in Germany and abroad that things were not exactly as reported. Hitler ordered an official day of mourning and Rommel was buried with full military honors, with his wife receiving letters of condolence from every high-ranking government official. Hitler did not personally attend the funeral, sending Field Marshal von Rundstedt as his representative (Marshall 189). After the war, von Rundstedt claimed that he knew nothing of the forced suicide (Wheeler-Bennett 688). This is possible, as von Rundstedt would not have been officially informed, though he would have heard the rumors. It is likely he simply never asked what had really happened to Field Marshal Rommel—because he did not want to know.

There may be more to this story than is generally known. "On July 15 Rommel saw the hopelessness of the Normandy situation and demanded that Hitler negotiate an armistice. Forty-eight hours later two planes with British markings attacked Rommel's car and shot it off the road. The one volley hit the car and knocked Rommel out onto the road. The Field Marshal lived but suffered a fractured skull, a broken cheekbone, an eye injury, and a concussion of the brain. The curious thing is, according to British records, no RAF plane could have been involved. It is possible that Hitler had been planning Rommel's death for some time" (Wallechinsky and Wallace 50). This suggestion is obviously pretty far fetched and no original source is given beyond "British records," but stranger things did happen during the war.

There is another dubious version of exactly how Rommel died: "Rommel was given a choice to face the People's Court or to be shot by the German police. Rommel chose the latter because, he explained to his wife and son, it would be better to die immediately with honor rather than die after facing national humiliation at the People's Court. He was then taken to a secret place in or around Berlin where he was shot by two Gestapo officials. He was then hailed as a national hero who died as a result of sustaining injuries" (see www.statemaster.com/encyclopedia/Erwin-Rommel). This account has been cited as coming from Shirer's *The Rise and Fall of the Third Reich*; however, the story is not in the book.

Churchill said, on hearing of Rommel's death, "He also deserves our respect, because, although a loyal German soldier, he came to hate Hitler and all his works, and took part in the conspiracy to rescue Germany by displacing the maniac and tyrant. For this, he paid the forfeit of his life. In the sombre wars of modern democracy, there is little place for chivalry" (Churchill 370).

An edited version of Rommel's diary was published by Basil Henry Liddell Hart as *The Rommel Papers* after the war. His well-tended grave is in Herrlingen, just west of Ulm.

Members of the SS were generally excluded from conspiracy circles since they had already sworn a personal oath of loyalty to Hitler, promising to defend him even to death. There is, however, one well-known exception: SS General (Gruppenführer) Artur Nebe. Born in Berlin on November 13, 1894, he was the son of an elementary school teacher and volunteered for military service during World War I in the 17th Pioneer Battalion, being injured twice in poison gas attacks.

Before joining the SS, Nebe was a civilian police detective and personally observed the heavy-handed incompetence of the SS security police (the SD). In 1920 he joined the civilian Berlin detective division of the Kriminalpolizei (KriPo), being promoted to police commissioner four years later. Nebe was particularly critical of the KriPo's methods after it became a part of the SS, even though by that time he had himself become a member of the Nazi party and the SS on July 1, 1931 (Wistrich 177). He soon became the party's primary contact with the Berlin KriPo and established a working relationship with Kurt Daluege, who would rise to become deputy Reichsprotektor of Bohemia and Moravia after Reinhard Heydrich's assassination. In early 1932 Nebe helped found the National Socialist Civil Service Society of the Berlin Police Department. Soon after the Nazis took control of the government, Daluege endorsed Nebe for a supervisory position in the State Police; years later, as the chief of KriPo, he would be involved in the investigation of the 1942 murder of SS Obergruppenführer Heydrich (at which time Nebe would conclude that the Gestapo was rather more interested in retaliations than in investigating the murder).

In October 1933 Nebe was ordered by Rudolf Diels, the Gestapo chief (who would marry Reichsmarshal Göring's stepsister's daughter, Ilse, in 1943), to arrange the assassination of Gregor Strasser, one of the original founders of the Nazi party, who had begun to openly voice his opposition to Hitler. Nebe could not justify this killing to himself and began to incrementally lean toward the resistance, such as it existed at the time. In 1936 he was selected to become chief of KriPo, which would later become the Criminal Police of Department V in the RSHA, and in 1937 a corresponding department was created for the entire Reich. The Gestapo then became one of the two main components of the new SD. Nebe, acutely aware of his position, would write a book on the criminal police, with Heydrich providing the introduction (Reitlinger 35).

When the KriPo was absorbed into the SD, Nebe was promoted to Gruppenführer. He continued to work in the SD, and his position there allowed him to observe directly the methods of Heydrich and Himmler. What he saw turned him further toward the resistance, leading him in the same year to be introduced to Gisevius, who was an official in the Berlin Gestapo headquarters. Gisevius became a close friend and introduced Nebe to Major General Hans Oster (Reitlinger 182).

Nebe was one of the ranking officers sympathetic to Dr. Karl Sack's (the Wehrmacht judge advocate general and a long-time member of the opposition) efforts in defending General Werner von Fritsch in 1938 (von Schlabrendorff, *The Secret War*, 173). This was no doubt looked upon with suspicion and disapproval by Reichsführer Himmler, but there were many in the regime who openly supported von Fritsch at the time, so no direct action was taken against Nebe. In September of the same year, Nebe joined Oster as part of the September 1938 coup attempt, which was to take place if Hitler went to war with Czechoslovakia over the Sudetenland. Nebe's role was to provide information on SS troop strengths, logistics, and the location of safe places throughout the Berlin area where conspirators could hide away temporarily. Ironically, the next year Nebe was put in charge of the investigation of the Elser assassination attempt.

In 1941 Nebe was ordered by Himmler to lead Einsatzgruppe B behind Army Group Center in support of Operation Barbarossa. Nebe knew what this would mean and asked for a transfer, but (as the story goes) Generals Beck and Oster convinced him to accept the command so that he could continue supplying the resistance with information. Nebe's Einsatzgruppe was reportedly responsible for the murder of hundreds, if not thousands, of civilians and military personnel (www.holocaust-education.dk/ordforklaringer/artur_Nebe.html). But another author, Fabian von Schlabrendorff, states that Nebe also "invented a thousand pretexts for sabotaging Hitler's murderous orders" (von Schlabrendorff, *They Almost Killed*, 37). It is believed that Nebe intentionally inflated the numbers he reported and that "SS detachments not subordinate to him were sent into his district to carry on their butcheries" (quoted in von Schlabrendorff, *They Almost Killed*, 37, and *The Secret War*, 174). Nebe returned from Russia convinced that the war was lost and that Germany would suffer because of the atrocities he himself had seen and been part of. An unreferenced Public Broadcasting Station (PBS) story that credits Nebe with inventing the use of carbon monoxide to kill Jews after coming home drunk and passing out in his garage with his car running just does not ring true (www.pbs.org/auschwitz/40-45/killing/). Perhaps the story originated with the work of a chemist named Dr. Albert Widmann assigned to Nebe's KriPo; he once related a story to Nebe in 1939 of a case of death by fume inhalation and advised that such a method using carbon monoxide might be used for mass extermination (Burleigh 385).

Nebe was to lead a team of a dozen policemen to kill Himmler as part of the July 20 coup, but the order to act never reached him. After the failure of the assassination attempt, he faked his own suicide and went into hiding on an island in Motzenmühle (on Lake Motzen, south of Berlin) with the Frick family, but he was later arrested by his own people after a mistress, Adelheid Gobbin, betrayed him to the Gestapo (Burleigh 715). However, Gobbin claimed that she was the one who had arranged for Nebe to stay with the Frick family and that the Gestapo threatened to shoot her, her mother, and her sister if she did not reveal Nebe's location (Weigelt 153).

After Nebe's arrest, Walter Frick and his family were arrested and their property confiscated (Gisevius, *To the Bitter End*, 587). Nebe was prosecuted by Paul Lämmle and Alfred Köhler, who drew up the indictment of treason against him (Jacobsen 2: 770). At his trial before the People's Court, he was sentenced to death and was hanged in Berlin at Plötzensee Prison, along with Walter Frick, on March 21, 1945 (Reitlinger 472; Wistrich 178). It is a bit of a mystery as to why Nebe was kept alive for so long—unless it was believed that he had more information on the other conspirators. There are also somewhat fantastic reports that Nebe was not executed and escaped with Otto Skorzeny to Italy and then Ireland (Wistrich 178).

4
Courts and Judges

Contrary to popular belief, the German government and its court system did not instantly change when Adolf Hitler became chancellor in January 1933. Paul von Hindenburg was still president, and the Weimar Republic's judges still interpreted the law and ruled accordingly, even though the law had already been substantially weakened by a series of "emergency" legislation decrees that were passed in an attempt to hold the country together. Hitler's National Socialist Party was not nearly strong enough to influence the Reichstag appreciably when Hitler first took office, but throughout 1933, with one act after another (all marginally legal), Hitler was able to seize enough control to essentially legislate his opposition out of existence. The Reichstag, which at the time was still made up of various political parties (though not many), passed the "Act to Relieve the Distress of the People and the Reich" on March 24, 1933, which gave the government power to write laws without parliamentary approval. Many jurists, including the respected German philosopher of law Carl Schmitt, openly approved of its passage (see *Deutsche Juristen Zeitung,* March 25, 1933, and www.esoteric.msu.edu/VolumeVII/Schmitt.htm). The seats held by the Communist Party had already been declared invalid, and many of the Communist members of the Reichstag had been arrested for dubious reasons.

The professed "Enabling Acts" repealed the established doctrine of basic rights: personal liberty, the right of free speech, and other basic rights (Koch 52–53). This resulted in the wholesale arrests of Communists, socialists, Jews, Social Democrats, labor union members, and even elected politicians. The "Act for the Restoration of the Professional Civil Service" of April 7, 1933, then called for the sacking of Jewish civil servants, of whom there were a considerable number. Civil servants in the judiciary were influenced by the overwhelming national public support of the legislation and encouraged their professional peers not to make disparaging comments on the changes being made by the new government. The "Act to Secure the Unity of Party and State" of December 1, 1933, ultimately substituted the traditional national loyalty of civil servants with loyalty to the party alone.

New laws were no longer based on the German constitution or established by acts of the Reichstag. They were created by Hitler's chosen legal experts, who quoted the Führerprinzip (leader principle, which was in fact not invented by the Nazis) as justification. This was the end of open political opposition to the Nazis and the end of basic rights guaranteed by a constitution and enforced by the government. Most ordinary Germans did not notice this evolution, seeing only the headlines in party-controlled newspapers announcing the latest "protection" legislation. These protectors of German law used the decrees to eliminate all political opposition and to ostensibly protect the community from foreign races, particularly Jews.

Changes in the criminal justice system followed soon after the new laws were passed. The Gestapo, for example, was given the authority to arrest suspects with little or no evidence and imprison them indefinitely until their cases came up in the courts. These were the so-called protective custody laws that were used to justify arrests for such things as listening to foreign radio programs and using defeatist language in public or private. These laws were often interpreted on the spot by Gestapo agents or police officers who had little or no legal training. Doing so was technically legal under the decrees and effectively meant that neither the courts nor the judicial authorities could limit the actions of the police, the Gestapo, or any other security branch that had a connection to the Nazi party. All security agencies would eventually have party-affiliated members in their ranks. Sentencing became effectively a political matter as well, with the criminal's *intent* playing as large a role as the actual crime in determining the punishment. If a political motive could be construed for the violation, then the sentence could be increased substantially.

> The death penalty became one of the deadliest weapons of the judicial system under National Socialism. Although the death penalty had existed before the National Socialists came to power in 1933, it had been used sparingly since the mid-nineteenth century, and was generally reserved for murder. In the fourteen years of the Weimar Republic, 1141 death sentences were passed, of which only 184 were actually executed. In those days, influential experts doubted whether the death penalty was ethically permissible and effective in terms of criminal policy. They demanded it be eliminated. In contrast, National Socialists like Alfred Rosenberg or Roland Freisler dramatically demanded that the state have the unrestricted right to conduct a political "purge" with its own "rope and gallows" and thus bring about the "removal of alien characters and foreign nature." The National Socialist German Workers Party found widespread sympathy for this thinking among voters. When Hitler came to power in January of 1933, the death penalty was a preferred means of demonstrating government brutality and for settling scores with political opponents [www.gdw-berlin.de/ged/ geschichte-e.php].

Any discussion of the trials of the officers and nobility accused of being involved in the July 20 conspiracy must include details of the specific branch of the Nazi regime's justice system that handled the cases and the judges who served in it. The system was extremely simple once party-aligned judges and their superiors at the Reich Ministry of Justice were in place. Sondergerichte (Special Courts) were established within the jurisdictions of the Oberlandesgerichte (High Courts) of each German state beginning in 1933. A year later, the Volksgerichtshof (VGH [People's Court]) was created to augment the High Court's prosecution of cases that had significant political implications. Almost all legislation passed after 1938 gave jurisdiction to the Special Courts (I. Müller 155). The VGH severely limited the legal rights of the defendant and his defense counsel, frequently curtailing or eliminating pretrial procedures such as issuing a written indictment against the defendant, while at the same time suppressing evidence that could clear him. Appealing the court's decision was not advisable, as this could in fact result in a harsher sentence for the defendant. Later, beginning in 1939, the party-assigned "political observer" could have any decision vacated and ask for a retrial if he thought the pronounced sentence was insufficient punishment. This was all perfectly legal regardless of how unjust it was. Those in the judicial system were following the law as it was written at the time, which was the argument used by the judges as a defense at their trials after the war. This conflated rationalization allowed many former Nazi jurists to practice law unquestioned after the surrender.

The VGH was formally established as a regular court early in Hitler's reign, in 1934, but in truth the idea of a "People's Court" goes back to 1922, when the Justice Ministry streamlined the legal system to counter the incessant political influence being exerted by the Weimar Republic. This action was generally supported by German citizens, because most of them believed that the First World War had been lost because of traitors that lived among them who were never punished—the "stab in the back." The reincarnated VGH was initially chartered by Hitler to hear cases involving treason of any sort and violations of the "Decree for the Protection of the German People" of February 4, 1933, and the follow-up decree of March 24, but in practice any offense that could be construed as having an opposing political angle could be tried by the court. The notion of a People's Court is also mentioned in Hitler's *Mein Kampf*: "One day a German national tribunal must condemn and execute several tens of thousands of the criminals who organized and are responsible for the November treason [namely, the November 1918 armistice that ended the First World War] and everything connected with it." The court heard cases ranging from the crime of listening to forbidden radio broadcasts to the attempted assassination of Hitler. The VGH had nineteen judges when it was first established; in two years that number rose to forty-three. These were lay judges, with little or no legal training: thirteen SA and SS leaders, ten party leaders, seventeen military officers and three senior police officers. In 1939 there were ninety-five judges, and by July 20, 1944, there were 173. Military officers, however, were no longer in the majority by this time. Eighty-two of the 173 judges came from the SA, the SS, the NSKK (the National Socialist Motor Corps), and Hitler Youth leaders (Koch 228).

> One must see—and this must be done with a lesson and by action on the part of the supreme judicial authorities—that the nation is made aware that the state is determined to eradicate any attempt at interference—with the most barbaric means, whereby one must bear in mind that the unavoidable lack of respect for human life at the front and the overvaluation of the lives of bad elements is a reality that represents an overriding danger. The judge is the bearer of racial and national self-preservation.... If on the other hand, I do not mercilessly annihilate the filth, then one day there will be a crisis.... There are certain ideological crimes that remove a person from the community of the people.... One must eradicate the notion that the judge is there to administer law even at the risk of letting the world go to pieces [Adolf Hitler, August 20, 1942, to Otto Thierack, Minister of Justice, quoted in Oleschinski 16].

By far the best-known president of the VGH was Roland Freisler, but the first permanent president was Fritz Rehn, who was appointed on July 13, 1934. He died two months later, on September 18, and was replaced by Wilhelm Bruner, who served as acting president until the appointment of Dr. Otto Thierack. Thierack presided from 1936 until 1942, when Freisler took over. The last president was Harold Haffner, who was appointed after Freisler's untimely (or timely) death in February 1945. The jurisdiction of the court seems to have been determined loosely by state borders, but the race of those involved could also be a consideration. It extended to the population of Bohemia and Moravia, as well as Poles in annexed territories, but also to Germans in Alsace-Lorraine and Eupen-Malmedy and to non–Germans arrested under any one of Hitler's "Nacht und Nebel" (night and fog) decrees. Basically, anyone arrested could find themselves appearing before the court if a high-ranking party member desired it. The Special Courts were, according to a statement made in 1938 by the vice president of the VGH, Dr. Wilhelm Crohne (sometimes spelled Krohne), "the swiftest and most effective means of eliminating gangster elements from the community at one stroke, either permanently or temporarily" (I. Müller 155).

The People's Court system operated within, and was a formal part of, Nazi Germany's established legal system; however, these courts were primarily run by judges who were committed National Socialist party members. The convening of a People's Court was typically requested for a specific reason, and the request had to be approved by the VGH president acting as chief justice. It was the president's job to divide the court into senates, see that they were staffed, and distribute cases among them. The trials themselves could then begin. The president of the VGH could also choose to hear individual cases himself, with a handpicked team of other judges assisting. A People's Court (even before Hitler's order of 1936) was established after the Reichstag fire in February 1933 to handle political criminal charges such as treason. Hitler's objective was to try any case that had underlying political implications in a court staffed with party members. The court had jurisdiction over a broad array of crimes that were labeled "political offenses." These included crimes like black marketeering, work slowdowns, defeatism, or anything that might contribute to a decrease in the defensive capability of the country (Wehrkraftzersetzung). The courts made no pretense of being impartial and made a point of ruling with party ideology as the guiding principle. Trials were over quickly, as there was no jury and only an ill-advised right to an appeal. Those few who were found not guilty or received light sentences by the court were often set free just long enough to be arrested again on another charge. Those who were found guilty were sentenced to prison terms, concentration camps, or executed—typically by hanging or beheading (Shirer, *The Rise and Fall*, 269–70).

More than twelve thousand death sentences were delivered by the VGH between 1934 and 1944 alone, although Judge Freisler was quoted in 1940 as saying that less than 4 percent of the cases presented resulted in a death sentence (quoted in Shirer, *The Rise and Fall*, 269). Most of the death sentences were passed after 1942, when the war began to turn against Germany and the organized resistance movements gained renewed momentum. The assassination attempt of July 20 significantly increased the number of cases referred to the court, as might be imagined. Many of the formal executions took place at Berlin's Plötzensee Prison; a detailed narrative describing that infamous Nazi institution is available at www.gdw-berlin.de/pdf/englisch-screen.pdf.

On April 24, 1945, the court moved from Potsdam to Bayreuth because of the bombing, but no trials were held there; the end of the war also meant the end of the VGH. The regular Berlin judicial system, however, was back in business on May 18, 1945, just ten days after the surrender, and courts began hearing cases, mostly involving burglary and looting. The first murder trial was opened in June and involved a man accused of killing another man who was fighting with a German soldier in uniform just before the end of the war. The defendant was sentenced to death and, after a series of appeals, was executed at Plötzensee with the same guillotine used on some of the lesser-known conspirators of July 20. "The guillotine, dismantled and neatly packed, is still in Berlin, awaiting the reintroduction of the death penalty in West Germany" (Kuby 316). On October 20, 1945, the VGH was formally dissolved by Proclamation 3 of the Allied Control Council for Germany. In 1985 the German Bundestag declared all decisions made by the VGH null and void. With the stroke of a pen, all VGH court decisions were vacated, the good ones with the bad (Burchard 800).

The military Court of Honor (Ehrengericht), which was separate from the civilian court system, was reserved for higher crimes committed by the military.

> Though immune from the jurisdiction of the civil courts and the public police, members of the Officer Corps stood in awe and respect of their own Court of Honor. For breaches of military regulations the punishment was fortress detention, but for offence against the Code of Honor of an officer and a gentleman—and the offences included failure to assert the superiority of the Corps over mere civilians—the ultimate and most dreaded punishment was to degrade the offender to civilian status. This indeed was to afflict him with social leprosy. "Stripped of his commission, despoiled of all his prerogatives as an officer, deprived of his right to wear uniform, he was an outcast. The places that had known him, knew him no more. As a soldier he was dead or worse than dead. For in Germany it was not better to be a living dog than a dead lion. The only course open to him, if he wished to avoid a life-long disgrace was to shoot himself. He usually did" [Wheeler-Bennett 11, citing Morgan].

It was through this Court of Honor that many of the members of the July 20 military conspiracy passed in order to be tried by the VGH, which was not constrained by traditional military formalities (or many others).

The Presidents of the People's Court

Dr. Otto Georg Thierack was born the son of a prosperous businessman on April 19, 1889, in Wurzen, Saxony; after his Arbitur he studied law at Marburg and Leipzig Universities. He passed the state examination for law in 1913, and then volunteered for the army and served throughout the First World War, often on the front line (Weiß 458). He was decorated with the Iron Cross Second Class before being discharged as a lieutenant. After the war, he completed his law degree in 1920 and was immediately hired as a court assessor in Saxony (Wistrich 256).

Thierack joined the Nazi party in 1932, and after the Nazis seized power a year later, he rose through the ranks quickly from prosecutor to president of the National Socialists Jurist Association to justice minister of Saxony, and finally to president of the Volksgerichtshof in 1936. He also joined the SA and was eventually promoted to Gruppenführer in 1942 (Wachsmann 216).

As Saxony's justice minister, part of Thierack's job was to firmly instill Nazi principles throughout the legal system. When the Second World War began, he was already serving as president of the VGH but still managed to serve two tours in the military while accomplishing this task. On August 20, 1942, he was promoted to Reich minister of justice, replacing the aging Franz Schlegelberger. Thierack's position at the VGH was subsequently filled by Freisler. Thierack's first action as the Reich's justice minister was to create monthly summaries of cases with comments on how National Socialist doctrine could be applied to similar decisions in the future. These were then distributed to judges throughout the Reich, serving as not-so-subtle hints regarding upcoming cases. Thierack also required higher court judges to submit cases of public interest that had political implications to the VGH for review before the court handed down its final decision. In this way, Thierack ensured that the "correct" verdict would be delivered. This resulted in tougher sentences or the defendant simply being handed over to the SS (as per an agreement with Himmler) if he happened to be of the wrong ethnicity. All these changes resulted in the legal system responding quickly when presented with a case, so that the public saw criminals prosecuted immediately and sentences (including death sentences) handed out before the crime was forgotten. Justice may have been denied, but it certainly was not delayed.

To increase the rate at which death sentences could be carried out, in December 1942 Thierack had eight iron hooks installed in the execution chamber at Berlin's Plötzensee Prison so multiple hangings could occur simultaneously. (Contrary to what is often reported, these hooks were not installed on Hitler's orders after July 20.) A guillotine was also available if needed. The largest mass execution occurred on September 7, 1943, when 186 condemned prisoners were hanged by candlelight in what must have been (even by Nazi standards) a macabre event. An Allied air raid on the night of September 3 had done considerable damage, and the electricity was still not working everywhere in the prison. Dr. Goebbels is recorded as having said, "That is the last thing we need, that after the air raids a few hundred condemned to death would be let loose on the population in the Reich capital" (Wachsmann 316). However, Goebbels had no reason for concern: Thierack had all those sentenced to death hanged in a single night.

Protestant pastor Harald Poelchau and his Catholic colleague Peter Buchholz witnessed the hangings. Poelchau described what he witnessed that night:

> As darkness fell on September 7 the mass murders began. The night was cold. Every now and then the darkness was lit up by exploding bombs. The beams of the searchlights danced across the sky. The men were assembled in several columns one behind the other. They stood there, at first uncertain about what was going to happen to them. Then they realized. Eight men at a time were called by name and led away. Those remaining hardly moved at all. Only an occasional whisper with my Catholic colleague and myself.... Once the executioners interrupted their work because bombs thundered down nearby. The five rows of eight men already lined up had to be confined to their cells again for a while. Then the murdering continued. All these men were hanged. ... The executions had to be carried out by candlelight because the electric light had failed. It was only in the early morning at about eight o'clock that the exhausted executioners paused in their work, only to continue with renewed strength in the evening [quoted in Oleschinski 19].

Poelchau was the chaplain of the Tegel Prison and also associated with the resistance, although he was never suspected of participating in the July 20 conspiracy (Manvell and Fraenkel, *The Men Who Tried*, 210). Unfortunately, this was not to be the end of the executions, as dozens more followed over the next five days, for a total of more than 250.

The Allies arrested Thierack after the war, but he committed suicide on October 26, 1946, by taking poison while incarcerated in the British Eselheide POW camp (Sennelager) near Paderborn, *or* by hanging himself at Neumünster camp (Hitler, *Speeches and Proclamations*, 3184; Weiß 458; Wistrich 257). Whatever the circumstances, if not for his suicide, he would certainly have been *the* major defendant at the Nürnberg Judges' Trials of 1947. As evidence of his faith in Thierack, Hitler named him in the political testament written just before his death, dictating that Thierack should retain his position in the new Dönitz government (Wachsmann 216).

Roland Freisler was born October 30, 1893, in Celle, Lower Saxony and at age 21, he volunteered to serve in the military. He saw action in the First World War and was promoted to lieutenant in early 1915. He was taken prisoner by the Russians later that year, in October, and held in Russia until 1918. He spent that time learning the language of his captors and studying their political system, which was in transition after the Russian Revolution of 1917. He was soon made a lower-level commissar by the Bolsheviks and placed in charge of food supplies for the prison (Knopp 220–21; Wistrich 64). The title of commissar was only a practical one and not a political appointment by any means. It has been said that Freisler became a true Bolshevist at this time, but his latter deeds dispute that claim. More accurately, one author says, "Freisler was never a Communist, though in the early days of his National Socialist career, he belonged to the NSDAP's left wing." Freisler himself later rejected all suggestions that he had even tentatively approached the hated enemy, but he never fully escaped the stigma of being labeled a "Bolshie" (Koch 29). Even Hitler referred to him on occasion as "nothing but a Bolshevik" (Hitler, *Table Talk*, 376).

Freisler returned to Germany from Russia in 1920 to study law at the University of Jena and became a doctor of law in 1922. He then worked as a lawyer in Kassel and also as a city counselor for the "Völkisch-Sozialer Block," an early nationalist party whose philosophy was not so different from that of the Nazis. In 1928 he married Marion Russegger, and they had two sons, Harald and Roland.

Freisler joined the National Socialist Party in July 1925 and was registered as member 9679. He denounced any group that supported the Weimar Republic and was often defense counsel for members of the Nazi party. He later became a delegate to the Prussian Landtag, and eventually a member of the German Reichstag.

> With his fanatical behavior and loud-mouthed over-zealousness he made some friends in the Party, but also enemies. Behind his back the Gauleiter of Hesse-Nassau [probably Karl Weinrich, Gauleiter of Hessen-Nassau-Nord from 1928 to 1943] complained of Freisler's "temperamental nature which shows him to be unsuitable for a senior position." His coziness and intrigues with deputies, city worthies and businessmen brought him a reputation for mixing private with political interests [Knopp 216].

In February 1933 Freisler was awarded a judicial position and became a department chief in the Prussian Ministry of Justice. He was secretary of state in that ministry from 1933 to 1934 and served as the Reich Ministry of Justice representative at the infamous Wannsee Conference chaired by Reinhard Heydrich in January 1942. Freisler was not one to oppose Nazi intrusion into the legal system and enthusiastically approved the proposals put forth at the meeting for dealing with the Jewish question.

Freisler's dominating personality and sharp legal mind quickly made him the most feared judge in the Reich and the very image of Nazi justice. However, Freisler was in reality an outsider who had little real support within the Nazi inner circle. He had a brother, Oswald, also a lawyer and party member, who made a point of being an embarrassment by defending those accused in high-profile cases that the Nazis wanted to use for political gain. Oswald Freisler brazenly wore his party badge during court sessions, which surely sent conflicting messages to observers of the proceedings, and that could not be tolerated. Dr. Goebbels was one of Judge Roland Freisler's only supporters in the Nazi upper echelon, but he did not hesitate to reprimand the judge for his brother's behavior, and when Hitler heard about the goings on, he had Oswald ejected from the party. In spite of Freisler's energetic support of National Socialist policies, Hitler continued to have doubts about him because of his earlier connection to the Bolsheviks (Knopp 221).

One example of Freisler's eagerness to please his superiors is revealed in an article he wrote, translated loosely as "The Racial-Biological Aspect of the Reform of Juvenile Criminal Law." Freisler, who was then secretary of state in the Reich Ministry of Justice, argued that "racially foreign, racially degenerate, racially incurable or seriously defective juveniles" should be sent to juvenile detention centers or correctional education facilities and be segregated from those who are "German and racially valuable" (quoted in Knopp 207). This opinion was publicized in October 1939 with a decree from Freisler, which provided the legal basis for imposing the death penalty and prison terms on juveniles. From 1933 through 1945 the People's Court sentenced at least seventy-two German juveniles to death. This decree was preceded by another, equally punitive diktat called "The Decree against National Parasites" (September 1939), which introduced racial and biological traits as metrics to be used in determining sentences.

On August 20, 1942, Hitler promoted Otto Thierack to Reich justice minister and named Freisler to succeed him as president of the VGH, probably because there was no one else available. Freisler made his presence known immediately, chairing the First Senate of the People's Court, acting as prosecution, judge, and jury, as well as writing up the proceedings, adding a bit of Nazi philosophy to every summary.

During Freisler's tenure, the absolute number of death sentences rose dramatically, even if his 1940 claim is correct that less than 4 percent of the verdicts were for death. In only about 10 percent of the cases placed before him was the defendant found innocent. The rest received long prison sentences or death. This trend had already begun in Thierack's court, a fact that is often overlooked (Koch 229). More often than not, the verdict and sentence were determined before the trial even began. Between 1942 and 1945 more than five thousand death sentences were handed out by the VGH, with at least half of them coming from Freisler's First Senate Court. Often, however, statements like this need to be taken with a grain of salt, especially if declared soon after the war, when it was commonplace to credit "the dead Freisler with many appalling actions in order to shift blame to one who could not respond" (quoted in Koch 145 and 230).

Freisler's courtroom behavior became unpredictable (or, rather, just got worse) the longer he served; he was known to humiliate defendants and occasionally screamed at them, earning him the nickname "Raving Roland." However, "even in the middle of his wildest outbursts, Freisler was able to argue coherently ... his worst ravings were still articulate" (quoted in Herzog 177). His best-known trials were those of the White Rose resistance members in 1943 and the July 20 conspirators in 1944. Nonetheless, by that time Freisler had already created a reputation for himself within the party as the overzealous and arrogant president of the VGH.

In 1942, Helmuth Hübener, at the age of seventeen, became the youngest opponent of the Nazis to be executed as a result of a trial by the VGH. Freisler also ordered several White Rose members (including Sophie Scholl, Hans Scholl, Alex Schmorell, Willi Graf, Christoph Probst, and Kurt Huber) executed by guillotine. Julius Fucik—a Czech journalist, Communist Party leader, and a member of the anti–Nazi resistance—was tried for high treason on August 25, 1943, found guilty, and guillotined on September 8, 1943. Karlrobert Kreiten, a German musician, was indicted and tried in 1943 for making disparaging remarks about Hitler and the war to a friend of his mother's, who promptly denounced him (German Resistance Memorial Center). Kreiten was found guilty of treason, sentenced to death by Freisler, and executed in Plötzensee Prison—along with 185 others. Father Dr. Max Josef Metzger, a German Catholic priest and the founder in 1938 of the "Una Sancta Brotherhood" (an ecumenical movement pledged to bringing Catholics and Protestants together), was arrested on June 29 after being denounced by a Gestapo agent. He was brought to trial on October 14, 1944, found guilty of treason, and sentenced to death, though he was not executed until April 17, 1945, at Brandenburg-

Görden Prison (Steinbach and Tuchel 137–38). During the trial, Freisler supposedly stated that people like Metzger (clergy) should be "eradicated," but this quote, while often repeated, is never referenced. It is recorded, however, that upon hearing his sentence, Metzger replied quite calmly, "I should like to say once more that I have a clear conscience before God and before my people and that I have only tried to serve them ... now it is done. I am at peace; I have offered up my life to God for the peace of the world and the unity of the Church" (quoted in Leber 211).

Freisler's showmanship reached a peak when he had several of the trials of the July 20 conspirators recorded on film with accompanying audiotape. Unaccustomed to being recorded, his shouting often went beyond the dynamic range of the tape recording equipment (Koch 198). This was Freisler's opportunity to be center stage, but the relatively composed demeanor of many of the defendants overshadowed Freisler's behavior, and the result of his portrayal on film was often the exact opposite of his intent. Of course, it should be mentioned that only those films that portray Freisler as history has already judged him are easily found. Those that show him behaving with dignity toward the accused brought before him are rarely referenced, and many quotes attributed to Freisler are pure fabrication. One of the most common quotes has Freisler calling von Witzleben a "dirty old man" in court, but there is no evidence that this incident ever occurred (Toland 818; Shirer, *The Rise and Fall*, 1070).

During the trials of the July 20 conspirators the principles guiding Freisler's decisions, were stated by him as follows:

> The People's Court takes the view that the mere failure to report defeatist utterances like [Helmuth James] von Moltke's, coming from a man of his reputation and position, already amounts to treason. It is already tantamount to treason to discuss highly political questions with people who are in no way competent to deal with them, especially if they do not in any way actively belong to the Party. It is already preparation for high treason to arrogate to oneself any judgement in a matter which is for the Führer to decide. Anyone who objects to acts of violence, but prepares for the case that another, that is, the enemy, removes the government by force, thereby engages in preparation of high treason; for then he counts on the force of the enemy [quoted in von Moltke, *Letters*, 400].

Freisler's opinion on this subject did not exclusively apply to failing to report defeatist utterances of a *well-known* conspirator. Ehrengard Frank-Schultz, who was the landlady of a certain Lieutenant Wendelstein (one of the minor conspirators), was hauled before the VGH on November 6, 1944, for making defeatist remarks. The fact that she was Wendelstein's landlady likely prompted the investigation. She was reported to the Gestapo by a German Red Cross nurse, and Freisler showed no mercy at her trial:

> Mrs. Frank-Schultz told a Red Cross nurse she was sorry that the attempt to murder our Führer had failed, and had the audacity to claim that a few years of Anglo-Saxon rule would be preferable to "the current reign of terror." She therefore made common cause with the traitors of the twentieth of July. Through this, she has been dishonored forever. She will be punished with death [quoted in I Müller 151].

In a letter to Reichsleiter Martin Bormann dated September 8, 1944, Reichsminister of Justice Thierack was critical of Freisler's behavior in court:

> The Chairman's [Freisler's] directing of the trial was unobjectionable and objective with the defendants Wirmer and Goerdeler; somewhat nervous with Lejeung-Jung. He did not let Leuschner and von Hassell finish their statements. He repeatedly shouted them down. That made quite a bad impression, especially so as the court president had given about 300 persons permission to

attend. Which individuals got admission tickets will still have to be gone into. Such an arrangement at such a session is very precarious. The political conduct of the trial was otherwise unobjectionable. Unfortunately, however, he addressed Leuschner as a quarter-portion and Goerdeler as a half-portion, and spoke of the defendants as small fry. This detracted considerably from the serious atmosphere of this important occasion. Constant long speeches by the chairman, aiming only at making propaganda, had a repulsive effect in this situation. Here, too, the seriousness and dignity of the court suffered. The president completely lacks the ice-cold air of superiority and reserve that alone is called for in such a trial [quoted in Zimmermann and Jacobsen 201].

Freisler was killed on February 3, 1945, when American bombers led by Lieutenant Colonel Robert Rosenthal dropped three thousand tons of bombs in the heaviest air raid on Berlin of the entire war. The Reich Chancellery, Gestapo headquarters, the Party Chancellery, and the People's Court all sustained substantial damage. There are conflicting stories as to exactly how Freisler was killed, but there is no doubt that he died as a result of the bombing. It is perhaps appropriate that, at the time of the air raid, Freisler was hearing the case against Fabian von Schlabrendorff, one of the July 20 conspirators, who became a judge himself after surviving the war. Ironically, the nurse who attended the mortally injured Freisler was the sister of Andreas Albrecht Theodor Graf von Bernstorff, who had already been scheduled to be tried in the VGH as a conspirator (Zimmermann and Jacobsen 308). In a final rejection by the man he idolized, Hitler refused to order a state funeral for Judge Freisler and, according to Jerje Granberg, a Swedish reporter in Berlin, "No one either was sad at the news of the Nazi executioner's death" (*Charlotte News*, February 23, 1945). His obituary appeared in the February 16 bulletin of the Reich Ministry of Justice (*Deutsche Justiz, Rechtspflege und Rechtspolitik*), and his wife sent cards to his associates and friends thanking them for attending his funeral. In death, Freisler became yet another alibi for the Germans after the war, with former judges pointing to him as Hitler's alter ego in the judicial system. The trials, however, continued after Freisler's demise, with the vice president of the People's Court, Dr. Wilhelm Crohne, taking over temporarily (Manvell and Fraenkel, *The Men Who Tried*, 217).

Dr. Harold Haffner was the last president of the People's Court, serving from March 12 to April 24, 1945. He was born on May 28, 1900, at Uslar, Lower Saxony and after completing his legal training, he worked as a prosecutor in local and regional court systems. He joined the Nazi party on May 1, 1933, and became a member of the SA thereafter. Haffner rose to the position of state prosecutor in Kattowitz in Upper Silesia in January 1944 and seems to have had an unremarkable and short tenure there. It is known that he and other judges visited the Auschwitz concentration camp on June 28, 1944, and in his report he commented on the favorable conditions there and the good health of the inmates (Koch 227).

It is not known why Haffner was chosen to replace Freisler; perhaps he was the only available placeholder during this hectic time. Hitler and Goebbels initially favored Hans Frank, minister of justice and former governor-general of Poland (Goebbels 45). At this time, the Third Reich was being bombed and shelled out of existence, and the pool of reliable party judges to accept the position was probably small—with the certain knowledge that their names would be on someone's list after the war. Haffner himself only presided over two cases during his tenure as president (neither of them particularly significant) involving government officials who had abandoned their offices when the Russians began their final assault.

Haffner survived the war and went into hiding, changing his name and profession;

in 1954, under the name Heinrich Hartmann, he surfaced in Uslar, near Hanover, and even petitioned the government to allow him to begin drawing his pension (see Ernst Klee, "Deutscher Menschenverbrauch," *Zeit Online*, November 28, 1997, and DR, 55). His request was granted without any investigation into his past. Haffner was eventually exposed but was not prosecuted as a war criminal and lived free until his death on October 19, 1969 (Koch 227).

Other Judges of the People's Court

Judges from any court could be drafted to serve in the VGH for varied lengths of time, and, importantly, they were not allowed to refuse the appointment. Judges were chosen for their political reliability over their legal training and experience; most were not well known to the public. Wilhelm Crohne was the only vice president of the VGH, serving throughout the Nazi period to the end of the war, committing suicide on April 26, 1945.

None of the judges in the VGH were successfully prosecuted after the war, although several were tried. A final trial was attempted more than forty years after the fact. One of the elderly would-be defendants, Paul Reimer, obligingly committed suicide before the trial began (Koch 240; *Pittsburgh Post-Gazette*, October 22, 1986, 32). Only one of the senior public prosecutors of the People's Court was tried and found guilty at Nürnberg. This was Oswald Rothaug, himself a one-time assistant judge in the ordinary German judicial system but never a judge on the People's Court. People's Court chief prosecutors (not judges) Paul Barnickel and Ernst Lautz were tried and acquitted at the Nürnberg trials, along with one lay judge (Hans Peterson, who served on the First Senate) and one chief justice (Günther Nebelung of the Fourth Senate).

The most publicized trial of a People's Court judge, however, took place in the late 1960s. The ruling made international news when Hans-Joachim Rehse was finally acquitted on December 6, 1968 (see *Time*, December 20, 1968, www.time.com/time/magazine/article/0,9171,844696,00.html). The court said that the ruling was made "with a retrospective view of that time" (quoted in Wyden 121).

In looking through a comprehensive list of the judges, it is apparent that a large number of them continued serving in the legal system as judges and lawyers long after the end of the war (Klee; National Council; Wieland). Some experienced difficulties due to their Nazi pasts, but most served without interruption up to their retirement. This was in part due to the fact that there was a critical shortage of trained lawyers and judges immediately after the war, and it was relatively easy for those judges who were mostly unknown to the Allies to avoid investigation.

5

Trials by Any Other Name

Trials of Former (Expelled) Military

Hitler ordered a Court of Honor convened to formally and legally expel those in the military who were involved with the July 20 assassination attempt, thereby making them civilians. It was a clever move, as this expulsion allowed the People's Court to try the cases and avoid established military procedures that even Hitler would have had trouble circumventing. The Court of Honor was chaired by Field Marshal Gerd von Rundstedt, and he was seconded by Field Marshal Keitel and General Heinz Guderian. There were no legally trained judges on the court—only military personnel. The accused were not present during the proceedings, and no witnesses were called. The court relied primarily upon documentation resulting from Gestapo investigations, which often involved torture. Each hearing lasted only a few minutes. In almost all cases, the defendant was expelled from the military. There were four hearings in total, beginning on August 4 and finishing on September 14. Twenty-two officers were ousted on the first day, including several who had already been executed or committed suicide; being dead was not a valid defense. After the final hearing, a total of fifty-five officers had been expelled from the military. Trials of those expelled who were still living began three days later. Those ousted include the following (microfilm "July 20, 1944" at the Institut für Zeitgeschichte, München; Zimmermann and Jacobsen 196–98):

August 4, 1944, Hearing

Erwin von Witzleben, Erich Fellgiebel, Paul von Hase, Hellmuth Stieff, Henning von Tresckow, Georg-Alexander Hansen, Robert Bernardis, Egbert Hayessen, Friedrich Karl Klausing, Fritz-Dietlof Graf von der Schulenburg-Tressow, Albrecht von Hagen, Peter Yorck von Wartenburg, Friedrich Olbricht, Claus Graf von Stauffenberg, Albrecht Merz von Quirnheim, Werner von Haeften, Ludwig Beck, Eduard Wagner, Wessel Freytag von Loringhoven, Werner Schrader, Fritz Lindemann, and Joachim Kuhn

August 14, 1944, Hearing

Carl-Heinrich von Stülpnagel, Fritz Thiele, Joachim Meichßner, Bernhard Klamroth, Karl Ernst Rahtgens, Joachim Sadrozinski, Günther Smend, Ludwig von Leonrod, Johannes-Georg Klamroth, Wilhelm Friedrich Graf zu Lynar, Hermann Kaiser, Ulrich-Wilhelm Graf Schwerin von Schwanenfeld, and Hans Ulrich von Oertzen

Abschrift
1 L 292/44
O J 3/44 gRs.

Im Namen des Deutschen Volkes!

In der Strafsache gegen

1.) Bernhard K l a m r o t h , ehem. Oberstleutnant i.G. aus Zossen, geboren am 20. November 1910 in Berlin,
2.) Hans-Georg K l a m r o t h , ehem. Major d.R. und Kaufmann aus Halberstadt, geboren am 12. Oktober 1898 in Halberstadt,
3.) Egbert H a y e s s e n , ehem. Major aus Nedlitz, geboren am 28. Dezember 1913 in Eisleben,
4.) Wolf Heinrich Graf H e l l d o r f , ehem. General der Polizei und Polizeipräsident aus Berlin-Lichterfelde, geboren am 14. Oktober 1896 in Merseburg,
5.) Dr. Adam von T r o t t zu S o l z , ehem. Legationsrat im Auswärtigen Amt aus Berlin-Dahlem, geboren am 9. August 1909 in Potsdam,
6.) Hans Bernd von H a e f t e n , ehem. Vortragender Legationsrat im Auswärtigen Amt aus Berlin-Dahlem, geboren am 18. Dezember 1905 in Charlottenburg,

sämtlich zur Zeit in dieser Sache in Polizeihaft, wegen Landesverrats u.a.

hat der Volksgerichtshof, 1.Senat, auf die am 11. August 1944 eingegangene Anklageschrift des Herrn Oberreichsanwalts in der Hauptverhandlung vom 15. August 1944, an welcher teilgenommen haben

als Richter:

Präsident des Volksgerichtshofs Dr.Freisler, Vorsitzer,
Volksgerichtsrat Lämmle,
General der Infanterie Reinecke,
Gartentechniker und Kleingärtner Kaiser,
Ingenieur Wernecke,

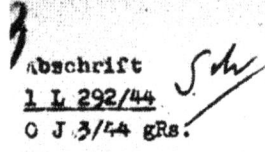

Indictment against Bernhard Klamroth, Hans-Georg Klamroth, Egbert Hayessen, Wolf-Heinrich von Helldorf, Adam von Trott zu Solz, and Hans Bernd von Haeften charging them with treason (among other things). Signed and initialed by Judge Freisler.

August 24, 1944, Hearing

Eberhard-Ludwig Finckh, Kurt Hahn, Ottfried von Listow, Rudolf Graf Marogna-Redwitz, Alexis Freiherr von Rönne, Karl-Heinz Engelhorn, Hans Erdmann, Carl-Hans Graf von Hardenberg, Wilhelm Kuebert, Gerhard Knaak, Max-Ulrich Graf von Drechsel-Deuffenstein, Bernhard Letterhaus, Theodor Strünck, and Siegfried Wagner

September 4, 1944, Hearing

Georg Schulze-Büttger, Gerd von Tresckow, Hans-Jürgen Graf von Blumenthal, Friedrich Scholz-Babisch, Busso Thoma, and Jens Jessen

On August 7 the first VGH conspiracy trial was called to order by Roland Freisler. The defendants were Field Marshal Erwin von Witzleben, First Lieutenant Peter Yorck von Wartenburg, Colonel General Erich Hoepner, Lieutenant General Paul von Hase, Major General Hellmuth Stieff, Captain Friedrich Karl Klausing, Lieutenant Colonel Robert Bernardis, and First Lieutenant Albrecht von Hagen. The trial was over in two days, and all of the defendants were found guilty and sentenced to death. They were executed immediately at Plötzensee Prison. However, this was just the beginning. As a final desecration, Himmler personally ordered that the remains of all prisoners executed in connection with July 20 be cremated and their ashes scattered over the sewage fields.

There is little doubt that Major General Henning von Tresckow would have been among this group had he not committed suicide on July 21. His brother, Lieutenant Colonel Gerd von Tresckow, was not directly involved in the events of July 20 and was not immediately under Gestapo investigation; however, he confessed to his commanding officer that he had general knowledge of the conspiracy. That was sufficient to land him in the Moabit Lehrter Strasse Prison after being arrested on July 27. He committed suicide in prison on September 6, 1944.

A series of more than fifty trials that would end with more than 110 death sentences occurred from October 1944 through the end of the war. A total of ninety people who were involved directly in the assassination attempt, supported those who were, or belonged to the resistance were executed in Plötzensee Prison between August 8, 1944, and April 9, 1945. Their names and dates of execution are known (Jewish Virtual Library; Perk and Deutsch 90–213). The "Murder Register (Mordregister) gives a few additional names that are not listed elsewhere" (Zimmermann and Jacobsen 202–9). "The register of executions kept by the Reich Ministry of Justice from 1871 to 1945 was known as the 'murder register' because, until 1933, the death sentence was only exacted for common murder" (Hoffmann, *The History*, 16).

Well-known defendants involved with the conspiracy as well as those accused of aiding and otherwise providing support for the accused were brought before Freisler, who personally presided over most of these trials. Today, anyone can view selected video recordings of some of the high-profile cases. The defendants were not allowed to hire their own legal representatives, nor did they learn the specific charges against them until just before their trials. In reading some of the statements made by their lawyers, it is obvious that they did not want the job and had no interest in putting up a real defense for their clients. Apparently Freisler thought the entire world would want to be informed, and especially Hitler, so he insisted that the first trials be given extensive coverage in the government-controlled press, where much of the testimony and Freisler's rebuttal was quoted in full. When it became apparent that the trials would continue for many months, the media lost interest and only select individuals attended the proceedings, not necessarily by choice.

Defendants in the First Conspiracy Trial, Held August 7/8, 1944

On August 7 and 8, Erwin von Witzleben, Erich Hoepner, Hellmuth Stieff, Albrecht von Hagen, Paul von Hase, Robert Bernardis, Friedrich Karl Klausing, and Peter Yorck von Wartenburg were executed by hanging. Inmate Viktor von Gostomski was on duty in the Plötzensee Prison library and later recorded his observations:

> Murmurs of a special action went through the building. Special action—that meant prominent people. Wardens spoke of a major event. I assumed they were men involved with the 20th of July. All the prisoners were locked in their cells at about six in the evening. Nobody worked anymore. Even we librarians were in our cells. We placed the table under the window and peeked out into the courtyard. It was probably about seven o'clock. The heavy iron gates of the prison opened. Men in striped prison clothes walked out with their hands tied, their bare feet in wooden shoes, and their heads bare. Each of them was led by two wardens. But they walked upright; they did not need any support. A lot of civilians walked behind the condemned men, probably Gestapo. SS men were filming. A warden spotted us at the window. He shouted, "Get away from the windows!" We held up a little mirror so that we could keep watching. How much time had passed? Ten minutes, or was it fifteen? I was too excited to notice. This was the special action. Wooden shoes clacked again and again the sad procession began. They were coming from within the prison. Probably the death warrant had been read. One after the other was led into the execution shed, hands tied behind his back and jacket loosely thrown over. It took about five minutes, and then it was the next one's turn. The Gestapo people were in the shed, and so was the camera-man. The whole thing was over within a good forty minutes [quoted in Oleschinski 35].

Generalfeldmarshal Job-Wilhelm Georg "Erwin" von Witzleben was born on December 4, 1881, in Breslau to a Thuringian military family. In 1901 he joined Grenadier Regiment No. 7 as a lieutenant after completing his cadet training at Whalstatt and Lichterfelde, and in 1910 he was promoted to first lieutenant. He married Else Kleeberg, and the couple had two children (Das-Ritterkreuz). Von Witzleben was to have been the commander in chief of the armed forces in a post–Hitler government. He served as brigade adjutant in the 19th Reserve Infantry Brigade at the beginning of World War I and was promoted to captain and company chief in the Reserve Infantry, Regiment 6, in October 1914; he later became battalion commander. Von Witzleben fought at both Verdun and Flanders, was seriously wounded in battle, and received the Iron Cross Second Class and the Iron Cross First Class before being transferred to General Staff training. At the end of the war he was first general staff officer of the 121st Division (Weiß 493).

Von Witzleben remained in the army (the Reichswehr) after the war as a company chief, being promoted to major in 1923 while on the Fourth Division staff in Dresden. In 1928 he became battalion commander in Infantry Regiment 6 and was promoted to lieutenant colonel in 1929. He received another promotion in 1931, this time to full colonel, and became the commander of Infantry Regiment 8 in Frankfurt (Weiß 493). Von Witzleben was promoted to major general in the new German Wehrmacht in 1934 and moved to Potsdam as the commander of the Third Infantry Division, replacing General von Fritsch as commander of Military District (Wehrkreis) III, which included Berlin (Fest, *Plotting*, 399). He was subsequently promoted to lieutenant general and in September 1935 became the commanding general of III Army Corps in Berlin. In 1936 he was promoted to general of the infantry (Das-Ritterkreuz).

As early as 1934, von Witzleben became a thorn in the Nazis' collective side when he, Erich von Manstein, Gerd von Rundstedt and Wilhelm Ritter von Leeb demanded an investigation into the murders of Kurt von Schleicher and Ferdinand von Bredow during the Night of the Long Knives. Notwithstanding this publicized call for an investigation, there are still questions regarding just how much advance information the generals were given about the purge (Wheeler-Bennett 321). Von Witzleben's prominent objection to the fabricated persecution of von Fritsch for homosexuality was the last straw, and Hitler had him retired. His retirement did not last long, however, even though his association with the likes of Colonel General Ludwig Beck, General Erich Hoepner, General Carl-Heinrich von Stülpnagel and Admiral Wilhelm Canaris was well known. None were fervent Nazis, but if war came, every general with battlefield experience would be needed. Hans Oster, part of Canaris' Abwehr since 1933, had a plan in 1938 to recruit this group of high-ranking officers and oust Hitler in a military coup to prevent a war over the Sudetenland (Parssinen 5). The Munich Agreement put an end to that notion. Von Witzleben was later involved in a coup planned in 1939 by Colonel General Kurt Freiherr von Hammerstein-Equord, who proposed kidnapping Hitler, leaving it to von Witzleben to secure the Nazi party headquarters, but this scheme never got past the planning stage.

In September 1939 von Witzleben was given command of the First Army, which was stationed in the west. His army was a part of Army Group D when Germany attacked France on May 10, 1940 (von Hassell and MacRae 324). Von Witzleben's First Army breached the Maginot Line on June 14 and within three days captured several French divisions, earning him the Knight's Cross of the Iron Cross, and on July 19 he was promoted to Generalfeldmarshal (Stockhorst 451). He was appointed commander in chief of the west in 1941 but was replaced after Operation Barbarossa. The official reason was his health, but it could easily have been because of his criticism of the attack that Hitler himself had ordered (Steinbach and Tuchel 245).

Von Witzleben was essential in plans made by the July 20 conspirators, as he was well known and was to become the supreme commander of the armed forces after the coup (Wistrich 180). He was, however, arrested on July 21 at his estate after going to the OKH headquarters in Berlin the previous day to assume command, only to find that things were not going according to plan. A Court of Honor was quickly convened to remove him from the Wehrmacht so that he could be tried in the People's Court. He was in the first group of conspirators to be arraigned on August 7. Freisler sentenced him to death and had him hanged the next day in Plötzensee Prison, with the event being video recorded—supposedly for Hitler's viewing, although there is no first-hand evidence that he ever watched the film (Toland 818). The following are said to be von Witzleben's closing words in court to Freisler: "You can hand us over to the hangmen but in three months the disgusted and harried people will bring you to book and drag you alive through the dirt in the streets." There is no recording, in either audio records or transcripts of the trial, that confirms von Witzleben ever made this statement; however, it has become part of the history of these events and has been reported as both truth and fiction (quoted in

Hoffmann, *The History*, 526; Koch 210). Von Witzleben's prophecy, whether actually made or not, didn't exactly come true, but Freisler was nevertheless quite dead six months later.

> [Von Witzleben] is perhaps best described as an unpretentious, straightforward soldier with a good fund of common sense. To his downright nature, answers came simply: Nazism was a criminal abomination, the military oath a swindle, Hitler's chosen path the road to national disaster. Others agonized and procrastinated where he was prepared to act [Deutsch, *Hitler*, 44].

First Lieutenant Peter Yorck von Wartenburg was born the fifth of ten children to Heinrich Graf Yorck von Wartenburg, in Klein-Öls near Ohlau in the Province of Silesia, on November 13, 1904. His ancestry included the philosopher Paul Yorck von Wartenburg (his grandfather) and the generals Prince Louis Ferdinand of Prussia and Johann (Hans) David Ludwig Graf Yorck von Wartenburg, who were his great-great-grandfathers (Shirer, *The Rise and Fall*, 1015; von Meding 104). Peter Yorck (as he was most commonly known) studied law at the prestigious Klosterschule (monastery school) Roßleben, in Thuringia, and then continued his law studies in 1923 in Bonn and Breslau, passing the law examination in 1926. He successfully passed the graduate law examination in 1930, and in 1932 he became part of the Osthilfe (Eastern Aid) organization, a Weimar Republic program created to stimulate the agricultural economy of East Prussia. He became an official at the Breslau Oberpräsidium (administrative office) in 1934, and in 1936 he was appointed to a position in the government price control office (Leber 184). Although he received commendations for his work, he was never promoted beyond this position because of his refusal to join the Nazi party.

Von Wartenburg became acquainted with his distant relative Helmuth James von Moltke and his closer cousin Berthold von Stauffenberg in 1938. It was about this time that he was also introduced to Adam von Trott zu Solz, Fritz-Dietlof von der Schulenburg-Tressow, and Ulrich-Wilhelm Graf Schwerin von Schwanenfeld. Their self-imposed undertaking involved creating a new constitution to be recognized after a purge of the Nazis. Von Wartenburg was a lieutenant when World War II began, and he was assigned as a tank regiment adjutant. He soon learned that two of his brothers had been killed in Poland, which no doubt contributed to his decision to actively participate in the resistance in whatever capacity was required. He became one of the original members of the Kreisau Circle in 1940 (Leber 184).

Being afflicted with a debilitating spinal problem in 1942, von Wartenburg was assigned to the Reich Armaments Ministry. When von Moltke's Berlin apartment building was damaged in the bombings of 1943, he moved into von Wartenburg's apartment in Berlin-Lichterfelde. Von Moltke was arrested in January 1944 (tried and executed a year later), which caused von Wartenburg to push his fellow conspirators to move ahead with plans to eliminate Hitler. He was to be the vice chancellor's (Wilhelm Leuschner) secretary of state in the post–Hitler government; however, he was arrested the day after the assassination attempt of July 20. His wife Marion (née Winter) was also arrested and held for a short time, but she was reasonably well treated (Steinbach and Tuchel 246; Steinhoff et al. 398).

Von Wartenburg was tried by the People's Court on August 8, showing no fear of Freisler and demonstrating that his knowledge of the law was superior to that of his judge. He was nevertheless hanged that same day at Plötzensee Prison, saying just before his execution:

I hope my death will also atone for all my sins; that it will be a sacrifice for what we have all had to bear. May it contribute to God becoming a little less remote in these days. I too am dying for my country, and even if it seems to all appearances a very inglorious and disgraceful death, I shall hold up my head and I only hope that you will not believe this to be from pride or delusion. We wished to light the torch of life and now we stand in a sea of flames [quoted in Leber 186].

Von Wartenburg's wife survived the war and, poignantly, became a judge in West Berlin. She died in Berlin on April 13, 2007, at the age of 102 (*The Telegraph* [London], May 17, 2007).

Colonel General Erich Hoepner was born in Frankfurt/Oder on September 14, 1886, the son of Kurt Hoepner (an army medical officer) and Elisabeth Kienast. After his arbiter examination in 1905, he joined Dragoon Regiment 13 in Metz; in 1906 he was promoted to second lieutenant. In 1910 he married Irma Gebauer, and they had two children (*Allgemeine Deutsche Biographie*). Hoepner's name appeared on Goerdeler's list as commander in chief of the Wehrmacht in the post–Hitler government (Wheeler-Bennett 623).

Hoepner was a company commander and a general staff officer in World War I; after the war he joined the Freikorps. In the Weimar Republic government, he rose to the rank of colonel, and in 1933 he was appointed chief of staff for District I, Königsberg. In 1936 Hoepner was promoted to major general of the Reichswehr and, in 1938, was made the commander of the 1st Light Division, which was part of the invasion of Czechoslovakia and Poland.

Prior to the invasion of Czechoslovakia, Hoepner gave his backing to General Franz Halder in his plans for a coup against the Hitler regime, volunteering himself and his men to disarm the SS should they try to interfere (Wistrich 123). The Munich Agreement put a temporary hold on these plans. Hoepner was awarded the Knight's Cross after the successful invasion of Poland and replaced Heinz Guderian as commander of the 16th Army Corps in 1939. In May 1940 he led his men in chasing British troops to Dunkirk, and a few weeks later he was promoted to colonel general (Das-Ritterkreuz). Hoepner commanded the 4th Panzer Army in Operation Barbarossa in 1941, and his troops attacked Leningrad before he was transferred to Army Group Center under the command of Field Marshal Günther von Kluge for the assault on Moscow. Hoepner "adopted Hitler's terminology of extermination in the military orders and instructions they issued and did not recoil from echoing the Führer's extreme anti–Semitism" (Mommsen 269). It was obviously not sympathy for the Jews that led him to the resistance. In an order he issued on May 2, 1941, Hoepner wrote:

> The war against Russia is an important part of the German people's battle for existence. It is the old fight of Germans versus Slavs, the defense of European culture against the Muscovite-asiatic flood; and the repulse of Jewish Bolshevism. This war must have as its goal the destruction of today's Russia and for this reason it must be conducted with unheard-of harshness. Every clash must, in its conception and execution, be guided by the iron will to completely and mercilessly annihilate the enemy. In particular, there is to be no mercy for the carriers of the current Russian-Bolshevik system [Jewish Virtual Library].

Hoepner was only twenty miles north of the Russian capital on December 5, but, following a strong counterattack by the Russians, he decided to withdraw his troops to save them from assured destruction. Hitler was furious when he heard of this decision and dismissed Hoepner immediately from the Wehrmacht (German Resistance Memorial Center). Hoepner was publicly humiliated in an official "order of the day" and even denied the right to wear his uniform (Wistrich 123). Senior officers objected so strongly to this treatment that Hitler rescinded his dismissal and allowed Hoepner to retire instead. In the period from 1942 to 1944, Hoepner was an active member of the Beck conspiracy group and was designated to take over command of the home forces if General Friedrich Fromm refused to join the coup. He was in the Bendlerblock the night of July 20 and was offered the opportunity to commit suicide by Fromm when it was obvious that the coup would be a failure, but he declined. He was arrested that night and taken to a Wehrmacht lockup instead of being delivered to the Gestapo (Dulles 194). He was tortured by the Gestapo before his trial, but there is no evidence that he divulged anything they did not already know. Hoepner's name does not appear on the list of fifty-five officers expelled from the Wehrmacht because he had already been forced to retire (Zimmermann and Jacobsen 196–98).

On August 8, 1944, Hoepner was tried in Freisler's People's Court, found guilty of treason, and was hanged the same day at Plötzensee Prison. His brother, Horst, was also arrested, but he survived the war as one of the 139 prominent prisoners held in Tyrol.

Lieutenant General Paul von Hase, born July 14, 1885, in Hannover, was a career German army officer and an uncle of Dietrich Bonhoeffer (Bonhoeffer's mother was von Hase's sister) (Stockhorst 179; Manvell and Fraenkel, *The Men Who Tried*, 74). Married to Margarethe Freiin von Funck, the von Hase marriage produced two daughters and two sons. In early 1933 von Hase commanded a battalion in Neuruppin and was transferred in 1935 to the garrison at Landsberg on the Warthe River (Steinbach and Tuchel 88). By the spring of 1938 he was well aware of plans by Canaris, Oster, von Witzleben, and Halder to do away with Hitler. Von Hase fought in the campaigns in Poland and France, but in 1940 he became ill and no longer fit for front-line duty. He was subsequently appointed commandant of the city of Berlin, a position that allowed him to interact with Beck's military opposition clique, particularly General Olbricht, without attracting attention. Von Hase was a critical member of the conspiracy, being recruited by von Stauffenberg and Olbricht because, as city commandant, he could issue orders to any military personnel posted there (Reitlinger 316). Two other men in von Hase's command were also informed of the plot: Lieutenant Colonel (General Staff) Hermann Schöne and Major Adolf Friedrich Graf von Schack. On July 20 von Hase issued the initial orders to seal off the government quarter, putting the coup in motion, and he was among the first taken into custody after it fell apart. On August 8 von Hase was tried by the VGH and, revealing nothing of the participation of others, declared that he alone was responsible for the coup attempt (Zeller 441). Freisler was not convinced. Von Hase was sentenced to death and hanged later that day in Plötzensee Prison.

Major General Hellmuth (sometimes written Helmuth) Stieff was born June 6, 1901, in Deutsch Eylau in West Prussia. He graduated from the Munich Infantry School at age 21 and was commissioned as a lieutenant. By 1927 he was working for the General Staff of the Reichswehr, and in 1938, as a general himself, he was posted to the General Staff of the Reichswehr (Steinbach and Tuchel 197). He was appointed chief of organization (Organisationsabteilung) at the OKH in October 1942. While serving in Warsaw in 1939, Stieff witnessed the brutal treatment of the Poles by the German army and was appalled by the way Hitler was running the war. He wrote many letters to his wife Cäcilie (née Gaertner) during the war while he was in prison, and the few that survive are "among the most moving accounts of the period" (Fest, *Plotting*, 397; Jacobsen 2: 798). At least one historian, however, records Stieff's willingness to participate in ethnic cleansing during Barbarossa (Mommsen 269). In a letter dated November 21, 1939, he wrote, "I am ashamed to be German. This minority, which is casting a slur on the German name through murder, burning and pillage, will bring misfortune upon the whole German nation if we do not put a stop to their actions soon" (quoted in von Schlabrendorff, *The Secret War*, 185). Stieff joined von Tresckow's resistance group that same year. In his position, he had access to explosives, both German and foreign made, and he had occasional access to Hitler as well (Steinbach and Tuchel 197). Stieff was also involved in trying to recruit Field Marshal Günther von Kluge into the resistance, although with limited success, and he ultimately volunteered to assassinate Hitler himself in a suicide mission (Fest, *Plotting*, 397). The opportunity was yet another "uniform display" that was finally held on July 7, 1944, at Klessheim Palace near Salzburg, but Stieff did not go through with the plan (Hoffmann, *Hitler's Personal Security*, 191).

Stieff was arrested in East Prussia at the Wolf's Lair on the night of July 20 and interrogated by the Gestapo in their search for information about other members of the conspiracy. Stieff was sentenced to death by Freisler's VGH on August 8, 1944, and executed the same day in Plötzensee Prison. At his trial, he claimed to have been misled by the conspirators (Manvell and Fraenkel, *The Men Who Tried*, 198). Freisler was not moved.

Captain Friedrich Karl Klausing was born May 24, 1920, in Munich, making him one of the youngest members of the July 20 conspiracy. His early training in the Hitler Youth was an overture to becoming a career officer, and in 1938 he joined the illustrious 9th Infantry Regiment in Potsdam as a cadet (Steinbach and Tuchel 112). When World War II broke out, Klausing fought in Poland and France and, in 1942–1943, was part of the failed Stalingrad rescue mission, being seriously wounded twice. He was subsequently transferred to Berlin and the OKH in April 1944 (Stockhorst 234).

Klausing was introduced into the conspiracy by Fritz-Dietlof von der Schulenburg-Tressow, and on July 11, 1944, he accompanied Claus von Stauffenberg to the Berghof as his adjutant. Von Stauffenberg carried a bomb, intending to assassinate Hitler, Himmler, and Göring, with Klausing being responsible for the getaway after the explosion. This attempt was called off, however, because all three of the targets were not present. The exercise was repeated four days later at the Wolf's Lair with the same result. On July 20 Klausing did not accompany von Stauffenberg, instead waiting at the conspirators' base at the Bendlerblock in Berlin. It would be his responsibility to relay Operation Valkyrie orders throughout the Reich, which he did, even if there were typical bureaucratic delays (Wheeler-Bennett 650; Zimmermann and Jacobsen 149). The storming of the conspirators' Bendlerblock headquarters after the failed attempt to assassinate Hitler rounded up most of the principal players, but Klausing escaped, only to turn himself in to the Gestapo the next day, expecting to be brought before a military hearing. This act of surrender would not be rewarded with leniency. He was imprisoned and dismissed from the Wehrmacht on August 4 (Zimmermann and Jacobsen 196).

Klausing's father, Professor Friedrich Klausing, who was rector of Charles University in Prague and had been a member of the Nazi party since 1933, was also a member of the SA. When he heard of his son's arrest, he went to Governor Hans Frank and asked if there was anything he could do to save his son, even volunteering to fight on the Russian front. An SA tribunal decided that he had to commit suicide to atone for his son's treason, which he obligingly did on August 6; however, that did not save his son (Demetz 182). Dr. Klausing wrote a final letter to his son on the day of his suicide expressing his undying belief in Germany, the German spirit, the German soldier, the SA, and Adolf Hitler (Jacobsen 2: 801).

Friedrich Karl Klausing was sentenced to death by the People's Court on August 8, 1944, and was hanged the same day in Plötzensee Prison, two days after his father's suicide.

Lieutenant Colonel Robert Bernardis was born August 7, 1908, in Innsbruck, Austria. As a young man, he graduated from prominent military institutes in Enns and Klosterneuburg, Austria, before starting his career as a lieutenant in Linz, later attending the War Academy in Berlin (Steinbach and Tuchel 26). He married Hermine Feichtinger in 1932, and the couple went on to have two children. Bernardis accepted the Anschluss of 1938 and became a confirmed Nazi party member. He served in Poland, France, and Russia, being promoted to major in 1942. After a serious illness, he was transferred to the Allgemeines Heeresamt (General Army Office) of the OKW in Berlin, where he was promoted to lieutenant colonel on the General Staff in 1943 and made responsible for personnel (German Resistance Memorial Center). When he became convinced of the ruthless treatment of civilians, particularly in Poland and Russia, he made contact with the resistance. His official duties at the high command made the connection with von Stauffenberg inevitable, and his OKW position allowed him to build up the resistance movement by assigning key personnel where they could best be used by those planning the coup. Early in 1944 he was included in the schemes for assassinating Hitler, and he did his part by completing tasks assigned to him, leading up to ensuring that the Valkyrie plan was transmitted to Vienna (Hoffmann, *The History*, 356).

On July 20 Bernardis was in the Bendlerblock headquarters, where he communicated the Valkyrie Order to Lieutenant Kurt Delius of the Großdeutschland Reserve Brigade in Cottbus (125 kilometers southeast of Berlin) (Hoffmann, *The History*, 430). He was arrested when the building was stormed and, along with von Wartenburg, von der Schulenburg-Tressow, Schwerin von Schwanenfeld, Berthold von Stauffenberg, and Eugen Gerstenmaier, was taken to the same courtyard where four of their fellow conspirators had been executed an hour earlier (Manvell and Fraenkel, *The Men Who Tried*, 241). Orders arrived from Kaltenbrunner, however, countermanding those of General Fromm, stating that there would be no more executions that night and that the men were to be delivered to the Gestapo for interrogation (Galante and Silianoff 194).

On August 8 Bernardis was tried in the People's Court, where he freely admitted his guilt, gaining for himself a death sentence and an execution in Plötzensee Prison that same day (Manvell and Fraenkel, *The Men Who Tried*, 198). His entire family was arrested by the Gestapo and sent to concentration camps; nonetheless, they all survived the war. His letters to his wife and mother-in-law, written on the day of his execution, appear in the Kaltenbrunner papers (Jacobsen 2: 796–97).

First Lieutenant Albrecht von Hagen was born into a noble family on March 11, 1904, in Langen, Pomerania. He studied law in Heidelberg, joining the Saxo-Borussian Heidelberg Corps, a civilian student organization. He finished a law apprenticeship in Königsberg and began working for the government-sponsored Osthilfe (Eastern Aid) Program, where future fellow conspirator Peter Yorck von Wartenburg would also work a few years later. Von Hagen eventually became a district judge, but he chose to resign that position in 1931 to become a corporate lawyer (Zeller 217). He married Erica Marianne von Berg, and the couple ultimately had a daughter and two sons. Von Hagen enrolled in military officer training courses in 1935, and in 1939 he was drafted into the

Wehrmacht as a lieutenant in the reserves, eventually fighting in France and Russia from 1940 to 1942. Early in 1943 he was posted to Angerburg, East Prussia, for a period and then temporarily assigned to North Africa, where he became acquainted with von Stauffenberg. The conspirators in Berlin then arranged his posting to the OKH (in Berlin) under Major General Stieff (Steinbach and Tuchel 81). His fortuitous assignment there was to investigate methods for updating the military command structure. He was also in charge of the dispatch service between military posts in Berlin and the Wolfsschanze in East Prussia. This put him in an ideal position to carry out the responsibilities he would soon be given. In November 1943, von Hagen and Major Joachim Kuhn took possession of the first two bombs, procured through Stieff's connections, to be used in killing Hitler (Zeller 264). Von Hagen delivered the explosives to Stieff, who passed them on to von Stauffenberg in May 1944.

Von Hagen and his immediate family were arrested by the Gestapo soon after the failed July 20 attempt. On August 8, 1944, he was tried by the People's Court, found guilty and straightaway hanged at Plötzensee Prison. In his defense at trial, von Hagen claimed that he had not known what the explosives were to be used for (Manvell and Fraenkel, *The Men Who Tried*, 198). Apparently Freisler was not convinced. Von Hagen's final letter to his wife reveals his acceptance of his role in the conspiracy. In it he states that "with my fate I cannot quarrel" (quoted in Albrecht 1).

Defendants in the Second Conspiracy Trial, Held August 10, 1944

The second trial began on August 10, mere days after the first one concluded, with death sentences being handed out for officers Erich Fellgiebel, Fritz-Dietlof von der Schulenburg-Tressow, Berthold Schenk Graf von Stauffenberg, Alfred Kranzfelder, and Georg-Alexander Hansen. This trial and the next two, like the first, were extensively reported in the Nazi press. Even though the public was no longer mesmerized, this was still the news of the day for the average German, who was glad to read anything that was a distraction from the bombings. Many of those average Germans believed the traitors to be indirectly responsible for their miseries and directly responsible for the downturn in the war.

General Erich Fellgiebel was born October 4, 1886, in Pöpelwitz, Silesia. He began his military career in September 1905, serving as an officer cadet in a signal battalion in the Prussian army. In the First World War, he was assigned to the General Staff; after the war, he remained in the Reichswehr, where he was in frequent contact with Generals Beck and von Stülpnagel (Fest, *Plotting*, 383; German Resistance Memorial Center). He was subsequently ordered to Berlin as a General Staff officer, where he was promoted to major in 1928.

Fellgiebel's elevation to lieutenant colonel came in 1933, and he was promoted to full colonel a year later. In 1938 he earned the rank of major general and was also appointed chief of the army's Signal Command and chief of the Wehrmacht's intelligence liaison to the OKW. He was promoted to general of the Signal Command in 1940, where he quickly became a technical expert, even being noticed by Hitler, who believed him to be too "independent minded" (Steinbach and Tuchel 57).

Fellgiebel became acquainted with members of the resistance through his direct superior, Colonel General Ludwig Beck. In his positions of responsibility, he had access to a range of classified information that would be useful to the conspirators. He played a critical role in the July 20 attempt, tasked with cutting communications between the Wolf's Lair and Berlin. This he was able to do for a short period of time; however, he had to restore communications to inform the Berlin conspirators that the assassination had not succeeded. His communication of "Something fearful has happened. The Führer is alive. Block everything" soon gave away his role in the attempt, and he was arrested at midnight (quoted in Zeller 347). His communication was quite clever, however, and could have been interpreted in written form two ways, depending on who was reading it. Perhaps he intended it that way, or it was just a fortunate choice of words. Unfortunately, the ruse (if that's what it was) did not work indefinitely. On August 10, he was tried in Freisler's People's Court, with Fellgiebel telling Freisler at one point that he had better hurry and hang him before he himself was hanged (Hoffmann, *The History*, 527). Fellgiebel was found guilty and executed on September 4 at Plötzensee Prison. His wife, daughter and sons were taken into custody and held for more than a month (Loeffel 131).

Lieutenant Fritz-Dietlof Graf von der Schulenburg-Tressow was born September 5, 1902, in London. His father, Friedrich Bernhard Graf von der Schulenburg (the brother of Friedrich-Werner Graf von der Schulenburg), was Germany's military attaché there. His mother was Freda-Marie von Arnim. Fritz-Dietlof, his four brothers, and his sister Tisa grew up being educated by a governess in Berlin, Potsdam, Münster, and at the family mansion, Castle Tressow near Wisma. He joined the growing Nazi party in 1932 and married Charlotte Kotelmann in March of the following year (Fest, *Plotting*, 396).

Von der Schulenburg-Tressow chose not to follow family tradition as a career military officer after completing his Arbitur in Lubeck in 1920, opting instead to study law in Göttingen and Marburg, where he became a member of the Corps Saxonia Göttingen student organization. He successfully completed the state law examination in Celle in 1923 and secured a government civil service trainee position in Potsdam and Kyritz for five years, after which he found permanent employment as an assessor in Recklinghausen. He became aware of the Nazi party, particularly the writings of Gregor and Otto Strasser, in 1930, and he and his entire family joined the party two years later. This was an important move for the family—and for Hitler, since he was by this time overtly courting German nobility for support. In 1932, von der Schulenburg-Tressow was transferred and made responsible for promoting party membership in East Prussia. His accomplishments in that undertaking caused him to be noticed by members of the Nazi elite. In March 1933, von der Schulenburg-Tressow's authority as a government official and party member significantly increased when he was appointed to the government council in Königsberg. His assignment was to create affiliations with existing government officials and in due course replace some of them with party members.

Von der Schulenburg-Tressow's continued success did not go unobserved by his superior, Erich Koch, the Gauleiter of East Prussia, who became wary of this rising star and had him transferred in 1934 to Fischhausen as a district administrator (Steinbach and Tuchel 177). Koch eventually had him transferred even farther away in 1937, to the Reich Interior Ministry in Berlin. Von der Schulenburg-Tressow's superior there was Wolf-Heinrich Graf von Helldorf, who would soon be involved in planning the Kristallnacht devastation of Jewish businesses—and later, oddly enough, in the July 20 conspiracy. In 1939, von der Schulenburg-Tressow was made acting Oberpräsident of Upper and Lower Silesia, but his observation of and comments on the Kristallnacht action got him expelled from the Nazi party and labeled "politically unreliable" (Leber 248). A relative,

Oskar von Arnim, had already been arrested once in 1935 and thrown in prison for his association with a planned putsch (Hoffmann, *The History*, 31). In spite of this incident, or perhaps because of it, von der Schulenburg-Tressow volunteered for service at the front as a lieutenant and was assigned to the reserve battalion of the renowned Infantry Regiment 9 in Potsdam. He was later involved in a far-fetched strategy to shoot Hitler in June 1940 as he and the troops paraded down the Champs-Elysees in France (von Hassell and MacRae 80). The parade was ultimately cancelled, and so was the plan. He later received the Iron Cross First Class for his service in Russia; however, this assignment and what he saw there caused him to become even more critical of the war and Hitler's leadership. He soon made contact with others of similar thinking.

In time, von der Schulenburg-Tressow would become a member of the so-called Gräfengruppe (Count's Group), which included Peter Yorck von Wartenburg, and by 1942 he was regularly attending meetings of the Kreisau Circle. Von der Schulenburg-Tressow had contacts in all the right places, owing to his position as a nobleman and government official, which he used to recruit new members to the resistance while acting as liaison between Carl Goerdeler and Julius Leber of the Social Democrats. In 1943 von der Schulenburg-Tressow was briefly detained by the Gestapo for suspected anti-government activities but, because of his aristocratic status and family influence, was soon released.

The planning of Operation Valkyrie was done with von der Schulenburg-Tressow's assistance and knowledge that he was to lead the Interior Ministry as state secretary after Hitler's assassination. On July 20, he was at the Bendlerblock and arrested after the attempt failed, although one member of the conspiracy seems to imply that he was in Paris at this time (von Hassell and MacRae 231). In any case, on August 10 von der Schulenburg-Tressow was tried and sentenced at the People's Court. During his trial, he spoke pompously to Freisler: "We have accepted the necessity to do our deed in order to save Germany from untold misery. I expect to be hanged for this, but I do not regret my action and I hope that someone else in luckier circumstances will succeed" (quoted in Hoffmann, *The History*, 526). Other remarks often attributed to him cannot be verified (Koch 216).

Von der Schulenburg-Tressow was hanged at Plötzensee Prison on August 10 as soon as his trial was concluded. His wife Charlotte and their six children would survive the war (MacDonogh, *After the Reich*, 350; Steinbach and Tuchel 177). His uncle, Friedrich-Werner Graf von der Schulenburg, who was a former ambassador to Moscow and also a member of the resistance, would be executed on November 10 (Zimmermann and Jacobsen 338).

Berthold Graf Schenk von Stauffenberg (the older brother of Claus von Stauffenberg) was born March 15, 1905, in Stuttgart. He studied law at Tübingen and was appointed assistant professor of international law at the Kaiser Wilhelm Institute of Foreign and International Law in 1927. Years earlier Berthold and his brother had been introduced to the poet Stefan George by their boyhood friend, Albrecht von Blumenthal, a cousin of Hans-Jürgen von Blumenthal. Many of the followers of this messianic lyricist became members of various resistance groups, and Berthold would arrange to have a book of George's poems (dedicated to him) published in 1928, titled *Das neue Reich*, which became George's best-known work. Berthold worked at The Hague from 1930 to 1932 and during that period married Maria Classen (*Allgemeine Deutsche Biographie*). In 1939 he joined the German navy and was appointed to the High Command as a staff judge and consultant in international law.

Berthold's apartment at Tristanstrasse in Berlin was a regular meeting place for the July 20 conspirators, which included his cousin Peter Yorck von Wartenburg. After the assassination attempt by Claus, von Wartenburg flew to Rangsdorf Airfield south of Berlin, where he met with Berthold; the two of them then went to the Bendlerblock headquarters to join up with the other members of the conspiracy (Manvell and Fraenkel, *The Men Who Tried*, 149). Berthold and his brother were both arrested there that night. Claus was quickly executed by firing squad, but Berthold's execution was stopped by Kaltenbrunner (Manvell and Fraenkel, *The Men Who Tried*, 154). He was subsequently tried in the People's Court with Judge Freisler presiding on August 10. Berthold and eight others involved in July 20 were hanged at Plötzensee Prison later that day.

Lieutenant Commander Alfred Kranzfelder was born February 10, 1908, into a family of Bavarian jurists; as a young adult, he joined the Reich Navy in 1927. He was encouraged by his superiors to apply to the German Naval College, and, if admitted, he foresaw making a career of the navy. His first posting was to the battleship *Admiral Scheer* as a lieutenant in 1937. In early 1940 Kranzfelder was transferred to Berlin, to the Operations Department of the Naval High Command (OKM), as a liaison officer to the Foreign Ministry. While serving in this capacity he was introduced to Berthold von Stauffenberg, and the two men soon became friends (Steinbach and Tuchel 119). In his new position, Kranzfelder was able to gauge the real status of the war and see how incompetently it was being directed. This revelation steered him toward becoming an active member of the resistance—while in the process being promoted to lieutenant commander. Although he did not participate directly in the events of July 20, he contributed to much of the planning and spoke with Claus von Stauffenberg just two days before the final attempt (Fest, *Plotting*, 253). The Gestapo got involved after securing telephone records confirming the existence of these conversations (Zeller 226). Kranzfelder's task was to discern the reaction of high-ranking naval officers, particularly Admirals Dönitz and Meisel, after the coup and report back to von Stauffenberg whether he believed the two would follow Field Marshal von Witzleben's orders as their new supreme commander. Kranzfelder was arrested by the Gestapo on July 24 and was likely dismissed from the military by a naval court of honor, or some other means, since the "Murder Register" refers to him as "former" naval lieutenant commander Alfred Kranzfelder (Zimmermann and Jacobsen 203). Kranzfelder's name does not appear on the list of fifty-five officers dismissed in the Courts of Honor held between August 4 and September 14 (Zimmermann and Jacobsen 196–98). Perhaps the navy convened a separate Court of Honor to deal with officers involved in July 20, as Berthold von Stauffenberg's name does not appear on the list either, and he is also referred to as "former" naval lieutenant commander by the "Murder Register." Lieutenant Commander Kranzfelder was sentenced to death by the People's Court two weeks after his arrest and hanged on August 10 in Plötzensee Prison.

Colonel Georg-Alexander Hansen was born July 5, 1904, in Sonnefeld and studied law after completing his Arbitur, but in 1924 he chose to pursue a military career. He was selected for General Staff training at the Berlin War Academy in 1935 and afterward assigned to the Foreign Armies East Department of the Army, where he remained until 1943. Hansen was then named chief of the Military Counterintelligence Office under Major General Oster, the Stabschef (Canaris' chief of staff) of the Abwehr. After Canaris was dismissed in January 1944, Hansen became acting chief, replacing Oster until June 1 of that year, when the Abwehr was enveloped by the RSHA (Dulles 80). He was heavily involved with the final planning of the July 20 coup (with Fritz-Dietlof von der Schulenburg-Tressow, Adam von Trott zu Solz, Peter Yorck von Wartenburg, Colonel Ritter Merz von Quirnheim and Lieutenant Colonel Cäsar von Hofacker) that took place on Sunday, July 16, at Claus von Stauffenberg's house at Wannsee (Fest, *Plotting*, 249). The next day Caen and St. Lo fell to the Western Allies, and Rommel was seriously injured in an air attack on the staff car he was riding in. On the day of the attempted coup, Hansen was in Bamberg. He returned to his office a few days later, unsure of whether his role had been discovered; it had, and he was immediately arrested by the Gestapo. A Court of Honor ousted Hansen from the military on August 4, allowing him to be tried by Freisler's VGH on August 10. He was predictably found guilty of treason and executed on September 8 in Plötzensee Prison (German Resistance Memorial Center).

Defendants in the Third Conspiracy Trial, Held August 15, 1944

On August 15, the third trial began, with death sentences being handed out the same day to the Klamroths (Bernhard and Johannes Georg), Egbert Hayessen, Wolf-Heinrich Graf von Helldorf, Adam von Trott zu Solz, and Hans Bernd von Haeften, brother of Werner von Haeften. Several of these men were close friends of Marie Vassiltchikov, a White Russian living and working in Berlin at the time of the assassination attempt. She and her sister, Tatiana, had moved to Berlin in 1940, looking for work; Marie soon found a job in the German Broadcasting Service, transferring later that year to the Information Department of the Foreign Ministry, where she worked for von Trott and became acquainted with other nobles involved in the events of July 20. As Russian nobility herself, she had the confidence of Germans of similar standing, and her sometimes casual references in her diary to resistance members she personally knew provides substantial insight into who these men were. Marie's brother, George Vassiltchikov, wrote in the preface to her diary (published decades after the war) that his sister may have been much more heavily involved in the conspiracy than her diary indicates (Vassiltchikov 202).

Lieutenant Colonel Bernhard Klamroth was born November 20, 1910, in Berlin and joined the Reichswehr in 1930. He was married to Ursula Klamroth, a cousin with whom he had a son. In the Polish campaign, he served as a company commander of the 10th Panzer Division, and in March 1942 he became a general staff officer with the 4th Army on the Eastern Front, where his commanding officer was Major General Hellmuth Stieff (Steinbach and Tuchel 111). Stieff was posted to the OKH in Berlin in October 1942 and soon requested Klamroth's transfer to a department under his command. It was there that Klamroth was introduced to Generals Olbricht, Lindemann, Fellgiebel and others from the von Witzleben clutch of conspirators. "In his department, Stieff was able to count on three officers: Lieutenant Colonel Bernhard Klamroth, Major Joachim Kuhn and First Lieutenant of the Reserve, Albrecht von Hagen" (Zeller 217). In May 1944, Klamroth was involved with von Hagen in acquiring the explosives for the planned assassination by von Stauffenberg. On July 10, 1944, he made the mistake of telling his father-in-law (and cousin), Johannes Georg Klamroth, about the plans; this knowledge would later cost Johannes his life. Bernhard Klamroth was arrested by the Gestapo on July 21, expelled from the military by a Court of Honor on August 14, and then tried in the People's Court on August 15. He was executed that same day in Plötzensee Prison (Stockhorst 234; Zimmermann and Jacobsen 197; German Resistance Memorial Center).

Major Johannes "Hans" Georg Klamroth was born October 12, 1898, in Halberstadt. He was an established businessman and a Hitler devotee from the beginning, joining both the Nazi party and later the SS. He was also a major in the Wehrmacht and became an intelligence officer in the Reserve Army, serving in counterintelligence (Abwehr III) in Denmark and Russia (Zimmermann and Jacobsen 197). Hans was involved in the July 20 plot only in that his aforementioned cousin (and son-in-law), Bernhard Klamroth, told him about the planned assassination and he did not report it or do anything to prevent it. For this offense he was arrested on July 21, expelled with his cousin from the military by a Court of Honor on August 14, and tried with him and Adam von Trott zu Solz on August 15. Hans was executed with von Trott on August 26 in Plötzensee Prison (German Resistance Memorial Center; Zimmermann and Jacobsen 197; and Hoffmann, *The History*, 529).

Major Egbert Hayessen was born December 28, 1913, in Eisleben and grew up in Mittelhof near Felsberg-Gensungen. He successfully completed his Arbitur at the Roßleben Monastery School in 1933 (the same school attended by Peter Yorck von Wartenburg) and finished his military training with Artillery Regiment 12 in Schwerin. Hayessen eventually rose to the rank of major on General Fromm's Ersatzheer staff, working in the same office as Robert Bernardis and Friedrich Klausing. Hayessen was a late member of the July 20 conspiracy, only hearing about it from Bernardis a few days before the attempt. His responsibility was maintaining uninterrupted contact between Berlin's military commander, Paul von Hase, and the city's police chief, Wolf-Heinrich von Helldorf (German Resistance Memorial Center). This was a particularly important task, for without the military and civilian police in Berlin being onboard, the coup would have no hope of success.

On July 20, Hayessen gave von Hase the news that General Fromm had been arrested and was being held for safekeeping at the conspirators' headquarters on Bendlerstrasse in Berlin. Hayessen was also a member of the group assigned the critical tasks of taking over the powerful Berlin radio station and arresting Propaganda Minister Joseph Goebbels, neither of which actually occurred; however, his obvious involvement in July 20 was ample cause for his arrest after the failed attempt (Jacobsen 1: 47). He was in fact arrested by one of his co-conspirators, Lieutenant Colonel Hermann Schöne, who was himself arrested soon afterward for having failed to stop Hayessen and Major Adolf-Friedrich Graf von Schack from burning incriminating papers (Hoffmann, *The History*, 512; Zimmermann and Jacobsen 148).

On August 4 Hayessen was expelled from the military by a Court of Honor, and on August 15 he was sentenced by the People's Court to death by hanging. The sentence was carried out that day at Plötzensee Prison (Zimmermann and Jacobsen 196).

Wolf-Heinrich Graf von Helldorf was born October 14, 1896, in Merseburg to a wealthy landowning family. He served as a lieutenant in the First World War, and after the surrender he volunteered for West Prussia's Freikorps Roßbach. In 1920 he was part of the Kapp Putsch and, when it failed, fled to Italy for several months to avoid arrest. From about 1921 to 1928 von Helldorf worked in farming and became a member of the Mitglied des Preußischen Landtages (representative parliament), first for the National Socialist Freedom Party in Prussia, and from 1925 for the Nazi party. He joined the SA early and, in 1931, was made the SA leader for Berlin-Brandenburg and elected to the Reichstag (Stockhorst 186–87). In March 1933 he was made police president of Potsdam, and in July 1935 he was assigned the same position in Berlin (Fest, *Plotting*, 388). Von Helldorf was one of the organizational planners behind the arson and looting of Berlin's synagogues and Jewish businesses during the Nazi-instigated Kristallnacht riots. He was not present in Berlin at the time; nonetheless, he later went so far as to reprimand some of his men for not having been even more ruthless (Fest, *Plotting*, 388). This, among other actions, caused him to be labeled "Germany's number two Jew-baiter", with the notorious Julius Streicher occupying the number one position throughout the Nazi era (quoted in Hollister and Strunsky 114).

In the Field Marshal Werner von Blomberg affair, von Helldorf withheld information from the Nazis that would have contradicted the Gestapo's claim that von Blomberg's new wife had a criminal record for prostitution. He then convinced Wehrmacht investigators that the Gestapo was withholding information about the incident from them. Von Helldorf devised a similar treachery when General von Fritsch was investigated for homosexual behavior. He had information that would have cleared von Fritsch but withheld it until after the general had been dismissed as commander in chief of the Wehrmacht. When it was convenient, von Helldorf then leaked the vindicating information to Wehrmacht officials (Gisevius, *To the Bitter End*, 220).

As early as 1938, von Helldorf was likely in some sort of collusion with the resistance, but, even if this is true, his motives were plausibly self-serving. As late as the first days of July 1944 he was considered unpredictable and more concerned with keeping his position as police president of Berlin. Vassiltchikov, however, records that von Helldorf had the confidence of some in the resistance, particularly Gottfried von Bismarck, the grandson of the former chancellor (Vassiltchikov 134). In any case, he carried out his critical assignment, keeping the Berlin police from interfering with the coup attempt, putting him forever in the books as a member of the German resistance. However, no streets will be found named for him in Germany today. Von Helldorf was arrested for his participation in the treason and tried by the People's Court on August 15. "We will all have to jump off the Hitler bandwagon someday," he is said to have told Judge Freisler at his trial (quoted in Dulles 179). Von Helldorf was executed at Plötzensee Prison that same day. As additional punishment, Hitler ordered that he be forced to watch the hangings that preceded his own.

Adam von Trott zu Solz was born August 9, 1909, in Potsdam. His parents were August von Trott zu Solz (the Prussian minister of education) and Emilie Eleonore von Schweinitz. He was awarded a Rhodes Scholarship in 1931 and went to Great Britain to study law at Balliol College in Oxford. After completing his studies, he spent six months in the United States. His maternal grandfather was General Hans Lothar von Schweinitz, who had been an ambassador during Bismarck's reign, and his grandmother was an American citizen, Anna Jay, the daughter of John Jay, the American minister in Vienna who was himself a grandson of the American founding father (and chief justice) of the same name (Rothfels 129; MacDonogh, *The Good German*, 13). In 1937 von Trott was assigned to a position in China and spent nearly two years there. With his position and name, he appealed to world leaders during his travels to see the Nazi government in Germany for what it was. In 1939 von Trott went through Lord Lothian and Lord Halifax in an attempt to reverse the British government's appeasement policies; that same year, he traveled back to America to plead his case in Washington. He was "bitterly disappointed by the indifference of the Western Allies" (Fest, *Plotting*, 398).

In 1940 von Trott returned to Germany, ignoring the counsel of friends, and joined the Nazi party so as to gain inside information for the Kreisau Circle (Weiß 465). With his freedom of travel, von Trott had ample opportunity to avoid returning to Germany, but he was "drawn as if by a magnet back to Germany where he considered his duty to lie" (Leber 252). He volunteered for the Sonderreferat Indien (Special Indian Bureau) commanded by Undersecretary of State Wilhelm Keppler. Subhas Chandra Bose (who was married to an Austrian) had fled India for Germany in January 1941 with the intent of raising a pro–Nazi Indian army from among prisoners captured by Rommel's Afrika Korps and then training them for an attack on India. The Nazi government supported this effort, more for propaganda purposes than actually raising an army; nevertheless, von Trott's involvement with Bose's "Free India" movement was a convenient way to maintain his standing in the party without contributing substantially to Nazi war aims.

The British Foreign Office wasn't quite sure what to make of von Trott and had evidence suggesting that he was in reality a German spy and not a member of the resistance at all. They did not officially respond to his various offers of information in trade and did not believe he represented the resistance. It is known, however, that he met with British and American diplomats several times through 1943–1944 in Switzerland and warned the Allies that if they did not make separate peace arrangements with the Germans, the resistance would turn to the Russians for aid. Evidence that came to light after the war confirmed that von Trott was always an anti–Nazi and never a spy (Wistrich 262).

Von Trott was directly involved with the events of July 20, being a part of the contingent responsible for occupying the Nazi Foreign Ministry. He was to be the undersecretary in the Foreign Office in the post–Hitler government, and written evidence to that effect was sufficient to ensure his full investigation (Leber 252). Not knowing what to do after the failed attempt, he simply went on with his regular routine. His office was searched by the Gestapo on July 25, and he was arrested later that day (Vassiltchikov 201). There was more than enough evidence by that time to get him tried before the People's Court. He was found guilty of treason and condemned to death on August 15. He was hanged on August 26 at Plötzensee Prison. His death sentence was delayed so that it could be determined whether he possessed additional information (Vassiltchikov 219).

Dr. Hans Bernd von Haeften was born in Charlottenburg on December 18, 1905. Lieutenant Werner von Haeften, von Stauffenberg's adjutant, was his younger brother, and his mother Agnes was the sister of Field Marshal Walther von Brauchitsch. Hans Bernd was to become state secretary in the post–Hitler Foreign Office, which all but guaranteed his name on a list ultimately found by the Gestapo (Fest, *Plotting*, 386). He studied law in Germany before becoming an exchange student at Oxford. After returning to Germany, von Haeften secured a position as a lower-ranking diplomat under Franz von Papen, first in Vienna and then in Berlin during the war. He became a faithful member of the Confessing Church in 1933 and was later employed by German Foreign Offices in Denmark, Austria, and Hungary, rising to the position of chief of the Cultural Department in 1940. By 1941 von Haeften had become well aware of the abuse suffered by Jews in conquered Belgrade, and that was enough to sway him toward the resistance (von Hassell 223). In 1943 he was appointed director of the personnel office in the Information Division of the Foreign Ministry in Berlin (Vassiltchikov 89). This is where he became acquainted with Marie Vassiltchikov and, according to her diary, she came to know him well. Through her, von Haeften met Adam von Trott zu Solz and Adolf Reichwein, who introduced him to von Moltke and the Kreisau Circle (Vassiltchikov 23). His advancement within the Foreign Ministry was severely limited, however, as he refused to join the Nazi party because of his strong Christian beliefs. Nevertheless, he was firmly committed to the coup, and on July 20, he, von Stauffenberg and von Trott zu Solz were to seize control of the Foreign Ministry after the initial military action. However, they never had the opportunity, and, instead of attempting to escape, von Haeften and von Trott zu Solz simply said farewell to their friends and families, resumed their jobs, and waited to be arrested (Vassiltchikov 219). They did not have long to wait.

Von Haeften was arrested on July 25 and tried on August 15 in Freisler's VGH. His wife was also arrested and held for several weeks (Leber 227). He, unlike many of the other conspirators, put up a forceful defense of his opposition to the Nazi regime, at one point declaring to the court that Hitler was the greatest perpetrator of evil in all of history. Predictably, he was found guilty of treason and hanged on August 15 in Plötzensee Prison (Jewish Virtual Library). His younger brother, Werner, had already been executed with von Stauffenberg on the night of July 20.

Other Military Trials

Between August 21 and September 29, thirty people, both military and civilian, were sentenced to death in another seven trials. There were military defendants in at least six of them: those that took place on October 5, 10, 12, and 20 and November 7 and 13, with Judge Freisler presiding. None of these trials received much publicity—and for a very good reason. With the number of cases being heard, it would have been hard for anyone in the Nazi bureaucracy to continue justifying Hitler's statement about a "small clique of traitors without any conscience," as he described them on the night of July 20. Four Wehrmacht officers were among those sentenced and executed on August 30: Carl-Heinrich von Stülpnagel, the military governor of France; Colonels Eberhard Finckh and Hans-Otfried von Linstow, who were both a part of the Paris operation; and Lieutenant Colonel Karl Ernst Rahtgens, a nephew of Field Marshal von Kluge.

Colonel General Carl-Heinrich von Stülpnagel was born January 2, 1886, in Darmstadt and joined the military in 1904, rising to become a General Staff officer in the First World War (Stockhorst 418). After the war he remained in the military and served in the Reichswehr, being promoted to captain in 1924 and major in 1925. Soon after Hitler came to power, he was promoted to colonel and commander of the 2nd Battalion of the 5th Infantry Regiment based at Neuruppin. In 1936 von Stülpnagel was promoted to major general and made commander of the 30th Infantry Division based in Lübeck. He was promoted again, to lieutenant general, in 1937, and on August 27 of that year he was made deputy chief of the General Staff of the Wehrmacht (Das-Ritterkreuz). Von Stülpnagel was a rising star who was destined for even higher positions, but he became disenchanted with the inner workings of the Nazi hierarchy in 1938 after the von Blomberg and von Fritsch investigations and the Wehrmacht's march into the Sudetenland. When Operation Barbarossa was launched, he led the 17th Army across southern Russia to routs in the battles of Uman and Kiev, and along the way he apparently did his part in eliminating Jews and other undesirables. When his men marched into Galicia, he encouraged them to recruit the anti–Communist and anti–Jewish inhabitants of the city to do the dirty work for them (Mommsen 270).

Von Stülpnagel's initial association with the military opposition to the Nazis came by way of General Erich Hoepner and Colonel General Kurt von Hammerstein-Equord in 1938. He had also been a friend of General Beck's since the early 1930s and took a supporting role in the first Abwehr plan to kidnap Hitler (Fest, *Plotting*, 397). This attempt was directed by General Oster and involved von Witzleben, von Helldorf and several others. The idea was to kidnap Hitler in Berlin as soon as the order for the Czechoslovakia offensive was given. This plot fell apart after the Munich Agreement. Von Stülpnagel's involvement with such intrigues came about because of his lack of faith in Hitler's leadership, not because of any moral opposition to the Nazis' overall goals. As commander of the 17th Army, he signed orders demanding reprisals against civilians for partisan attacks and ordered cooperation with the SS Einsatzgruppen in their "cleansing" campaigns, which followed the military occupation of Russian territory. He was awarded the Knight's Cross on August 21, 1941 (Das-Ritterkreuz).

In March 1942, Operation Barbarossa was in full swing and Hitler was convinced the Russians were beaten, going so far as to reduce personnel committed to the operation. Von Stülpnagel was transferred to France and made military governor of the country, replacing his cousin, General Otto von Stülpnagel, who had held that position since France's capitulation (Wistrich 254). He took along Lieutenant Colonel Cäsar von Hofacker, and together they continued collaborating with those in the military resistance. Von Hofacker became von Stülpnagel's contact with von Stauffenberg during this time when it seemed to ordinary Germans that Hitler could do no wrong.

Von Stülpnagel's role on July 20 was ordering the arrest and detention of all SS and Gestapo officers in Paris. The order was given to Hans Otfried von Linstow, who had not been a part of the coup planning at all and was only told of it on July 20. He was, however, expected to follow the orders of a superior officer, and he did so. Von Linstow was successful beyond expectations and had his prisoners under guard within a few hours of receiving the order. His command caught the SS and Gestapo chiefs by surprise, giving them little opportunity to resist. Things were going quite well for the conspirators in Paris—much better than in Berlin. When definite news of Hitler's survival of the assassination attempt spread, von Stülpnagel was unable to convince Field Marshal Günther von Kluge to support the uprising and was forced to release his prisoners, though he did so only after being threatened by Admiral Theodor Kranke, who assured the conspirators that he would send his men to free the prisoners if necessary. Von Stülpnagel received orders to immediately report to Berlin, knowing that he would be arrested and probably tortured until he either died or gave up others in the resistance. He attempted suicide at Verdun on his way back to Berlin but only succeeded in seriously wounding himself. While being tended to, the obviously muddled von Stülpnagel mentioned his friend Field Marshal Rommel's name (Speidel 116). His delirious rambling placed Rommel under serious suspicion.

Von Stülpnagel and von Hofacker were both soon arrested by the Gestapo. Still not fully coherent, von Stülpnagel was tried by the People's Court on August 30. He was found guilty of high treason and hanged that day at Plötzensee Prison. His cousin Otto was arrested after the war for ordering the execution of Jews and Communists in France early in the war while he was military governor there. He was brought to Paris for trial but committed suicide by hanging himself in his cell on February 6, 1948 (Wistrich 254).

Oberstleutnant Dr. Cäsar von Hofacker was born March 11, 1896, in Ludwigsburg and studied law as a young man (Stockhorst 203). He volunteered for service in Ulhan Regiment 20 and in the German Replacement Flying Corps, the FEA (Flieger Ersatz Abteilung), in the First World War and was captured by the French in early 1918. He was not released until March 1920 (Hoffmann, *Stauffenberg*, 9). His brother Alfred had been killed at Verdun in 1917. Cäsar and Alfred were sons of Eberhard von Hofacker and Albertine Gräfin von Üxküll-Gyllenband, the sister of Claus von Stauffenberg's mother. (As noted earlier, declaring that all the major conspirators were related somehow would not miss the mark by much.) After the war, von Hofacker took a supervisory position in the German steel industry before being recalled to the Luftwaffe in 1939. After the German occupation of France, he served in Paris as a group commander in the Luftwaffe and as chief of the iron and steel office in the military government. In his official Luftwaffe position, he was a personal advisor to von Stülpnagel, becoming an important liaison between him and von Stauffenberg, while at the same time trying to solidify backing of the resistance by Field Marshals Rommel and von Kluge. Von Hofacker referred to Hitler's treatment of France as "short-sighted and imprudent, and in every moral respect disastrous" (quoted in Zeller 231).

On July 20, von Stülpnagel took von Hofacker along with him to notify von Kluge (at La Roche Guyon) that the coup was taking place and that SS and Gestapo personnel in Paris were being rounded up and held. The two men attempted to convince the field marshal to make a choice for the resistance and proclaim orders ("after the action had been taken," as Captain Hermann Kaiser had put it a year earlier), but von Kluge refused to commit. The two conspirators returned to Paris with every intention of carrying on without him. The coup proceeded as planned in Paris until it was known for certain that Hitler had survived—and that the simultaneous insurrection in Berlin was falling apart. The threat of intervention by Admiral Theodor Krancke's naval marines to put down the uprising convinced von Hofacker and von Stülpnagel to release their prisoners. The two of them hastily conspired to invent a believable story that would keep them from being shot by the SS, and both men destroyed incriminating documents related to the coup attempt.

Von Hofacker did not leave Paris, but for some reason he was not arrested until July 26. He was tortured until he admitted that he had talked to Rommel, but apparently he did not provide many details, for if he had, those details would certainly have been transmitted to Kaltenbrunner and documented in his reports (Jacobsen 1: 101 and 267). Stories that von Hofacker somehow betrayed Rommel to the Gestapo are a gross simplification of what likely happened. His interrogators called von Hofacker "the most dangerous internal enemy to the regime in all of France" (quoted in Zeller 231). Major Friedrich Georgi, General Olbricht's son-in-law, was the only other well-known Luftwaffe collaborator, and he was at the Bendlerstrasse on July 20, though he was not arrested until five days later (Hoffmann, *Stauffenberg*, 509; Stockhorst 203).

Von Hofacker was dragged before the VGH on August 30, with Judge Freisler presiding. He was well beyond being intimidated by his accusers by this time and openly harangued the Nazi regime. He made it clear to the court that he wished that he could have taken von Stauffenberg's place and completed the assassination. Hoffmann quotes him as saying:

> Be silent Herr Freisler for today it is my head at stake. In a year, it will be yours. I uncommonly regret that I could not take the place of my cousin von Stauffenberg, who was prevented by his disabilities sustained in combat from completing the deed [Hoffmann, *Stauffenberg*, 279].

Predictably, the VGH found von Hofacker guilty of treason and ordered the death sentence. He was hanged at Plötzensee Prison on December 20 (Stockhorst 203). His wife, Ilse Lotte von Hofacker (née Pastor), and children were sent to concentration camps after his arrest and were among those transferred from Dachau on April 24 and finally liberated from their detention in Tyrol by Wehrmacht troops.

Hauptmann Ulrich-Wilhelm Graf Schwerin von Schwanenfeld (often referred to as Schwerin) was born the son of a Catholic diplomat, Ulrich Carl Wilhelm Graf von Schwerin, and his wife, Freda Elisabeth Helene von Bethmann-Hollweg, in Copenhagen on December 21, 1902. The family's estates in Göhren (Mecklenburg-Strelitz) and Sartowitz (Pomerelia, East Prussia) were large agricultural establishments. Ulrich-Wilhelm married Marianne Gräfin Sahm in 1928, and the couple went on to have five sons. Marianne's father, Heinrich, was senate president of the Free City of Danzig and Oberbürgermeister of Berlin until 1936 (Band 662). Ulrich-Wilhelm attended the Roßleben Monastery School, completing his Arbitur in 1921. (This was the same prestigious school attended by von Wartenburg and Hayessen.) He then attended Munich University and Berlin University, where he studied agriculture. He subsequently graduated from Breslau University with a degree in agronomy in 1926 and then managed his family's estates. He was not an early follower of the National Socialists, having experienced the Munich Beer Hall Putsch first-hand on November 9, 1923 (German Resistance Memorial Center).

Schwerin was a friend and early resistance ally of von Wartenburg and von der Schulenburg-Tressow, even before the invasions of Czechoslovakia and Poland, becoming an important link between multiple civilian and military opposition groups after these offensives. With his many connections in the Foreign Office and the Office for Foreign Affairs (Counterintelligence) in the OKW, he acquired access to reports describing the heavy-handed treatment of civilians in Eastern Europe. Schwerin knew of (and possibly witnessed) the execution of Polish Christians and Jews on his Polish estate in Sartowitz, which served to galvanize his commitment to the resistance (German Resistance Memorial Center; forum.axishistory.com/viewtopic.php?t=54853). Being convinced of Schwerin's anti–Nazi sentiments, von Wartenburg soon introduced him to the Kreisau Circle.

Schwerin was drafted into the Wehrmacht in 1939 as a reserve captain and assigned to the staff of von Witzleben (until his involuntary retirement in 1942), later becoming an important liaison between him and the von Stauffenberg group (Gisevius, *Valkyrie*, 194). In 1943 Oster had Schwerin reassigned to the Abwehr office of the OKW in Berlin (Hoffmann, *The History*, 259). Schwerin was one of the more radical members of the resistance, ready at any time to participate in an assassination attempt, and he enthusiastically took part in planning the events of July 20 (Zeller 296). He was at his assigned position at the Bendlerblock on July 20, in his office, along with Berthold von Stauffenberg, von Wartenburg, and von der Schulenburg-Tressow, when Claus von Stauffenberg returned from Rastenburg and announced that Hitler was dead (Hoffmann, *The History*, 422). Schwerin and the others later attempted to destroy all documents related to the coup when they learned that Hitler was alive, but their association with von Stauffenberg was already well known. The Gestapo arrested Schwerin that night, and he was tried by the VGH on August 21 (Fest, *Plotting*, 397). He was found guilty of treason and sentenced to death by Judge Freisler. He insisted in court that his participation in the coup stemmed from a purely moral standpoint in objection to the many illegal killings authorized by the Nazi regime at home and in occupied countries. That well-stated position garnered him no consideration from Freisler.

Ulrich-Wilhelm Graf von Schwerin von Schwanenfeld, designated to be the state secretary to Beck in a post–Hitler government, was executed on September 8 at Plötzensee Prison (Hoffmann, *The History*, 367). In a final letter to his wife, he wrote, "I am going to my death with the firm conviction that I have wanted nothing for myself and everything for our Fatherland; of this you must be sure, always, and you must tell our sons again and again" (quoted in Zeller 230). A year after his death, he was given a proper funeral, but it had to be announced simply as the funeral of a "fallen soldier" (Fest, *Plotting*, 322).

Colonel Eberhard Finckh was born on November 7, 1889, in Kupferzell, Baden-Württemberg, and he joined the Imperial Army in 1917, serving for a year during the war. After the surrender, he remained in military service as a member of the Reichswehr until 1927, when he entered the War Academy in Berlin, where he first met von Stauffenberg and von Quirnheim (Jacobsen 1: 296). Finckh was married to Annemarie von Weyrauch, and the couple had two daughters and a son (Steinbach and Tuchel 57; German Resistance Memorial Center). Finckh was initially a solid supporter of the Nazi movement, and when Poland was invaded, he served on the Eastern Front as quartermaster of the 6th Army (Zeller 220). Later, in 1943, he served at the same rank in Army Group South and, after being promoted to colonel, as chief quartermaster under General Günther Blumentritt's command in Paris. His direct connection to the attempt of July 20 came through von Stülpnagel and von Hofacker, with all three men coordinating the concurrent uprising in Paris. On June 25 Finckh reported to Rommel that von Stauffenberg was ready for the attempt on Hitler (Zeller 282). Although the field marshal had not participated in the planning, he was made aware of the imminent insurrection.

Finckh was in Paris on July 20 and informed by phone that Hitler was dead. He then reported this information to General Blumentritt. In a later meeting with von Stülpnagel, he was ordered to carry on with arresting all high-ranking Gestapo and SS personnel in Paris. He and his detail followed their orders and promptly made the arrests, only to be ordered to release the prisoners a short time later. Finckh himself was subsequently arrested by the Gestapo and held until he could be discharged from the Wehrmacht by a Court of Honor, which put him in the hands of the People's Court. He was tried on August 30 with von Stülpnagel, von Hofacker, and Otfried von Linstow. He was sentenced to death by the court, with Judge Freisler presiding, and executed by hanging the same day in Plötzensee Prison (Fest, *Plotting*, 280 and 313; Hoffmann, *The History*, 529).

Colonel Hans Otfried von Linstow served in the First World War, and after the surrender he remained in the military as a member of the Reichswehr until the beginning of World War II, being assigned to the 15th Infantry Division in 1939 and to the 10th Army Corps the following year. In 1941 von Linstow was with the 9th Army Corps during Operation Barbarossa. In April 1944 he was reassigned to Paris as the chief of staff to General von Stülpnagel (Zeller 280). The coup was to take place at the next opportunity to kill Hitler, so von Linstow was hastily recruited by von Stülpnagel and von Hofacker to participate in the Paris phase of the insurrection. The final plans were not revealed to him until the coup had essentially begun. Von Linstow had a heart ailment, and it was felt that the gravity of the situation might be too much for him (Wheeler-Bennett 663). Nevertheless, on July 20 von Linstow and others began arresting members of the Paris Gestapo and SS as soon as the Valkyrie code word was transmitted to his superiors and then to him. He heard by phone from von Stauffenberg late that day that the assassination had failed and reported the news to the other Paris conspirators (Zeller 330). "At eleven o'clock Colonel Linstow staggered into the room on the fourth floor of the Raphael [Hotel]. His heart was affected and he could barely breathe. The men gathered there rushed to help him reach a chair. 'It's all over in Berlin,' he gasped. 'Stauffenberg's just been on the phone. He told me the terrible news. His murderers were actually hammering on the door'" (quoted in Manvell and Fraenkel, *The Men Who Tried*, 153). The Paris operation was quickly called off and the prisoners at the Hotel Continental were released.

Von Linstow was arrested by the Gestapo in Paris on July 23 and promptly dismissed from the Wehrmacht by a Court of Honor. He was sentenced to death by the People's Court in Berlin on August 30, 1944, and executed that same day in Plötzensee Prison (Hoffmann, *The History*, 529).

Oberstleutnant Karl Ernst Rahtgens joined Infantry Regiment 1 in Potsdam in 1928, soon after completing his Arbitur, and became an officer cadet (Fahnenjunker), senior grade. He and his wife, Johanna von Cramon, were the parents of a daughter and two sons (German Resistance Memorial Center; Steinbach and Tuchel 159). He was admitted to the War Academy in Berlin in 1937, intending to make the military his career, and began General Staff training the next year. After the war began, Rahtgens was assigned to a number of different commands, which would have been typical for someone on his career path, and in 1942 he was promoted to lieutenant colonel on the general staff of the Führer's headquarters at Rastenburg in East Prussia (Vierhaus 102). Here he met and became friends with Lieutenant Colonel Günther Smend, who was already involved in the resistance. Smend was adjutant to General Kurt Zeitzler, the Wehrmacht chief of staff, who would himself be dismissed from the Wehrmacht by Hitler on July 20, though not for involvement in the coup attempt (Speer 499). Rahtgens' uncle was General Field Marshal Günther von Kluge, who, for the time being, indicated support of the resistance (Zeller 377 and 445). Rahtgens was a member of the group that planned parts of the July 20 coup and, after its failure, was arrested by the Gestapo in Belgrade a few weeks later and dismissed from the Wehrmacht by a Court of Honor on August 14 (Zimmermann and Jacobsen 197). Karl Ernst Rahtgens was tried by the People's Court on August 30, 1944, and sentenced to death for treason. He was executed later that day at Plötzensee Prison (German Resistance Memorial Center).

Major Busso Thoma was born October 31, 1899, in St. Blasien-Immeneich, Schwarzwald. He served in the First World War, retired from military service as a lieutenant in 1920, and became a businessman. He was recommissioned in 1939, like many other former officers, when the war with Poland began, rising to the rank of major and becoming a Luftwaffe liaison to the Wehrmacht (Jacobsen 2: 723). In 1941 he met and became friends with Captain Hermann Kaiser (who was already a member of the conspiracy) in his official capacity as the officer responsible for keeping the war diary of the OKW. Thoma soon became an active member of the resistance himself and an accessory in the July 20 attempt. He was in the Bendlerblock in Berlin, assigned to lead his men against the pro-Nazi forces (which would be commanded by Major Otto Ernst Remer) sent to occupy the building. Thoma was immediately arrested when the coup fell apart, but he was not summarily executed or even charged (German Resistance Memorial Center). Though released during the chaos, he was re-arrested by the Gestapo on September 14 after they determined he was not simply following the orders of his superiors but was in fact a member of the resistance. He was eventually tried by the People's Court on January 17, 1945, and found guilty of treason. He was executed on January 23 in Plötzensee Prison (Stockhorst 422).

Oberleutnant Heinrich Graf von Lehndorff-Steinort was born June 22, 1909, in Hanover, to an aristocratic agricultural Prussian family of considerable means, being related to the von Haeftens and Wagners (including Colonel Siegfried Wagner). He was also the grandson of Wilhelm I (Wilhelm the Great, Wilhelm Friedrich Ludwig) (Wheeler-Bennett 515; Zimmermann and Jacobsen 327). As a young man, he studied economics and business at Frankfurt University and put his education to use in managing the family estate at Steinort, East Prussia. It was at this family citadel that Henning von Tresckow first met Claus von Stauffenberg, soon after the surrender at Stalingrad (Fest, *Plotting*, 201). Von Lehndorff-Steinort was married to Gottliebe Gräfin von Kalnein (called "Mausi"), and the couple would go on to have four daughters (MacDonogh, *After the Reich*, 72). He was drafted into the Wehrmacht soon after the invasion of Poland as a reserve lieutenant and sent to the front. Von Lehndorff-Steinort was eventually made adjutant to Field Marshal Fedor von Bock and followed him back to the Eastern Front when von Bock was made commanding officer of Heeresgruppe Mitte (Army Group Center). This was the renamed Army Group B and one of the three major army groups to lead the invasion of Russia. Von Lehndorff-Steinort was then made an aide to General von Tresckow (von Bock's nephew) in Posen and immediately brought into von Tresckow's resistance cadre, along with Major Carl-Hans Graf von Hardenberg and Colonel Bernd von Kleist (son of the field marshal). Von Kleist would ultimately survive the war (von Schlabrendorff, *The Secret War*, 189).

Von Lehndorff-Steinort observed first-hand the treatment of Russian Jews by SS Einsatzgruppe personnel and local collaborators—often trained by members of the Einsatzgruppe. Of particular disrepute was Einsatzgruppe B, which was responsible for training local volunteers who subsequently murdered most of the Jewish population of Barysau on October 20, 1941. From an airplane, von Lehndorff-Steinort witnessed for himself the results of that massacre of more than seven thousand (Fest, *Plotting*, 180).

Von Lehndorff-Steinort was designated by von Stauffenberg as the post–Hitler liaison officer for Wehrkreis I (Königsberg) (Hoffmann, *The History*, 349). Thanks to this list of reliable Wehrkreis officers and teletype messages identifying him, von Lehndorff-Steinort was arrested the day after the failed coup, but he managed to escape and hide out until betrayed and re-arrested (MacDonogh, *After the Reich*, 164). He was tried by the VGH on September 3 and found guilty of treason. Judge Freisler sentenced him to death, and the punishment was carried out the next day at Plötzensee Prison.

Von Lehndorff-Steinort's wife, Gottliebe, was remanded to a concentration camp and his daughters were taken from their mother, given new names, and placed in orphanages in Thuringia, but they all survived the war (Fest, *Plotting*, 304). His cousin, Hans Graf von Lehndorff-Steinort, was captured by the Russians on April 13, 1945, and would survive captivity at the infamous Rothenstein camp near Königsberg. He was a medical doctor, and during his two-month imprisonment he did his best to treat inmates who had been abused by the Russians (MacDonogh, *After the Reich*, 166). Hans Graf von Lehndorff-Steinort died in Bonn in 1987.

Major Hans-Jürgen Graf von Blumenthal was born February 23, 1907, to a noble family headed by Graf Hans von Blumenthal XII, who would be made governor of the Neufchateau district in Belgium after the First World War. His mother was a von Schulenburg. The family was prosperous until the inflation of the mid–1920s, when, like many others, they lost almost everything. Hans-Jürgen was slated to be the military liaison officer for District II (Stettin) in the post–Hitler government (Wheeler-Bennett 744). His name on that list was enough to guarantee his investigation after July 20.

Von Blumenthal attended the Potsdam Gymnasium until 1928 and the Neustrelitz Realgymnasium when his family moved there, and he later studied law and economics at Königsberg and Munich Universities. He presently became involved with the Stahlhelm veterans' association and worked in the organization's publications division until the National Socialists took control of it in 1935. Earlier, in 1930, he had the good fortune to visit the United States, which led him to have a greater appreciation of Germany's position in the world. Von Blumenthal wasn't always critical of the Nazis or Hitler; in fact, he joined the SA and was promoted to Sturmbannführer. He did not stay in the SA, however, and after finishing his university education in 1935, he went back to Neustrelitz and joined the Wehrmacht as a second lieutenant in the 48th Infantry Regiment. He was soon promoted to lieutenant and was made a company commander in 1938, with a short-term assignment at the War College in Munich that same year (*Allgemeine Deutsche Biographie*).

Von Blumenthal became involved with the resistance even before the Sudetenland Crisis and was a member of the largely unknown 1938 Beck/Oster/von Witzleben plan to storm the Reich Chancellery and arrest Hitler, and then have him "accidentally" shot during the fighting (Parssinen 160 and 215). The plan was detailed and had a good chance of success, but it did not get implemented because of the German people's continued admiration of Hitler and the unwillingness of the British to intercede militarily and stop Hitler's successful invasion of Czechoslovakia. An assassination at that time would have been seen by all of Germany as high treason rather than an action taken to rid the country of a despot.

In August 1939 von Blumenthal was promoted to captain and came in contact with members of the Abwehr conspirators group. The invasion of Poland began on September 1, and he married Cornelia von Schnitzler eight days later. The couple would have one son, Hubertus, born in May 1942 (German Resistance Memorial Center). Cornelia was from a wealthy family: her mother was a von Borsig of the Borsig-Werke factory, the first German manufacturer of locomotives. Von Blumenthal was stationed at Saarbrücken during the interim after the Polish invasion and before the actual shooting war began. When the German army started to move, he was with the initial strike force in Alsace for several months; then, in July 1940, his regiment was moved to Tomaschew (Tomaszowo) Poland and he was made a battalion commander. When Barbarossa commenced, he was on the front line and led his battalion to within a few kilometers of Kiev before he was severely wounded (Steinbach and Tuchel 28). He was confined to the military hospital in Leipzig for more than a year, until December 1942. During his recovery, he reconnected with members of the resistance; after being released from hospital, he was transferred to the Reserve Army in Berlin, where one of his superiors was Colonel Siegfried Wagner. Von Blumenthal was already well acquainted with von Dohnanyi and Oster, and he was a childhood friend of Albrecht von Mertz von Quirnheim (Zeller 213). He came to know Claus von Stauffenberg through his cousin, Albrecht von Blumenthal.

In April 1943 von Blumenthal was promoted to major and became the connection between resistance members in Berlin and Stettin. He was regularly in communication with von Stauffenberg and Goerdeler in the period before July 20, but he was not directly involved in the attempted coup. The Gestapo was nonetheless quick to arrest him on July 23 while he was with his family in Kümmernitz. He was imprisoned and interrogated but did not reveal information about others involved in the plot. Hans-Jürgen von Blumenthal was ousted from the military by a Court of Honor on September 14 and tried on October 13 by the VGH, found guilty of treason, and executed that same day at Plötzensee Prison (German Resistance Memorial Center; Zimmermann and Jacobsen 198). His cousin Albrecht would ultimately survive the war.

Major Roland-Heinrich von Hößlin was born February 21, 1915, in Munich and was another one of the young members of the resistance involved in July 20. He was from a well-established military family and in 1933, at the age of seventeen, joined the Reichswehr and became a Fahnenjunker in Regiment 17, the von Stauffenberg family's traditional regiment based in Bamberg (Fahnenjunker is a rank that designates the holder as an officer candidate and was not commonly used in the Third Reich, but it is roughly equivalent to second lieutenant in the infantry).

By 1936 von Hößlin had been drafted into the Wehrmacht and was promoted to first lieutenant during the invasion of Poland in 1939. He was then sent to North Africa in March 1941 as an orderly officer in the Afrika Corps at Tripolitania under Rommel (Steinbach and Tuchel 95). In August 1941 he was assigned to Pz. AA 33 (Panzer Aufklärung Abteilung, Reconnaissance Battalion) and, a year later, was promoted to captain. von Hößlin was seriously wounded on July 12, 1942. He was awarded the Knight's Cross for bravery on July 23, promoted to major, and transferred back to the Bamberg 17th Cavalry Regiment (Das-Ritterkreuz).

In February 1944 von Hößlin was made commander of Armored Reconnaissance Battalion 24 in Meiningen, East Prussia (Hoffmann, *The History*, 441). By that time he was already a member of the resistance, but until April 1944 he had not been asked to actively participate in any of the assassination attempts. Von Stauffenberg gave von Hößlin the task of having his battalion occupy assigned buildings in East Prussia after the coup and defend them against those loyal to the Nazis if the need arose. Von Hößlin's role in the events of July 20 was not immediately discovered, and on August 1 he was transferred back to Meiningen (Steinbach and Tuchel 95). The Gestapo exposed his connection to the conspiracy three weeks later, arresting him in Meiningen on August 23, and a Court of Honor promptly discharged him from the Wehrmacht. He was tried by the VGH on October 13 and found guilty of treason. At his trial, von Hößlin was able to protect Claus von Stauffenberg's friend Peter Sauerbruch to some degree by convincing Judge Freisler that information on the conspiracy that had been presented at his trial came only from the already dead von Stauffenberg (Hoffmann, *Stauffenberg*, 202). Von Hößlin was hanged at Plötzensee Prison immediately after his trial (German Resistance Memorial Center).

Colonel Alexis Freiherr von Rönne was born into a devout Protestant family of Baltic heritage on February 22, 1903. In 1943, he was head of the Fremde Heere West (OKH Foreign Armies West), which was responsible for military reconnaissance of the Western Front (and later the Atlantic Front.) His superior was Major General Reinhard Gehlen, who chose von Rönne to be his liaison with the Abwehr (Jörgensen 125). In his station on the Western Front, von Rönne had a good view of the overall military situation, correctly perceiving that, ever since 1939, the German forces had been tied up with Poland and Russia while their enemies had ample opportunity to fashion effective air war tactics—which would be used to great effect in the future. He was correct in believing that this development would be decisive in the war. His strong Christian beliefs and the Nazis' opposition to all forms of established religion meant it was only a matter of time before he became involved in the resistance.

Prior to the Allied invasion of 1944, von Rönne was chief of military intelligence in the West and intentionally sent false information back to Berlin regarding estimated Allied troop strength in England (Mitcham, *Retreat*, 24). Often von Rönne would double the actual estimates, misleading Hitler about the coming invasion already known to be codenamed Overlord. It was through his association with the economic advisor in annexed Regierungsbezirk (administrative district) Kattowitz, Reserve Captain Michael Graf von Matuschka (a collaborator with Fritz-Dietlof von der Schulenburg-Tressow), that von Rönne first became aware of the July 20 coup plans (Zeller 220; German Resistance Memorial Center).

Von Rönne refused to participate directly in an assassination because of his religious beliefs, but he was nonetheless involved in the planning. His link to the conspirators was quickly discovered after July 20, which guaranteed his apprehension, but he was soon released, only to be re-arrested two weeks later and this time imprisoned. Before his second arrest, he had the opportunity, through his contacts, to go underground with the aid of the French Resistance, but he chose to face the consequences of his actions, saying that a Prussian officer did not break his oath (Liss 29). Throughout his interrogation by the Gestapo, von Rönne insisted that it had been the anti–Jewish and anti–Christian policies of the National Socialists that persuaded him to join the resistance. He was tried by the VGH on October 5 and found guilty of treason. Von Rönne was executed on October 14 at Plötzensee Prison, although October 12 is given in another source (Stockhorst 350; German Resistance Memorial Center). The day before his execution, he wrote to his mother, saying, "You have sometimes been tormented by fear of death simply because of the physical process of the events, and so I wanted very much to let you know that our Lord can wipe that too completely away if we ask him to. So do not be in the least afraid" (quoted in Zimmermann and Jacobsen 257).

Von Matuschka was also arrested after July 20. He was tried by the VGH on September 14, found guilty of treason and executed that same day (with Colonel Nikolaus Graf von Üxküll-Gyllenband, General Heinrich Graf Zu Dohna-Tolksdorf, and Father Hermann Wehrle) at Plötzensee Prison (Steinbach and Tuchel 136).

Rittmeister (Cavalry Captain) Friedrich Scholz-Babisch was born April 10, 1890, and, as an adult, became a moderately wealthy Silesian landowner and agriculturalist. After the Nazis came to power, he served in the Wehrmacht as a reserve Rittmeister in Wehrkreis VIII. Claus von Stauffenberg personally recruited Scholz-Babisch in December 1943, and he soon became a confirmed member of the conspiracy (Hoffmann, *Stauffenberg*, 202). His name would ultimately be found on the list of reliable Wehrkreis liaison officers proposed for District VIII (Hoffmann, *The History*, 350). This was a crucial appointment because of the sizable SS contingency in the Wehrkreis that would have to be dealt with. After July 20, the Gauleiter and Oberpräsident of Lower Silesia, Karl Hanke, wanted Scholz-Babisch arrested immediately, but his commanding officer, General Koch-Erpach, objected, stating that he himself would be responsible for any disciplinary action (Hoffmann, *The History*, 450). Nevertheless, Scholz-Babisch was arrested, though he was not tried until October 13, after first being expelled from the military by a Court of Honor on September 14 (Zimmermann and Jacobsen 198). The VGH subsequently found him guilty of treason, and he was hanged October 13 at Plötzensee Prison.

Lieutenant Colonel Karl-Heinz Engelhorn, a General Staff officer, was born September 6, 1905, and became a member of Canaris' Abwehr at the beginning of the Second World War (Stockhorst 123). He was another conspirator who was guilty of little more than knowing of the plans for July 20 and not reporting what he knew to the Gestapo. His superior on that date was Colonel Georg-Alexander Hansen, who was Canaris' temporary replacement in February 1944 before the Abwehr was absorbed into the SD (and thus the RSHA) (Zeller 219). Through Colonel Hansen, Engelhorn became aware of the planned coup (Steinbach and Tuchel 53). Multiple higher-ranking Abwehr officers had been under Gestapo surveillance for more than a year, and Engelhorn's guilt by association was enough to warrant his arrest after July 20. He was charged by Judge Freisler with treason in a VGH trial that also heard the cases of Major Adolf Friedrich Graf von Schack, Lieutenant Colonel Wilhelm Kuebart, and Colonel Alexis Freiherr von Rönne. Kuebart was one of the few conspirators to be sentenced to a prison term and survive the war, but Engelhorn, Schack, and von Rönne received death verdicts (see *Yank Magazine*, June 1, 1945). Engelhorn was executed by firing squad or hanged (reports disagree on what actually happened) on October 24 in the Brandenburg-Görden Prison (Stockhorst 123; German Resistance Memorial Center).

Colonel Rudolf Graf von Marogna-Redwitz was born August 15, 1886, in Munich and became a career officer in the Imperial German Army, serving in the First World War and remaining in the military after the surrender. After completing additional officer training, he was posted to the nascent Reichswehr military counterintelligence office. He was married to Anna Gräfin von Arco-Zinneberg, and the couple would have a daughter and two sons. He met von Stauffenberg in the late 1920s while serving with Reichswehr Regiment 17 in Bamberg. Von Marogna-Redwitz became one of the early members of the Abwehr after being reactivated just prior to the Polish invasion. He was stationed in Vienna as chief of counterintelligence, where he became acquainted with groups of conservative Catholics in the city; their influence no doubt contributed to his desire to be involved in Abwehr resistance efforts (Steinbach and Tuchel 135; German Resistance Memorial Center). He remained with the Abwehr until it was consolidated under Himmler in 1944, by which time he had become an intimate of both Claus and Berthold von Stauffenberg. After the Abwehr was essentially dissolved, von Marogna-Redwitz asked to be relocated, as did many of Canaris' men, and he was soon posted to the OKW in Berlin, with General Olbricht becoming his direct superior. On July 20, in Vienna, he and fellow conspirators Karl Seitz and Josef Reither were responsible for arresting the city's Nazi officials, as per the general coup plan, but von Marogna-Redwitz himself was arrested by the Gestapo shortly after the failure in Berlin. His name was on von Stauffenberg's list to become a liaison officer for Wehrkreis XVII (Vienna) (Hoffmann, *The History*, 350). This list was discovered by the Gestapo on July 20 at the Bendlerblock, which was enough to justify von Marogna-Redwitz's dismissal from the military by a Court of Honor on August 24 (Zimmermann and Jacobsen 197). He was sentenced to death by the People's Court on October 12, 1944, and executed later that day in Berlin's Plötzensee Prison. Photographs taken of von Marogna-Redwitz in the VGH show bandages on his face covering injuries sustained during the Gestapo interrogations (Zimmermann and Jacobsen 299). "Some day, when the history of the Austrian liberation movement is written, his name will take one of the first places. There will be many witnesses in the countries of southeastern Europe to testify to the devotion which this splendid man, a true European, lavished upon the cause" (Gisevius, *To the Bitter End*, 426). A book on his life, written by his daughter Elisabeth von Loeben, was published in 1984.

Lieutenant Colonel Georg Schulze-Büttger was born October 5, 1904, in Posen and grew up in Hildesheim. He attended the Andreanum Gymnasium and completed his Arbitur in 1922. Soon after, he joined the Reichswehr with the intention of making the military his career. Schulze-Büttger was married to Jutta Neumann, with whom he had a daughter and two sons (German Resistance Memorial Center). He received rapid promotions in the military and, in 1935, was made adjutant to General Ludwig Beck, the chief of staff of the army (Generalstabschef des Herres). In due course he became acquainted with members of the resistance around him, but it was the Kristallnacht destruction in 1938 that convinced him that something had to be done. After Beck's resignation, Schulze-Büttger was transferred to the Chief of Staff Office of Army Group Center (Heeresgruppe Mitte), where Henning von Tresckow was his direct superior. Schulze-Büttger was von Tresckow's operations officer from December 1941 to the end of February 1943. His replacement was Lieutenant Colonel Hans-Alexander von Voß. Schulze-Büttger then became senior operations officer to Field Marshal Erich von Manstein in Army Group South (Goerlitz 437). Von Manstein was, at best, a lukewarm supporter of the resistance, and it seems Schulze-Büttger had little success in convincing his new commander to take an active role.

Schulze-Büttger has been described as someone whom von Tresckow could depend on when the events of July 20 began to unfold (Hoffmann, *The History*, 265). No doubt his name was discovered on some list after the failure of the coup, because he was arrested and then expelled from the Wehrmacht on September 14 by a Court of Honor (Zimmermann and Jacobsen 198). He was tried by the VGH on October 13, sentenced to death for treason, and subsequently executed that same day at Plötzensee Prison (German Resistance Memorial Center).

In rendering judgment on Schulze-Büttger, von Hößlin, von Blumenthal, and Scholz-Babisch, Judge Freisler was clear:

> In the name of the German People: Georg Schulze-Büttger, Hans-Jurgen Count Blumenthal, Roland von Hößlin, and Friedrich Scholz-Babisch, knew well beforehand of the planned betrayal of 20 July. They revealed nothing and thus allowed the plot to come to maturity. Thus they are forever without honor, jointly guilty of the heaviest betrayal known to history. They stand together as traitors with the assassin Count von Stauffenberg. With him they betrayed everything that we are and for which we fight. They betrayed the sacrifices of our soldiers, betrayed the people, the Führer and the Reich. They had a part in a betrayal which would have delivered us defenseless to our mortal enemies. For this, they are sentenced to death [quoted in Williamson and Bujeiro 24].

Generalleutnant (Lieutenant General) Karl Freiherr von Thüngen was born June 25, 1893, in Mainz and served honorably in the First World War. He remained in the Reichswehr after the surrender, and in the Second World War he served on the Eastern Front with the 18th Panzer Division, being decorated with the Knight's Cross of the Iron Cross in April 1943 (Das-Ritterkreuz). Von Thüngen was an unenthusiastic conspirator, but he was nonetheless proposed as military commander of Wehrkreis III in Berlin (under Major Hans Ulrich von Oertzen), replacing General Joachim von Kortzfleisch, the current commander of the Berlin military district (Steinbach and Tuchel 203). Von Kortzfleisch made it clear to the conspirators on July 20 that he was not interested in participating, which led to his arrest by Olbricht as a precaution (Fest, *Plotting*, 274). Von Kortzfleisch was killed less than a year later, on April 20, 1945, by advancing American forces.

Von Thüngen was not given much time to become convinced that he should back the coup of July 20 and, as a result, delayed acting, but he did go to his assigned command post on the Hohenzollerndamm. Von Thüngen and the chief of staff, General Otto Herfurth, were both suspicious of the orders they had been given (Fest, *Plotting*, 270). When news arrived that Hitler had survived, von Thüngen refused to accept additional orders from the conspirators. He was not suspected of having been involved in the attempt and even assisted in the interrogation of Major von Oertzen (www.lexikon-der-wehrmacht.de/Personenregister/T/ThuengenKarlFrhrv.htm). Nonetheless, von Schlabrendorff identifies von Thüngen as a fellow conspirator (von Schlabrendorff, *The Secret War*, 289), and his name appears on a plaque in Bamberg Cathedral underneath those of von Stauffenberg, von Marogna-Redwitz, von Leonrod, and von Hößlin. Von Thüngen was soon arrested by the Gestapo in any case, primarily because of his guarded behavior after the failed attempt, and dismissed from the Wehrmacht by a Court of Honor. He was tried by the VGH on October 5, found guilty of treason, and sentenced to death. He was executed by firing squad (the more honorable option) at Brandenburg-Görden Prison on October 24 (Zimmermann and Jacobsen 342).

General Otto Herfurth was arrested on August 14, dismissed from the Wehrmacht by a Court of Honor on September 28, tried by the VGH the next day, and then hanged at Plötzensee Prison, alongside Joachim Meichßner, Fritz von der Lancken, Wilhelm-Friedrich zu Lynar and Joachim Sadrozinski (German Resistance Memorial Center). There are claims that Herfurth initially supported the coup but later switched sides (Brakelmann 259).

Major Adolf Friedrich Graf von Schack was born in St. Goar on August 3, 1888, and was the fourth of five children of Ulrich Graf von Schack (1853–1923). Adolf Friedrich was an officer in the First World War, during which he was seriously wounded. He requested a discharge in 1920 to manage the family investments and was married to Else Dorothea Freiin von Werthern in 1928. The couple had three sons and a daughter (German Resistance Memorial Center). During this time he also joined the Stahlhelm, as did many other veterans. Von Schack was recalled to active duty prior to the invasion of Poland, being ultimately promoted to major and posted to the Wehrmacht Archives Office in Potsdam. He had joined the Nazi party in 1936 but was never an active member or appointed to any party office. He was involved in the events of July 20 through his superior, Lieutenant General von Hase, the Berlin city commandant, and was part of the contingent that was to be responsible for securing the government district. However, military intervention by Major Remer's Großdeutschland Infantry Division prevented him from completing this assignment (Zeller 224).

Von Schack destroyed as many conspiracy-related documents as he could immediately after the failed coup, and for this he was arrested the next day (Hoffmann, *The History*, 512). Kaltenbrunner's report of July 31 to Reichsleiter Martin Bormann mentioned von Schack as being one of the conspirators, and that was enough to seal his fate (Jacobsen 1: 112). He was tried by the VGH on October 10 and sentenced to death for treason. However, he was not immediately executed but sent to Tegel Prison until his execution by firing squad on January 15, 1945, at Brandenburg-Görden Prison (German Resistance Memorial Center).

Hauptmann Professor Jens-Peter Jessen was born December 11, 1895, to Jes and Maria (née Andersen). He attended the Flensburg Gymnasium, completing his Arbitur in 1914, and immediately joined the military. After the First World War, he continued his education at the universities of Hamburg and Kiel; married Käthe Scheffer in 1921, with whom he would have four sons; and became a university instructor in Göttingen in 1927, later serving as a professor of political science there in 1932. He also taught political science in Keil and Marburg in subsequent years. His final academic position was professor of economics and political science at Berlin University in 1936 (*Allgemeine Deutsche Biographie*). One of his students at Kiel was Otto Ohlendorf, who would later become an SS Obergruppenführer, assigned by Heydrich to lead the infamous Einsatzgruppe D. Ohlendorf was hanged for multiple war crimes in 1951. "He [Ohlendorf] was an intellectual and had not lost contact with his old teacher who liked to be kept informed of the attitude of the SS; there were in their ranks young intellectuals who thought of themselves as an elite and as the pioneers of a genuine revolution, and who regarded Hitler and his personal following corrupt" (Ritter 299).

Jessen was recalled to the military in World War II and made a reserve captain on the staff of Quartermaster General Eduard Wagner (Fest, *Plotting*, 389). His position there allowed him to create travel opportunities for the major conspirators without attracting attention. Jessen had initially supported the Nazis, but he became an avowed anti–Nazi after seeing them destroy the economy with their uncontrolled military spending. He soon joined the Wednesday Society along with Johannes Popitz and Erwin Planck. The three of them were responsible for writing the initial drafts of an extremely right-wing constitution for post–Hitler Germany (Ritter 209). In late May or early June 1944, Jessen was seriously injured in an automobile accident, which prevented him from being able to travel widely, and this factor probably contributed to the final planning for July 20 taking place at his house (von Hassell 360). His name was on many of the documents produced by the resistance, which was more than enough to warrant his arrest when these records were found, and it did not take the Gestapo long to connect Jessen directly with the July 20 attempt after its failure. Interrogations revealed the link between those conspirators and the Wednesday Society, whose members were already under constant surveillance. Jessen was dismissed from the military by a Court of Honor on September 14, tried in the People's Court on November 7, and found guilty of treason (or, rather, not reporting treason he was aware of). Professor Jessen was executed on November 30 at Plötzensee Prison (Zimmermann and Jacobsen 322).

Captain Bernhard Letterhaus was born July 10, 1894, in Barmen and after completing a textile apprenticeship in the Rhineland, he attended the Prussian College for Textile Workers, an advanced technical school of design (Leber 107). He was married to Grete Thiel, and the couple had one daughter. After serving in the First World War, during which he was severely wounded and awarded the Iron Cross First Class, he became active in the Association of Christian Textile Workers and a good friend of Heinrich Brüning, the Reich chancellor (Leber 108). Otto Müller, of the Association of Catholic Workers and Miners, convinced Letterhaus to become secretary of the central office of the Catholic Labor Movement in München-Gladbach in 1927. Müller served as a Center Party representative on the city councils of München-Gladbach and Cologne from 1919 to 1933 (Mommsen 285). The Catholic Labor Movement would survive until 1938. When the organization moved its headquarters to the Kettelerhaus in Cologne, Letterhaus met Nikolaus Groß; the two would become key leaders of the Cologne Circle. His function was to also serve as a liaison between the military and the circle during this time (Zeller 219). Later, just after Hitler became chancellor, Letterhaus represented the Center Party in the Prussian Parliament, where he attempted to block Hitler's initial legislative actions, thus attracting additional scrutiny from the party. After the invasion of Poland, Letterhaus was drafted into the Wehrmacht again, as a captain, and in 1942 he was transferred to the OKW in Berlin. He soon made contact with resistance leaders Ludwig Beck and Carl Goerdeler, though he still maintained his connections with the Cologne group. Letterhaus would have been, in the post–Hitler government, the minister of reconstruction or the political representative for Military District VI (Münster) (Zeller 249). He was arrested on July 25, tried in the VGH on November 13, and executed the next day at Plötzensee Prison (Steinbach and Tuchel 128).

Captain Dr. Hermann Kaiser was born May 31, 1885, to a family of Protestant educators. His father was Dr. Ludwig Kaiser, a career educator and school administrator, and, at one time, director of the Oranienschule in Wiesbaden and superintendent of education in Kassel. After Hermann completed his Arbitur, he entered the University of Halle and later studied physics and math at the University of Göttingen, earning a doctorate in 1912. General Beck was his "old schoolfellow" (Gisevius, *To the Bitter End*, 533).

At the beginning of World War I, Kaiser joined the 11th Field Artillery Regiment as an officer cadet and served on the Western Front and later on the Romanian and Russian fronts. He was promoted during his service, to regimental adjutant and ordnance staff officer. During the war, Kaiser was awarded multiple decorations, including the Iron Cross Second Class. After the surrender, he returned to Wiesbaden to teach. In 1920 he became a member of the Nazi party, but that was very early, long before the church, which he strongly supported, became a target of the Nazis. By 1934 Kaiser had become fully aware of the Nazis' aims and began actively defending the church, which did not go unnoticed in Berlin. Later he was turned down for a faculty position at the Protestant University of Marburg because he was considered politically unreliable. Twenty professors had already been expelled at the urging of the party.

Kaiser was drafted in 1939 as an Oberleutnant (first lieutenant) and assigned as regimental adjutant in a cavalry regiment based in Darmstadt; in 1940 he was assigned to OKH in Berlin. He was soon promoted to captain and served under General Fromm, whom he knew well from the First World War (Rothfels 69). Fromm assigned him to keep the office war diary, which was an essential task in all German commands. In one instance, he recorded a quote from von Kluge regarding his participation in the coup: "Children, you've got me," referring to the younger group of conspirators (quoted in Ritter 291). This unambiguous commitment would not stand the test of time.

In his position, Kaiser soon met established members of the resistance under Fromm's command, and in a post–Hitler government he would have been the minister of culture and liaison officer in Military District XII (Wiesbaden). Kaiser was often frustrated by the lack of action on the part of the generals, writing prophetically in his diary on February 20, 1943, "One wants to act when he receives orders and the other to give the orders when action starts" (quoted in Rothfels 69). There are slightly different versions of this famous quote (Zeller 424). Kaiser was investigated in 1943 for making negative comments about Hitler, but a fellow resistance member (and another former comrade in arms from the First World War), Judge Advocate General Karl Sack, helped him remain free, no doubt with a warning that he was being watched. In that same year, Kaiser informed Goerdeler about large sums being paid to General Guderian and Field Marshals von Kluge and von Rundstedt to ensure their loyalty (Goda).

Kaiser's task on July 20 was to act as liaison between the groups of civilian and military resistance forces in his hometown military district of Wiesbaden. The day after the failed coup, Kaiser and his brothers Heinrich and Ludwig were arrested in Kassell. The diaries he had been keeping for Fromm were seized by the Gestapo, which led to even more arrests. An entry in one of the diaries about Field Marshal von Manstein, saying, in so many words, that he "must be written off once and for all" (for any aid to the resistance), probably saved von Manstein from Gestapo scrutiny after July 20 (quoted in Hoffmann, *The History*, 290). Kaiser was not tried until January 17, 1945 (Wistrich 224; German Resistance Memorial Center). One historian gives the trial date as October 20, 1944, and states that he was tried with General Fritz Lindemann and Theodor Haubach, but that is obviously an error, as Lindemann died before he could be tried and there is no mention of a "post-mortem" trial (Fest, *Plotting*, 313). Freisler sentenced Kaiser to death for treason and had some choice words for him at trial, charging him with shamefully breaking three solemn oaths: as a civil servant, as a party member, and as an officer. Kaiser was executed on January 23, 1945, in Berlin Plötzensee Prison. Fabian von Schlabrendorff, it is said, wrote that "Hermann Kaiser was ready to take the consequences of his actions. He went to his death with an unwavering calm and inner strength." This certainly reads like something von Schlabrendorff would have said; however, the quote is not in any of his three books. Hermann Kaiser's cousin (mistakenly referred to as his brother), the Christian Trade Unionist Jakob Kaiser, survived the war, as did several of his relatives who were imprisoned after July 20 (Rothfels 831).

General der Artillerie Fritz Lindemann was born April 11, 1894, in Charlottenberg, the son of artillery officer Friedrich Lindemann and his wife Gertrud (née Reinecke). He completed his Arbitur at the Victoria Gymnasium in Potsdam in March 1912, and before the war began, he volunteered for the 4th Guard, Field Artillery Regiment, in Potsdam, being promoted in 1913 to lieutenant. His active service in the war began in April 1914, when he was stationed on the Western Front. Later that same year he was awarded the Iron Cross Second Class, and in 1916 he was promoted to first lieutenant. The following year Lindemann was awarded the Iron Cross First Class (Deutsches Historisches Museum). On December 6, 1918, he was transferred to the 35th General Infantry Division East. After the truce, Lindemann and five other officers were members of a security detachment sent with the German peace delegation to Versailles in 1919. On October 2, 1922, he married Lina von Friedeburg, and together they would go on to have three children (two sons and a daughter). He also completed a General Staff training course (which was a violation of the Treaty of Versailles) offered by the Reichswehr in 1922 and personally trained other officers through the end of the decade (*Allgemeine Deutsche Biographie*). In 1926 Lindemann became General Kurt von Schleicher's direct subordinate and was assigned to work with Friedrich Olbricht. In 1929, he commanded the 15th Battery of Artillery Regiment 3 in Sprottau. He completed a training class for General Staff officers in 1932 and later studied economics at Berlin University.

Although Lindemann was critical of the Nazi government when it took over, he approved of Hitler's rearmament programs. In the early years of the new government, 1933–1936, he taught history and military tactics at the War Academy in Berlin. In 1937 he was promoted to colonel; the following year, he retired from the Wehrmacht and became a member of the Nazi party. Lindemann was reactivated when the war with Poland began two years later, becoming commander of Artillery Regiment 27. He was promoted to the rank of artillery general (only two ranks below field marshal) and fought in Poland, France and the Soviet Union (Battle of Sevastopol), ultimately being appointed chief of staff of artillery at the OKH (World War II Database). He was awarded the Knight's Cross on September 4, 1941. With his rank and position, he could use official military travel opportunities to meet with members of the resistance, including von Stauffenberg, von Tresckow, and Hellmuth Stieff, who was already a close friend (Zeller 216).

By the time of the von Stauffenberg assassination attempt, Lindemann was chief of the ordnance office and one of the key men von Stauffenberg needed. He was scheduled to make the first radio announcement to the public after the coup (Gisevius, *To the Bitter End*, 554; Fest, *Plotting*, 272). That opportunity never came. After the insurrection had been put down, he managed to get away and hide with relatives in Dresden. The Gestapo soon connected Lindemann to the plot and he was expelled from the Wehrmacht, but by that time he was being hidden in Berlin by Erich and Elisabeth Gloeden. However, there was an enormous 500,000 Reichsmark bounty on his head, and he was soon betrayed (Zeller 215). Lindemann was shot and seriously wounded during his capture by the Gestapo on September 3. In spite of several operations at a Berlin hospital, Lindemann died of his wounds on September 22, 1944. He would certainly have been tried and executed had he lived.

Lindemann's oldest son, Friedrich, a lieutenant in the Wehrmacht, was sentenced to seven years for defeatist remarks, and his youngest son, Georg, an Oberfähnrich (sergeant first class) in the Hitler Youth, was sentenced to five years for knowing of his father's plans and not reporting him (Koch 219). A cousin, Hermann Lindemann, was sentenced to ten years' imprisonment, and an uncle, Wehrmacht Major Max Lindemann, was released and went on to win the Knight's Cross in the closing days of the war (Das-Ritterkreuz).

The Civilian Trials

THE CIVILIAN CONSPIRACY LEADERS

On September 7 and 8, Freisler's People's Court heard cases involving the civilian leaders arrested soon after July 20. They included Carl Friedrich Goerdeler, Wilhelm Leuschner, Josef Wirmer, Ulrich von Hassell, and Paul Lejeune-Jung. These men are well known today as members of the resistance, and a number of books have been written by and about them. They were leaders, not just of the resistance but also in their individual professions, long before Hitler came to power. Trials of other, less prominent civilians also took place in the VGH throughout the month of September.

One additional case stands out in the history of civilians tried in the VGH—that of Catholic clergyman Father Hermann Wehrle, who was among those tried and executed on September 14, 1944 (Zimmermann and Jacobsen 205). His only involvement in the conspiracy of July 20, 1944, was that he had heard of the planned assassination attempt in a confession given by Ludwig von Leonrod and did not advise him to report what he knew, although some claim that Wehrle encouraged him and others say the information was not given in confession (Zeller 220; Koch 218). When von Leonrod, who was to have been made liaison officer for Wehrkreis VII (Munich), spoke of his confession in court, Wehrle was called as a witness. Shortly after that, Wehrle himself was charged as an accessory and sentenced to death. His execution took place three weeks after von Leonrod's (Zeller 427; Zimmermann and Jacobsen 204).

Carl Friedrich Goerdeler, a name that has become almost synonymous with resistance to the Nazis, was born to a conservative family of Prussian civil servants in Schneidemuhl, Germany, on July 31, 1884 (Stockhorst 158). If the July 20 plot had not failed, he would have been chancellor in the new government. Goerdeler was, without question, the major civilian figure and chief anti–Nazi intellectual involved in the final plans to do away with Hitler. He has been described recently as a "liberal conservative monarchist," and that seemingly contradictory depiction is appropriate (Burleigh 861).

Goerdeler studied economics and law at the University of Tübingen from 1902 to 1905, and in 1911 he accepted a civil service position in Solingen. That same year, he married his cousin, Anneliese Ulrich, the daughter of a well-established optometrist, and together they had five children—two daughters and three sons (Steinbach and Tuchel 71).

His brother, Fritz Hermann, married Anneliese's sister, Susanne. When World War I began, Goerdeler joined the German army and served as a junior officer on the Eastern Front, being promoted to the rank of captain before the end of the war. After the war ended in November 1918, Goerdeler served at the headquarters of the XVII Army Corps based in Danzig for six months. In June 1919 he submitted a memo to his superior officer, General Otto von Below, in which he recommended the destruction of Poland as the only way of preventing land losses on Germany's eastern border (a bit of information not widely recounted). Goerdeler joined the nationalistic German National People's Party (the DNVP) after being discharged from the army, and, like most of the politically astute of Germany at the time, he vehemently opposed the Treaty of Versailles, which, among other things, required Germany to give up land in the creation of a restored Polish state (Fikentscher et al. 203).

Goerdeler served as the vice mayor of Königsberg in East Prussia beginning in 1922, and on May 22, 1930, he was elected lord mayor of Leipzig, where he was already well known and a respected politician. On December 8, 1931, German chancellor Heinrich Brüning appointed him to the post of price commissioner, making Goerdeler's name soon recognized throughout Germany. He left the DNVP in 1931 when the party initiated a tenuous relationship with the Nazis. The Brüning government collapsed on May 30, 1932, and Goerdeler was thought to be next in line for chancellor. Brüning recommended him to von Hindenburg, but General Kurt von Schleicher's endorsement of Franz von Papen effectively put an end to the appointment. Goerdeler was offered a position in Papen's cabinet, but he declined it.

After Hitler became chancellor in 1933, Goerdeler was one of few politicians who openly questioned his policies. Hitler's nationalistic views were nonetheless initially appealing to him, and Goerdeler convinced himself that the new chancellor would listen to the advice of the intellectuals when it came to implementing policies—an optimistic conviction that would stay with him. Goerdeler sent Hitler long memos offering his advice on economic policy, which Hitler either ignored or passed off to subordinates for criticism. Goerdeler had an "unshakable belief that by virtue of human reason and vision, good would finally prevail" (Leber 164). By the mid-1930s, however, Goerdeler realized that his recommendations were not being taken seriously and that the Nazis' economic policies would soon ruin the country.

In November 1934, Hitler reappointed Goerdeler as Reich price commissioner, tasking him with doing something about inflation—which Goerdeler already knew was caused by out-of-control rearmament spending. The reappointment was seen by the German public as a step in the right direction; however, Goerdeler was given little authority to do anything meaningful. His opinions were rarely in agreement with the economics minister and Reichsbank president, Dr. Hjalmar Schacht, who advocated a devaluation of the currency to disguise the government's inflationary policies—a common practice in the world even today. Goerdeler became cynical from having to serve in a position where he was routinely ignored, so he resigned in 1935 (Wistrich 80). As a farewell message in October 1935, he sent Hitler a report in which he warned that continuing the present course (of increasing state involvement in the economy and financing high military spending) would result in the complete collapse of the economy and a lowering of the German standard of living. Hitler ignored this report just like the others.

Goerdeler later declined to accept his reelection as lord mayor of Leipzig and resigned from office on March 31, 1937. The final straw had been the destruction of a statue of Felix Mendelssohn in front of the Gewandhaus concert hall while he was away on a business trip sponsored by the German Chamber of Commerce. He had previously been assured, by both Hitler and Goebbels, that the statue would remain, though it would be moved to a less conspicuous location. Shortly after his resignation, Goerdeler became heavily involved in anti–Nazi activities. He was asked to be head of the finance department at the firm of Krupp AG, which at the time was Germany's largest corporation, but Hitler intervened and ordered Krupp to withdraw the offer. Goerdeler instead became director of the overseas sales department at the Robert Bosch Corporation (Steinbach and Tuchel 71). Bosch, who was a long-time friend of Goerdeler's, was willing to overlook his anti–Nazi sentiments. Goerdeler worked to build an opposition out of his circle of business and civil servant friends and sent a torrent of unsolicited memoranda to Hitler and other high-ranking Nazis, trying to persuade them to reevaluate the country's economic and foreign policies.

In 1937 and 1938 Goerdeler made several Bosch-financed business trips to France, the United Kingdom, the United States, the Balkans, the Middle East and Canada (Burleigh 681). He took this opportunity to voice his concern to all he came in contact with regarding Germany's aggressive foreign policies, while simultaneously promoting a peaceful expansion of the Reich's boundaries (Wistrich 80). At the same time, he became a member of General Ludwig Beck's undercover intelligence network. Goerdeler's secret reports were sent directly to Generals Beck and von Fritsch. During one of his visits to London, in June 1937, Goerdeler told Robert Vansittart that he would like to see the Nazi regime replaced by a military dictatorship that would pursue British friendship in exchange for supporting German appropriation of parts of Poland and Czechoslovakia (Weinberg 43). In October 1937, during a visit to the United States, Goerdeler stayed with the British historian John Wheeler-Bennett at his home in Virginia and revealed his passion for a restored monarchy in Germany (Wheeler-Bennett 386). During this same trip to the United States, Goerdeler drafted his "Political Testament" attacking Nazi economic policies and criticizing the regime for its anti–Christian stance, widespread corruption, and lawlessness (Rothfels 85). Thanks to the Gestapo, this document was probably read in Germany before it was read in the United States. There is little doubt that Goerdeler was being watched carefully, but he seemed oblivious to such things and continued his denunciation of the Nazi government. Apparently he could not imagine that his educated criticism could be taken any way but constructively; unfortunately, criticism (educated or otherwise) was quickly being silenced in Germany.

The sham court martial of General Werner von Fritsch, which even the enemies of Germany ridiculed over the airwaves a month after the war officially began, was enough to push Goerdeler to the edge. He began to actively use the von Fritsch crisis in an attempt to turn the army leadership against the Nazi regime, to the point of planning a putsch in the spring of 1938 with the aid of Hans von Dohnanyi, General Hans Oster, and Johannes Popitz. The planned invasion of Czechoslovakia (Case Green, as it was called) was not a closely kept secret, and Goerdeler intended to use this event, should it occur, as the catalyst for a military revolt. He began passing information to the British via spies and relayed to them the news that Hitler intended to launch the invasion in September 1938, but the British did not have evidence that the resistance in Germany was even remotely well organized enough to carry off the putsch and refused to give their full support; besides, it was felt that if German leaders got wind of British support of the resistance, that might start a war in and of itself.

Goerdeler, to some degree, believed that Hitler would not actually go through with the invasion of Czechoslovakia, but history has revealed that he was serious from the beginning and that the date had already been set for October 1. The Munich Agreement with Chamberlain, which essentially gave Hitler what he wanted—namely, the Sudetenland—cancelled the invasion and postponed the war for a year. This victory by Hitler, without a shot being fired, destroyed any hope for a putsch that would include the military. The British, placated by Hitler's claims that his expansion of the Reich was at an end, had no further interest in Goerdeler's forewarnings. Even the Kristallnacht bloodshed, which Goerdeler wrote about in detail, did not incite the British to act. He devoted the winter of 1938–1939 to aggressively rebuilding his network and making new connections. There was no shortage of people opposed to Hitler and his Nazis, but it was hard to argue against the successes they had put together—without a drop of German blood being shed. Goerdeler's closest circle now included General Beck, Ulrich von Hassell, and Erwin Planck.

By this time Hitler was becoming annoyed with all the uninvited memos from Goerdeler (sent directly to him) containing advice on everything from economics to foreign policy. He referred to Goerdeler (along with Dr. Schacht, General Beck, von Hassell, and the economist Rudolf Brinkmann) as an "overbred intellectual" who should someday be exterminated. Goerdeler composed and sent written warnings to British officials that Hitler was bullying Italy into attacking France and that a surprise British air bombardment was in the works for February 1939. The report went on to say that an attack on Switzerland and the Low Countries would be used as a prelude to a general attack in the West (Robertson 231). This notion must have seemed pretty fantastic at the time, but, unknown to Goerdeler, he was being used by the Abwehr to transmit false information. Canaris was hoping that these reports might lead to a change in British foreign policy. Later, in February 1939, Chamberlain (to his credit) announced that any German attack on France, Switzerland, or the Low Countries would mean war between Great Britain and Germany.

Goerdeler was aware of secret meetings being held between Soviet representatives and the Nazi foreign minister, Joachim von Ribbentrop, and that the goal was an agreement to divide Eastern Europe between them. Von Ribbentrop continued to assure Hitler that Great Britain was in no military position to be a factor in any case (Ritter 86). In May 1939 Goerdeler transmitted what he knew to the British Foreign Office, and later that month he went to London to deliver the message in person to Winston Churchill. The future prime minister listened, but those in power at the time were of the opinion that a firm declaration of Anglo-French support for Poland, along with Goerdeler's predicted German economic collapse, would bring about Hitler's downfall soon enough, and without a war.

Goerdeler contacted General Walther von Brauchitsch in early 1939, trying to recruit him for a planned overthrow of the government should Germany attack Poland. Goerdeler was convinced the result would not be the restricted war Hitler had guaranteed, but rather a world war with Germany facing Britain and France. Von Brauchitsch ignored Goerdeler's solicitations, declaring that he, like Hitler, believed the war, if it came, would be localized (Ritter 85). Goerdeler was of course proven more than accurate on all counts. Britain and France were joined by Australia and New Zealand in declaring war on September 3, but none of these countries did anything to immediately aid Poland, which was quickly overrun. In October 1939 Goerdeler wrote a draft of what he believed would avert a widespread shooting war:

In return for the "restitution of the reign of law" (Rechtsstaat) the new regime in Germany should receive the German-Polish frontiers of 1914, Austria and the Sudetenland. Independence was to be restored to the remainder of Poland—that is to say, the remainder of the Polish territory occupied by German troops, for, of course, it was not suggested that Germany and the Western powers should embark on a crusade against the Soviet Union for the liberation of Poland's eastern provinces—and to the rump Czechoslovakia, and there were certain nebulous ideas about general disarmament and the restoration of world commerce [quoted in Wheeler-Bennett 485].

Goerdeler approached General Franz Halder, the chief of the General Staff, in April 1940, before the real shooting war with Britain and its allies began, and asked him to consider leading a putsch while there was still time, but Halder refused. Undeterred, Goerdeler and his supporters composed a future constitution for Germany (with Goerdeler promoting a British-style monarchy), and in 1941 he recruited leading Social Democrats Wilhelm Leuschner and Hermann Maaß to the cause.

Goerdeler's second son, Christian, was killed in action on the Eastern Front on May 15, 1942, after being posted there as retribution for being involved with the composition of an anti-government document (Ritter 243). If Goerdeler wasn't totally committed to doing away with the Nazis before, he was then (Zeller 405).

In 1943, after the Battle of Stalingrad, Goerdeler redoubled his efforts to provoke a revolt against the Nazis, and that year he wrote a letter addressed to several German army officers, appealing to them directly. This act was enough to seal his fate, if it hadn't been sealed already. He soon grew impatient with the military element of the conspiracy, complaining that the officers involved in the opposition were better at finding excuses than reasons for action. He wrote long letters to General Friedrich Olbricht and Field Marshal von Kluge, urging them to take action (Wheeler-Bennett 567–69 and 571–74). Goerdeler was "deeply disappointed at first by the Allied demand for unconditional surrender, since he had been hoping for separate peace negotiations with the Western powers" (quoted in Fest, *Plotting*, 386).

Goerdeler, the eternal optimist, for some curious reason believed that if only he could meet with Hitler, he could intelligently point out examples of the Führer's poor leadership in military and economic matters and persuade him to resign. His co-conspirators thought him insane and adamantly opposed any such meeting. It is likely that Goerdeler would have found himself in a concentration camp or meeting with a fatal "accident" a short time after such a confrontation. By this time those in Hitler's inner circle were well aware of Goerdeler's intrigues, and it would not take much for Hitler to order Himmler and his minions to act. Goerdeler, however, was a well-known and connected public figure among Germany's elite who could not just disappear without questions being asked and official inquiries being made.

In May 1944, Goerdeler again proposed to his circle his far-fetched idea of talking Hitler into bringing about a peaceful end to his rule by resigning. He still believed that he could convince Hitler, in a face-to-face meeting, to acknowledge that someone else (namely, Goerdeler himself) would be better able to lead the country. He thought that "the practical solution is to bring about the conditions, even if only for twenty-four hours, in which the truth can be told, to restore confidence in the resolve that justice and good government shall again prevail" (quoted in Leber 165). Goerdeler hoped that Hitler would then resign and appoint him as successor. Again, his compatriots talked him out of this irrational idea. There was only one sure way to be rid of Hitler, and plans to that effect were already being finalized.

On July 16, 1944, Goerdeler departed Leipzig for Berlin and stayed at the home of General Beck in the Berlin suburb of Lichterfelde, with supreme confidence in von Stauffenberg's ultimate success. However, whatever spectator plans Goerdeler might have had were forgotten the next day when news of his pending arrest arrived and he went into hiding. The Nazi hierarchy (and, more important, Hitler) had finally had enough of him. After the failure of the July 20 attempt, the Gestapo searched Goerdeler's room at the Anhalter Bahnhof hotel and discovered a collection of documents related to the putsch, including Goerdeler's planned radio address to the German people as the new chancellor. This was more than enough to bring him to trial, even with the public outcry that such an action might incite. It would be difficult for any German to countenance treason, even from the likes of Goerdeler.

Goerdeler managed to get out of Berlin, but a million Reichsmark reward was offered for his capture (Zimmermann and Jacobsen 229). He was arrested on August 12, 1944, when he visited his mother's grave in Marienwerder, a town where he was easily recognized. He was given up by a female support member of the Luftwaffe (a Blitzmädchen, as they were called) when he stopped at an inn in the town of Konradswalde (Ritter 291). After his arrest, six members of his family were sent to concentration camps, but they were not harmed and were among the 139 prominent prisoners freed in the closing days of the war by Wehrmacht troops, on April 30, 1945.

On September 8, 1944, after a trial in Freisler's People's Court, Goerdeler was predictably sentenced to death (Steinbach and Tuchel 71). After being tortured for months by the Gestapo in an effort to learn the names of other conspirators, he was finally hanged on February 2, 1945, at Plötzensee Prison, not at the Prinz Albrecht Strasse Gestapo headquarters lockup (Wistrich 81). While awaiting his death sentence, Goerdeler—always the writer—composed a farewell letter, which ended with "I ask the world to accept our martyrdom as penance for the German people" (quoted in Rothfels 152). His brother, Fritz Hermann, who was heavily involved with the military resistance in East Prussia, was executed on March 1, 1945 (Wheeler-Bennett 745; Steinbach and Tuchel 71). It would be decades before men of Carl Goerdeler's stature would again hold positions of authority in Germany.

Judge Freisler had a few choice words to say about Goerdeler in a letter: "Some of those, like that fellow Goerdeler, have nothing better to do after their conviction than to inundate us with memoranda and information implicating an almost countless number of others in the reactionary plot" (quoted in Koch 239). Goerdeler's attempt to deal rationally with an irrational system by telling the truth no doubt led to the arrest of many who might otherwise have escaped notice. In 1957, Eberhard Zeller, a fellow member of the resistance who survived the war, had this to say about Goerdeler:

> Goerdeler was a few years younger than Beck, East Prussian by origin and birth; tall, broad shouldered, somewhat heavily built, and surprisingly efficient in hardship conditions of any kind. His stimulating influence on all around him was a talent that could only ripen to such a degree in the rotting soil of the governmental and private circumstances in which he and his colleagues lived. These circumstances roused him from his normal human limitations to pursue a great mission. He developed the power to appeal to consciences and turn them toward a fear of God and a passion for honesty, right, law, and decency [quoted in Zimmermann and Jacobsen 229].

Karl Friedrich Wilhelm Leuschner was born into poverty on June 15, 1890, in Bayreuth; as an adult, he became an influential member of the Sozialdemokratische Partei Deutschland (German Social Democrat Party [the SPD]). His parents were Wilhelm, a stove fitter by trade, and Marie (née Dehler).

At age thirteen, Leuschner began an apprenticeship as a wood sculptor, completing his training in 1907 and joining the trade union representing his skill. Soon after, he moved to Darmstadt and found employment in furniture manufacturing. Around this time he became seriously involved with the trade union movement (Leber 103). He joined the SPD in 1910 and became a prominent member of his local union. He married Elisabeth Batz in 1911 (Steinbach and Tuchel 129).

Leuschner served on the Eastern Front in the First World War; after the surrender, he became a city council member and chairman of the Darmstadt Unions in 1919. In 1924 he was elected as a member of the Hesse Landtag (Legislature) for the SPD, eventually becoming Hesse's interior minister in 1929 (Leber 104). Hermann Maaß, who had previously worked for Leuschner, would become his assistant (Ritter 104; Leber 106). It was in the Landtag that Leuschner first became acquainted with the National Socialists, and he often decried the proposals of jurist and fellow Landtag member Dr. Werner Best, who represented the Nazis. Leuschner was elected to the board of the National German Union Federation (Allgemeiner Deutscher Gewerkschaftsbund) in 1933, just before Hitler won the March 5 election (Mommsen 297).

Leuschner was forced to resign from the legislature in April 1933, after the Nazis came to power, and give up his office as Hessian interior minister. Within a month he was arrested after refusing to cede control of his unions to Dr. Robert Ley, the Nazi Labor Front leader. He was soon released but arrested again in June and detained for a year in the Börgermoor and Lichtenburg concentration camps. Ley personally questioned every union leader arrested and gave orders regarding what was to be done with each of them (Zimmermann and Jacobsen 236; Leber 104).

When he was finally released in June 1934, Leuschner began to assemble resistance groups within the unions (Wistrich 154). In 1936 he became the manager of a small manufacturing workshop that made pub utensils as a cover for his full-time commitment to anti–Nazi union endeavors. Leuschner's major contribution to the broader conspiracy was in solidifying connections between the trade unionists and the conservative and military resistance (Burleigh 673). He created affiliations with other organizations such as the Kreisau Circle and, in 1939, with the circle ostensibly led by Goerdeler. Leuschner was to become Germany's vice chancellor after the July 20 coup, but after its failure, he was arrested by the Gestapo on August 16 and brought before the People's Court, although he had little or nothing to do with the actual assassination attempt. He was sentenced to death by the court on September 8 and executed on September 29 at Plötzensee Prison (Steinbach and Tuchel 129). On his way to the gallows, he transmitted a single word in sign language to those present: "Unity" (quoted in Zimmermann and Jacobsen 238).

Josef Wirmer was born into an established Catholic family on March 19, 1901, in Paderborn, and he would have been justice minister after July 20 had the coup succeeded. His father, Anton, was the Marianum Warburg Gymnasium headmaster. After receiving a diploma in Warburg, Wirmer studied law in Freiburg and Berlin, where his democratic views were in stark opposition to the monarchists who largely populated academia at the time. Nevertheless, he successfully completed the examinations for law (1924) and civil service (1927) and obtained a position as a lawyer in Berlin. Wirmer opposed the National Socialists on democratic and constitutional grounds and was dismissed from the Nazi-backed Rechtswahrerbund (National Socialist Lawyers League) because of his defense of those subject to racial persecution (Wistrich 277). As a Catholic, he also opposed the Reichskonkordat (agreement) between the Nazis and the Vatican and sought to have it revoked.

Wirmer came into contact with the trade unionist resistance group led by Jakob Kaiser in 1936, spending considerable time in discussion with another prominent trade unionist, Max Habermann (Leber 138). Kaiser was the primary liaison between the trade unionists, the Social Democrats, and the aristocrats, and in due course he came to be affiliated with Goerdeler and his resistance circle in 1941. Wirmer was arrested on August 4, 1944, as part of the roundup of anyone remotely related to the July 20 conspiracy. His confidence and quick wit when faced with the People's Court are illustrated by dialogue recorded at his trial in response to Freisler's accusations:

"When I hang, I'll have no fear, but you will!"

"You will be in Hell soon," Freisler screamed.

Wirmer answered, "It will be a pleasure for me when you come soon afterward, Mr. President" [quoted in Hoffmann, *The History*, 526; Leber 136].

On September 8, 1944, Josef Wirmer was predictably sentenced to death, and within two hours he was hanged at Plötzensee Prison. Roland Freisler was killed five months later; however, it is doubtful that the two met soon thereafter.

A descendent of German nobility, Christian August Ulrich von Hassell was born in Anklam, Pomerania, on October 12, 1881, to Prussian Oberstleutnant Ulrich von Hassell and his wife Margarete (née von Stosch). Christian August earned his diploma at the esteemed Prinz Heinrich Gymnasium in 1899 and studied law and economics at the University of Lausanne and the University of Tübingen from 1899 to 1903, becoming active in the Tübingen Studentenverbindung (student organization) (*Allgemeine Deutsche Biographie*). He began his civil service career in 1909 as an assessor in the German Foreign Office and was to have been foreign minister in the post–Hitler government (Hoffmann, *The History*, 367).

In 1911 von Hassell was appointed a vice consul in Genoa, Italy, and married Ilse von Tirpitz, Grand Admiral Alfred von Tirpitz's daughter. The couple ultimately had four children. Von Hassell volunteered for the First World War and was seriously wounded in the First Battle of the Marne on September 8, 1914. After recovering from his injury, he worked as von Tirpitz's advisor and private secretary; later he went on to write the admiral's biography (*Allgemeine Deutsche Biographie*).

Von Hassell joined the DNVP immediately after the war and returned to work for the Foreign Office until the early 1930s, being assigned to Barcelona, Rome, Copenhagen, and Belgrade. In 1932 he was appointed German ambassador to Italy (Stockhorst 180). He became a member of the Nazi party in 1933, but in 1937 he opposed the party regarding the Anti-Comintern Pact between Germany, Italy, and Japan. Von Hassell was recalled as ambassador to Italy in 1938 but remained in the diplomatic service. After the German invasion of Poland in 1939, he led a delegation to ameliorate tensions and managed to convince other European governments that similar military strikes were not in store for them. As part of his government (and party) duties, von Hassell was appointed to the Central European Economic Congress, and over the next few years he used this position to get a sense of how other member countries might react to any coup that expelled the Nazis from power.

After the British declaration of war, von Hassell learned of the various resistance groups and eventually became a mediator between the Goerdeler and Beck groups—and another (soon to be well-known) association, the Kreisau Circle led by von Moltke (Wistrich 98). Both conservative and liberal members of this group shared the ultimate goal of seeing Hitler removed. Von Hassell submitted reports to the group based on his experience as a member of the Economic Congress. He, Goerdeler, Beck, and Popitz drew up a disclosure paper for Lord Halifax, which von Hassell delivered to a British contact in Arosa, Switzerland, on February 23, 1940. The aim of the conspirators was to confirm the presence of a resistance movement in Germany and give a sense of its objectives. This paper has come to be known as the "Arosa Memorandum."

Confidential

I. All serious minded people in Germany consider it as of utmost importance to stop this mad war as soon as possible.

II. We consider this because the dangers of a complete destruction and particularly [because] a bolshevization of Europe is rapidly growing.

III. Europe does not mean for us a chess-board of political or military action or a base of power but it has "la valeur d'une patrie" [the value of a fatherland] in the frame of which a healthy Germany in sound conditions of life is an indispensable factor.

IV. The purpose of a peace treaty ought to be a permanent pacification and reestablishment of Europe on a solid base and a security against a renewal of warlike tendencies.

V. [A] condition necessary for this result is to leave the union of Austria and the Sudeten with the Reich out of any discussion. In the same way there would be excluded a renewed discussion of occidental frontier questions of the Reich. On the other hand, the German-Polish frontier will have to be more or less identical with the German frontier of 1914.

VI. The treaty of peace and the reconstruction of Europe ought to be based on certain principles which will have to be universally accepted.

VII. Such principles are the following:
  1. The principle of nationality with certain modifications deriving from history. Therefore:
  2. Reestablishment of an independent Poland and of a Czech Republic.
  3. General reduction of armaments.
  4. Reestablishment of free international economic cooperation.
  5. Recognition of certain leading ideas by all European states, such as:
     a. The principles of Christian ethics.
     b. Justice and law as fundamental elements of public life.
     c. Social welfare as leitmotiv [a basic theme].
     d. Effective control of the executive power of state by the people, adapted to the special character of every nation.
     e. Liberty of thought, conscience, and intellectual activity [von Hassell 117–18].

Von Hassell was not involved in the July 20 coup attempt; nonetheless, he was arrested by the Gestapo at his office nine days later. As a known member of the Kreisau Circle, he expected no less (Wistrich 99). He was brought to trial in the People's Court on September 6, and two days later Freisler sentenced him to death for treason. He was immediately executed at Plötzensee Prison.

Von Hassell's diaries survived the war and serve as one of the few accounts written as the various plots developed, with the final entries composed just days before he was arrested (von Hassell 355). There was also a *Colonel* Hassell (without the "von"), who, according to Zeller (who cites the Kaltenbrunner papers), "had been in league with Olbricht since 1943 and had undertaken to have twenty officers ready for the coup; their task was to operate the communications of the Foreign Office, Ministry of Propaganda, RSH, Broadcasting Station, etc." (Zeller 353). A book has recently been published by one of Ulrich von Hassell's grandsons on the secret connections and communications between members of the German Abwehr and the American OSS (von Hassell and MacRae).

Dr. Paul Adolf Franz Lejeune-Jung (not directly related to Edgar Julius Jung, killed in the Night of the Long Knives) was born March 16, 1882, in Cologne to a family of Huguenot origin; however, he and his siblings were raised Catholic. His mother was a Catholic Rhinelander, and his father Hugo was a captain in the British Merchant Marines. The family finally settled in Rathenow an der Havel. Lejeune-Jung graduated from the Theodorianum Gymnasium in Paderborn and afterward studied theology with the intention of becoming a Catholic priest. However, he soon changed his mind and left theology studies for the University of Bonn, pursuing degrees in philosophy and history, ultimately earning a doctorate in the former (*Allgemeine Deutsche Biographie*). His formal training was not at an end however. He went on to study economics at Humboldt University in Berlin and worked as an economic assistant in the Imperial Colonial Office and for the German Colonial Company. He eventually landed a permanent job at the Feldmühle Paper Corporation, where he quickly gained a management position. In 1913 Lejeune-Jung married Hedwig Foltmann from Breslau, and they had a large family together (three daughters and five sons). He would have been the economic minister in the post–Hitler government (Hoffmann, *The History*, 369).

Lejeune-Jung was elected to the Reichstag in 1924 as a member of the DNVP (Stockhorst 267). As part of his duties, he was a member and chairman of the trade policy board and participated in the International Parliamentary Conferences in London (1926), Rio de Janeiro (1927), and Berlin (1929). He was a true conservative Catholic and often at odds with the Catholic Center Party of the time because he personally favored a monarchical form of government. He eventually split with the DNVP over disagreements regarding the Young Plan (a program for settling German reparation debts after World War I, written in 1929 and approved in 1930) and joined a new party called the People's Conservative Party, which in the end had little influence on the elections of September 1930 (Steinbach and Tuchel 127). In 1931 Chancellor Heinrich Brüning named Lejeune-Jung to the German-French Economic Commission, where his education in economics proved invaluable. As a member of this commission, Lejeune-Jung advocated for a European market with German industries playing a central role, which was a popular idea at the time and after the war.

Lejeune-Jung was not initially opposed to the National Socialists, but when they came to power, he was unceremoniously removed from his government position; later, in 1941, he began to associate with members of the resistance movement. Through the trade unionist Max Habermann, he was introduced to Goerdeler, who assigned him the task of drafting an economic plan for a post–Hitler Germany. Lejeune-Jung created a strategy to socialize the mines and give the new state authority over all mineral and water rights (Ritter 253; Zeller 248). This work put him in contact with Hermann Kaiser, Wilhelm Leuschner and Julius Leber as well as Friedrich-Werner Graf von der Schulenburg (an uncle of Fritz-Dietlof von der Schulenburg-Tressow) and Josef Wirmer. As can be imagined, the idea of socializing these vital industries was not popular among the trade unionists.

Lejeune-Jung was not part of the assassination attempt of July 20, but his close association with known opposition members landed him in Freisler's People's Court. He was arrested on August 11 and thrown into the Moabit Lehrter Strasse Prison in Berlin, being charged on September 3 with high treason. His co-defendants were Goerdeler, Leuschner, and Wirmer, all prospective members of the new government. Lejeune-Jung, von Hassell, and Wirmer were hanged at Plötzensee Prison on September 8. On Hitler's orders, their bodies were cremated and their ashes scattered (Stockhorst 267).

OTHER CIVILIAN TRIALS

Professor Johannes Popitz was born the son of a pharmacist on December 2, 1884, in Leipzig, and he studied political science and law in Dessau, Lausanne, Leipzig, Halle, and Berlin. He was retained by the German government as a lawyer from 1907 to 1918, and that year he married Cornalia Slot. The couple would have three children. After the elections in 1919, Popitz worked in the Finance Ministry of the Weimar government as a privy councilor (Geheimrat) and became an honorary professor of tax law and financial science at the University of Berlin in 1922 (German Resistance Memorial Center). "He was a man of personal integrity and humanistic education, a respected scientist in the field of political and financial economy who had also made his name as an archaeologist" (Rothfels 89). At one point, Popitz was named to be the minister of culture in the post–Hitler government, but he was replaced by Eugen Bolz before the July 20 coup attempt.

From 1925 to 1929 Popitz was acting state secretary in the German Ministry of Finance under Finance Minister Rudolf Hilferding until both were asked to resign because of their radical political views. Popitz was later appointed to Kurt von Schleicher's cabinet as state minister without portfolio, as well as a member of the Prussian Finance Ministry. On April 21, 1933, he became the Prussian finance minister, although he was not yet a member of the Nazi party (Steinbach and Tuchel 157). Popitz offered his resignation in protest after Kristallnacht, but it was refused by Hitler—Popitz was still needed. This was the beginning of his movement toward the resistance, leading to his association with Goerdeler's resistance group and the Wednesday Society. Popitz had his own ideas about who should supplant Hitler, promoting Crown Prince Wilhelm (Kaiser Wilhelm II's oldest son) as his replacement. Popitz was in truth not entirely trusted by many members of the resistance, probably due to his long government service (Rothfels 89).

Popitz went so far as to assist in writing a provisional post–Hitler constitution (the *Vorläufiges Staatsgrundgesetz* [Preliminary State Constitutional Law]), which was nevertheless still very dictatorial in structure and opposed by most members of the resistance (Rothfels 99). Popitz, often referred to as the "Gray Eminence" by party insiders, was always a controversial figure among the conspirators, and in late 1943 he was bold (or foolish) enough to engage in private talks with Himmler in an attempt to gain his support for a general coup, stating that he and others in the conspiracy had decided that the Reichsführer should be Hitler's successor (Havas 28). Popitz was being liberal with the facts here, as few members of the conspiracy would see this eventuality as an improvement. Himmler reported the talks to Hitler to avoid him hearing of such things from a third party and was told to continue (Speer 485). No details of these talks are known except for those given under interrogation (Dulles 150). In any event, the Reichsführer made no overt move toward the resistance; however, the Gestapo's surveillance of Popitz increased.

Popitz was arrested in Berlin the day after von Stauffenberg's final assassination attempt. "At his trial, Freisler seems to have used all his skills to prevent Popitz from making his relations with Himmler the focus of his defense" (Koch 222). On October 3 he was sentenced to death at the People's Court by Freisler, and his hanging (along with that of Carl Langbehn) was scheduled for October 12, but Popitz was actually not executed on that date (Zimmermann and Jacobsen 206; Steinbach and Tuchel 157). Himmler probably believed that Popitz might yet be of use in making contact with the Allies, but with the acceleration of the Allied advance on Berlin, Popitz became redundant. He was finally hanged on February 2, 1945, at Plötzensee Prison in Berlin.

Dr. Carl Langbehn was born December 6, 1901, in Padang-Bedagei, Sumatra; he studied law as a young man and opposed National Socialism from his very first exposure to it. Sometimes, however, strange relationships develop as a result of children and family: his daughter attended the same school as Himmler's daughter, Gudrun, giving him inside contact with the Reichsführer (Gisevius, *To the Bitter End*, 433). Langbehn is often referred to half-seriously as "Himmler's lawyer" (Ritter 326). Popitz indicated to Langbehn in 1943 that Himmler might be interested in negotiating peace terms with the Allies without Hitler. There is speculation as to which came first—Himmler's supposed interest or Popitz's insinuation to him of a coming coup. In August 1943, Langbehn organized the initial meeting between Popitz and Himmler, but Himmler was not reassuring and gave no indication of approval. However, this does not mean that he wasn't interested, for he, better than most in Hitler's inner circle, had a clear vision of the future, even if he did not have the fortitude (or the ideal opportunity) to act. "That the Allies would have demanded his head even as part of the terms of a negotiated peace was something Himmler was incapable of seeing" (Reitlinger 124).

Langbehn had freedom of travel during this period and was reportedly sent by Himmler in the summer of 1943 to Stockholm "to explore possibilities of a separate peace with a Germany led by himself and the military" (von Klemperer 262). Langbehn also met with Allen Dulles of the U.S. Office of Strategic Services in Switzerland in September 1943. Dulles had no words of reassurance for Langbehn and told him that an unconditional surrender would be demanded regardless of any nebulous conspiracies for removing Hitler. As soon as he returned from Switzerland, Langbehn was arrested. Information indicating Himmler's association with Langbehn had been intercepted by the Gestapo and forwarded to Hitler through Obergruppenführer Heinrich Müller and Martin Bormann (Dulles 163). Himmler did not want the details of his connection to either Popitz or Langbehn to be revealed to others by a third party, which forced him to create his own spin on the matter for the Gestapo. Himmler was one of the few who had Hitler's absolute trust, and his version of the story was accepted without question.

Langbehn had little or nothing to do with the events of July 20; however, after the coup attempt he was tried for treason by the VGH and found guilty. It is likely that Himmler delayed the execution—just in case Langbehn was needed in future contacts with the Allies. Langbehn was sentenced to death on October 3 but not executed until October 12 in Plötzensee Prison.

The indictment of Popitz and Langbehn was found after the war and has been published in Dulles' book (Dulles 150). It is typical of many others that can be found in the Kaltenbrunner papers (see both volumes of Jacobsen). The indictment illustrates just how little hard evidence of illegal activity was needed to gain a death sentence after July 20, for by that time even defeatist leanings could prove fatal for anyone in the military or government. The indictments of many of the conspirators brought to formal trials were detailed legal documents reflecting extensive investigation, but they also included hearsay evidence and third-hand rumors. Information obtained through torture or the threat of torture was also admissible at trial. As mentioned by Dulles, the indictment glosses over Himmler's direct connection to either of the accused. It was dated September 25, 1944, and signed by Dr. Ernst Lautz, the prosecuting attorney. In reading the full transcript of the interrogations, it is apparent that both Popitz and Langbehn attempted to avoid implicating others who had not yet been arrested.

Friedrich-Werner Graf von der Schulenburg (the uncle of Fritz-Dietlof Graf von der Schulenburg-Tressow) was born November 20, 1875, in Kemberg, Saxony-Anhalt, the son of Bernhard Friedrich Wilhelm Graf von der Schulenburg and Margarete (née von Waldenfels). He studied law in Munich, Berlin, and Lausanne; after graduating, he joined the Foreign Office as an assessor (junior grade lawyer) in 1901, rising to become Germany's vice consul in Barcelona two years later. Other consulate positions followed in Lviv, Tbilisi, Prague, and Warsaw. He married Elisabeth von Sobbe in 1908, and the couple had one daughter (Steinbach and Tuchel 177). However, the marriage would only last two years. In 1914 von der Schulenburg volunteered for military duty and fought at the First Battle of the Marne, earning a promotion to captain and the command of an artillery battery in that same year. During the Russian Revolution, he led the Georgian Legion until it was destroyed in battle against Russia in 1917 (German Resistance Memorial Center). He was finally captured by the British and imprisoned on the island of Prinkipo until 1919. When released, von der Schulenburg resumed his Foreign Office position and was appointed German consul in Beirut, then emissary to Tehran and Bucharest. The high point of his diplomatic service came in 1934 when he was made the (last) German ambassador to the Soviet Union, where he became a key figure in creating the German-Soviet Nonaggression Pact of August 1939. Because of his extensive experience in foreign affairs, he was considered for the office of foreign minister in the post–Hitler government (von Hassell 321).

The German (and Russian) invasion of Poland in 1939 put von der Schulenburg in a precarious position when he began using his influence as German ambassador to persuade Moscow to allow Polish diplomats to leave Russia. Later he tried to convince the German government to drop its plans for invading Russia, but Hitler gave no credence to von der Schulenburg's claims of Soviet military and industrial capacities—which all of Germany would soon come to realize were accurate. When the invasion began on June 22, 1941, the Soviets arrested von der Schulenburg, but they treated him well. He was released after a few weeks and immediately began advocating for an agreement of some sort with the Russians, volunteering to negotiate the deal himself. Even after the war with Russia had begun, von der Schulenburg believed it was still possible to come to terms with Stalin (von Hassell 327). "The Soviet Government had expressed a wish to conduct peace negotiations with Schulenburg, but Hitler had invariably refused" (quoted in Hoffmann, *The History*, 245). Later, von der Schulenburg went so far as to suggest going on his own to speak to Stalin, "with the backing of the resistance movement. He now placed himself at Goerdeler's disposal and said he was ready to slip through the German lines to see Stalin" (quoted in Ritter 267). His knowledge of Russia and the exposure of his tentative position in the post–Hitler government led to his arrest after July 20. He was tried by the VGH on October 23 and sentenced to death. Von der Schulenburg was hanged on November 10 in Plötzensee Prison. He was 69 years old at the time, making him the oldest member of the conspiracy to be executed.

In addition to Friedrich-Werner and Fritz-Dietlof, there was one other rarely mentioned von der Schulenburg involved in the conspiracy: Ehrengard Martha Gräfin von der Schulenburg. She was the daughter of Albrecht Karl Werner Graf von der Schulenburg and Erna (née von Pelken), and the secretary for General Joachim von Kortzfleisch (Hoffmann, *Stauffenberg*, 197). She married Friedrich August Graf von Rantzau in June 1944, and they both survived the war.

Wilhelm Bernardo Walter Cramer was born May 1, 1886, the son of Wilhelm Cramer and Josepha Sala. He was educated at the Humanistisches Thomasschule in Leipzig, the oldest public school in Germany. As an adult, he joined the DNVP in 1920 and went on to become a successful textile merchant and a member of the board of directors of the Stöhr Worsted Spinning Mill in 1923 (German Resistance Memorial Center). Cramer was married to Charlotte Weber, with whom he had two daughters and a son (Steinbach and Tuchel 41). He served in the reserves in the First World War and fought on both the western and the eastern fronts. After the war, his position at Stöhr allowed Cramer to travel extensively in Germany and abroad, which would prove to be a valuable benefit in the years to come.

Soon after Hitler was elected, Cramer dissociated himself from the National Socialists and became involved with Carl Goerdeler (whom he already knew) and his resistance circle (Gisevius, *To the Bitter End*, 501). He was vocal in his opposition to the war, particularly the Nazis' treatment of the mentally ill, and he was well acquainted with ranking officers who opposed Hitler. After his business was threatened with government takeover, Cramer became active in efforts to aid persecuted Jews in Germany and Jewish employees in his firm's branches in Southeastern Europe. The death of his only son in Poland in 1941 affected Cramer profoundly, causing him to turn even more toward the resistance (Steinbach and Tuchel 41). Goerdeler had high regard for Cramer and asked him in 1943 to become the political advisor in Wehrkreis IV (Dresden) in a post–Hitler Germany (Hoffmann, *The History*, 357).

In April 1944 Cramer was brought before the Leipzig District Court, charged with undermining the war effort; comments he had made about the occupation of Hungary had been reported to the Gestapo. After the unsuccessful July 20 assassination attempt, Cramer fled to Württemberg, but he was arrested by the Gestapo in Leipzig two days later on his way to visit his daughter in Vienna. He was taken to Dresden and from there to the Moabit Lehrter Strasse Prison in Berlin, where he was interrogated by the Gestapo and mistreated by SS guards. Cramer was subsequently transferred to Tegel Prison in Berlin to await arraignment. The Catholic priest Peter Buchholz managed to smuggle Cramer's diaries out and deliver them to his family. Cramer was sentenced to death by the People's Court, with Roland Freisler presiding, on November 14, 1944, and executed that same day in Plötzensee Prison (German Resistance Memorial Center). Eberhard Zeller wrote about Cramer:

> It seems to me that for years Cramer had lived with a premonition of how frightfully they would torture him to death. Did he also guess, this cultivated businessman spoiled by luxury, who had reached an age when he was certainly no longer any too strong—did he also guess how he would rise above himself during his suffering? Did he suspect that some day the few survivors of the prison near the Lehrter railroad station would mention his name with admiration whenever they recalled those days of horror? [Zeller 501].

Dr. Eduard Robert Wolfgang Brücklmeier was born in Munich on June 8, 1903; beginning in 1923, he studied law in Leipzig, Munich, Lausanne, and Würzburg, earning a doctorate from the University of Würzburg in 1927 (Schwerin, *"Dann sind's,"* 24). He accepted a civil service position in the German Foreign Office that same year. Over the next four years, he was assigned to Tehran, Baghdad, Colombo (Sri Lanka), and eventually Katowice. In early 1936 he was reassigned to London, where von Ribbentrop would be installed as German ambassador later that year. In 1937 Brücklmeier married Klotilde von Obermayer-Marnach; they would go on to have one child, a daughter (Steinbach and Tuchel 36). Brücklmeier left London in mid-1938, following von Ribbentrop back to Berlin, and took a position in his office. Undersecretary of State Ernst von Weizsäcker's anti-war rhetoric of 1938–1939 appealed to a number of the younger anti-war diplomats, including Brücklmeier, who was arrested after making his opinions known and being reported to the Gestapo (Schwerin, *Die Jungen*, 296). Someone in the Gestapo office must have thought Brücklmeier was particularly important because he was interrogated personally by Heydrich and brought before a hearing. He was fortunately given the option of retiring and did so, but with the knowledge that the Gestapo was very much aware of him. By this time Brücklmeier had already formed a close relationship with other members of the resistance, including Ulrich-Wilhelm Graf von Schwerin von Schwanenfeld and Albrecht von Kessel. Brücklmeier's involvement in the conspiracy began with his introduction of Goerdeler, Maaß, Leuschner, and von Stauffenberg to his former superior in Teheran, Ambassador Friedrich-Werner Graf von der Schulenburg. Although he was not directly involved in the events of July 20, Brücklmeier was arrested in Prague seven days later and found himself facing Freisler's People's Court on September 20 charged with treason. He was sentenced to death and executed a month later at Plötzensee Prison (German Resistance Memorial Center).

Dr. Julius Leber was born November 16, 1891, in Biesheim, Upper Alsace, to an unmarried woman named Katharina Schubetzer who later married Jean Leber; Jean adopted Julius as his own son. Julius Leber attended a vocational school in Breisach, completing his initial training in 1908. He continued his education, thanks to an honorarium, in 1910 at Freiburg Oberrealschule (an upper-level vocational school), completing his Arbitur in 1913 (*Allgemeine Deutsche Biographie*). Leber proved himself academically capable of more and went on to study economics and history in Straßburg and at Freiburg University in Breisgau. He volunteered for military service at the beginning of the First World War and was promoted to lieutenant and twice wounded. After the war, he remained in the military (the Reichswehr), serving with border patrol units along the eastern perimeter. The Kapp Putsch in 1920 drove Leber to resign from military service when he discovered that some of the Reichswehr's most respected officers had been behind the attempted coup. He then went back to school, earning a doctorate from the University of Freiburg. Leber became editor-in-chief of a Social Democratic newspaper, the *Lübecker Volksboten*, in 1921, and he also became a member of the Lübeck city council. In 1924 he was elected to the Reichstag (Steinbach and Tuchel 126).

Leber's life was threatened and he was arrested multiple times after Hitler came to power. "From February 1, 1933 onward, with only a short break just before the March elections of that year, until the summer of 1937, he was dragged through prisons and concentration camps, always in danger of his life" (Leber 255). He worked as a coal dealer in Berlin-Schöneberg after his release, which camouflaged his resistance work with Gustav Dahrendorf (Ralf Dahrendorf's father), Ernst von Harnack, and Ludwig Schwamb. Leber had the respect of civilian resistance groups by 1940, and he soon became acquainted with von Stauffenberg, Goerdeler, and other members of the Kreisau Circle. Leber was slated to become minister of the interior in the new government after the assassination of Hitler, although von Stauffenberg preferred him over Goerdeler to become chancellor (Fest, *Plotting*, 392; Zimmermann and Jacobsen 240).

Leber was actually arrested on July 5, 1944—two weeks before July 20—after he was reported to the Gestapo by Anton Saefkow, a member of an underground Communist group. "His arrest moved Colonel von Stauffenberg, who was politically very close to him, to carry out the attempt on Hitler's life himself, on July 20, with a view at the same time to rescuing Leber" (Zimmermann and Jacobsen 240–41). On October 20, Leber,

Adolf Reichwein, Hermann Maaß and Gustav Dahrendorf were brought before the People's Court. Leber was sentenced to death, though he was not executed until January 5, 1945, at Plötzensee Prison (Zimmermann and Jacobsen 238). There exist many quotes from Leber, but one appropriate for the ages is this: "You have got to govern or be in clear opposition. Not to be ready to assume responsibility for the one or to have the courage for the other, but to prefer a policy of sailing with the wind rather than of taking a firm line is the biggest mistake a political party can make" (quoted in Zeller 90). Before his death, Leber was married to Elfriede Nebgen (née Nebgen), and the couple's daughter Annedore survived the war and wrote the first biographies of members of the German resistance (Mommsen 285; Leber).

Hermann Maaß was born October 23, 1897, and grew up the son of a railway official in Bromberg (Wistrich 281). He volunteered for military service in the First World War after completing school and was seriously injured in a poison gas attack a short time before the armistice. He recovered and went on to study psychology, philosophy, and sociology in Berlin. After his Arbitur, Maaß enrolled in the newly founded Hochschule für Politik (school for political studies) (German Resistance Memorial Center). He later took a position as the director of German youth associations (Reichsausschusses der deutschen Jugendverbände) and authored a book on the topic in 1931, *Geistige Formung der Jugend unsere Zeit* (Zimmermann and Jacobsen 218). His position was abolished when Hitler came to power and it was decreed that the Hitler Youth would replace all other youth organizations. Soon Maaß became an open critic of the Nazis and a close associate of Wilhelm Leuschner in the state government of Hesse (Mommsen 283). His conscience persuaded him to turn down the offer of a visiting professorship at Harvard University to stay in Germany and work in the resistance movement. Maaß eventually went into the publishing business and became Leuschner's business partner in a metallurgical company (Mommsen 208). This position allowed him to use business trips to create free labor union resistance groups throughout Germany. He and Goerdeler rarely agreed on the ideal form for a post–Hitler government, but both Maaß and Leuschner recognized Goerdeler's "superior gifts and character" (Ritter 252). Maaß was also unsure of von Stauffenberg's concept of a post–Hitler Germany and believed the "Counts" would claim their birthrights soon after a successful coup (Mommsen 123 and 199).

Even though he was not directly connected to the events of July 20, Maaß was arrested on August 8, 1944, because of his close association with the Goerdeler and Kreisau circles. At his trial on October 20, he twice tried to speak, with Judge Freisler cutting him off both times (Zeller 409). Hermann Maaß was sentenced to death and executed that same day in Plötzensee Prison.

Dr. Adolf Reichwein was born October 3, 1898, in Bad Ems and grew up in Oberosbach. He was the son of a teacher; as an adult, he became an educator, economist, and policymaker for the SPD. He would likely have become culture minister in the post–Hitler government. His education at the Universities of Frankfurt am Main and Marburg under Hugo Sinzheimer (who wrote the Weimar constitution) and Franz Oppenheimer (the political economist) prepared Reichwein for an academic career. However, World War I changed those aspirations, with Reichwein being drafted into the military at the outbreak and then seriously wounded (Leber 62).

After the war, Reichwein became active in education reform in Berlin and Thuringia; he founded the Volkshochschule (a new upper education prototype) and the Arbeiterbildungsheim (a worker's vocational training facility) in Jena and directed them both until 1929 (Vierhaus 270). During that same time period he was the cultural advisor to the Prussian culture minister, Carl Heinrich Becker, and from 1930 to 1933 he was a professor at the newly established Pedagogical Academy in Halle. Reichwein's membership in the SPD caused him to lose his appointments after the Nazis came to power, and he was eventually sent to Tiefensee in Brandenburg as an elementary school teacher (Wistrich 198). He worked there until 1939, writing and implementing many of his progressive educational ideas. He was the author of four books (Leber 62). In 1939 Reichwein took an academic position at the Folklore Museum in Berlin and used his work as a cover for resistance undertakings with the Kreisau Circle. He and Leber went so far as to contact a Communist resistance group to ask for endorsement of their post–Hitler government ideas, but, unknown to anyone, the Communist cabal had been infiltrated by the Gestapo (Fest, *Plotting*, 395).

On July 4, more than two weeks before the attempt on Hitler's life, Reichwein was arrested by the Gestapo; in a trial by the VGH held on October 20, he was found guilty of treason and sentenced to death (Leber 64). He was executed with Hermann Maaß that same day at Plötzensee Prison (Zimmermann and Jacobsen 208). Eberhard Zeller saw fit to mention Dr. Reichwein in his postwar book:

> His almost magic power of attraction came not on practice, not only from the fullness of his experience and his toughness in bearing various vicissitudes, which is reminiscent of the similarly wiry and redhaired T.E. Lawrence, not only from his great and varied abilities but, above all, from the purity of his nature, which lay beneath it all and was always shining through [Zeller 410].

Carl Wentzel-Teutschenthal was born December 9, 1876, in Brachwitz into an agricultural business family settled on an estate at Teutschenthal, Saxony. He studied agriculture as a young man, eventually expanding the family business into a substantial farming enterprise after World War I, specializing in sugar processing, and he also became a high bailiff in the Prussian province of Saxony (Rothfels 88). He was married to Ella (nèe von Zimmerman) in 1908, herself an agricultural heiress, and the couple had one son (German Resistance Memorial Center). Wentzel-Teutschenthal was well connected with other large business owners like Paul Reusch, the chief executive of GHH (Gutehoffnungshütte) Steel (the parent company of Maschinenfabrik Augsburg-Nürnberg, also known as MAN Industries). In 1942 Reusch was dismissed from his position for (among other things) refusing to supply the Hermann Göring Works with raw material. He also had a powerful enemy in Julius Streicher, the infamous Jew-baiting Gauleiter of Franconia.

German businesses did well when Hitler first came to power, securing large government contracts and expanding their assets, but within a few years many of the business leaders realized where Hitler was leading the country. Wentzel-Teutschenthal was the most radical of those businessmen connected to Reusch, hoping aloud that someone in the officer corps would just shoot Hitler, while at the same time distancing himself from direct participation in such activities for religious reasons. In late 1943, Goerdeler met with the Reusch group of would-be revolutionaries at Wentzel-Teutschenthal's estate and spoke to them regarding the post–Hitler economy. Goerdeler came away from the meeting with the group's moral support, but nothing else. It is likely that most of Reusch's people thought themselves too old or too dependent on government contracts to get involved personally. However, in another meeting, Wentzel-Teutschenthal did supply Goerdeler with the names of those who might be of value in the new government (Rothfels 88)— and of interest to the Gestapo. The Gestapo knew of this meeting, as they were following

Goerdeler's movements closely by this time and were notified of the event by an informant.

Wentzel-Teutschenthal was arrested after July 20, even though he had nothing to do with the attempt on Hitler's life. His wife was also arrested and sent to Ravensbrück. His arrest was provoked by the (well-known at the time) Dresden-based SS Gruppenführer (and major general of the police) Ludolf von Alvensleben, who, coincidentally, happened to owe Wentzel-Teutschenthal a considerable sum of money (German Resistance Memorial Center). Wentzel-Teutschenthal was tried for treason in the VGH, with Freisler presiding, on November 13 and sentenced to death. He was executed on December 20, 1944, in Plötzensee Prison. He was 68 years old. He wrote a letter to his wife shortly before his execution, declaring that he was going to his death "upright, confident, and innocent" (quoted in Zimmermann and Jacobsen 344). In 1981, a book was published (in German) on the life of Carl Wentzel-Teutschenthal (Olbrich).

Dr. Erich Gloeden was born August 23, 1888, in Berlin, the son of well-known Berlin bronze foundry owner Siegfried Loevy (1859–1936). Erich studied architecture and earned a doctorate at the Dresden University Technical College in 1915. His research was in city planning, and he published a book on the topic in 1923 (*Die Inflation der Gross-Städte und ihre Heilungusmöglichkeit*) (Lees 341). In 1918 he took the name Erich Loevy von Gloeden to conceal his Jewish ancestry—fifteen years before the Nazis came to power. His namesake was a teacher and friend of his parents. In 1938 he married the court lawyer Dr. Elisabeth Charlotte Kuznitzky, known by the nickname Lilo (born December 9, 1903, in Cologne). Gloeden joined the Organization Todt (OT) at the outbreak of World War II, where his training in architecture made him a valuable member of this Reich engineering and construction organization. While stationed in Poland, he saw first-hand the crimes being perpetrated against the inhabitants, and this knowledge moved him to discard all Nazi philosophies and become particularly sympathetic to the fate of the Jews. He and his wife then began helping Jews evade persecution and aided them in living underground or escaping Germany altogether (www.loevy.de).

On July 29, 1944, Gloeden, on the recommendation of his friend, Hans Ludwig Sierks, allowed General Fritz Lindemann to stay with him. Gloeden thought Lindemann was a Jew hiding from the Gestapo, which would not have made him suspicious, as by that time he and his wife had been helping Jews avoid the concentration camps for years. Lindemann stayed for five weeks in a house next to the Gloedens' in Charlottenberg. On September 3 the house was stormed by the Gestapo and everyone was arrested and interrogated, including Lilo's mother, Elisabeth (Liliencron) Kuznitzky (P. West 316). Erich Gloeden was brought before Freisler's People's Court on November 27 and sentenced to death for being aware of Lindemann's true identity and treason and not reporting his location (Stockhorst 156). Gloeden had successfully hidden the involvement of his wife and mother-in-law, but both declared after hearing the sentence that they were fully aware of who Lindemann was. On November 30 all three were beheaded at Plötzensee Prison (Leber 76).

Hans Ludwig Sierks was born July 24, 1877, in Seeth, Schleswig-Holstein, and studied industrial engineering, becoming an authority on city planning and publishing two books on the subject: *Wirtschaftlicher Städtebau und angewandte kommunale Verkehrs-Wissenschaft* (1926) and *Grundriss Der Sicheren Reichen Ruhigen Stadt* (1929). He later became a representative of the SDP, but he left the political party in 1931 to join the short-lived Sozialistische Arbeiterpartei Deutschlands. Sierks had reasonable freedom of travel even after the Nazis took over and spent considerable time in neighboring European countries as an advisor on major industrial building projects. He was arrested for a short time after Hitler became chancellor because he publicly complained about political writings (which he had authored) being declared verboten. In 1943 he joined the Free Germany Movement (Bewegung Freies Deutschland) and became a member of the relatively unknown resistance group led by Georg Schumann, but he was also a member of Goerdeler's wider circle (Zeller 405).

After the failed assassination attempt (which he had nothing to do with), Sierks assisted General Fritz Lindemann by helping him hide from the Gestapo. Sierks knew Lindemann's cousin, Hermann Lindemann (the former Social Democrat mayor of Senftenberg), who had asked for his help. Sierks was arrested on September 3 and tried on December 1 in the VGH. He was found guilty of aiding a known member of the conspiracy and sentenced to death by Judge Freisler. Lieutenant Colonel Horst von Petersdorff was arrested for the same offense but acquitted for lack of evidence, as was a woman, Frieda Pilat (Koch 219; Jacobsen 1: 571). Sierks would probably have been arrested anyway, even without the Lindemann affair, because of his association with others known to be members of the resistance. For some inexplicable reason, Sierks was not immediately executed but held by the Gestapo at Lehrter Strasse until the night of April 22, 1945, when he and several others were executed by a detachment of SS from the RSHA (Ueberschär 239).

Carl Marks was a relatively unknown, nonpolitical businessman caught up in the Gestapo's wide net after July 20. Is there a more unfortunate name to have as a German accused of aiding a member of the resistance to the Nazi regime than "Carl Marks" (sometimes written Karl Marcks)? Marks was a Charlottenberg-area businessman and World War I veteran who had nothing to do with the events of July 20, but he and his secretary were nonetheless arrested on August 21 along with Max Lindemann (General Fritz Lindemann's uncle) and his wife Elsa (*Der Spiegel*, December 5, 1966). On November 27, Erich and Elisabeth Gloeden, Elisabeth Kuznitzky, Hans Sierks, and Carl Marks were sentenced to death by the People's Court for helping to hide General Fritz Lindemann after July 20 (Jacobsen 1: 570). "Two of them were 'Jewish half-castes, first grade' and another, the widow of a Jew" (Hoffmann, *The History*, 517). Marks, like Sierks, was not immediately executed but was among those executed by the SS on the night of April 22 (1:00 a.m. on the 23rd), 1945 (Hoffmann, *The History*, 532). It is not known why he was held for so long. Marks would have been of no value as a hostage in any sort of negotiation with the Allies. Neither Marks nor Sierks could have had further information about the conspiracy, and neither had powerful friends who could have delayed their executions. Perhaps, with so many other more important defendants to be executed, they were simply forgotten. Their executions seem to have been an afterthought prompted by the chaos in Berlin created by the advancing Russian army.

Erwin Planck was born March 12, 1893, in Berlin. He was the fourth child of the eminent physicist Max Planck and his first wife, Marie (née Merck). Max Planck's second wife was Margarethe von Hößlin, whose parents were Georg von Hößlin and Elisabeth Merck. (Intermarriage among Germany's aristocratic families was the norm rather than the exception.) Erwin Planck joined a fusilier regiment in Schleswig-Holstein as a cadet in 1911 after his Arbitur, with the intention of pursuing a career as an officer; however, he was severely wounded and taken prisoner by the French very early in the First World War. He was released in a prisoner exchange in 1917 (Leber 142). After the war, Planck remained in the military (the Reichswehr) and was attached to the General Staff. This is where he first met Major Kurt von Schleicher, who was director of the political office and a man looking forward to a career in politics. Planck was married to Cornelie Schöller in Berlin in 1923 and held various positions within the defense ministry over the next three years. He left the Reichswehr in 1926 to become a government advisor, rising in 1932 to undersecretary of state in the von Papen government and remaining in that position when von Schleicher became chancellor (Gisevius, *To the Bitter End*, 432).

Planck left the government and went to East Asia for a year after the Nazis took control in 1933. A year later, he came back to Germany just prior to the Night of the Long Knives massacre, in which von Schleicher was assassinated. Planck requested an official investigation, but that went nowhere, and his repeated inquiries became an embarrassment for the Nazis. Von Schleicher had been a powerful enemy of the Nazis, especially Reichsmarshal Göring, who used the Long Knives purge to get rid of him. When asked at a press conference late on June 30, 1934, what had happened to von Schleicher, Göring replied, "Ah yes, you journalists always like a special headline story; well here it is, General von Schleicher had plotted against the regime. I ordered his arrest. He was foolish enough to resist. He is dead" (quoted in Wheeler-Bennett 323).

Planck remained out of government service, eventually taking a position with the Cologne-based Otto Wolf Corporation in 1936, and in 1939 he was promoted to director of the company's Berlin office (Weiß 351). In that position, he became associated with Prussian finance minister Johannes Popitz and Reichsbank president Hjalmar Schacht. In 1939 the three of them had a meeting with General Georg Thomas, chief of the Defence Economy and Armament Office, to ask whether there was anything they could contribute to averting the coming war (*Allgemeine Deutsche Biographie*). Thomas did write a memorandum to the chief of the OKW, Field Marshal Wilhelm Keitel, detailing their concerns, but Keitel responded in August with the assurance that Hitler had no plans for a war. Germany invaded Poland less than a month later.

In 1940 Planck, von Hassell, Popitz and Beck drafted a new German constitution, with the expectation that German generals would soon take care of Hitler. That wasn't the case, but Planck continued his involvement with the resistance, four years later being peripherally connected to the attempt of July 20. The Gestapo quickly linked Planck to the known conspirators, and he was arrested on July 23 and interrogated for three months. He was tried in the People's Court on October 23 and sentenced to death for treason. He was hanged at Plötzensee Prison on January 23, 1945 (Weiß 351). Hans Graf von Kress said of his friend, "Atonement must be made for the injustice that has been done and in this spirit he accepted his fate" (quoted in Leber 144).

The Kreisau Circle Conspiracy Trials

The trial of the primary members of the Kreisau Circle took place between January 9 and 11, 1945. Helmuth James Graf von Moltke was sentenced to death together with Franz Sperr and Alfred Delp. Eugen Gerstenmaier was sentenced to seven years at hard labor (but was liberated by the Americans at the end of the war). A few days later Freisler sentenced Theodor Haubach, Theodor Steltzer, and Nikolaus Groß to death, but not all of them were executed.

Helmuth James Graf von Moltke was born in Kreisau (Silesia Province) on March 11, 1907. He was the great-great nephew of Helmuth von Moltke, the celebrated German field marshal in the Austro-Prussian and Franco-Prussian wars, and the proprietor of the family's Kreisau estate in Prussian Silesia. His mother, Dorothy Rose-Innes, was the daughter of Sir James Rose-Innes, the chief justice for the Union of South Africa (von Moltke, *A German*, 7).

Beginning at age twenty, von Moltke studied law in Breslau, Vienna, Heidelberg, and Berlin until 1929; in 1931 he married Freya Deichmann. In 1934 he passed the junior law examination but chose not to pursue government law practice, as he would have been required to join the National Socialist Party. He instead opened a private law practice in Berlin, specializing in international law, and covertly aided the emigration of many trying to escape the Nazi regime. Von Moltke completed his law studies via London and Oxford universities in 1938 (von Moltke, *Letters*, 12).

Von Moltke was drafted by the Abwehr in 1939 when the war began and served in the counterintelligence division under Canaris—specifically, the Amt Aussland (Foreign Office) within the OKW (Wheeler-Bennett 443). His responsibilities included gathering intelligence from publicly available sources, writing reports on his findings for the Wehrmacht and advising on matters of international law. He also observed first-hand some of the crimes being committed in occupied Poland and began writing memoranda advocating the recognition of Geneva Convention rules. In an October 1941 letter, von Moltke wrote, "Certainly more than a thousand people are murdered in this way every day, and another thousand German men are habituated to murder.... What shall I say when I am asked: And what did you do during that time?" (von Moltke, *Letters*, 175). Von Moltke continued writing during the war with Russia, promoting his view that Germans should follow both the Geneva Convention and the Hague Convention so as to ensure the fair treatment of their prisoners of war. It was pointed out to him by Field Marshal Keitel that Russia had not signed these agreements (which was true) and was therefore not entitled to protection under them. This exchange led von Moltke to personally arrange the deportation of Jews to countries that were considered safe and to begin passively opposing all things Nazi related. He began revealing information about the concentration camps and the war to members of the organized resistance and making contact with the British government through his friends from Oxford. The unofficial British response called for a show of action by the resistance rather than more words. The well-known American journalist and radio broadcaster Dorothy Thompson addressed her weekly radio program to him as "Hans," and in these broadcasts she openly encouraged him and his friends to act instead of talking: "I said that one day you would have to demonstrate by deeds, drastic deeds, where you stood, as if the salvation of Germany depended on the answer to that question. And I remember that I asked you whether you and your friends would ever have the courage to act" (quoted in D. Thompson 284).

A letter written in 1942 from von Moltke to Lionel Curtis, a friend in Great Britain, reveals much about his state of mind at that time:

> Today, not a numerous, but an active part of the German people are beginning to realize, not that they have been led astray, not that bad times await them, not that the war may end in defeat, but that what is happening is sin and that they are personally responsible for each terrible deed that has been committed—naturally, not in the earthly sense, but as Christians [quoted in Rothfels 112].

Von Moltke had become fundamentally opposed to the Nazis on many levels, bolstered by his strong religious principles—of which, he was convinced, the Nazis were completely devoid. Before the war, he had held the opinion that belief in God was not essential to maintaining the struggle against the Nazis, but later he confessed that his opinion was totally wrong: "The readiness to make sacrifices that are demanded of us presupposes more than sound ethical principles" (quoted in Leber 232).

The anti-Nazi group to which von Moltke belonged met primarily at predesignated locations in Berlin, but on occasion they met at Kreisau. The meetings were not particularly secret, and it was not difficult for anyone with connections to gain admission. Meetings covered everything from how educational and religious institutions were allowing Nazism to spread to the post-Hitler reconstruction of the country after a lost war and how war crimes trials might be regarded by the public. Von Moltke wrote two volumes titled *Principles for the New Order* and *Directions to Regional Commissioners* based on these meetings. His wife, Freya, was given these documents and told to hide them in a place unknown to him (F. von Moltke 35).

Von Moltke did not approve of the proposed assassination of Hitler, primarily on religious grounds, but he also realized that Hitler could well become a martyr for the Nazi cause. In his thinking there was no political benefit to killing Hitler. Von Moltke's expressed opinions and objections to Hitler's violation of international law finally got him arrested by the Gestapo in January 1944, and he was held for a year without being charged. He, Delp, and Sperr were finally brought before Freisler's VGH in January 1945. Von Moltke's only substantial defense was that "all he had done was to organize resistance movements to be mobilized in the eventuality of enemy occupation" (Koch 223). Freisler was not taken in by the ruse, but still there was no hard evidence that von Moltke had participated in any plans for a coup. However, Freisler decreed that von Moltke's participation in discussions of a Germany without Hitler was itself treason and punishable by death—a charge that would have been upheld if contested. Von Moltke saw this sentence as punishment for his ideas, not his actions, which would never have had standing in German courts before Hitler came to power. He was sentenced to death on January 11 and hanged on January 23 at Plötzensee Prison. Many of his letters to his wife were smuggled out of Tegel Prison by Pastor Harald Poelchau and were subsequently published in book form under the title *Letters to Freya*. When the American OSS learned of von Moltke's death sentence, strategies were connived for rescuing him, but the execution took place before plans could be set in motion (von Hassell and MacRae 250).

Franz Sperr was born February 12, 1878, and became a career officer in the Bavarian army. He was posted to Berlin on October 27, 1918, and reassigned as a military advisor serving on the Reich Council. This position was eliminated the following year, and Sperr joined the Bavarian State Foreign Ministry, where he served until the end of 1934 as an envoy to Berlin (German Resistance Memorial Center). Sperr was instrumental in forming and sustaining the Bavarian resistance groups, which were generally inclined toward independence, preferring to distance their region's leadership from Germany's at every occasion.

Sperr's own daughter, a member of the Hitler Youth, informed the Gestapo of her father's resistance activities in December 1939; earlier that year he is known to have met with von Hassell (von Hassell 30). This led to a warning for Sperr, though not an arrest (von Hassell 96). In late 1942 Sperr became associated with members of the Kreisau Circle, particularly the Jesuit fathers Alfred Delp and Augustinus Rösch, and he also met with von Moltke on multiple occasions (Steinbach and Tuchel 191). On June 6, 1944, Sperr saw von Stauffenberg in Bamberg and was told that "the goal was a federal state with very considerable autonomy of the member states with much autonomy in administration, with social reforms, with participation of workers in settling wages, working hours and holidays and the like" (quoted in Hoffmann, *The History*, 321). Later in the month Sperr met with von Stauffenberg again, and he once more voiced his ethical opposition to killing Hitler. By this time, the Gestapo were well aware of Sperr's activities, and on July 28, after the coup attempt, he was arrested as a conspirator, but he was not tried in the People's Court until January 11, 1945. He was found guilty of the familiar charge of not informing the Gestapo of what he knew about the coup. He was executed on January 23 at Plötzensee Prison in Berlin.

Father Dr. Alfred Delp was born September 15, 1907, in Mannheim. His mother was a Catholic and his father a Protestant. Delp was baptized in the Catholic Church as a baby, but he attended a Protestant school and was confirmed in the Lutheran Church in 1921. He later left the Lutherans, became a Catholic and studied at the Goetheschule in Dieburg. He bore no animosity toward the Lutherans and would later become an advocate of better relations between the two churches. Delp joined the Bund Neudeutschland Catholic youth organization and, after graduating in 1926, the Society of Jesus. He studied philosophy at a Jesuit college in Pullach (Bavaria) and worked for three years at the Stella Matutina College in Feldkirch, Austria (*Allgemeine Deutsche Biographie*). It was in Austria that Delp was first exposed to National Socialism. Even before the annexation of Austria in 1938, German students living there were being coerced into attending Reich schools in Germany. To sidestep this situation, the Jesuits opened a college in the Black Forest, called St. Blasien, to console the expelled students. Delp completed his theology education in Valkenburg, Holland and Frankfurt, graduating with a doctorate in philosophy in 1937 (Leber 224). He was ordained a Catholic priest in Munich that same year. From 1939 until the Nazis closed it down and arrested him in 1941, Delp wrote for the Jesuit publication *Stimmen der Zeit* (Voices of the Times). He then became the rector of St. Georg Church in the Munich suburb of Bogenhausen and began secretly helping Jews escape to Switzerland. By this time, any priest was subject to arrest for disparaging the National Socialists, which would often result in the seizure of church property as well.

Augustinus Rösch, Father Delp's direct superior in Munich, was already active in the underground resistance, and he introduced Delp to the Kreisau Circle (Rothfels 110). From 1942, Delp met regularly with the group, often in his own apartment, and worked with von Moltke to create a model for a new post–Hitler German social order (Koch 223). Delp injected Catholic social philosophy into the plan and arranged meetings between von Moltke and major Catholic leaders such as Archbishop Konrad von Preysing of Berlin.

After July 20, Delp was arrested by the Gestapo in Munich on July 28 as part of the general roundup of Kreisau Circle resistance members. Despite not having been involved with the assassination attempt, Delp was locked up in Tegel Prison in Berlin, and then transferred to the Moabit Lehrter Strasse Prison. Many of his letters written there were smuggled out before his trial (Leber 224). He volunteered to serve as a spiritual advisor for others imprisoned at Moabit even though he was offered his freedom by the Gestapo if he would leave the Jesuits. On December 8 Delp made his final confession to Father Franz von Tattenbuch, who had been mistakenly admitted to the prison as a visitor. Delp wrote on the same day, "It was too much, what a fulfillment, I prayed for it so much, I gave my life away. My chains are now without any meaning, because God found me worthy of the Vincula Amoris (chains of love)" (Delp 63).

Delp was tried along with von Moltke, Sperr, and Eugen Gerstenmaier in Freisler's People's Court during the session of January 9–11, 1945. Delp was tried on the last day

(Weiß 83). Only Gerstenmaier was not sentenced to death for treason. Father Delp was hanged at Plötzensee Prison on February 2, the day before Freisler himself was killed (Stockhorst 37–38). In his last letter, he wrote, "The actual reason for my conviction here is that I am a Jesuit and have remained one" (quoted in Zimmermann and Jacobsen 248). Delp's deeply held religious convictions rivaled those of the widely venerated Dietrich Bonhoeffer.

Dr. Theodor Haubach was born September 15, 1896, in Frankfurt am Main and grew up in Darmstadt, attending the Ludwig-Georg Gymnasium. After finishing school in 1914, he joined the military and was wounded and decorated for bravery during the First World War. Haubach became a university student at Heidelberg in 1919 and studied economics and philosophy with the intention of becoming a journalist. He joined the SPD in 1920 and was an active member of the university-based Young Socialists (*Allgemeine Deutsche Biographie*). In 1924, Haubach became an assistant editor of the *Hamburger Echo* daily newspaper and held that position until 1929, when he took a position at the Interior Ministry, eventually becoming chief press officer (Stockhorst 180). He was an active supporter of the Weimar democracy movement from 1924 onward and a leading member of the Hamburg branch of the Reichsbanner Schwarz-Rot-Gold (black, red, and gold) group, which openly opposed the National Socialists (Leber 244). As soon as the Nazis came to power in 1933, Haubach was high on their list of people to watch, and he was repeatedly arrested on fabricated charges, eventually being held at the Esterwegen concentration camp in Lower Saxony for two years as a final warning (Steinbach and Tuchel 89; Leber 244).

After his release, Haubach worked as an insurance agent to avoid further scrutiny. This position allowed him to travel extensively without attracting suspicion, and he soon made contact with members of the Kreisau Circle through Adolf Reichwein. Haubach was referred to by the circle as "The General" because of his knowledge of military law. He, Leber, and Leuschner were the key members of the SPD involved in organized resistance (Zimmermann and Jacobsen 244). Haubach was also responsible for recruiting his friend Carlo Mierendorff into the Kreisau Circle. Mierendorff would become a major leader in the circle for a short period of time and one of the first to be arrested soon after Hitler came to power. Mierendorff was held for five years, released, and then killed in an air raid on Leipzig on December 4, 1943 (Fest, *Plotting*, 157; Leber 238). "He was a doomed man and the bomb only saved him from Freisler's death sentence" (Leber 242). Haubach's association with Kreisau was enough to get him arrested on August 9 after von Stauffenberg's failed attempt to kill Hitler. He was also listed as minister of propaganda in the proposed post–Hitler government, which would have led to his apprehension in any case (Rothfels 95). Haubach was tried and sentenced by the VGH on October 20, though he was not executed until January 23, 1945 (at Plötzensee), along with Eugen Bolz, Reinhold Frank, Nikolaus Groß, Hermann Kaiser, Helmuth von Moltke, Ludwig Schwamb, Erwin Planck, Franz Sperr and Busso Thoma (Fest, *Plotting*, 313).

Nikolaus Groß was born September 30, 1898, in Niederwenigern and grew up intending to become a coal miner like his father. However, as an adult, he chose to further his education and completed classes through an organization called the People's Association for a Catholic Germany. At the age of twenty, he founded the first youth groups of the Christian Miners Movement, which were affiliated with the Mineworkers Trade Association based in Oberhausen (Leber 49). The next year Groß moved to Essen to become an assistant editor for the association's newspaper, the *Bergknappen*. Two years later he began a long-running career as a trade union secretary, being posted to several major union cities, including Zwickau (Saxony) and Bottrop (Rhineland), and his reputation as an organizer continued to grow. In 1927 he was offered a position with the *Westdeutsche Arbeiterzeitung*, a widely circulated union newspaper in western Germany that was also affiliated with the Catholic Workers Front (Wistrich 87). Soon Groß was made chief editor, but because of the newspaper's anti–Nazi positions, its successor, the *Ketteler Wacht*, was banned for a short time after Hitler came to power (Stockhorst 165). The newspaper was on thin ice for the next few years and was eventually shut down altogether on November 19, 1938. Groß then became the general leader of the Catholic Workers Front in Düsseldorf; in this position, he had the funds and cover to travel throughout Germany, meeting various members of the resistance movement, notably those of the Cologne Circle, which by this time was already in contact with Goerdeler's group of resisters.

Goerdeler invited Groß to contribute to the planning of a post–Hitler government, believing his support and that of another resister, Bernhard Letterhaus, would be useful in dealings with trade unions and Catholics after the coming coup (Leber 50). Groß's name appeared on documents seized by the Gestapo after July 20, which was sufficient evidence to warrant his arrest on August 12. He was brought before the VGH finally on January 15, 1945, and sentenced to death by Freisler. He was beheaded (or hanged) at Plötzensee Prison on January 23. In his last letter to his family, written two days before his execution, Groß said, "Have no grief over me—I hope that the Lord will accept me. Has he not disposed everything miraculously? He left me in a place where, even in confinement, I received much love and human fellow-feeling" (quoted In Zimmermann and Jacobsen 254). On October 7, 2001, Nikolaus Groß was beatified by Pope John Paul II as a martyr for the faith (www.vatican.va/news_services/liturgy/saints/ns_lit_doc_200110 07_beat-gross_en.html).

THE BONHOEFFER CONSPIRACY GROUP TRIAL

On February 2, 1945, the loosely organized resistance group that included Klaus Bonhoeffer was brought to trial. The "Bonhoeffer Circle" (generally referring to Dietrich Bonhoeffer) is often incorrectly referred to as the Freiburg Circle (Bonhoeffer, *Dietrich*, 662). When tried by the VGH after July 20, Klaus Bonhoeffer was sentenced to death, and so were his brother-in-law Rüdiger Schleicher, Hans John, and Friedrich Justus Perels. February 2 would be the last full day of trials conducted by Freisler, as he was killed during proceedings the following day.

Contrary to the usual sequence of events, those found guilty in this trial were not immediately executed. The Russians were already in the suburbs of Berlin, and Himmler believed some of those being held might yet be useful. By April 22, though, he realized that it was too late for negotiations. When some twenty prisoners were being marched on foot from the Moabit Lehrter Strasse Prison to the Gestapo lockup at Prinz Albrecht Strasse late on the night of April 22 (early morning of the 23rd), they were stopped along the Invaliedenstrasse by an SS detachment from the RSHA led by Sturmbannführer Kurt Stawizki (who managed to change his name and evade prosecution after the war). The prisoners were killed by being shot in the back of the head—probably on orders from Obergruppenführer Heinrich Müller. Certainly someone gave direct orders to carry out the executions, since the fact that some of those executed had already been sentenced to death by the VGH would not have been enough to convince the SS men to unilaterally take on this culpability so late in the war.

Two members of the party escaped in the confusion, but among those who died were Albrecht Graf von Bernstorff, Klaus Bonhoeffer, Karl Ludwig Freiherr von und zu Guttenberg, Albrecht Haushofer, Hans John, Franz Kempner, Richard Künzer, Franz Leuninger, Carl Marks, Wilhelm zur Nieden, Friedrich Perels, Rüdiger Schleicher, Ernst Schneppenhorst, and Hans Ludwig Sierks (Wheeler-Bennett 685). Other authors provide a slightly different account, with Colonel Wilhelm Staehle, Lieutenant Colonel Ernst Munzinger, Major Hans Victor von Salviati, a Russian prisoner named Sergei Sossimov, Carlos Moll, and two Communists (Max Jennewein and Herbert Kosney) being added to the list and the executions taking place over two nights, with von Bernstorff, von Guttenberg and Schneppenhorst being executed during an ordered SS raid of the prison on the night of April 23 (early morning of the 24th) (Shirer, *The Rise and Fall*, 1073; Hoffmann, *The History*, 523–33). There is yet another story that the events took place on the nights of April 23 (early morning of the 24th) and April 24 (early morning of the 25th) with no survivors (Fest, *Plotting*, 320). This last account is obviously erroneous, as one of the survivors (Herbert Kosney) later told his story (Boehm 48). The most accurate account of what probably transpired—or, at any rate, the easiest to follow—is given by James Douglas-Hamilton (Douglas-Hamilton 253).

Dr. Klaus Bonhoeffer (Dietrich's brother) was born January 5, 1901, in Breslau. His parents were Karl and Paula (née von Hase) Bonhoeffer. Karl was a well-known and respected professor of psychiatry and neurology (Stockhorst 71). Of the couple's seven children, Klaus was the third son. As a child, Klaus went to the prestigious Grunewald-Gymnasium in Berlin, where one of his classmates was future fellow conspirator Hans von Dohnanyi. All the Bonhoeffer children were home schooled by their mother until old enough for the gymnasium.

Bonhoeffer studied law at Heidelberg University and received a doctorate for his dissertation on workers' cooperatives ("Die Betriebsräte als Organ der Betriebsgenossenschaft"). He continued his training at the University of Geneva and married Emilie Delbrück on September 3, 1930. She was Hans Delbrück's daughter, and Justus and Max Delbrück's sister—as well as a cousin of Ernst von Harnack (Leber 146; Steinbach and Tuchel 32). Hans was professor of history at Berlin University and is best known for his four-volume set titled *The History of the Art of Warfare*. Max received a doctorate in physics from Göttingen University in 1930 and left Germany in 1937 for the United States, becoming a well-known scientist and winning the Nobel Prize in 1969. Justus remained in Germany, becoming a lawyer (and a member of the resistance). Bonhoeffer worked as a lawyer after his marriage, and in 1935 he became a legal advisor for Lufthansa, rising to chief councilor in 1937 and remaining in that position until 1944 (Stockhorst 71). His position allowed him to travel extensively even after the war began.

In 1940 Bonhoeffer began contacting established resistance circles, introduced to many of them by his brother Dietrich, brother-in-law Justus, and former classmate von Dohnanyi. Bonhoeffer, in turn, introduced his friend Otto John, whom he had known for three years, to the resistance. Bonhoeffer's wife's cousin, Ernst von Harnack, put him in contact with the Social Democrat resistance group. Von Harnack's cousin, Arvid von Harnack and his American wife Mildred (née Fish), would both be executed (December 22, 1942, and February 16, 1943, respectively) as members of the Red Orchestra. Bonhoeffer's connection to the military opposition came through resistance members in

Canaris' Abwehr organization. Bonhoeffer, who did not share his brother's moral objections to assassinating Hitler, was in complete agreement with the plans of July 20. By this time, he was well known by many members of the various resistance groups, so, after the failed attempt, it was only a matter of time before the Gestapo ran him to ground. The arrest came on October 1, but Bonhoeffer didn't appear before the People's Court until February 2, 1945. He was held for those four months at the Lehrter Strasse Prison complex, and one of his letters to his children written during that time has been published in *Auf dem Wege zur Freiheit* (On the Road to Freedom) (Leber 147; Bonhoeffer et al.). Klaus Bonhoeffer was sentenced to death by the court but was not immediately executed. He was ultimately shot by Stawizki's SS detachment; a first-hand account of the executions was later provided by Herbert Kosney. A bullet was also meant for Kosney, but he claimed that in the darkness the bullet only wounded him, and he lived (barely) to tell his story (Boehm 48). Stories of Kosney dodging a bullet at the last second and escaping uninjured are inaccurate.

Dr. Rüdiger Schleicher was born the son of a civil servant in Stuttgart on January 14, 1895, and in 1923 was married to Ursula Bonhoeffer, Karl Bonhoeffer's daughter (Dietrich and Klaus Bonhoeffer's sister) (Stockhorst 382; Schlingensiepen 39). In 1943 Schleicher's daughter Renate would marry Dietrich Bonhoeffer's good friend, Eberhard Bethge (who survived the war and would write the first Bonhoeffer biography). Schleicher was seriously wounded in the First World War and afterward, at age 28, graduated from Tübingen University with a doctorate in law, specializing in international aviation treaties. He then became a civil servant in Württemberg and later a member of the Foreign Office, serving on the German-American Arbitration Committee; he was eventually appointed to the Reich Ministry of Aviation and made chief of the Institute for Aeronautical Law in Berlin in 1933 (Steinbach and Tuchel 173). Hans John (Otto's brother) was Schleicher's technical assistant (Hoffmann, *The History*, 246). In 1935 Schleicher was appointed chief of the Ministry of Aviation's legal department. The Nazis removed him from the ministry just before the war with Poland began, assigning him to a lower position in the General Air Office. It seems that Schleicher's published positions in matters of international law (specifically, his support of the Kellogg-Briand Pact and the Hague Convention) did not meet with the approval of the new Nazi government.

Schleicher volunteered to become the director of the Institute for Aviation Law at the Berlin Friedrich-Wilhelm University in 1939, and he directed the publication of the legal journal *Archiv für Luftrecht* (Leber 150). He and his immediate associates later became one of the dozens of smaller, loosely connected circles of underground resistance. Schleicher was cited as the person to be responsible for the reconstruction of Germany's air travel after the coup of July 20. His name was thus among those recorded during meetings where a post–Hitler government was discussed, and that was sufficient evidence to get him arrested as one of the conspirators, even though he had nothing directly to do with the assassination attempt. Schleicher was detained by the Gestapo on October 4, 1944, and held until his trial on February 2, 1945. He was found guilty of treason by the People's Court, with Freisler presiding (Steinbach and Tuchel 173). Schleicher (along with his brother-in-law, Klaus Bonhoeffer) was among those shot by Stawizki's men near the Lehrter Strasse Prison complex. The case against him was based on the emergency decrees of February 28, 1933, "for which the Reichstag fire had been the original justification" (Steinbach and Tuchel 173; Leber 151).

Dr. Hans John was born August 1, 1911, in Ziegenhain, Hesse. He studied law at the

University of Berlin as a young man and in 1939 became a legal apprentice at the Aviation Law Institute, also in Berlin (Steinbach and Tuchel 102). He was drafted by the Wehrmacht in June 1940 and seriously wounded on the Eastern Front in March 1942. After recovering from his injury, he was discharged from the Wehrmacht and resumed his law studies. He and his brother Otto, who worked for Lufthansa, were both involved in resistance activities masterminded by conspirators in the Abwehr and the Office of Foreign Affairs of the OKW (Zeller 219). By this time the Abwehr was being closely watched by the Gestapo, leading to the arrest of Hans Oster and Hans von Dohnanyi in the spring of 1943. Both John brothers were directly involved in planning operations that ran to July 20, and they had previously hidden a fellow Abwehr conspirator, Captain Ludwig Gehre, who escaped after being arrested during the Solf tea party roundup.

Hans John was arrested in August 1944, interrogated and manhandled by the Gestapo, and finally sentenced to death by the People's Court on February 2, 1945. He was another who was among the group executed by Stawizki's SS on the night of April 22, 1945 (Manvell and Fraenkel, *The Canaris Conspiracy*, 244). His brother Otto escaped arrest and left Germany on a Lufthansa flight on July 24, four days after the assassination attempt.

Dr. Friedrich Justus Perels was born November 13, 1910, and studied law as a young adult; however, after successfully completing his state examinations in 1933 and 1936, he was refused entrance into the judicial service on "racial grounds," as his great-grandparents had been Jews (Steinbach and Tuchel 154). Perels was married to Helga Kellermann, with whom he had a son. He had been a member of the Protestant Church since his youth and served as legal counsel for members of the Confessing Church when they began being harassed by the Nazi government (Stockhorst 320). He opposed the "Germanization" of the church, saying that it was not the duty of the church to serve the people, but rather to serve God (Leber 212). To that end, Perels, with pastors Martin Niemöller and Dietrich Bonhoeffer, aided in the escape of persecuted Jews whenever possible. He was a reliable friend of both the von Dohnanyis and the Bonhoeffers (Manvell and Fraenkel, *The Canaris Conspiracy*, 170). Perels made contact with the resistance group in the Office of Foreign Affairs (through Bonhoeffer) in 1940 and immediately became involved in "Enterprise Seven," which was the plan to help Jews escape to neutral countries by passing them off as Abwehr agents. It was called Enterprise Seven (Unternehmen Sieben) because the initial plan was for aiding just seven people (Steinbach and Tuchel 208). Perels was, according to Bishop Dibelius, "the only man we still had in Berlin who could keep the door open to other people, groups and powers" (quoted in Leber 213).

Perels was arrested by the Gestapo on September 5, 1944 (Manvell and Fraenkel, *The Canaris Conspiracy*, 242). He was sentenced to death by the People's Court on February 2, 1945, at which time Judge Freisler screamed at him, "After the war the Church will be wiped out." "The Church will endure" was Perels' reply (quoted in Leber 215). As it came to be, the church endured and Freisler himself was wiped out the next day.

Friedrich Justus Perels was among those executed by Stawizki's men on the night of April 22. Perels' father, Dr. Ernst Perels, a professor at Berlin University, "fell victim to the Gestapo at the same time" (Leber 212). According to his biographer, Dr. Ines Oberling, "Ernst Perels was arrested for being a member of the family, in October of the same year, and taken to a concentration camp. In May 1945, he died, shortly after his release, of the effects of the strains of the camp in Flossenbürg" (Oberling 225; *Allgemeine Deutsche Biographie*).

The Final Trials

The vice president of the People's Court, Dr. Wilhelm Crohne, began hearing and assigning cases soon after Freisler's death; Harold Haffner, who would become the new president, was not appointed until March 12. The public sensationalism of the earlier trials had faded considerably by this time, even if the determination of the prosecutors had not. By now the average Berliner had more pressing things to worry about.

Ernst von Harnack was tried on February 1, 1945; Ewald von Kleist-Schmenzin on February 23; and Friedrich (Fritz) Voigt, Franz Leuninger, and Oswald Wiersich on February 26. All were sentenced to death. However, with the pending change in leadership of the VGH after Freisler's death, several of those who had been tried received reduced sentences instead of the death penalty. That did not apply to SS Gruppenführer Nebe and General Fromm, who were both sentenced to death in March. Nebe was sentenced on March 2 and hanged March 21 and did not "die before capture and his planned trial" (Jacobsen 2: 771; Hoffmann, *The History*, 528; Wistrich 178; and Bloxham 196). Fromm was sentenced on March 7 and executed by firing squad on March 12 (or March 19) in Brandenburg-Görden Prison (Hoffmann, *The History*, 528; Wistrich 69).

Ernst Wolf Alexander Oskar von Harnack was born July 15, 1888, in Marburg, the son of the prominent theologian Adolf von Harnack and Amalie Thiersch (Wistrich 97). His mother's grandfather was the distinguished chemist Justus von Liebig. Ernst von Harnack was married to Änne Wiggert, the daughter of the Prussian secretary Ernst Wiggert and his wife Elizabeth (née Schmidt), on October 5, 1894. Ernst and Änne would have two sons and three daughters (German Resistance Memorial Center).

Von Harnack attended the Joachimsthalsche Gymnasium in Berlin, completing his Arbitur in 1907, and then studied law at the University of Marburg. He took the first law examination in May 1911 and began practicing in Lichterfelde (a Berlin suburb). He entered military service that same year, prior to World War I, as an Einjährig-Freiwilliger (a one-year volunteer) and served until 1912. After the invasion of Poland, he served in the military administration of that country and, in 1913, as an apprentice lawyer in Oppeln. In mid–1918, he accepted a position as a Regierungsassessor (government assessor) in the Ministry of Science, Art, and Education, eventually being promoted to Regierungsrat (government councilor) and Landrat (state official) in Hersfeld-Rotenburg. Von Harnack was elected to the Federation of Religious Socialists on November 27, 1921. On June 1, 1925, he was made an assistant in the regional government of Hanover; later, in April 1927, he was moved to a similar position in Cologne. On August 8, 1929, he was appointed president (Regierungspräsident) of the provincial government of Merseburg. However, with provocation from the emerging Nazi party, Chancellor Franz von Papen dismissed von Harnack from government service on July 20, 1932 (Wistrich 97).

Von Harnack was arrested and held for a short time in 1933 after being investigated by an embryonic Gestapo because of his repeated inquiries into the murder of the former prime minister and SPD executive Johann Stelling during the Night of the Long Knives. He was a confirmed member of the resistance by the winter of 1938–1939 (Hoffmann, *The History*, 103).

Von Harnack was arrested on July 20 after the assassination attempt, and his entire family was arrested soon afterward (Hoffmann, *The History*, 520). He was a known associate of conspirators Klaus Bonhoeffer, Otto John, Hans von Dohnanyi, and Wilhelm Leuschner, but in truth he had nothing directly to do with the coup attempt. Nonetheless, on February 1, 1945, he was brought before the VGH and found guilty of treason. He was sentenced to death and executed on March 5, 1945. Today the name von Harnack is well represented in German resistance history. Major Fritz von Harnack was one of Olbright's staff officers and directly involved in July 20, although without explicit knowledge of what was transpiring (Ritter 387 and 501). His cousins Arvid and Mildred von Harnack have already been mentioned in connection with the Red Orchestra.

Ewald von Kleist-Schmenzin was born March 22, 1890, in Dubberow, Pomerania. He was a descendant of Prussian royalty, through his parents Hermann Otto von Kleist and his wife Elisabeth Alice von Kleist. He was a wealthy conservative aristocratic German lawyer who supported the DNVP, wanted nothing to do with Hitler's National Socialist party, and was in fact arrested many times for his outspoken opposition—a "pietist Pomeranean Junker," as described by one modern-day historian (Burleigh 674). The year before Hitler became chancellor, von Kleist-Schmenzin published a broadside for widespread distribution outlining the threats he perceived in National Socialism (von Schlabrendorff, *The Secret War*, 357). He knew the law better than those who wanted to silence him and used his legal training to get himself released quickly after each arrest. Before the invasion of Poland, von Kleist-Schmenzin made several trips abroad, warning government leaders of the probable invasion of that country. In 1938, he secretly traveled to Great Britain as a representative of Admiral Canaris, with the intent of informing the English regarding the existence of opposition to Hitler even at this early date. He aimed to persuade Churchill and Robert Vansittart to actively oppose British appeasement of Hitler's policies (Fest, *Plotting*, 390). This was to be done through Great Britain supporting Czechoslovakia, using force if necessary. Both Churchill and Vansittart were open to his ideas, but neither was in a position to set policy. All Churchill could do was compose a letter to Hitler expressing his concern over German military belligerence.

Von Kleist-Schmenzin's connection to established resistance cells came via Carl Goerdeler in 1942, through whom he first became aware of detailed plans for a coup. Von Kleist-Schmenzin was clear in his view regarding how to overthrow the Nazi regime, encouraging an assassination attempt immediately, to the point of condoning his son Ewald Heinrich's attempted suicide mission in January 1944. He was well aware of von Stauffenberg's planned attempts and his son's involvement. The senior von Kleist-Schmenzin was to become deputy political advisor to the military Wehrkreis commander in Wehrkreis II (Stettin) in a post–Hitler government (Hoffmann, *The History*, 357).

Ewald von Kleist-Schmenzin was arrested by the Gestapo the day after the failed assassination attempt, but he was not immediately tried. He was eventually brought before the People's Court on February 23, 1945, and sentenced to death for treason, but not before having a few last words for Judge Freisler: "Yes, I have pursued high treason since 30 January 1933 [the day Hitler became chancellor], always and with every means. I have made no secret of my struggle against Hitler and National Socialism. I regard this struggle as a commandment from God. God alone will be my judge." These were to be the last words from a defendant that Freisler would hear, as the air raid that would shortly kill him was just beginning (Burleigh 715). Regarding von Kleist-Schmenzin, Judge Crohne, the vice president of the VGH, had to admit, "Disagreeable as he was during his trial, he was great in the manner of going to his death" (von Schlabrendorff, *Revolt*, 164). Ewald von Kleist-Schmenzin was hanged at Plötzensee Prison on April 9. His son would survive the war after enduring four months in the Ravensbrück concentration camp before the

July 20 conspiracy case against him was dropped. He would end the war fighting the Americans in Italy.

Friedrich (Fritz) Voigt was born November 18, 1882, in Treba and became a skilled construction worker while completing his education and before serving in the military for three years, from 1902 to 1905. After his discharge, he became active in the Deutschen Bauarbeiterverbandes (German Construction Workers Association). He was married to Magda Kruse, with whom he had a son.

At age thirty-two, Voigt rejoined the military and fought in the First World War from beginning to end; after the surrender, he became a labor union activist in Breslau (Osterroth 318; www.fes.de/archiv/adsd_neu/inhalt/stichwort/harnack-wiersisch-voigt.htm). He was soon nominated by the Silesian Social Democratic Party (SPD) to become a candidate for the National Assembly (Steinbach and Tuchel 209). Voigt joined the Nazi party in 1919, before it was a recognized party, but resigned in 1921 when it became obvious to him that the Nazis would not be sympathetic to labor. He also held the post of police president in Breslau for a year (Stockhorst 432). During the Kapp Putsch in 1920, there was a call by the German government for a general strike to help suppress rebel activities and also to possibly deter union members from joining them. Voigt did not support the dissidents, but he did not permit his union members to actively oppose them. Beginning in 1933 he was imprisoned by the Nazis in the concentration camps of Breslau-Dürrgoy, Esterwegen, and Lichtenburg, and he was not released until 1934 (Steinbach and Tuchel 209).

After the Second World War began, Voigt established communication with other labor leaders who were members of the resistance; among them were Jakob Kaiser and Wilhelm Leuschner in Berlin, and Franz Leuninger and Fritz-Dietlof Graf von der Schulenburg-Tressow in Breslau. The conspirators came to recognize his leadership abilities and designated him to be the political representative for Lower Silesia in Wehrkreis VII (Breslau) under Dr. Hans Lukaschek in the post–Hitler government (Hoffmann, *The History*, 357). Voigt was arrested along with other union leaders soon after July 20 and imprisoned, but he was not tried until February 26, 1945. He was found guilty of treason and executed on March 1, 1945, in Plötzensee Prison (German Resistance Memorial Center).

Franz Leuninger was born December 28, 1898, in Mengerskirchen and, as a young man, learned the trade of bricklaying, later becoming involved in local politics through the Christian labor (trade) unions in the Weimar Republic, eventually being elected as one of their representatives. He served in World War I and married Anna Paulina Meuser in 1924, with whom he would have three sons (*Allgemeine Deutsche Biographie*). His political activity and respectability in the area led him to be elected a member of the Breslau city assembly for the Center Party in 1930, and he ran as a Center Party candidate in the Reichstag elections of March 1933 (Stockhorst 269). Leuninger was never tempted to join the Nazi party, primarily because of its policies regarding labor unions, which were amplified soon after Hitler became chancellor.

Leuninger took a job as the manager of a labor-based cooperative housing association after the Nazis took control of the government, which put him in daily contact with men in the labor front being terrorized by the party, including fellow Christian trade unionist Jakob Kaiser. Goerdeler recruited Leuninger to the organized resistance because of his multiple contacts with labor leaders, and had the coup been successful, Leuninger would have been a political appointee in Silesia. After the failure of the assassination attempt, he was arrested on September 26 and held in the Moabit Lehrter Strasse Prison in Berlin for several months, where he was ruthlessly interrogated (Jacobsen 1: 466). He was tried by the VGH on February 26, 1945, and sentenced to death. Franz Leuninger was hanged on March 1, 1945, in Plötzensee Prison (*Allgemeine Deutsche Biographie*).

Oswald Wiersich was born September 1, 1882, in Breslau and was another critical resistance member who advocated support of the movement throughout the labor unions. He joined trade unions when he was very young while working as an intern mechanical engineer (rising to some prominence in the profession), and he was eventually made a labor leader (Stockhorst 447). Wiersich was an elected representative of the German Metalworkers Union from 1912 until the Nazis came to power, and in 1923 he was named secretary of the German Labor Unions in Silesia. Later he became a member of the Prussian State Parliament as a representative of the SDP (Steinbach and Tuchel 243). All the shrewd resistance leaders realized early on that they needed men like Wiersich, Voigt, and Leuninger (who had the support of labor) if their future post–Hitler government was to survive, and they actively involved the labor leaders in planning for that eventuality. Unfortunately, labor leaders were also conspicuously mentioned in documents discovered by the Gestapo after July 20. The Kaltenbrunner papers are filled with reports of their interrogations after the failed coup.

Two months after the National Socialists came into power, Wiersich and other labor and Social Democrat leaders were arrested and held for a month—as a warning to those who followed them. Wiersich had no job after his release but found menial employment while continuing his underground resistance work in Silesia, organizing labor opposition to the Nazis. He had the support of Leuschner, who soon introduced him to Beck and others in larger resistance circles. Wiersich had nothing to do with the events of July 20, but he was arrested on August 22 in the general muster of resistance members. His association with Michael von Matuschka, Fritz-Dietlof von der Schulenburg-Tressow, and Fritz Voigt was well known by the Gestapo, and that, along with the documents seized, was enough evidence against him (Steinbach and Tuchel 243). Wiersich was tried by the VGH on February 28, 1945, and found guilty of treason. The verdict was death, and the sentence was carried out on March 1, 1945, in Plötzensee Prison (German Resistance Memorial Center; Zimmermann and Jacobsen 316).

Lieutenant Colonel Hasso von Böhmer was born August 9, 1904, and rose to become a member of the General Staff in World War II. He had something in common with many of the other organizers of the military resistance: he, too, was a member of Wehrmacht Infantry Regiment 9, based in Potsdam. His superiors in the regiment were von Tresckow and von der Schulenburg-Tressow. Von Böhmer was married to Käthe Torhorst, and the couple would have two sons and a daughter (German Resistance Memorial Center; Zimmermann and Jacobsen 282).

Von Böhmer was recruited to the resistance by von Tresckow, who nominated him to become the military representative for Wehrkreis XX (Danzig) after the coup (Hoffmann, *The History*, 349). His direct superior in Danzig prior to July 20 was General Bodewin Keitel, the brother of the field marshal. Von Böhmer's critical role in the coup was to ensure that all the conspirators' orders from Berlin were passed on to his superiors in Poland. This was not to be a localized insurrection. After the collapse of the coup, he was not immediately implicated, but his name did exist on yet another document, signed by Colonel General Erich Hoepner, naming him to the above-mentioned position in the post–Hitler Wehrmacht (Jacobsen 1: 81). When Gestapo investigations discovered that document, von Böhmer was arrested (on August 22) and sent to the Lehrter Strasse Prison in Berlin. An illness caused him to be transferred to a medical clinic in Sachsenhausen. He was dismissed from the Wehrmacht, though not tried immediately, being imprisoned until his trial by the VGH on February 28, 1945. He was found guilty of treason and sentenced to death. Von Böhmer was executed March 5, 1945, at Plötzensee Prison (Grzesinski 364; Stockhorst 66).

THE SS AND GESTAPO TRIALS AND EXECUTIONS

There were many more executions as a result of SS and Gestapo trials (or direct orders from above) than those officially conducted by the People's Court. Often these trials took place with only the accused and a few SS men or Gestapo agents present. There was no defense representation and no appeal. In other cases, there was no trial of any sort. The accused were simply held by the Gestapo until executed on Himmler's orders to subordinates (or on Hitler's orders as relayed through Himmler). The best known of these trials was held at Flossenbürg concentration camp on the night of April 8, 1945. Those tried included several conspirators who were being held either because they were thought to possess information or because Himmler believed they might be useful in bargaining with the Allies. SS judge Otto Thorbeck presided, with SS lawyer and chief interrogator Walter Huppenkothen prosecuting, when Admiral Canaris, Hans Oster, Karl Sack, Ludwig Gehre, Theodor Strünck, Friedrich von Rabenau, and Dietrich Bonhoeffer were tried and sentenced to death. The sentences were carried out the next day, April 9 (Manvell and Fraenkel, *The Canaris Conspiracy*, 224). Two other conspirators being held at the time, Andreas von Bernstorff and Albrecht Haushofer, were among those whose death sentences were carried out later in the month by Stawizki's SS detachment.

Andreas Albrecht Theodor Graf von Bernstorff was born March 6, 1890, in Berlin to a noble family of ambassadors, politicians, and lawyers. His father, also Andreas, was the son of Albrecht Graf von Bernstorff, the eminent Prussian statesman who had served as foreign minister, Prussian ambassador to London, and finally German imperial ambassador until his death in 1873 (*Allgemeine Deutsche Biographie*).

Von Bernstorff was well educated, being chosen as a Rhodes Scholar to Oxford before the First World War. He was employed as a member of the von Ribbentrop Bureau (the Nazi rival to the German Foreign Office) at the German embassy in London from 1923 to 1933, when he was forced, because of his outspoken opposition to the Nazis, to retire from his position. His closest associates in the office were Herbert Mumm von Schwarzenstein and Eduard Brücklmeier. Von Bernstorff could easily have remained in England but chose to return to Mecklenburg, where he became a board member of the longstanding (Jewish-owned) Wassermann Bank (Stockhorst 55). This decision was not looked upon favorably by the National Socialists, who were just coming to power. On June 1, 1940, he was arrested on suspicion of treason after a week-long trip to Switzerland, where he met with ex-chancellor Josef Wirth. It is suspected that a Nazi-sympathizing sister-in-law might have had something to do with his detention, possibly reporting him to the Gestapo for having anti–Nazi sentiments—with an eye on a piece of the von Bernstorff estate. He was soon transferred to Dachau and remained there until September 27 (*Allgemeine Deutsche Biographie*). His sisters and Gräfin Reventlow secured the help of a well-connected lawyer, Carl Langbehn ("Himmler's lawyer"), who met with Himmler,

Heydrich, and SS Obergruppenführer Karl Wolf and negotiated von Bernstorff's release—after a modification of the family's inheritance agreement was signed (Broderskeil and Vollmer 251).

Von Bernstorff went back to his position at Wassermann and managed to stay out of the hands of Gestapo agents (who were watching him closely) until 1943, when he was arrested on July 30 after another trip to Switzerland. By this time the Gestapo had connected him to the Solf and Kreisau circles and their efforts in helping Jews escape the country (Hoffmann, *The History*, 32). Von Bernstorff's close association with known resistance activists Adam von Trott zu Solz and Carl Langbehn was well established by the Gestapo, and that alone would have been enough to warrant his arrest in any case (von Hassell 336).

Von Bernstorff's contribution to the active resistance was his many foreign contacts, which he had secured in his ten years of service in London, as well as his ability to communicate with other members of resistance circles. He maintained contact and shared information with Abwehr agents through Otto Kiep and with other circles through Goerdeler. Members of the Solf Circle were taken into custody on January 12, 1944, and in February 1944, von Bernstorff was transferred to Ravensbrück, where Hanna Solf was being held, and remained there until December 1944. He was then moved to the Moabit Lehrter Strasse Prison complex in Berlin, where others involved in the assassination attempt were being held. Von Bernstorff was interrogated and tortured for weeks and scheduled to be tried by the VGH, but the bombing that killed Judge Freisler delayed his trial indefinitely (Wheeler-Bennett 595). He was executed by the SS on the night of April 23, 1945. Possibly von Ribbentrop ordered the execution because von Bernstorff's name had appeared in an Allied report obtained by his office saying that von Bernstorff would be a member of the post–Hitler government (Hill 223).

Professor Dr. Albrecht Georg Haushofer was born January 7, 1903, one of two sons of Dr. Karl Haushofer and his half-Jewish wife Martha (née Mayer-Doss) (*Allgemeine Deutsche Biographie*; Stockhorst 181). Albrecht Haushofer and Rudolf Hess (who would become Hitler's deputy) became friends and together studied political science under Haushofer's father at Munich University in the early 1920s. Hess was imprisoned along with Hitler at Landsberg Prison after the Beer Hall Putsch in 1923, but the prison had a very liberal visitor policy and Haushofer visited him often, even though he had strong reservations about the embryonic National Socialist Party. Haushofer and Hess stayed friends long after Haushofer graduated from Munich University two years later and had found employment with Germany's Geographic Society. He held his position there until 1940, becoming the editor of the society's journal (Steinbach and Tuchel 89). His job with the society allowed him extensive national and international travel. In 1931, Hess named Haushofer his advisor on foreign affairs, which was a career-making opportunity, notwithstanding Haushofer's personal opinion of the party (Wistrich 100). In his new position, Haushofer functioned as an advocate of German foreign policy throughout Europe, and when war came in 1939, he was heavily involved in trying to negotiate non-aggression agreements with the British and the French. In 1940 he was named professor of geopolitics and political geography at the University of Berlin and taught in Berlin at the Hochschule für Politik (School of Political Science) (Zeller 63). Haushofer was also a member of the International Sciences faculty of Friedrich Wilhelm University, but he remained in close contact with Hess, and in all probability he and his father knew about (or even encouraged) Hess' flight to Scotland on May 10, 1941. According to Albert Speer,

Hitler put the blame for Hess' flight on the corrupting influence of the elder Professor Haushofer (Speer 241).

Because of his close association with Hess, the younger Haushofer came under scrutiny after the Scotland flight, and it was not long before his Jewish ancestry caused him problems. He was arrested in April 1941, though not charged with any crime, and soon released. He was, however, kept under surveillance by the Gestapo. His and his father's protector was in an English prison, and the younger Haushofer soon found his way to conservative resistance circles, where he was involved in plans for a coup and forming a new post–Hitler government (Weiß 187).

After July 20, Haushofer managed to get to Bavaria, but the Gestapo caught up with him in mid–December, and he was arrested and brought back to Berlin. His father was also arrested and sent (without charges or a trial) to the Dachau concentration camp. Haushofer was held in Moabit Lehrter Strasse Prison and, like his father, was never charged or tried. He spent his imprisonment writing sonnets that were only discovered after the war; they remain popular reading (Clifford). Albrecht Haushofer was among those executed near the Moabit prison complex on the night of April 22. His body was discovered by his brother Heinz on May 12. At the time of his death, he had on him a sonnet titled "Schuld" (Guilt). Professor Karl Haushofer was investigated after the war for possible war crimes but was cleared. He and his wife committed suicide on March 10, 1946 (*New York Times*, March 14, 1946, 3). Another source gives the suicide date as March 13 (Wistrich 101).

Dr. Johann (Hans) von Dohnanyi was born January 1, 1902, in Vienna and was the "instigator and guiding spirit of the movement to eliminate the Führer" (Leber 119). His parents were both famous musicians, the Hungarian composer Erno von Dohnanyi and the pianist Elisabeth Kunwald. However, the marriage did not last, and his parents divorced when Hans was young. He grew up in Berlin and went to the same exclusive gymnasium (Grunewald) as Dietrich and Klaus Bonhoeffer.

After his Arbitur, von Dohnanyi studied law in Berlin, receiving a doctorate in 1925 at the young age of 23. His specialty was international law. He married Christine Bonhoeffer, Dietrich's sister, in 1925 after passing his initial state law exam. The couple would have three children: Klaus, Christoph and Barbara. Von Dohnanyi began his career as a legal assistant, working his way into the Reich Ministry of Justice in 1929 as a consultant to several justice ministers. Von Dohnanyi's Jewish ancestry was "corrected" personally by Hitler, and he rose quickly through the ranks, although he was not allowed to join the Nazi party (Koch 252). In 1932 he became the adjutant to the Reichsgerichtspräsident (Prussian court president in this case), Erwin Bumke, and was the chief author of the Prussian legal grievance against the German Reich after Vice Chancellor von Papen's dissolution of the Prussian government earlier in the year (the Preußenschlag). Von Dohnanyi had become a well-respected legal advisor by this time, and his career in government service appeared secure. In 1938 he became the youngest member of the Reich Supreme Court (I. Müller 193).

Hitler's first purge of the ranks, the Night of the Long Knives, was a bellwether for von Dohnanyi, making him fully aware of the lengths to which the Nazis were willing to go to gain absolute control of the government. The murders of Ernst Röhm and the SA leadership are well known, but the purge's victims also included many of those loyal to von Papen and others Hitler believed to be political challengers. Eighty-five people were known to have been murdered, only fifty of whom were Röhm's SA men. Some have estimated the total casualties to be between 150 and 200 (Kershaw 517). This slaughter was enough to drive von Dohnanyi toward the resistance, and as future ammunition against the Nazis, he kept detailed accounts of all the crimes he suspected were being committed by them. He intended to present his evidence to a court that would try the Nazi leadership after a coup. Von Dohnanyi was soon labeled "politically unreliable" and transferred to the court in Leipzig as an advisor, perhaps so that he could be watched more closely.

In 1939, before the invasion of Poland, Hans Oster offered von Dohnanyi a position in the Abwehr. He accepted and found himself surrounded by like-minded resistance members. He was protected in his Abwehr station and was able to aid dozens of Jews in their escape from the Nazis. Under the Enterprise Seven program, he personally arranged for two well-known Jewish Berlin lawyers—Friedrich Arnold and Julius Fliess (and their families)—to escape to Switzerland in 1942.

By early 1943, von Dohnanyi was fully involved in assassination attempts and worked with von Tresckow on his airplane bomb plans for March of that year. Von Dohnanyi was arrested by the Gestapo on April 5 for financial irregularities, which were (unknown to the Gestapo) actually related to his aid of Jews fleeing Germany. Luckily, he had a friend in the judiciary, Karl Sack, who was able to postpone the hearing, but in 1944 von Dohnanyi was re-arrested and sent directly to Sachsenhausen without being formally charged with a crime. He remained there until after July 20, giving the Gestapo an opportunity to discover his name on documents seized from the conspirators (Hoffmann, *The History*, 369). There was nothing to be done for him at this point. Von Dohnanyi tried to delay the proceedings by deliberately making himself ill eating contaminated food brought to him by his wife, but to no avail. He was tried on April 6 at Sachsenhausen by Judge Thorbeck and SS Standartenführer Walter Huppenkothen and sentenced to death. He was executed on or around April 9, 1944 (Hoffmann, *The History*, 530).

Israel has honored Hans von Dohnanyi for his efforts in saving the lives of many Jews during the war and has recognized him as one of the "Righteous Among Nations." A revealing interview with von Dohnanyi's son, Christoph (who is today a well-known German conductor), appears in the October 12, 2013, issue of the *Boston Globe*.

Major General Hans Oster was born August 9, 1887, in Dresden to a devoutly Christian (Calvinist) family; his father was a Protestant minister. He was educated at the Humanistisches Gymnasium zum Heiligen Kreuz (Holy Cross) in Dresden, and after graduation he joined a Saxon artillery regiment (Leber 173). Oster served in the First World War as a General Staff officer and was decorated for bravery.

After the surrender, Oster remained in the military as a member of the Reichswehr until 1932, when he was dismissed as a result of an affair with a fellow officer's wife (spartacus-educational.com/GERoster.htm). He was married to Gertrud Knoop, and the couple would have two sons and a daughter. Soon after the Nazis came to power, Oster was recalled to the military and posted to the Reichswehr Office of Counterintelligence by General Halder, and he was soon promoted to lieutenant colonel. From this position, under the command of General Ferdinand von Bredow, Oster was able to see the danger Hitler posed for Germany. Von Bredow was murdered the day after the Night of the Long Knives, which (with additional details of the operation supplied by Gisevius) put Oster firmly in the resistance clique (Burleigh 679). His first overt action took place in 1938, when he and von Witzleben made plans to arrest or kill Hitler at the Chancellery. "As usual, when something out of the ordinary needed doing, the responsibility fell to Oster"

(Deutsch, *Hitler*, 307). This ambitious attempt is described in detail elsewhere (Parssinen). In 1939 Oster was made chief of the Central Office of Counterintelligence (Department Z) within the Abwehr and promoted to colonel. Unlike others in the resistance at the time, Oster advocated the immediate assassination of Hitler, and he became involved in planning every coup attempt that originated with the Abwehr.

> The so-called Oster Circle was treated inside the Abwehr with suspicion and often with open hostility. The other officers spoke contemptuously of the "civilians" by which they meant not so much the external matter of dress (since most of Oster's men were in military service) as the manner in which we worked together with a challenging disregard for epaulets and stripes [Gisevius, *To the Bitter End*, 425].

In 1940, a year after the Polish attack, Oster informed Bert Sas, a close contact of his (and also the Netherlands' military attaché in Berlin), of the planned invasion of the Low Countries (Fest, *Plotting*, 394). Sas duly reported this information to his superiors in the Dutch government; however, the invasion was postponed more than a dozen times, causing Sas to lose credibility with all concerned.

Oster was promoted to major general in 1941 and made chief of staff of the Office of Foreign Affairs, Counterintelligence Division, of the OKW. Albeit, he was forced to resign in 1943 because of alleged illegal foreign currency dealings, which earned him continued observation by the Gestapo. The foreign currency dealings were a result of his involvement in aiding Jews through Enterprise Seven. Oster was to become president of the Reich Court Martial following the successful assassination of Hitler, and his name appeared on the list found by the Gestapo on July 20 (Hoffmann, *The History*, 369). That was ample reason for arresting him the day after the assassination attempt. He was tortured by the Gestapo into giving up Canaris, but only after activities of the conspiracy were revealed to him that he could not attribute to Olbricht, who was already dead (Mueller 246). Oster was sentenced to death on April 8, 1945, by an SS summary court ordered by Kaltenbrunner and presided over by Otto Thorbeck in the Flossenbürg concentration camp. He was executed the next day (German Resistance Memorial Center; Leber 173). Von Schlabrendorff described Oster as "a man such as God meant men to be—lucid and serene in mind, imperturbable in danger" (von Schlabrendorff, *They Almost Killed*, 15).

Dr. Karl Sack was born June 9, 1896, and as a young adult he studied law in Heidelberg. He began his law career in Hesse and, after establishing his practice, became a judge there, eventually transferring to the military judiciary (Reichskriegsgericht) in 1934. He was married to Wilhelmine Weber, with whom he had two sons (German Resistance Memorial Center). The rapid expansion of the Wehrmacht accelerated Sack's career in the Reich War Ministry, and, as a judge in the Reich Military Court, he was assigned the task of investigating charges against the chief of the army high command, Colonel General Werner von Fritsch, in 1938. He believed von Fritsch to be innocent and was successful in delaying the proceedings (von Schlabrendorff, *The Secret War*, 75). Sack was assisted in his investigations by Oster and von Dohnanyi. Von Fritsch had been falsely accused by the Gestapo of homosexuality in an attempt to discredit him and, by association, the Wehrmacht high command. Sack was able to prove that the accusations were fabricated, but his arguments were ignored. All this drove him toward the resistance, especially Admiral Canaris' group, of which Oster and von Dohnanyi were already members. In the fall of 1942, Sack rose to the high position of judge advocate general of the army, and in this station he was able to misdirect the initial investigation of a number of those who would later be accused of treason, including Nikolaus-Christoph von Halem, Hermann Kaiser, and von Dohnanyi. Sack was at one time considered for the position of minister of justice in a post–Hitler government, but he was replaced in that position by Josef Wirmer by the time of the July 20 coup attempt.

Sack, having the wits of a trained lawyer, was able to postpone the arrest of Admiral Canaris for a short time by convincing Field Marshal Keitel that Himmler was attempting to take over not only the Abwehr but also the entire Wehrmacht (Zimmermann and Jacobsen 255; Dulles 79). In the various plans made earlier for kidnapping Hitler and putting him on trial, Sack was to be in charge of the prosecution. After July 20, he was arrested on August 9 and, on Hitler's direct orders, was executed in the Flossenbürg concentration camp on April 9, 1945. His recognition after the war as a member of the resistance was held up when some questionable rulings he had made while serving as judge advocate general under Hitler became known. Karl Sack is often confused with another (distinctively pro–Nazi) jurist, Alfons Sack; however, the two had nothing in common other than a last name (von Schlabrendorff, *The Secret War*, 155).

Captain Dr. Theodor Strünck was born April 5, 1895 (April 7 according to one source), in Pries and became yet another lawyer to be involved with the resistance (German Resistance Memorial Center; Stockhorst 417). He served in the First World War and, after the armistice, became an insurance broker. He initially supported the National Socialist movement, primarily because of its opposition to the Weimar Republic, but after 1933, when the Nazis took over, he observed the ruthless and illegal tactics they employed in order to get existing laws rewritten. This was enough to drive Strünck toward the opposition (German Resistance Memorial Center). His acquaintance with Hans Oster led him to join the Wehrmacht in 1937 as a reserve officer in the counterintelligence branch of the Office of Foreign Affairs of the Abwehr (Stockhorst 417). He immediately became involved in Oster's resistance work and, through him, met with Goerdeler and offered his support to any coup attempts being planned. Strünck became "the principal courier who carried information and instructions back and forth between Zurich and Berlin" (Hoffmann, *The History*, 237). Gisevius was the conspirators' contact (in Zurich) with Allen Dulles of the American OSS (Hoffmann, *Stauffenberg*, 255).

Strünck was not directly involved in the attempted assassination of July 20, but he did travel with Gisevius from Zurich back to Berlin on July 11 so as to be present in advance of that date (Hoffmann, *The History*, 239). Strünck's documented close association with those who were involved with the coup was enough evidence for the Gestapo to arrest him. In his position in the Foreign Affairs Office, Strünck could have fled under false travel papers, but he chose not to. He and his wife Elisabeth, who was also involved in the resistance, were both arrested on August 1. Strünck was expelled from the Wehrmacht, tried in the VGH on October 10 and sentenced to death. He was not immediately executed, but sent to Flossenbürg concentration camp, where he was tried again, this time by Thorbeck, in a quickly arranged trial, and then executed along with Canaris, Oster, Sack, Gehre, and Bonhoeffer on April 9, 1945 (Hoffmann, *The History*, 530; German Resistance Memorial Center).

If Goerdeler was the intellectual heart of the conspiracy and von Moltke the political, then surely Dietrich Bonhoeffer was the spiritual. He was a prolific writer as well, and his *Ethics* and *The Cost of Discipleship* are still required reading for students of theology at major universities. The cover of the enlarged edition of Bonhoeffer's *Letters and Papers from Prison* contains a quote from William Hamilton of *The Nation* that sums up

Bonhoeffer's enduring relevance: "Bonhoeffer is teaching a few Protestants what it means to say 'yes' to the 20th Century and still somehow stay recognizably Protestant" (quoted on Bonhoeffer, *Letters*, cover).

Dietrich Bonhoeffer and his twin sister Sabine were born February 4, 1906, in Breslau, Silesia. An older brother, Walter, would be killed in the First World War. His sister Christine married Hans von Dohnanyi in 1925, and another sister, Ursula, married Rüdiger Schleicher. In total, there were eight children born to Karl and Paula Bonhoeffer (Bonhoeffer, *The Cost*, xiii). It was expected that Dietrich would follow in his father Karl's footsteps and study psychiatry; however, he chose to study theology and spent a term in Rome when he was only eighteen. He received a doctorate in theology at the University of Berlin in 1927 at the unheard-of age of twenty-one, but Lutheran policy kept him from being ordained immediately because he wasn't yet twenty-five years old. *Sanctorum Communio* (The Communion of Saints) was the title of his dissertation, and it is still widely read (mostly by academics, as it is not light reading by any means). His family was reasonably wealthy, so he had the opportunity to travel, and he spent a year at the Union Theological Seminary in New York (Wistrich 17). Bonhoeffer learned about America by meeting as many people from as many different areas of the country as possible, traveling into the Deep South, where he first heard traditional African-influenced American Negro spiritual music. Bonhoeffer felt an instant connection to his new surroundings: "I heard the Gospel preached in the Negro churches" (quoted in Marsh 101). This was a time in America when a white man attending a Negro church service would have been a rarity anywhere, especially in the South.

Bonhoeffer was ordained a Lutheran pastor in 1931, but he became disillusioned with Lutheran Church liberalism. Within a few years, he, Karl Barth, and Martin Niemöller would found the Confessing Church, which emphasized scripture over the more humanistic Lutheran theology popular at the time. Bonhoeffer never completely broke free of liberal Lutheran theology, but he insisted that the ingrained liberal philosophy of the church ignored the realities of the time. He and Barth were advocates of the so-called neo-orthodox movement in Europe's Protestant regions. Bonhoeffer coauthored *Bethel Confessions* with Hermann Sasse in 1933, and since he was still able to travel freely at that time, he also served as pastor of two Protestant churches in London from 1933 to 1935. Bonhoeffer recognized the coming struggle between the national German church (supported by the Nazi regime) and the Confessing Church. To respond, he turned to scriptures and preached to his followers his confidence in God's final victory. He visited India to learn nonviolent resistance from Mohandas Gandhi and led seminars for other pastors of Confessing churches in Finkenwalde and at the von Blumenthal estate of Groß Schlönwitz, with the encouragement and consent of Albrecht von Blumenthal (the von Stauffenberg brothers' boyhood friend). Bonhoeffer's popularity did not escape the Gestapo, and he was soon prohibited from making any kind of public speech, including preaching at churches and teaching classes. The Confessing Church openly opposed the Nazis' treatment of the Jews, and, while it was small, it nonetheless became a leading voice of the Christian movement against the regime—and the regime took note (Leber, ix).

The year 1939 was a turning point in Bonhoeffer's life. While on a lecture tour in the United States, he could see from a distance exactly what was taking place in Germany. As an incentive to remain in the States, he was offered a professorship at New York City's Union Theological Seminary, but he chose to return to Germany (Leber 217). He soon joined the growing Abwehr military resistance circle planning to assassinate Hitler (Wheeler-Bennett 597). Bonhoeffer's primary interest at the time, however, was contributing to the Abwehr's efforts in helping Jews escape Nazi persecution. He volunteered to launder money used for that purpose, but in April 1943 funds used to help Jews escape to Switzerland were traced back to him. Bonhoeffer was arrested by the Gestapo, charged with conspiracy, and locked up in Berlin's Tegel Prison for a year and a half (Wheeler-Bennett 566). His connection to the Abwehr Circle was not discovered at the time, but after July 20 the connection was made and he was re-arrested, though never arraigned at a formal hearing. At the time of his arrest, Bonhoeffer was engaged to be married to von Schlabrendorff's cousin, Maria von Wedemeyer. He was held in a series of concentration camps and finally sentenced in a Gestapo trial at Flossenbürg on April 8, 1945, three weeks before the Russians occupied Berlin. The next day, he, Canaris, Oster, Sack, Strünck, and Gehre were executed by hanging. All had been tortured by the Gestapo and ridiculed by prison guards before being led naked to the gallows (von Hassell and MacRae 256).

The camp doctor at Flossenbürg was Hermann Fischer-Hüllstrung, and after the war he gave a first-hand account of the execution:

> I was most deeply moved by the way this lovable man prayed, so devout and so certain that God heard his prayer. At the place of execution, he again said a short prayer and then climbed the steps to the gallows, brave and composed. His death ensued after a few seconds. In the almost fifty years that I worked as a doctor, I have hardly ever seen a man die so entirely submissive to the will of God [quoted in Metaxas 532].

Dietrich Bonhoeffer was thirty-nine years old at the time of his death. His genuine moral and religious opposition to the Nazis has never been questioned. He had no political ambitions, and his name never appeared on any list of proposed post–Hitler cabinet members. His life has been well documented, and his letters and papers from prison were published in a series of books by his friend, colleague and biographer, Eberhard Bethge, with *Letters and Papers from Prison* being one of the most widely read.

Captain Ludwig Gehre was born October 5, 1895, in Düsseldorf and grew up with the intention of working in construction, but he soon changed his mind, choosing to make the military his career. He became an officer in the Reichswehr after the First World War and studied the history of warfare, publishing a book on Carl von Clausewitz in 1928: *Die Deutsche Kräfteverteilung Während des Weltkrieges: eine Clausewitzstudie*.

Gehre was drafted into the Abwehr under Canaris at the beginning of the war with Poland, at which time he was promoted to captain. He soon joined the Abwehr resistance group, working with Oster and von Dohnanyi, and was later instrumental in planning the March 1943 assassination attempt by von Tresckow. By this time the Abwehr was being closely watched by the Gestapo, and Oster and von Dohnanyi were arrested in the spring of 1943. Gehre was also involved in an indirect way with the Solf tea party on September 10, 1943: Helmuth Plaas, an Abwehr telephone-tapping expert and conspiracy member, had recorded the entire conversation between the Gestapo agent, Dr. Paul Reckzeh, and his superiors at the SD when Reckzeh made his report on the information he had gathered at the party. Plaas passed on the news to Gehre, who passed it on to von Moltke, so the attendees at the tea party knew almost immediately that the meeting had been compromised (Reitlinger 303). Von Moltke was arrested in January 1944, and Gehre was arrested two months later, but he managed to escape and was hidden for a time by the brothers Hans and Otto John (John 136).

After July 20, the Gestapo stepped up the search for Gehre and cornered him on November 2. In an effort to save himself and his wife from being arrested, Gehre shot and killed his wife and attempted to kill himself, but he was not successful (Steinbach and Tuchel 66). He was badly injured and was afterward held at the Prinz Albrecht Strasse Gestapo headquarters. The intense bombing of February 3, 1945, destroyed the Gestapo headquarters, with Gehre and other prisoners subsequently being sent to Buchenwald, and then Flossenbürg. Gehre was sentenced to death in an SS trial presided over by Thorbeck on April 9. He was hanged that day at Flossenbürg (German Resistance Memorial Center).

Karl Ludwig Freiherr von und zu Guttenberg was born March 22, 1902, into a venerated Franconian monarchist family dating back to the twelfth century (*Allgemeine Deutsche Biographie*). He studied law and history at the University of Munich, graduating in 1929 and marrying Therese Schwarzenberg that same year. The couple would have two daughters and a son.

Before the war, von Guttenberg oversaw the aristocratic publication *White Papers (Weisse Blätter): Journals on History, Tradition and State* beginning in 1934, and the meetings concerning its publication gave rise to a conservative (albeit academic) opposition to the National Socialists. Von Schlabrendorff was an occasional contributor to this periodical (von Schlabrendorff, *Revolt*, 37). Perhaps von Guttenberg's most relevant contribution to the active resistance was his introduction of Goerdeler to von Hassell in 1939.

In 1941, von Guttenberg was drafted into the Abwehr and assigned to the counterintelligence branch. He was on Oster's staff and worked side by side with von Dohnanyi and Delbrück, who by this time were both fully involved in various aspects of the resistance movement (Wachsmann 271). While von Guttenberg is never mentioned as one of the critical members of the resistance, he did provide a valuable link between the military resistance and the nobility, who generally preferred to remain aloof from such matters— that is, until near the end of the war, when the outcome was beyond doubt.

Von Guttenberg was arrested by the Gestapo soon after July 20 and imprisoned at Lehrter Strasse. As a member of the aristocracy, he was particularly abused during his incarceration, but there is no evidence that he revealed any information his captors did not already have. Von Guttenberg was never charged or tried, but he was among those executed by the SS on the night of April 23, 1945 (Steinbach and Tuchel 79).

Ernst Schneppenhorst was born April 19, 1881, in Krefeld, and as a young man he learned the trade of carpentry. During his training he traveled throughout Germany, Austria, Hungary, Italy and Switzerland, finally setting up shop in Nürnberg. He became secretary of the German Woodworkers Association there from 1906 to 1918. Schneppenhorst was also a member of the Bavarian State Parliament for the SPD from 1912 to 1920 and a member of the Reichstag, representing Bavaria for two years, 1932–1933 (German Resistance Memorial Center). During this time, he became interested in optical devices and opened a business manufacturing and marketing his own instruments. He also invented an improved beer tap, which Wilhelm Leuschner's factory produced (Rothfels 91). Schneppenhorst traveled extensively, using the marketing of his inventions as a ruse, while all the time recruiting members to the resistance (Dulles 106). The Nazis confiscated his business soon after they came to power, and he was arrested on dubious charges, being held for a year in 1937—probably because of his connection to labor unions. After he was released, Schneppenhorst became fully involved in resistance activities with Leuschner, which put him in contact with other anti–Nazis in the labor movements. He was arrested again in 1939 and held for a short time. In 1944, after July 20, Schneppenhorst was arrested, like many others, because of his connection to more prominent labor resistance members, not because he had anything to do with the attempted assassination. He was thrown into the Sachsenhausen concentration camp and later moved to the Gestapo prison on Lehrter Strasse. On the night of April 23, 1945, Ernst Schneppenhorst was executed by Stawizki's SS men (Hoffmann, *The History*, 533; Fest, *Plotting*, 320).

Lieutenant General Friedrich von Rabenau was born October 10, 1884, and became a career military officer, serving in the First World War and remaining in the Reichswehr after the surrender. He was married to Eva Kautz, and the couple had two daughters (*Allgemeine Deutsche Biographie*). He was a lifelong student of history and theology, so that when the National Socialists came to power, he had a preconceived impression of where Hitler would eventually lead the nation. In 1936, the chief of the General Staff, Generaloberst Beck, assigned von Rabenau the task of creating the Potsdam army archive out of the old Reicharchive. This was an ideal assignment for him, and he took to the task diligently, eventually writing a book on Hans von Seeckt in 1940 (*Seeckt, aus seinem Leben*). In this book he wrote that a Prussian general never broke his oath, with no idea that he "had completely failed to foresee that a few years later he was himself to be placed before the alternative of either breaking his oath or disobeying the dictates of his conscience" (Goerlitz 438).

Von Rabenau's theological background and Christian beliefs put him at odds with the Nazis early on. He was a trained Rechtsritter (literally, "Knight of Justice," an official interpreter of scripture in practice) in the Order of Saint John. In 1937 von Rabenau signed the damning *Declaration of 96 Protestant Church Leaders against Alfred Rosenberg* (*Die Erklärung der 96 evangelischen Kirchenführer gegen Alfred Rosenberg*) in reply to Rosenberg's anti–Christian *Protestantische Rompilger* (Protestant Pilgrims to Rome). Von Rabenau was a capable verbal tactician and even convinced Himmler to allow him to take over Maria Laach Abbey in Münster after it had been appropriated from Cardinal Clemens von Galen by the Nazis (*Allgemeine Deutsche Biographie*).

Von Rabenau cannot be attached to a particular resistance group, but he had contact with all the major civilian and military circles, often acting as liaison between Beck and Goerdeler. His power of persuasion was tested when he attempted to convince high-ranking officers in the OKW to turn against the Nazi government before Operation Barbarossa was launched, even approaching Commander in Chief von Brauchitsch and General Staff Chief Halder (von Hassell 172). Von Rabenau also tried to win over his long-time friend, Colonel General Heinz Guderian, reminding him that he was already involved and that "in the Third Reich it is not only he who lights the fire that is punished but also he who first reports its outbreak" (quoted in Wheeler-Bennett 647). Apparently, von Rabenau had no fear of speaking openly to higher-ranking officers who had expressed even a passing interest in undoing Hitler, but he was becoming something of a loose cannon and was removed from his office in June 1942, made a general of the artillery in reserve, and then retired permanently.

Von Rabenau returned to his study of theology, enrolling at the University of Berlin, where he wrote a dissertation on military chaplaincy in 1943. This did not mean he was finished with the resistance movement however; that same year he arranged meetings between Goerdeler and Guderian with the hopes that he might yet be able to sway the general. Von Rabenau knew of the plans of July 20, having been sent by Goerdeler to Major General Erwin Jaenecke to convince him to support the pending coup (Ritter 270).

Von Rabenau was arrested soon after the failed attempt. He was never charged or tried but was nonetheless executed at the Flossenbürg concentration camp sometime between April 9 and April 14, 1945 (German Resistance Memorial Center). Another, more definitive date of April 15, with the order coming directly from Gestapo Chief Heinrich Müller, is proposed by Professor Eberhard Dünninger, president of the Bayerischen Staatlichen Bibliotheken, in an article titled "Gefangene des Widerstands" (Prisoners of the Resistance) (see www.bayerischer-wald-verein.de).

The following account of the days after the liberation of the Flossenbürg concentration camp comes from Lieutenant Colonel Leslie A. Thompson, chaplain (retired), formerly of the U.S. 97th Infantry Division. This account was written on January 14, 1989, and a brief excerpt is given below (milewis.wordpress.com/chaplain-leslie-thompson-flossenbuerg/). Only minor grammatical corrections have been made to his text.

> In writing this account, I have had to rely on memory and several snapshots which were given to me by a young soldier who happened to have a camera available. My notes were lost in moving about; and in the closing days of the war, we were moving very fast and I did not have time to make an adequate account of happenings. At the time, I regarded my contacts with Flossenbürg as a normal part of military duty, although the shock of seeing this concentration camp firsthand and the memory of it are unforgettable.
>
> I was the Division chaplain of the 97th Infantry Division, which was in combat near the Czechoslovakian border, later crossing the border to Cheb and Pilsen in Czechoslovakia.
>
> Since retirement from Army service in 1967, I have become interested in reading the books written by and about Dietrich Bonhoeffer. In several of them, I found references to Bonhoeffer having been put to death by hanging in the Flossenbürg concentration camp on April 9, 1945. My interest in this changed from a wartime event to a very personal experience having great significance. A dedicated, widely known Christian pastor had been killed by the Nazi regime. An interesting account of the death of Bonhoeffer is given in the closing chapter of the book *Dietrich Bonhoeffer: Letters and Papers from Prison*. ...
>
> In April 1945, the 97th Division Headquarters moved to Wunsiedel, Germany, and the Division combat teams took up positions along the Czechoslovakian border. Division Rear, the service section of Division headquarters, was located at Weiden. A day or two after arrival at Weiden, the Jewish chaplain of XII Corps visited the chaplain's section. The news had come that a concentration camp had been liberated in our combat area. This was at Flossenbürg, a few miles from Weiden. I regret that I do not remember the chaplain's name. The Jewish chaplain, along with my assistant, Ervin Royse, and I drove to the camp at Flossenbürg. I expected to find some of our troops in charge, but none was there due to the fact that the camp had just been liberated. We found a Jewish lad of about thirteen or fourteen years of age who had been a prisoner. Fortunately, he and our Jewish chaplain spoke in Yiddish, which became our language of contact. Since this young boy seemed to be the only child around, I supposed the German guards had not harmed him. He was nicely dressed and not emaciated like the other prisoners. This young boy became our tour guide. We saw one of the barracks where the prisoners stayed. He told of sleeping on the bare wooden bunks. Sometimes the person sleeping next to him had died in the night. He told us that there were prisoners marked for death by starvation, but in whom the will to live was strong, and these were eliminated by holding their heads under water. He showed us the path from the main buildings where the prisoners had to remove their clothes before walking down a number of steps into a small open area where they had placed the gallows. Near this were buildings in which they stacked the bodies until they had time to burn them. There was a stack of many bodies here. Near this I observed a large cistern-like area with an opening of about six or eight feet in diameter. The furnaces were nearby. Looking down, I saw that it was almost full of small bones. I realized that this was the remains of all the bodies of persons who had been cremated. I

wondered how many thousands of bodies had been cremated in this manner. As I looked down, I prayed that God would have mercy on those who had been so mercilessly treated. ...

Bonhoeffer made a lecture tour in America in 1939. His friends urged that he not return to Germany, but he wanted to return to support the confessing church and the Resistance Movement.

Through his brother-in-law, Hans von Dohnanyi, Bonhoeffer learned of the conspiracy to overthrow the Nazi government, which involved Generals Werner von Fritsch, Ludwig Beck and several prominent government officials. Bonhoeffer came to realize that passive methods were not enough and that it would take an organized resistance movement to free Germany from Hitler and the Nazi Party; so with the encouragement of his sister and brother-in-law, he joined the conspiracy against Hitler.

The Resistance Movement is credited with many attempts on the life of Hitler. One was on March 13, 1943, when General von Tresckow and an aide planted a bomb on Hitler's private plane. The detonator failed and the bomb was discovered. Another attempt was on March 20, 1943. Colonel Rudolf von Gersdorff planned to detonate a bomb close to Hitler at the Zeughaus in Berlin. Hitler left the hall before the bomb exploded. On April 5, 1943, Bonhoeffer with his sister Christel and her husband Hans von Dohnanyi were arrested and thrown into a military prison in Tegel [a Berlin suburb].

The most serious attempt of the resistance group to which Bonhoeffer belonged failed on July 20, 1944. The bomb left Hitler dazed and slightly injured. Five collaborators were executed. In the investigation, implicating documents and interrogations of prisoners under torture indicated a nationwide network. Hitler became convinced of this and gave orders that their trials be prolonged in order that they might find other conspirators. After Tegel, Bonhoeffer was transferred from one Gestapo prison to another in Berlin, Buchenwald, Schonberg, and finally Flossenbürg, and all contact with the outside world was severed.

On Sunday, April 8, 1945, Pastor Bonhoeffer conducted a service of worship. As he ended his last prayer, two men came for him. He spoke to an English officer, "This is the end, but for me it is the beginning of life." The next day, April 9, 1945, he was hanged in Flossenbürg. Among those who died with Bonhoeffer were fellow participants in the Resistance Movement: Admiral Wilhelm Canaris, Major General Hans Oster, Judge Advocate General Karl Sack, Captain Ludwig Gehre, and a man named Strunk [Theodor Strünck]. Also executed on the same day was Bonhoeffer's brother-in-law, Hans von Dohnanyi at Sachsenhausen. It is difficult to understand the persistence of revenge at the time the German armies were falling apart. The allies were rapidly advancing; resistance was crumbling. Huppenkothen, a magistrate, was sent from Berlin with instructions to conduct a summary trial and to execute Canaris, Sack, Oster, Gehre, Strunk and Bonhoeffer, all prisoners in Flossenbürg. The prisoners were ordered to remove their clothing and were led down the steps under the trees to the secluded place of execution. Naked under the scaffold, Bonhoeffer knelt for the last time to pray. Within five minutes, his life was ended. Memorial services for Bonhoeffer were held at Holy Trinity Church in London on July 27, 1945, at the instigation of the Bishop of Chichester. The announcement of this service over the radio was the first word of Bonhoeffer's death that his family had received. Another memorial service was held in Berlin on April 9, 1946.

On Easter Sunday 1953, the pastors of Bavaria unveiled in the church in Flossenbürg a tablet with the simple inscription: "Dietrich Bonhoeffer, a witness of Jesus Christ among his brethren; born February 4, 1906, in Breslau; died April 9, 1945, in Flossenbürg."

This was my brief contact with the liberation of the camp at Flossenbürg. It was a small camp compared to Auschwitz, Dachau or Buchenwald. I do not know how to estimate the number of persons killed there. I would estimate it at several hundred thousand. Auschwitz is estimated as having killed 2,000,000. At one period, 24,000 Jews a day were received for mass slaughter.

After hostilities ended and the 97th Division completed its mission in Czechoslovakia, with the capture of Cheb and Pilsen, the Division was pulled back to Bamberg. At this time one of the regimental chaplains requested that a Jewish soldier be taken to Munich to visit his high school. He had managed to escape and make his way into the United States where he joined the U.S. Army. He had pleasant memories of his high school days. I desired to visit the chaplain of our next higher headquarters (Y Corps) and arranged for Chaplain Edwin Settle, the Jewish soldier whose name I cannot remember, my assistant, Ervin Royse, and me to drive to Munich.

First, we left the young man off at his high school. After a visit at Corps Headquarters, we returned for our passenger. He was disappointed. He had expected a pleasant visit to his school, but especially was he displeased as he met one of the teachers he had known before, and he was a Nazi. We asked him if he wanted to find anyone else. He said he would very much like to visit his former music teacher. We drove him to the residence, and he invited Chaplain Settle and me to go in with him. His music teacher was genuinely glad to see him. They had a pleasant visit. He asked her if she would play the piano for him. She graciously refused, then held up her hands to show us that they were gnarled and twisted. She explained that she had been forced to work in a factory. She then asked her former student to play for her, and she led us into an average sized room in which was a large grand piano. The young man seated himself and played. I listened and thought how the lovely bond of music could reunite two people after all that they had both suffered. It was a moving experience, and I never forgot it.

World War II was an expensive war, as to cost of lives and money. It was more expensive in its damage to the human spirit of mankind. The volume of hatred generated and released in the world affects us even today. Hate used as a political weapon is dangerous to the future of mankind. Somehow, we must learn to use love as an instrument in our lives and relationships. May God forgive us and help us to build our lives. It is the only way. We cannot afford another Holocaust.

Gestapo Interrogations

Regarding the methods employed by the Gestapo in interrogating those involved with the July 20 attempt, there is no shortage of first-hand descriptions of the brutal measures taken, but there were actual regulations regarding how these "sharpened" interrogation techniques (as they were called) were to be applied. Gestapo Chief Heinrich Müller's memo of June 12, 1942, on the subject survived the war (Zimmermann and Jacobsen 190). The original memos (in German) appear in *Proceedings against the Major War Criminals, Nürnberg 1948/49*, vol. 27, 326–27.

1. The sharpened interrogation may only be applied if, on the strength of the preliminary interrogation, it has been ascertained that the prisoner can give information about important facts, connections or plans hostile to the state or the legal system, but does not want to reveal his knowledge, and the latter cannot be obtained by way of inquiries.
2. Under this circumstance, the sharpened interrogation may be applied only against Communists, Marxists, members of the Bible-researcher sect, saboteurs, terrorists, members of the resistance movement, parachute agents, asocial persons, Polish or Soviet persons who refuse to work, or idlers. In all other cases my previous permission is required as a matter of principle.
3. The sharpened interrogation may not be applied in order to induce confessions about a prisoner's own criminal acts. Nor may this means be applied toward persons who have been temporarily delivered by justice for the purpose of further investigation. Once more, exceptions require my previous permission.
4. The sharpening can consist of the following, among other things, according to circumstances: simplest of rations (bread and water), hard bed, dark cell, deprivation of sleep, exhaustion exercises, but also [for] the resort to blows with a stick (in the case of more than 20 blows) a doctor must be present.

The members of the Gestapo made much use of the "among other things" phrase in the last point of the memo. They were also careful not to violate point 3 and would torture a defendant mercilessly to extract information about others involved in the resistance, while refraining from asking questions about the actions of the accused himself (Budde and Lütscher 33).

6

Suicides, Attempted Suicides and Unexplained Deaths

There were a number of suicides among the conspirators after July 20, and one colonel died of his injuries after attempting suicide. The details of the 1944 suicides of Colonel General Ludwig Beck on July 20, Lieutenant Colonel Werner Schrader on July 28, and Field Marshal Rommel on October 14 have already been cited, but there were many more. For some, suicide was the only way to be certain the Gestapo would not extract information from them. One of Canaris' direct subordinates, Colonel Egbert von Bentivegni, chose suicide after July 20 (Manvell and Fraenkel, *The Canaris Conspiracy*, 244). He was the Prussian chief of the Abwehr's Abteilung II in charge of sabotage and subversion up until Canaris was replaced. He and Walter Schellenberg had been instrumental in the arrest of several known Communist agents at a time when von Bentivegni was convinced that the war with Russia would be over within a few months of its beginning (Manvell and Fraenkel, *The Canaris Conspiracy*, 69).

There were also unexplained deaths among resistance supporters *after* the war. Some of the more unfortunate former conspirators were held in Russian custody, often in what had been German concentration camps, and committed suicide or died under mysterious circumstances. Not only the Russians but also most Allied commanders saw all Germans as Nazis first and treated them as such. This included the nobility, who would have nothing to do with the Nazis by the end of the war, and ordinary soldiers who were, for the most part, drafted into service with no choice in the matter.

August Ernst von Borsig was born October 16, 1906, at the von Borsig villa in Berlin (Tegel). The family was well known in Europe, his father Ernst having made his fortune in heavy industry, particularly in producing and then marketing the first German locomotives. His mother was Margaret Gründler. August Ernst was married to Barbara Freiin von Müffling, who was the daughter of Hans Freiherr von Müffling and Annette von Siemens (*Allgemeine Deutsche Biographie*). The senior von Borsig, like many German industrialists, was an early supporter of Hitler, though later he and other industrialists realized that the Nazis would simply nationalize their industries if they did not cooperate. August Ernst and his brother Karl were never taken in by the Nazis, but as members of the wealthy industry elite, they would never have directly participated in insurrection either. August Ernst, however, did join the Kreisau Circle and attended meetings irregularly from 1941, but he was not arrested after July 20 (van Roon 141). The von Borsig name probably kept him from being arrested and likely saved his life. At the end of the war he went back to the family estate and attempted to defend it against Russian invaders, who (apparently not impressed with his nobility) promptly arrested him and occupied the estate. He died under mysterious circumstances on September 30 while being held by the Russians at Landsberg Prison (Wheeler-Bennett 744).

Field Marshal Günther von Kluge was born in Posen on October 30, 1882, into a traditional Prussian military family. As expected of him, he chose the military as a career and was a staff officer in the First World War, participating in the battle at Verdun in 1916. He rose rapidly through the ranks, being promoted to lieutenant general in 1936; the next year he was given command of the 6th Army Group, which he led into Poland in 1939 as the renamed 4th Army (Wistrich 141).

Von Kluge was not mesmerized by Hitler, and did not support his plan of attack on France, but nonetheless followed his orders, leading the 4th Army through the Ardennes. Von Kluge, von Witzleben, von Rundstedt, von Bock, von Brauchitsch, Keitel, Ritter von Leeb, Wilhelm von List, and Walther von Reichenau were the heroes of the attack, and all were promoted to the rank of field marshal by Hitler on July 19, 1940, after France was defeated (Galante and Silianoff 115).

Von Kluge remained the commander of 4th Army, and in July 1941 he led his men in the offensive into Russia. He also took over command of Army Group Center in late 1941, when von Bock retired "because of health," and held both commands until he was severely injured in an automobile accident on October 27, 1943. Von Tresckow was his chief of staff. Von Kluge was aware of von Tresckow's strategy to simply shoot Hitler during a visit to Army Group Center, but he ordered his subordinate to stand down. Although von Kluge was not opposed to anyone doing away with Hitler, he was afraid an assassination would put Himmler in command and further degrade the Wehrmacht's ability (and will) to fight.

Von Kluge's extended recovery was complete by July 1944, and he was put in command of all German forces in the west, replacing von Rundstedt on July 2. This put Rommel's Army Group B under his command as well. Rommel and von Kluge did not see eye to eye, and being made Rommel's superior by Hitler gave von Kluge the opportunity to castigate the field marshal on his lack of faith in the Führer. However, this situation only lasted as long as it took von Kluge to actually visit the fronts, where he learned firsthand that Rommel was correct in his assessment of the overall military situation. After that, von Kluge moved closer to Rommel's opinion that the war was being lost due to Hitler's meddling—particularly his refusal to allow field commanders to respond immediately to circumstances as they developed.

German ground forces moving toward Normandy after the Allied invasion were under constant air attack, which allowed the enemy to break out of the beaches toward Granchiel and Avranches; there was little von Kluge could do. His headquarters was almost destroyed by USAAF fighter-bombers in one sortie (Mitcham, *Rommel's Desert*, 131). Since the beginning of the invasion, Rommel had been trying desperately to slow the Allies' march from the beaches, but their fighter-bombers (and the almost total absence of the Luftwaffe) harassed any relief forces sent to him. On July 17 Rommel was severely wounded by an air attack, and two days later von Kluge took over direct command of Army Group B.

On July 20 von Kluge was in his headquarters in La Roche-Guyon. Carl-Heinrich von Stülpnagel, the commander of German forces in France, along with Cäsar von Hofacker and Dr. Max Horst (a brother-in-law of Speidel) came to von Kluge's headquarters and informed the field marshal of the events taking place in Berlin and of von Stülpnagel's orders to arrest a large number of SS officers in Paris. By that time von Kluge had already learned that Hitler had survived the assassination attempt and refused to provide any support, saying only "Ja—wenn das Schwein tot wäre!" (Yes—if the Pig *were* dead) (quoted in Salewski and Schulze-Wegener 184). General Günther Blumentritt and Eberhard Colonel Finckh had telephoned von Kluge's chief of staff at Army Group B and informed him that Hitler was dead, but an hour later the radio announced that Hitler had survived the attempt, news that was confirmed by telephone from Hitler's headquarters (Speer 114). Von Kluge washed his hands of the event, saying, "Well, gentlemen, the attempt has failed. Everything is over" (quoted in Hart, *The German Generals*, 263).

Von Kluge was replaced by Field Marshal Walther Model (without von Kluge's knowledge) on August 17, and von Kluge was recalled to Berlin for a meeting with Hitler. Thinking that Hitler would immediately have him arrested as a conspirator, he committed suicide on August 19 by taking cyanide near the First World War battlefield at Verdun where he had fought—not far from the place where von Tresckow had committed suicide earlier.

> The unfortunate Kluge was ordered to return at once to Germany, and knowing what the Gestapo no doubt had in store for him (both because of the failure of the attack on Mortain and because of his contacts with some of those responsible for the July 20 assassination attempt against Hitler), he killed himself on the way home [Korda 511].

Von Kluge left Hitler a letter advising him to make peace and put an end to the hopeless struggle. Hitler reportedly handed the letter to Alfred Jodl and commented, "There are strong reasons to suspect that had von Kluge not committed suicide he would have been arrested anyway" (quoted in F. Gilbert 101).

Max Habermann was born March 21, 1885, and became a major labor leader after the First World War. He was married to Anni Stoffers, with whom he had five sons and two daughters. He was affiliated with the German National Union of Shop Assistants and recognized as one of its leaders (Ritter 187). This was a sizeable union of mostly lower-paid salaried employees. Habermann was an early strong supporter of National Socialism, seeing it as a vast improvement over the Weimar Republic's treatment of the people he represented. Even after the Nazis placed restrictions on the unions, he continued his support and believed that the unions would have a place in the new regime—that they would be protected from Jewish business competition (Hamerow 87). Unfortunately for Habermann, his enthusiasm was not rewarded by the National Socialists, who saw him as just another union leader to be eliminated. He was temporarily placed under house arrest without charges in 1933, and by the time he was released, he had no union to represent.

Habermann was well acquainted with other union representatives, and in late 1934 he had multiple meetings with Jakob Kaiser and Wilhelm Leuschner. The three men intended that union leadership would be an integral part of any government after the Nazis were overthrown. Habermann had his say in discussions between Leber, Kaiser, Wirmer, and Goerdeler regarding a post–Hitler government and abetted other members of the resistance, often acting as a courier for them (Hoffmann, *The History*, 391). After July 20, all previous union leaders came under increased scrutiny by the Gestapo, and Habermann was by this time well known to them. He and his wife hid with friends in Bielefeld initially, but the house was destroyed in a bombing raid. He was arrested by the

Gestapo on October 30 and committed suicide the next day in Gifhorn Court Prison because "he did not want to give away those who had given him asylum" (Leber 109).

Dr. Eduard Hamm was born October 16, 1879, in Passau and graduated from St. Stephan Gymnasium in Augsburg. He obtained a law degree from Ludwig Maximilian University in Munich and joined the Bavarian civil service, in due course being appointed minister of trade, transportation, and industry. He was made state secretary of the Reich Chancellery in 1922 (Rothfels 89). Hamm married Maria von Merz in 1907, and the couple would go on to have a son and two daughters.

Chancellor Wilhelm Marx appointed Hamm to his cabinet as minister of economics, and from 1925 to 1933 he was director of the Association of German Chambers of Industries and Trades (Zeller 120). In 1927 he was awarded an honorary doctorate by the University of Erlangen. Hamm was often critical of the Nazis' economic programs; as early as 1939, he saw Germany's fiscal state of affairs as extremely serious (von Hassell 96). After Hitler's appointment as chancellor in 1933, he refused to join the Nazi party and withdrew from politics. He established law offices in Berlin and Munich but maintained contacts with old friends in the resistance, including Otto Gessler, Franz Sperr, and Carl Goerdeler, who planned to appoint Hamm state administrator for Bavaria in the post–Hitler government (Steinbach and Tuchel 83). Hamm had nothing to do with the coup itself, but his name was on Goerdeler's list found after July 20. He was arrested on September 2 and repeatedly interrogated by the Gestapo.

Hamm chose to take his own life a few weeks short of his sixty-fifth birthday rather than face further torture and perhaps implicate others. He jumped from an upper window of the Gestapo prison on Lehrter Strasse on September 23, 1944 (Zeller 120; *Allgemeine Deutsche Biographie* [though the death date is wrong in this source]). Passau and Munich have chosen to honor Hamm by naming streets for him.

Major Georg Conrad Kißling was born July 20, 1893, into a wealthy agricultural family in Silesia (Stockhorst 233). As an adult, he managed the family estate and owned a large brewery. Kißling was married to the noblewoman Alice Freiin von Printz, and the couple produced a daughter and two sons. In 1935 Kißling published a book on the family brewery: *Hundert Jahre Conrad Kißling Bierhandlung, 1835–1935*. He served in the First World War and was a major in the reserves at the beginning of the Second World War while serving as an agricultural advisor to the OKH. Kißling was not a member of any particular resistance circle, but he supported von Stauffenberg and had agreed to become commander for Wehrkreis XXI (Posen) after Hitler's death (Hoffmann, *The History*, 350). When he got news of the failure of the assassination attempt, Kißling escaped arrest by committing suicide on July 22, although one historian says that he was executed on that date (Wheeler-Bennett 747; German Resistance Memorial Center; Stockhorst 233). Since he was certainly not a high-profile conspirator, there would have been no pressing reason for his execution (without a trial) so soon after July 20 even if he had been arrested.

Major Hans Ulrich von Oertzen was born March 6, 1915, in Berlin to a noble family and joined the Reichswehr (following his father Ulrich's example) when he came of age. His family's military history dated back to the seventeenth century (*Allgemeine Deutsche Biographie*). He gained promotions quickly after Hitler came to power due to his training as a General Staff officer. However, "his experiences in Russia changed him" (Zeller 426). Von Oertzen was soon promoted to major and assigned to the General Staff. In 1943 he joined the staff of Army Group Center, where Major General Henning von Tresckow was his direct superior. Under von Tresckow, von Oertzen worked on the Valkyrie plans with von Stauffenberg (who was by this time chief of staff in the Ersatzheer Army Office in Berlin) while trying to recruit those in the Berlin military district to the conspiracy (Wheeler-Bennett 583). He married Ingrid Langenn on March 26, 1944. Von Oertzen was to serve as commander of Wehrkreis III (Berlin) after the coup, and his name appeared on the list of Wehrkreis commanders found by the Gestapo at the Bendlerstrasse on July 20. Von Oertzen passed on the first Valkyrie orders to Paris and Vienna on July 20.

Von Oertzen was arrested immediately after the failed coup and interrogated by General Joachim von Kortzfleisch and Generalleutnant Karl Freiherr von Thüngen, a lukewarm supporter of the resistance—until its failure. Von Oertzen was not directly implicated in the coup and released, but the next day the Gestapo learned that he had previously been seen in the company of von Stauffenberg. That information, along with the Wehrkreis III appointment discovery, was more than sufficient reason to re-arrest him. Von Oertzen had a premonition that he would be picked up again and chose to commit suicide by exploding two grenades shortly before he was to be taken (Fest, *Plotting*, 293). However, that did not stop a Court of Honor from dismissing him from the Wehrmacht on August 14 (Zimmermann and Jacobsen 197). Von Oertzen wrote numerous letters to his wife during the planning of the coup, and many of those have been preserved and published (Kiel).

"Kurt Eugen Gustav Adolf Baron von Plettenberg was born on 31 January 1891 in Bückeburg as the second son of this aristocratic Prussian family" (Schmidt 9). Von Plettenberg would come to study forestry and law at the universities of Lausanne, Kiel, Hannoversch-Münden, Munich, Berlin, and Eberswalde. His education was interrupted by the First World War, in which he served as a first lieutenant in a machine gun company of the Second Garde-Ulanen Regiment and later in Infantry Regiment 408. He was highly decorated during his enlistment, winning the Iron Cross First and Second Class, the Knight's Cross of the Sächsischen Albrechtsordens with Swords, and the Schaumburg-Lippische Military Merit Medal. He was "as much esteemed for his unassuming nobility as his reliability" (Zeller 229). Von Plettenberg was married to Arianne Freiin von Maltzahn, with whom he had two daughters and a son, Karl Wilhelm (German Resistance Memorial Center).

After the war, von Plettenberg served in various government forestry services, becoming chief of the Department of Timber in Stralsund and East Prussia, finally succeeding Albrecht Friedrich Graf von der Schulenburg-Lieberose in the Forestry Department of Agriculture in the province of Brandenberg. In 1934 he was posted to the Office of Forestry of the Greater German Reich, eventually being promoted to Oberlandforstmeister (Steinbach and Tuchel 156). In 1937 he resigned from his position because of his opposition to the Nazis and returned to Bückeburg. Von Plettenberg was nevertheless drafted in 1939 and distinguished himself in service as a battalion leader in the 23rd Infantry Division of the previously cited Infantry Regiment 9 (German Resistance Memorial Center).

Von Plettenberg was heavily involved in planning the July 20 attempt and had regular contact with Claus von Stauffenberg, Johannes Popitz, Ulrich von Hassell, Ludwig Beck, Carl-Hans Graf von Hardenberg and Fabian von Schlabrendorff (Zeller 279). He was not initially implicated in the coup and was not arrested until early March 1945. Knowing that he had been designated to become a member of the new government (Generalforstmeister) and that he would be tortured into divulging information on others, he overpowered his guards and killed himself by jumping out a fourth-floor window of the Gestapo headquarters on Prinz Albrecht Strasse on March 10, 1945 (von Schlabrendorff, *They Almost Killed*, 143; Zeller 368). Two relatives, Walther Graf von Plettenberg-Lenhausen and his daughter Gisela, were held at Buchenwald until the end of the war (Wheeler-Bennett 685). A book has recently been published that includes details of the role of Kurt von Plettenberg in the July 20 assassination attempt (Schmidt).

Major General Henning von Tresckow was born January 10, 1901, in Magdeburg, the younger brother of Gerd von Tresckow. They were children of Hermann von Tresckow, a general under Helmuth von Moltke (the elder), and Marie-Agnes von Zedlitz-Trützschler, who would be among civilians killed during the Polish invasion of 1939. The von Tresckow brothers were also nephews of Field Marshal Fedor von Bock (Pejsa 60; Scheurig 11; Blanke 239; and Moorhouse 236). Henning volunteered for the military at the age of seventeen and served in the last two years of the First World War in his brother's regiment, the 1st Foot Guards, where he was decorated with the Iron Cross (Leber 178; Burleigh 705). He remained in the Reichswehr after the war for two years; then he left to study law. Four years later, he took over management of the family estate, Gut Wartenberg, in the Neumark region; two years later he rejoined the Reichswehr (Wistrich 260). He was married to Erika von Falkenhayn, and the couple had two sons and two daughters. Von Tresckow was not supportive of the Weimar Republic; regardless, he applied for General Staff training and was accepted. He endorsed the National Socialist victory in the elections but turned against the party and joined the resistance after Kristallnacht. Nonetheless, he is one of several conspirators who could have found himself facing war crimes charges had he not committed suicide (Heer and Naumann 127).

Von Tresckow was promoted to major and assigned to the command of Army Group G under General Gerd von Rundstedt in 1939, and he was chasing the British at Dunkirk at the end of May 1940 before he was ordered to stop (Galante and Silianoff 110). He was promoted to lieutenant colonel in 1940 and transferred as first General Staff officer to Army Group B, which in 1941 became Army Group Center prior to the invasion of Russia. In the resistance, von Tresckow was a primary liaison between the military faction and Ludwig Beck and Carl Goerdeler, soon becoming a key figure amid the officers involved in the opposition. He advocated simply "shooting Hitler like a mad dog," or, rather, having someone else shoot Hitler like a mad dog. To that end, he recruited several fellow officers who were willing to do the deed. He was described by Kaltenbrunner, in one of his reports on July 20, as "the driving force and the evil spirit behind the coup attempt" (quoted in Fest, *Plotting*, 398). Von Tresckow continued to gain promotions, and in 1942 he was made a colonel in the General Staff, while continuing to recruit officers for assassination attempts. His most daring attempt was in March 1943, when he, von Schlabrendorff, and von Gersdorff placed the bomb on Hitler's airplane.

Von Tresckow was transferred to the Ersatzheer, based in Berlin, in late July 1943, where he collaborated with von Stauffenberg and others on the Valkyrie plan. This arrangement ended in the fall of 1943 when von Tresckow was transferred to the southern end of the Eastern Front and appointed chief of staff of the 2nd Army, where he later earned a promotion to major general. Being so far removed from Berlin, von Tresckow could not contribute much to the events of July 20, but in communications with von Stauffenberg he continued to encourage attempting the assassination. His cousin, Arnold von Tresckow, was involved with procuring explosives for the job in late 1943. Arnold worked in the OKH in weapons testing and was able to obtain both German and British explosives, which he hid until April or May 1944, when they were requested by Henning (Hoffmann, *The History*, 335). After Henning got news that the coup had failed, he took his own life at the front near Ostrow on July 21, 1944, firing his pistols and exploding a grenade so as to imply a partisan attack. In his last conversation with von Schlabrendorff, having already made up his mind to kill himself, von Tresckow expressed no regrets.

> The whole world will vilify us now, but I am still totally convinced that we did the right thing. Hitler is the archenemy not only of Germany but of the world. When, in few hours' time, I go before God to account for what I have done and left undone, I know I will be able to justify what I did in the struggle against Hitler. God promised Abraham that He would not destroy Sodom if only ten righteous men could be found in the city, and so I hope for our sake God will not destroy Germany. No one among us can complain about dying, for whoever joined our ranks put on the shirt of Nessus. A man's moral worth is established only at the point where he is ready to give his life in defense of his convictions [quoted in Fest, *Plotting*, 289].

Von Tresckow was buried next to his parents, but when his role in the coup became known, his body was disinterred and used in what must have been a macabre scene to try to induce a confession from von Schlabrendorff (who was married to von Tresckow's cousin) (von Schlabrendorff, *They Almost Killed*, 133; Zeller 366).

Lieutenant Colonel Gerd von Tresckow was born March 21, 1899, in Lüben, Silesia, and grew up with his younger brother Henning on the family estate, Gut Wartenberg. He was educated by a private tutor until entering the Realgymnasium Alumnats des Klosters Loccum in Hannoversch-Münden, the same school attended later by Adam von Trott zu Solz. His marriage to Cornelia von Köller would produce two daughters and end in divorce; a second marriage to Erika Gräfin von Schlieffen would lead to three more daughters. His father was a cavalry general in the Imperial Army, and Gerd volunteered for service in the First World War as soon as he could, becoming a lieutenant and commander of the 7th Company of the 2nd Battalion (grenadiers) of the 1st Regiment Foot Guards. He was captured by the British on August 23, 1918, just before the end of the war. After the war (and his release) he remained in the Reichswehr as a member of the famous Infantry Regiment 9.

This von Tresckow was an Oberstleutnant (lieutenant colonel) serving in Italy at the time of the coup of July 20 and had nothing at all to do with it. He, however, confessed to his superior that he had known about the attempt, and at this time that was enough to get him arrested a week later (German Resistance Memorial Center). He was sent to the Lehrter Strasse Gestapo lockup, where he committed suicide on September 6, 1944 (Zeller 147). Another account states that he died as a result of his treatment by the Gestapo after attempting suicide by slitting his wrists (Orth 50).

Lieutenant Colonel Hans-Alexander von Voß (often referred to incorrectly as Albrecht) was born December 13, 1907 and as an adult he became an early member of the military resistance (von Schlabrendorff, *They Almost Killed*, 41). Von Voß was yet another conspirator who came by way of Infantry Regiment 9 (Hoffmann, *The History*, 265). He married Gisela von Stülpnagel, General Joachim von Stülpnagel's daughter, and the couple would have two sons and a daughter (von Schlabrendorff, *The Secret War*, 190). Von Voß was no theoretician, and as early as 1941 he volunteered to kill Hitler himself (Hoffmann, *The History*, 259). Von Witzleben, a personal friend of von Voß, was the commander in chief of all western forces at the time (Steinbach and Tuchel 211). He assigned von Voß the job of maintaining contact for him with others in the military resistance, particularly General Franz Halder. Von Witzleben believed that Halder would support the resistance once Hitler was removed and that he might be convinced to help bring about that event. Von Voß's assignment went beyond simply being a liaison; he was also to keep up the pressure on Halder to commit to the action itself.

In 1943 von Voß was transferred to the Eastern Front as part of Henning von Tresckow's staff in Army Group Center (Steinbach and Tuchel 211). In this position, surrounded by like-minded conspirators, he was involved in all of von Tresckow's plans; nevertheless, he was not immediately implicated in the July 20 coup and saw no urgent reason to escape or hide. He was informed in early November, however, that he would soon be arrested, and he chose to commit suicide on November 8, 1944, in Heinersdorf (Berlin suburb) (German Resistance Memorial Center).

General Eduard Wagner was born April 1, 1894, in Kirchenlamitz, Bavaria, and served in the First World War, being promoted and decorated regularly for his competence and bravery. After the war he remained in the Reichswehr and intended to make the military a career. When the Second World War began, he was already an experienced and respected officer. He was on the front lines during the invasion of Poland and, without qualms, approved of this operation and the subsequent occupation (M. Gilbert 170). Wagner would likely have faced war crimes charges after the war for issuing written orders that condoned the arrest and execution of Polish civilians (Megargee 13).

Wagner was made quartermaster general in 1941 and held that position until his death (German Resistance Memorial Center). This position in the German army is substantially different from similar-sounding ranks in the armies of other countries, as the quartermaster general had to be a high-ranking officer first (and his position had nothing to do with routine supplies, as the rank might imply). In the German army, a Quartiermeister was a noncommissioned officer in charge of anything related to equipment supporting operational planning. A Generalquartiermeister was the most senior officer below an army's chief of staff. The German rank was created by Erich Ludendorff during the First World War. Ludendorff himself was Paul von Hindenburg's quartermaster general when von Hindenburg was appointed chief of the General Staff in 1916. Wagner was subsequently made general of the artillery on August 1, 1943.

Wagner's turn toward the resistance came about after the invasion of Russia, but not immediately (M. Gilbert 242). Hitler's lack of planning for a winter campaign was Wagner's principal reproach. He was a well-experienced and tested officer who saw Hitler as nothing more than an amateur leading the German army to ruin. Later in the war, Wagner's greatest fear was the invasion of Germany by the Russians, and he lived to see Belarus recaptured on the march west. For some implausible reason, he seriously believed that the eradication of the Nazis would convince Stalin to come to even-handed terms, and with this mindset he encouraged von Stauffenberg to follow through with his assassination plans. Yet when von Stauffenberg had the opportunity to explode a bomb in an attempt to kill Hitler on July 15, 1944, it was Wagner who called off the attempt because Himmler was not present (Fest, *Plotting*, 247). Wagner was convinced that both men would have to be eliminated for the coup to be fully successful. On the day of von Stauffenberg's final attempt, Wagner agreed to arrange an airplane to fly von Stauffenberg from Rastenburg back to Berlin after the bomb exploded—and this time he agreed that the bomb would be detonated regardless of whether Himmler was present (Fest, *Plotting*, 253). Wagner telephoned Olbricht after the attempt and the two of them chose to delay further action until verification of Hitler's death was announced. When it was certain that Hitler had survived, Wagner realized that his arrest by the Gestapo was imminent and that he might, under torture, reveal the names of others involved. He committed suicide by shooting himself on July 23, 1944 (Hoffmann, *The History*, 513).

Oberst (Colonel) Siegfried Wagner (not the son, by the same name, of the composer Richard Wagner) was born February 16, 1881, and served throughout the First World War, being regularly promoted and decorated for bravery. After the war, he joined the Stahlhelm association of war veterans, where he was far from alone in his opinion of the coming Nazi takeover of the government (Meyer 376). Wagner was drafted when the Second World War began and served in the AHA (Allgemeines Heeresamt [General Army Office]) and later in the OKW Staff Duties Office. Wagner was picked by the conspirators to be the commander of Wehrkreis XI (Hannover) after the coup of July 20, and his name appeared on the list found by the Gestapo (Steinbach and Tuchel 213). He was of the unshakable opinion that martial law should be declared immediately after the Nazis were removed to give the new government a chance to establish itself. Wagner jumped from his third-floor window in an attempt to commit suicide when the Gestapo showed up at his office to arrest him on July 22. He was not successful in his suicide attempt, but he was badly injured and transferred to the Sachsenhausen concentration camp hospital, where he died on July 26 (www.scrapbookpages.com/Sachsenhausen/MemorialSite/Monument.html).

Arthur Heinrich Ludwig Zarden was born April 27, 1885, in Hamburg to a Jewish family of some means, and as a youth he was able to attend the Wilhelm Gymnasium in Hamburg, passing the Arbitur in 1904. He studied law at several major universities, including Munich, Kiel, and Berlin, passing the examination in law at Rostock in 1909 and his state examination in Hamburg in 1912. His specialty was tax legislation, and he became a certified government assessor in 1912. Zarden was appointed to an administrative position in 1914, and in 1919 he took a position in the German Finance Ministry. He married Edithe Orenstein, the daughter of the well-known Jewish industrialist Benno Orenstein, on July 24, 1920 (*Allgemeine Deutsche Biographie*). The early 1920s were trying times for German finance, as inflation and reparations after World War I had stagnated the economy, but through minimal taxation and creative increases in the debt, Zarden's office was able to contribute extensively to a strengthened national economy. Later, when the economy had indeed improved, Zarden sponsored simplified taxation and the lowering of rates to continue the recovery. He was regularly promoted within the Finance Ministry, finally becoming its state secretary in 1932 on the recommendation of Ludwig von Krosigk, the Reich finance minister (von Hassell 338). Zarden was also a prolific writer, submitting his articles to technical journals and trade magazines, but he never gained the recognition he deserved from his peers as the real intellect behind the economic recovery after the First World War. The Nazis were certainly not about to credit a Jew with contributing to the reemergence of Germany as an economic power.

After the Nazi takeover, Zarden stayed in his position until he was "temporarily retired" in late March 1933. The retirement became permanent the next month with the passage of the Law for the Restoration of the Professional Civil Service, which removed Jews (and often those married to Jews) from civil service positions and prohibited their hiring in the future (Koch 43).

Zarden's role in the resistance came through the Solf Circle, and he was at the famous tea party on September 10, 1943. His comments to the Gestapo spy, Dr. Paul Reckzeh, about the hopelessness of the war were sufficient to ensure his subsequent arrest. He was taken into custody on January 12, 1944, and interrogated by the Gestapo for almost a week. On January 18, Zarden committed suicide by throwing himself through an upper window of the Gestapo headquarters and falling to his death (Wheeler-Bennett 595).

Oberst Wessel Freytag von Loringhoven was born November 10, 1899, in Groß-Born, Courland, to a noble Baltic German family and grew up in Adiamünde, Livonia. After his Arbitur, he joined the military at the very end of World War I, serving in the Baltic-German Army, and after the war he joined the 13th Infantry Regiment of the (newly created) Latvian Army. He left Latvia in 1922 in order to join the German Reichswehr. Von Loringhoven was a fervent supporter of the National Socialists when they came to power in 1933, but the Night of the Long Knives turned him morally against the new government (Jewish Virtual Library). He was not an active member of the resistance, however, until the invasion of Russia, when he was in a position to know details of the systematic massacre of citizens by the Einsatzgruppen and SS following behind the Wehrmacht. Von Loringhoven was married to Elisabeth von Rauch, and the couple ultimately had four sons (Steinbach and Tuchel 61).

Before the war with Poland began, von Loringhoven served with the 4th Prussian Cavalry Regiment and then with the Abwehr's Department 44 under Admiral Canaris. In 1940 he was promoted to major and posted to the General Staff of the 11th Army Corps. In 1943 he was again promoted, this time to colonel, and (on the recommendation of Canaris) was posted to the OKH and made head of the Army Affairs Office (Hoffmann, *The History*, 516). By this time, von Loringhoven had known von Stauffenberg for a period and was aware of his assassination plans. He also had access to explosives and volunteered to procure British bombs from the Abwehr. After July 20, Kaltenbrunner's investigation of the source of the explosives used at Rastenburg led him to von Loringhoven. The Gestapo was sent to arrest him, but he committed suicide at Mauerwald in East Prussia (near Hitler's Wolf's Lair) on July 26 before they could take him (Steinbach and Tuchel 61; Wheeler-Bennett 745). One source gives the date of von Loringhoven's death as July 23 and references a Wehrmacht Personnel Office report (Hoffmann, *The History*, 516). After the suicide, his wife was arrested and imprisoned at Sachsenhausen and his four children were taken away; however, they all survived the war.

Wessel Freytag von Loringhoven's cousin, Bernd Freytag von Loringhoven, was not involved with the conspiracy and, in a rare gesture toward relatives, was not arrested after July 20. He had an unblemished military record and was actually one of the final occupants to leave the Berlin Führerbunker alive at the end of the war. He was subsequently captured by the British, being released soon after the war, and died on February 27, 2007, in Munich (New *York Times*, April 1, 2007).

7

Survivors

Not all of those involved in July 20 and earlier conspiracies were discovered, and not all of those discovered were executed or committed suicide. There were several well-known survivors among the conspirators, as well as their persecutors, and hundreds of lesser-knowns. In fact, there were considerably more survivors than historians usually report. Many of these individuals went on to become public servants or members of the postwar German military; others survived only long enough to die imprisoned by the Allies. A few of the survivors' stories are provided below, but an extensive list of names is available (Zimmermann and Jacobsen 216–19).

Count Fabian von Schlabrendorff and Dr. Josef Müller, both active members of the resistance, survived (although von Schlabrendorff suffered horrendous torture at the hands of the Gestapo). Hjalmar Schacht, Ewald Heinrich von Kleist-Schmenzin, Hans Fritzsche, Navy Commander Sydney Jessen, Ludwig von Hammerstein, Otto John (brother of Hans John), Eugen Gerstenmaier, Hans Bernd Gisevius, Delia Ziegler (Friedrich Olbricht's secretary), Axel von dem Bussche-Streithorst, Jakob Kaiser (cousin of Hermann Kaiser) and Colonel Rudolf-Christoph von Gersdorff also survived. Major Joachim Kuhn survived by (supposedly) defecting to the Russians on July 28, 1944 (Mitcham, *Retreat*, 235). The brothers Erich and Theodor Kordt, who were involved with the plans of von Witzleben and Oster in 1938 and warned the British government about the impending German-Russian Pact of 1939, managed to be out of the country on July 20 and their involvement in the earlier attempt was not discovered (Mommsen 286; Parssinen 277). Erich Kordt testified at the Nürnberg trials on behalf of Nazi state secretary Ernst von Weizsäcker and later became a university professor at Cologne (National Council 345). Theodor Kordt became the Federal Republic of Germany's ambassador to Greece.

In the last days of the war, no one wanted responsibility for the remaining political prisoners. On April 23 all of those in the Moabit Lehrter Strasse Prison were handed over by the Gestapo to the judicial authorities in an effort to wash their hands of any executions or releases yet to come. Plötzensee Prison had already been occupied by the Russians, so there was nothing for the authorities at Lehrter Strasse to do but release their prisoners—or execute them. The execution raid on the prison by the SS in the early morning hours of April 24 has already been cited, and the surviving prisoners were released at 6:00 p.m. on April 25. They included Colonel Otto Armster, Eberhard Bethge, Captain Helmuth Cords, Justus Delbrück, Professor Constantin von Dietze, Friedrich Ernst, Father Friedrich Erxleben, Dr. Maximilian von Hagen, Colonel Kurt Hassel, Dr. Andreas Hermes, Navy Commander Sydney Jessen, Professor Adolf Lampe, Friedrich

Leon, Dr. Fiszel Majnemer, Gustav Noske, Major Oskar Graf von Pilati, Jesco von Puttkamer-Nippoglense, Hans-Joachim von Reclam-Schlee, Professor Gerhard Ritter, Father Augustinus Rösch, Colonel Hans-Joachim von Steinäcker, Dr. Theodor Steltzer, Hans Detlof von Winterfeldt, Willi Wiegand, Berengar von Zastrow, and Friedrich-Carl von Zitzewitz-Muttrin (Hoffmann, *The History*, 533).

An account of the release of the prisoners is given by Pastor Eberhard Bethge:

> My trial was fixed for May 15, 1945 but on Tuesday morning April 24 the few of us left of forty-five political prisoners in the Lehrter Strasse prison noticed that our SS guards had left us and been replaced by the original prison warders who had "normally" been in charge. In some of the cells we discovered SS uniforms, evidently discarded by some of the men who were trying to avoid trouble by changing into mufti. But it took us another 24 hours to persuade the prison guards to let us go, our argument being that once the approaching Russians had arrived, they were likely to hurt them rather than us.
>
> So on Wednesday April 25, in the afternoon, we persuaded them to open the prison gates to us. One could already hear the Russian guns. Some of us were still apprehensive about being made to join a Volkssturm company, but there was no one to conscript us. So we were able to rush home, almost delirious with joy at being free and alive, though we had to run through a hail of shot.
>
> Home for me meant the Marienburger Allee, the Schleichers' house next to the Bonhoeffers. Only one of us had nowhere to go, a Jewish-Russian doctor whom the SS had taken from the concentration camp at Sachsenhausen to do all the most menial chores in the Lehrter Strasse prison. I took him to my mother-in-law's house, little realizing how useful this would turn out to be a few days later, when the Russians started on their brief period of unchecked raping and plundering. It was this Russian who saved us all from any form of molestation when the front engulfed the Marienburger Allee. Of course we had to take shelter in the cellar like everyone else, since the bombardment was still going on. But thanks to our protector, the Russians treated us with every consideration [quoted in Manvell and Fraenkel, *The Canaris Conspiracy*, 244].

Major Dr. Fabian Ludwig Georg Adolf Kurt von Schlabrendorff was born July 1, 1907, in Halle an der Saale and was the son of Carl Ludwig Ewald von Schlabrendorff and Ida Freiin von Stockmar. Fabian von Schlabrendorff married Luitgarde von Bismarck, who had been born in Frankenstein, Schlesien; the couple would have six children, four boys and two girls (German Resistance Memorial Center). Von Schlabrendorff was educated as a lawyer at the University of Halle, graduating in 1932. He then moved to Berlin to become an assistant to State Secretary Herbert von Bismarck, but he resigned soon after Hitler came to power and went into private law practice. By this time he was already a convinced anti–Nazi and sought out those of similar persuasion. He became friends with Ernst Niekisch, who was the editor of *Widerstand* (Resistance), a widely read anti–Nazi periodical. Niekisch was imprisoned by the Nazis for treason in 1937 and sentenced to life at hard labor. He survived and was freed from Brandenburg-Görden Prison by the Russians in 1945 (Stockhorst 308).

Von Schlabrendorff met with several high-ranking political and military leaders early in the Nazi era, including General von Rundstedt, in an attempt to recruit those who could help undermine the Nazis from within, but he didn't find backing for any overt plans. However, his first meeting with Pastor Niemöller was heartening and made him aware of just how widespread the resistance was becoming in the Protestant and Catholic churches. In the summer of 1939 von Schlabrendorff had the opportunity to fly to England and speak frankly with Baron Lloyd and Winston Churchill (Steinbach and Tuchel 172). He made the case for British support of the resistance in order to avert a war that von Schlabrendorff fully expected if Germany invaded Poland—an invasion, he told Baron Lloyd, that was imminent. In October 1939, a month after the beginning of the war, von Schlabrendorff was drafted as a noncommissioned officer and sent to the Siegfried Line near the French border. He remained there until early 1941, when von Tresckow had him transferred to Army Group Center in the east as his adjutant (Jewish Virtual Library). Von Tresckow and von Schlabrendorff soon became close friends, with each contributing opinions regarding how best to involve the military in removing Hitler (von Schlabrendorff, *They Almost Killed*, 29). Von Tresckow was transferred to the southern end of the Russian front in the fall of 1943, and he relied on von Schlabrendorff to be his liaison with Beck, Goerdeler, Oster, and Olbricht in Berlin (Fest, *Plotting*, 396).

Von Schlabrendorff was involved with the March 13, 1943, attempt on Hitler's life (bomb on the aircraft). It was he who set the fuse of the explosive and handed the "cognac" package to Colonel Brandt, who was traveling with Hitler. This was the best-planned attempt (and the most likely to succeed) made up to that point.

Von Schlabrendorff was notified of his imminent arrest on August 17 after the failed coup. He was still on the Eastern Front at the time. During his transport to Berlin, he had ample opportunity to escape but chose not to because of a premonition that he would survive (von Schlabrendorff, *They Almost Killed*, 123). He was locked up in solitary confinement at the Gestapo headquarters on Prinz Albrecht Strasse as soon as he arrived in Berlin, but in the washroom he had the opportunity to get acquainted with others being held there. Among them, he "recognized many familiar faces: Admiral Canaris, General Oster, Count von der Schulenburg, von Hassell, Count Lehndorff, Reichsbank President Schacht, Minister of Finance Popitz, Infantry General Thomas, Colonel General Fromm, Mayor Goerdeler, the lawyers Josef Müller and Langbehn, and Infantry General Alexander Ernst von Falkenhausen" (von Schlabrendorff, *They Almost Killed*, 124). Von Schlabrendorff was tortured for months by the Gestapo, in an attempt to learn of others involved in the coup, before being brought before the VGH in late December. There were five other individuals to be tried, causing his trial to be postponed. The case against him involved his knowledge of the conspiracy, not any actions of his, but von Schlabrendorff knew this would not prevent Judge Freisler from sentencing him to death.

On February 3, 1945, von Schlabrendorff was again brought before the VGH, with Judge Freisler presiding. The trial of Ewald von Kleist-Schmenzin had barely concluded, with Freisler sentencing him to death just before air raid sirens sounded. It would be a massive attack, leaving Freisler dead while still holding von Schlabrendorff's file. Freisler's death no doubt saved von Schlabrendorff's life. His trial was subsequently postponed five more times, but it finally began on March 16, with Judge Crohne, the vice president of the VGH, presiding. Von Schlabrendorff argued that since he had been tortured, which had been outlawed for two hundred years in Germany, he should be acquitted. Surprisingly, Crohne agreed, and the charges against him were dismissed. However, this verdict did not mean he was to be released. Von Schlabrendorff was moved from one concentration camp to another, from Sachsenhausen to Flossenbürg, Dachau, and Innsbruck. In late April he was transferred to Tyrol and joined the 139 "prominent prisoners" transferred from Dachau. They were liberated by the U.S. 5th Army on May 5, or May 4 according to another account (von Schlabrendorff, *They Almost Killed*, 149). At least one historian declares (without reference) that Hitler himself had earlier ordered their executions (Korda 577).

After the war, Fabian von Schlabrendorff became a judge of the Constitutional Court of West Germany from 1967 to 1975. He died on September 3, 1980, in Wiesbaden. During his lifetime he wrote three books: *They Almost Killed Hitler*; *Revolt against Hitler*; and *The Secret War against Hitler*. All three contain essentially the same information.

Ewald Heinrich von Kleist-Schmenzin was born July 10, 1922, at the family estate Gut Schmenzin, near Köslin, Pomerania. His father was Ewald von Kleist-Schmenzin, and both were heavily involved in the July 20 attempt. The older von Kleist-Schmenzin was a self-proclaimed opponent of the Nazis and editor of an anti–Nazi publication, which was swiftly shut down by the Nazis in 1933, chiefly because of a blistering article that von Schlabrendorff had written for it (Hoffmann, *The History*, 20). Out of a sense of tradition, Ewald Heinrich joined the Wehrmacht as an infantry officer at age eighteen in 1940, but what he knew of the Night of the Long Knives murders in 1934 had already turned him against the Nazis. His own father was to have been shot in that purge, but he was warned in time to escape (Hoffmann, *The History*, 20). Ewald Heinrich was almost immediately introduced to the resistance and later was personally recruited by von Stauffenberg. His most famous role, planning to blow Hitler and himself up with grenades during a uniform display, was only part of his overall contribution to the rebellion. He was one of the youngest members (if not the youngest) of the von Stauffenberg circle, but he was nonetheless as serious in his commitment as any of the others—and much more willing to act. He had just turned twenty-two years old when von Stauffenberg's final attempt was made.

Von Kleist-Schmenzin was at the Bendlerblock on July 20, but when questioned after the failed coup, he was able to convince the officers loyal to Hitler that he was not involved, and there was no paper trail connecting him to von Stauffenberg except along official duty lines (Steinbach and Tuchel 113). He was investigated anyway and charges were brought against him, but they were dropped in December by a Court of Honor for lack of evidence. As in many other cases, this decision did not mean that he would be set free. Von Kleist-Schmenzin was sent to Ravensbrück temporarily before being sent to the Eastern Front—probably to die. However, he survived the war in spite of the assignment and became a major publisher in Germany with the Ewald von Kleist Verlag Company. He also maintained an interest in international affairs and in 1962 founded the Wehrkundetagung (Conference on Defense Issues) in Munich, which became an annual event attended by major world leaders. He stepped down as chairman of the conference in 1998. He was living in Munich as of November 19, 2008, and was mentioned as being eighty-six years old in the Dutch newspaper *Algemeen Dagblad* (dated February 7, 2009), making him the last surviving member of the conspiracy. Ewald Heinrich von Kleist-Schmenzin died in Prien am Cheimsee on March 8, 2013 (*The Guardian*, March 15, 2013).

Eberhard Bethge was born August 28, 1909 in Warchau, fifteen kilometers west of Brandenburg, and studied theology after completing his Arbitur. He was one of the students at the now venerated Finkenwalde Seminary, founded by Dietrich Bonhoeffer in Pomerania, before it was closed down by the National Socialists in 1937 and twenty-seven of its students imprisoned. He was perhaps Bonhoeffer's closest friend and married Renate Schleicher, Bonhoeffer's niece, in May 1943 while Bonhoeffer was in prison; a year later the couple named their first child Dietrich. During Bonhoeffer's imprisonment, the two exchanged numerous letters, many of which have been published (Bonhoeffer, *Letters*).

Bethge was drafted into the Wehrmacht during World War II and served most of his time in Italy as a member of the Abwehr (Manvell and Fraenkel, *The Canaris Conspiracy*, 102). He was arrested in von Dohnanyi's house after the July 20 attempt because of his association with Bonhoeffer and imprisoned in Berlin, but he survived until the

Russians liberated him at the end of the war (Hoffmann, *The History*, 533). He continued Bonhoeffer's commitment after the war as pastor for the German-speaking Sydenham church in London that Bonhoeffer had pastored from 1933 to 1935. He was also closely associated with the Evangelical Church of the Rhineland and served as its pastoral college director from 1961 to 1975. Bethge held honorary academic positions at the Chicago Theological Seminary, the Union Theological Seminary (New York), the University of Bonn, and the Harvard School of Divinity, and he regularly gave lectures at each of them for as long as he was physically able.

Bethge was single-handedly responsible for ensuring Bonhoeffer's legacy through the many books he wrote on the young pastor. These are routinely used in religion classes at universities throughout the world and have never been out of print. After Bethge's death on March 18, 2000, his obituary appeared in major newspapers worldwide. An excerpt from one of them is given below:

Obituary appearing in the *Manchester Guardian*, April 3, 2000, by Edwin Robertson

The German theologian Eberhard Bethge, who has died aged 90, subordinated his reputation to that of his friend and colleague Dietrich Bonhoeffer, the Christian anti–Nazi who was hanged in April 1945, a few days before the end of Hitler's reign of terror. He became the editor of Bonhoeffer's works, his biographer and his interpreter to the world.

Born into a Lutheran parsonage in the Saxon town of Warchau, he studied theology in Konigsberg, Berlin, Vienna, Tubingen and Halle-Wittenberg. As a young man, he was a member of the Hitler Youth. But he soon became disillusioned and joined the Confessing church, the Christian movement in Germany that opposed those who accepted the support Hitler promised to subservient churches.

In 1935, Bethge volunteered, as a mature student, to go to the seminary for theological students within the Confessing church. It was there that he first met Bonhoeffer, the seminary's director and just three years his senior. The two men began in a very primitive, empty bible school in Zeist, on the Baltic, later moving to Finkenwalde, near Stettin, and developed a close friendship. When the Gestapo closed the seminary in 1937, Bethge became the student inspector for the scattered student groups, which until 1940 illegally continued their studies throughout Pomerania under Bonhoeffer's direction.

When Bonhoeffer was arrested in 1943, he kept in touch with his friend by smuggled letters—which Bethge preserved. While his friend was in prison, Bethge married Bonhoeffer's niece, Renate Schleicher, and a year later their first child, Dietrich, was born. Bonhoeffer had sent a sermon for their wedding, and now he sent, also from prison by hand of the jailer, a sermon for the child. It was one of Bonhoeffer's most important pieces of writing, condemning his church for fighting only for its own preservation....

The letters that Bonhoeffer wrote to Bethge changed the direction of theology in the western world, and have not been not without significance in Asia, Africa and Latin America. Bethge responded to these letters and stimulated his friend, because they both estimated the real contribution, which the other could make to the advancement of the church in the postwar world.

After his release from jail, Bethge held various positions as student pastor at Humbold University and the technical high school in Berlin. From 1953 until 1961, he was minister to the German-speaking congregation in London, a post which Bonhoeffer had held between 1933 and 1935, and, for the next 15 years, he was director of a pastoral college of the church of the Rhineland in Rengsdorf....

Once the world was awakened to the significance of Bonhoeffer's work, Bethge was in constant demand to lecture and to write, interpreting the theology they had discussed. This was not academic, but relevant to the reconstruction of Germany after its shattering wartime defeat. Bethge's interpretations were enriching. Through him, and the role of his wife, he has taken us beyond Bonhoeffer, enabling us to go on with that discussion the two men longed for.

Bethge's last visit to London was in 1998 for the unveiling of the 10 modern martyrs on the west front of Westminster Abbey—Bonhoeffer among them. Eberhard was surrounded by many grateful theologians and personal friends and family. He was frail but happy and knew, as we did, that that meeting was likely to be our last. We vainly hoped that he would join us in Berlin in August for the international Bonhoeffer conference.

He and Renate had one son and two daughters.

Dr. Theodor Steltzer was born December 17, 1885, to a middle-class family in Schleswig-Holstein. After a basic education, he studied economics and political science at Göttingen and Munich while teaching in various worker education programs (Mommsen 284). He volunteered for service before World War I and served on General Wilhelm Groener's transport staff. After the war he became a civil servant (Landrat) in Rendsburg in 1920. Steltzer was one of the early outspoken detractors of Hitler and his National Socialists, so when they came to power, he was ejected from his civil service position after the Gestapo searched his apartment and found anti–Nazi documents that he had authored. He was later accused of financial embezzlement and treason to justify a formal arrest. The treason charge came about because he had written a letter to the Austrian government reproving all things Nazi. The letter was subsequently leaked to the Gestapo, and even early in the Nazi era this evidence was enough to charge Steltzer with treason. He was held for months but never tried (Dulles 90).

Steltzer managed to stay out of prison after his release and, in 1936, became an official in the Protestant Brotherhood of St. Michael in Marburg. In 1939, like many others, he was recommissioned into the Wehrmacht. With the endorsement of Admiral Canaris, he was eventually promoted to lieutenant colonel on the General Staff of General Franz Friedrich Böhme, the Wehrmacht commander in chief of occupied Norway. Steltzer developed contacts with the Norwegian resistance movement at this time and soon came to know Otto Heinrich von der Gablentz, who introduced him to Helmuth von Moltke, who in turn introduced him to the Kreisau Circle (Dulles 91). In 1941, Steltzer, at great personal risk, was instrumental in organizing the escape of Norwegian and Danish Jews to neutral Sweden.

In 1942 Steltzer attended the first two conferences at Kreisau. He was proposed as a representative of Schleswig-Holstein in the post–Hitler government, but, fortunately for him, his name did not appear on Goerdeler's list found by the Gestapo (Hoffmann, *The History*, 357). After the unsuccessful coup attempt of July 20, Steltzer was called back to Berlin and promptly arrested by the Gestapo for his association with Kreisau. On January 15, 1945, he was sentenced to death by the People's Court, but his Swedish and Norwegian friends petitioned Reichsführer Himmler and the sentence was reduced to seven years' imprisonment (Mommsen 284). Steltzer was, however, released from the Moabit Lehrter Strasse Prison on April 25 when the Russians were overrunning the city. He survived the war, later becoming one of the founders of the Christian Democratic Party (CDU), and he was the regional commissioner of Schleswig-Holstein from 1945 to 1947. Steltzer died October 27, 1967 (German Resistance Memorial Center). His superior in Norway, General Böhme, committed suicide in May 1947 while in prison expecting extradition to Yugoslavia after standing trial in Nürnberg for war crimes.

Josef Müller was born March 27, 1898, in Steinwiesen, Upper Franconia, to a simple Catholic farm family, but he was able to study law after his Arbitur. Upon passing the law examination, he set up a private practice in Munich. Müller became a vocal member of the Bavarian People's Party during the Weimar Republic, and when the National Socialists came to power, he caught their attention by representing a number of people persecuted by them. He was a capable lawyer and often successful in keeping his clients out of prison. The so-called currency and immorality trials of 1935–1936 particularly singled out members of the clergy, and Müller was the lawyer for many of those accused (Westermeyer 139). These trials came after almost three hundred arrests of clergy, charged by the new Nazi government with homosexuality; the purpose being to slander all religious leaders in the press and eliminate them as opposition.

After the beginning of the war with Poland, Müller (with ulterior assistance from Hans Oster) was drafted into the Abwehr and allowed to travel reasonably unrestricted, making several visits to the Vatican on behalf of the resistance (Wheeler-Bennett 490). His primary contact at the Vatican was Cardinal Michael von Faulhaber (Dulles 78). By that time Müller was already well connected with the Catholic resistance movement and other members of the Abwehr resistance. His code name was X, and there are multiple references to him by that name (von Hassell 134; von Klemperer 173). In fact, his real name is never mentioned in period resistance documents. Müller's mission was to open a route of communication between German resistance and the British through the Vatican and to gain assurances from the British, which would hopefully incite the generals to act against Hitler. "On February 1 [1940], give or take a day, Josef Müller brought to Berlin the long awaited British answer on which rested the final hopes of the German Opposition in the Twilight War. On a single sheet of paper in the hand of Father Leiber was what the Pope had dictated to him about the peace Britain would negotiate with a post–Hitler government" (quoted in Deutsch, *The Conspiracy*, 289). This refers to the X-Report, which the Gestapo would find at Zossen after July 20.

Müller was arrested on April 5, 1943, along with Bonhoeffer and von Dohnanyi, and imprisoned at Flossenbürg (Hoffmann, *The History*, 298). He was not executed with them, however, but sent to Niederdorf, South Tyrol, probably by way of Dachau, as one of the 139 "prominent prisoners" (Steinbach and Tuchel 143). Possibly he was kept alive because someone in the Nazi hierarchy believed he would be useful in negotiating with the Allies. The prisoners held there were taken from the custody of the SS by Wehrmacht troops and protected until the arrival of the U.S. 5th Army.

After the war, Müller helped found the Bavarian-based Christian Social Union Party (CSU) as a Christian party hoping to appeal to both Catholics and Protestants, and he was its first chairman, serving from 1946 to 1949. The CSU polled well in the elections of 1946, but the party settled on Hans Ehard as the Bavarian minister instead of Müller. Müller was appointed minister of justice in 1947, and in 1950 he became deputy prime minister. He resigned from all government service in 1952 to become a private citizen. Josef Müller published his biography in 1967 and died in Munich on September 12, 1979 (Jewish Virtual Library; J. Müller).

This Josef Müller is easily confused with a Catholic priest of the same name who had nothing to do with July 20 but was nevertheless sentenced by Freisler to death soon thereafter. The priest was actually in Moabit Lehrter Strasse Prison at the time of the July 20 attempt, having been charged with undermining the war effort. He was beheaded for this offense in Brandenburg-Görden Prison on September 11, 1944: (newsaints.faithweb.com/year/1944.htm#Muller).

Hans Bernd Gisevius was born July 14, 1904, in Arnsberg, Westphalia, and studied law after passing the Arbitur. He was an early convert to National Socialism and joined the Prussian Interior Ministry immediately after the Nazis came to power, being assigned to the Gestapo (Steinbach and Tuchel 70). According to his own story, he did not fit in well and could not tolerate his superior, Rudolf Diels. Gisevius was soon able to effect Diels' reassignment with the help of Artur Nebe, who firmly believed that Diels was a communist and said he had evidence to prove this assertion (Zeller 49). Reitlinger comments, however, that "This is putting too high a valuation on the part played by Gisevius in history. He was ambitious and he was jealous of Diels, whom he had known in his student days at Marburg, but this jealousy served other masters" (Reitlinger 50). Gisevius was dismissed from his office when Himmler was given control of all Reich police functions in 1935 and transferred to the Reich Interior Ministry, but he maintained close contact with Nebe. In any case, Gisevius used his position to collect information on Nazi crimes that he personally observed being committed (Mommsen 297). This he passed on to members of the resistance such as Hans Oster of the Abwehr and Reichsbank president Hjalmar Schacht, who would not be directly involved with the resistance after 1941—although later his lawyer at Nürnberg claimed otherwise (Peterson 340).

Gisevius was drafted into the Abwehr at the beginning of the Second World War and was assigned to the German consulate in Zurich, which was the perfect location for acting as liaison between the American OSS and the Abwehr and for facilitating communication between the Vatican and resistance circles in Germany. He was soon appointed German vice consul to Switzerland and met personally with Allen Dulles of the OSS in 1943. In Zurich, far enough from Berlin, he was able to coordinate meetings between all the major leaders of the German resistance, the Vatican, the British, and the American OSS while maintaining a low profile (Fest, *Plotting*, 385). He retained close contact with Allen Dulles in particular and sent a report to him just a week before July 20 predicting the "dramatic developments" to come in some detail. However, the Allies did nothing with this information. Harold C. Deutsch, an American historian, asked the question "In which Washington waste-basket did these reports end their existence?" (quoted in Rothfels 143).

> It was several weeks [after July 20] before Dulles learned that Gisevius was alive and hiding in Berlin. In fact, Gisevius reported that while the coup had failed, conditions in Germany were very unstable. If the Allies would only "strike hard ... the entire German structure will collapse." But months went by without further word, so Dulles concluded that Gisevius must have been caught and executed. In his later account of the German opposition, Dulles permitted himself a fairly discreet expression of frustration. "Both London and Washington were fully advised beforehand on all the conspirators were attempting to do," he wrote, "but it sometimes seemed that those who determined policy in American and England were making the military task as difficult as possible by uniting all Germans to resist to the bitter end" [quoted in von Hassell and MacRae 232–33].

Gisevius was arrested in Berlin and held briefly for questioning by the Gestapo just before July 20, and he went so far as to go the Bendlerstrasse on July 20 to assist in the coup (Fest, *Plotting*, 385). It is not known exactly what his function was to have been, if indeed he had one. After the attempt, he fled back to Switzerland and went into hiding, thus avoiding arrest, and waited out the end of the war while working on his memoirs. He had little to do with the planning of July 20, but he knew that his involvement in other conspiracy matters would likely be revealed during the investigation. "Gisevius owed his life to the helping hand of Allen Dulles of the American Office of Strategic Services" (Deutsch, *The Conspiracy*, 360).

At the Nürnberg trials Gisevius was an important witness for the prosecution against Reichsmarshal Göring, Wilhelm Keitel, and Ernst Kaltenbrunner, all of who received death sentences. One author suggests, however, that if things had gone differently in

1933–1934, it would have been Gisevius in the dock instead of Kaltenbrunner (Reitlinger 50). He was a witness for the defense in the cases of Schacht and Wilhelm Frick, the former minister of the interior, as well as Karl Hermann, Hans Frank's replacement as Reichsprotektor of Bohemia and Moravia (Frank had replaced Obergruppenführer Reinhard Heydrich after his assassination in May 1942). Gisevius was charged with spying on the Swiss in 1946, but the charges were dropped.

His autobiography, *To the Bitter End* (published in 1946), was the first book of many to be written by survivors after the war—and he intended to be the first. There is always an advantage in telling a story first, even if you do not get it quite right, and Gisevius took full advantage of this fact. This book is an *auto*biography, so a certain amount of bias is to be expected, and the book has received its share of criticism from later historians, but the fact remains that Gisevius was there as the events unfolded and he did live to tell about them. Criticisms include the book's factual errors in names and dates, but that is a minor complaint compared with the criticism Gisevius received for his overall condemnation of the German people after the war and their claim that they did not know the details of the concentration camps and the outrages committed in them. Gisevius, more than any other survivor, has been accused of downplaying the roles of others in the resistance while embellishing his own (Rothfels 55). "The accuracy of numerous points has been disputed on the basis of other sources and of internal evidence" (Gisevius, *Valkyrie*, 7). In the 1950s, he moved briefly to the United States, but he returned to live the rest of his life in Switzerland, married to Gerda Woog, who was his Swiss protector immediately following July 20. Gisevius died February 23, 1974, in Baden-Württemberg, Germany.

Baron Axel Freiherr von dem Bussche-Streithorst was born April 24, 1919, in Braunschweig to an aristocratic Danish mother, Jenny Lassen, and a German father, Georg Clamor Freiherr von dem Bussche. He joined the Wehrmacht in 1937 and would become yet another veteran of Infantry Regiment 9. As a junior officer, he was immediately sent with the regiment to the Eastern Front in Poland (Steinbach and Tuchel 39). Von dem Bussche-Streithorst remained at the front and was promoted regularly, being made a captain by 1942 after receiving the Wound Badge in Gold, the German Cross in Gold, and the Iron Cross (both Second and First Class). In Poland, he was exposed first-hand to the cruel treatment of Jewish civilians by the Einsatzgruppen, which was enough to make him doubt the goals of those in Berlin. On October 5, 1942, he witnessed an SS and Ukrainian soldier massacre of more than five thousand Jewish civilians at the abandoned Dubno airport in western Ukraine (Hoffmann, *The History*, 324). This atrocity turned him permanently to the resistance and caused him to seek out fellow travelers in Army Group Center. They were not difficult to find.

Von dem Bussche-Streithorst was one of the young conspirators who preferred doing something over theorizing. He volunteered his services to von Stauffenberg in a plot to blow up Hitler in the first of the uniform display attempts in November 1943 at Hitler's headquarters near Rastenburg. At this time, he had only recently been introduced to von Stauffenberg by Fritz-Dietlof von der Schulenburg-Tressow (Fest, *Plotting*, 223). An Allied air raid on November 16 destroyed the new uniforms, putting the plan on hold, and von dem Bussche-Streithorst returned to his post at the Russian front on November 18. The event was rescheduled for February 1944, but he was seriously wounded in January, losing a leg (Hoffmann, *The History*, 328). He was awarded the Knight's Cross on March 7 for his sacrifice and bravery (Das-Ritterkreuz).

Von dem Bussche-Streithorst spent months in the Waffen-SS hospital in Lychen and was not at all involved in the events of July 20. The Gestapo never discovered his role in the earlier attempt and he was not arrested with the others. After the war he studied law at Göttingen University and eventually became a diplomat. He served four years (1954–1958) in Washington at the German Embassy (Fest, *Plotting*, 382). After returning to Germany he became involved in education, serving as headmaster of the Schule Schloss Salem boarding school in southern Germany. He married Lady Mildred Camilla Nichola Acheson in 1950. She was a daughter of the 5th Earl of Gosford and an American, Mildred Carter of Virginia. Lady Mildred Camilla had once been married to Hans von Stauffenberg, a cousin of Claus. She and von dem Bussche-Streithorst would have two daughters. He was elected a delegate to the Stockholm UN conference in 1972 and later became an advisor to the World Bank (www.geni.com/people/Axel-von-dem-Bussche-Streithorst/6000000004079761276).

Baron Axel Freiherr von dem Bussche-Streithorst died January 26, 1993, in Bonn. An excerpt from his London obituary is below.

> The first impression of Axel von dem Bussche was of a wounded lion. Everyone who was lucky enough to meet him will remember his physical and intellectual power. Tall, handsome, with piercing blue eyes and a voice like a cello, he made little of his war injuries—he had lost a leg and three fingers of his right hand. He was worldly, amusing and a fine raconteur. The fascination he held for people had something to do with the war record of his early twenties, but it came from the man himself. Children who knew little of the war always voted him the grown-up it was most fun to be with.
>
> With Bussche's death the President of Germany, Richard von Weizsäcker, lost his best friend. The country lost a man who came within hours of changing the course of German history. Yet most contemporary Germans had hardly heard of him. Marion Dunhoff, a friend of Bussche and founder of the great weekly paper *Die Zeit*, wrote: "If you read Axel von dem Bussche's story in the present political climate in Germany it seems like a mythical tale from another era."
>
> Bussche was one of the last surviving members of a group of Wehrmacht officers led by Colonel Claus von Stauffenberg who made a number of attempts on Hitler's life after 1943. What set Bussche apart from the other conspirators was that at the age of 24 he and Stauffenberg planned and tried to execute a suicide mission to blow himself up with Hitler. ...
>
> Not long after, Bussche was wounded and lost his leg. This helped save his life. He was in hospital (with the bomb under his bed until a friend managed to smuggle it out) when Stauffenberg's ADC, Klausing, visited him to warn him of the impending July attempt to kill Hitler. After Stauffenberg's death the visit alerted the SS and he was repeatedly interviewed. But his long hospitalisation and the brave silence of his fellow conspirators made things difficult for them. Bussche always felt guilty for having survived.
>
> Axel von dem Bussche was born in 1919 in Braunschweig to an ancient aristocratic Saxon family. His mother was Danish and much of his childhood was spent on his grandmother's estate in Denmark. His first cousin, Anders Lassen, who fought for the British in the Second World War, was one of the only foreigners ever awarded the VC. After school Bussche joined the army. His regiment, the 9th Infantry, was based in Potsdam and kept alive the spirit and best traditions of the Prussian army: justice, duty, self-esteem, courage. ...
>
> Throughout his life Axel von dem Bussche retained a special affinity for Britain. In 1985 he spent a year at St Antony's College, Oxford, encouraged by English friends to write his memoirs. But he had always wryly maintained that the German Resistance was an overcrowded ship and the idea of writing about it stuck in his throat [*The Independent*, February 20, 1993].

Major General Rudolf-Christoph Freiherr von Gersdorff was born March 27, 1905, in Lüben, Silesia. His father was General Ernst Freiherr von Gersdorff, and his mother was Countess Christine von Dohha-Schlodien (*Allgemeine Deutsche Biographie*). Rudolf-

Christoph joined the Reichswehr as an officer cadet between the world wars in 1923, just as National Socialism was gaining attention. His ancestors had served in the 1st Schlesisches Liebkurassiter Regiment, a famous Silesian cavalry regiment, and von Gersdorff furthered his training in Breslau, this regiment's home.

In 1926 von Gersdorff was promoted to second lieutenant, and in 1934 he married Renata Kracker von Schwartzenfeldt, an heiress to the von Kramsta industrial family. The couple would ultimately have one daughter. He was promoted to Rittmeister (cavalry captain) in 1938 and graduated from the Prussian Military School in Berlin in 1939, just in time to be deployed in the Polish campaign; von Gersdorff later served as a General Staff officer during the French offensive. In 1941 his cousin, Fabian von Schlabrendorff, arranged for him to be detailed to Army Group Center as an intelligence officer liaison with the Abwehr (Burleigh 704). This assignment brought him into contact with the organized military resistance, particularly von Tresckow. He learned of the wholesale shootings of Jews, prisoners, and commissars between June 1941 and May 1942, and von Gersdorff went so far as to include this information as an appendix to the war diary of Army Group Center (Mommsen 248). One historian, however, reports that "Gersdorff himself was formally responsible for the Secret Field Police (Geheim Feldpolizei) which, during October 1942, killed one thousand people, including 133 Jews, in Army Group Center's area" (Burleigh 710). Had this information been available directly after the war, von Gersdorff would likely not have been charged with war crimes, with so many other high-profile cases for Allied prosecutors to choose from, but his later prominence as a member of the resistance would surely have been challenged.

Von Gersdorff agreed to kill Hitler himself after the failure of von Tresckow's attempt on March 13, 1943. This would become the March 21 Zeughaus attempt, where he was to be in charge of the opening ceremonies (Galante and Silianoff 196). Hitler was scheduled to inspect a collection of captured Russian equipment, and von Gersdorff was slated to serve as his technical guide. He set the fuses on bombs he had hidden in his coat as soon as Hitler entered the exhibit. His intent was to grab Hitler and hold him until the bombs exploded, killing them both, but Hitler never got close enough, spending only a few minutes at the display before leaving. Fortunately, von Gersdorff was able to defuse the bombs in a bathroom before they exploded. This was his one and only opportunity, as he was soon transferred back to the Eastern Front (von Schlabrendorff, *The Secret War*, 238). His attempt was never discovered and he was never betrayed to the Gestapo after the arrests following July 20.

In April 1943, while still an Army Group Center intelligence staff officer, von Gersdorff discovered a mass grave containing the bodies of 4,242 executed Polish officers in a forest on Goat Hill near Katyn. The number would increase to more than 20,000 after other killing sites were found. The officers had been murdered on Stalin's orders in 1940 (Burleigh 455). This event has come to be called the "Katyn Massacre," and its true history, including Stalin's involvement, was finally acknowledged by the Soviet Union in 1990.

In mid–1944 von Gersdorff was transferred from the Eastern Front to the Atlantic Wall and became chief of staff in the 7th Army (Fest, *Plotting*, 385). Later that year he earned the Knight's Cross for his work in planning the successful escape of German forces from the Falaise pocket (Das-Ritterkreuz). He had already been awarded the Iron Cross First Class for bravery under fire. Von Gersdorff's role in July 20 was in helping hide the explosives he had received from Wessel Freytag von Loringhoven, procured through the Abwehr, that were to be used by von Stauffenberg. Once again, his involvement was not discovered and he was able to avoid arrest and trial. He was promoted to major general in 1945 before being captured by U.S. forces. He was not released until 1947, and when he tried to join the postwar German Bundeswehr, his service was refused by those in the Adenauer government who did not want to reward a traitor (von Gersdorff 210). Von Gersdorff chose then to dedicate his time to charities, particularly the Order of St. John and the Johanniter Unfall Hilfe (Accident and Humanitarian Aid) organization. He was seriously injured in a riding accident in 1967 that left him a paraplegic for the rest of his life. He was, however, able to write his memoirs ten years after the accident. He was awarded the Großes Verdienstkreuz (German Grand Cross of Merit) in 1979 for his charitable endeavors. Von Gersdorff died January 27, 1980, in Munich.

Dr. Hans Speidel was born in Metzingen on October 28, 1897, and was married to Ruth Stahl; the couple had two daughters and a son. Speidel joined the German army in 1914 at the outbreak of World War I, was soon promoted to second lieutenant, and fought at the Battle of the Somme (German Resistance Memorial Center). After the war he continued to serve in the Reichswehr and was eventually promoted to lieutenant colonel before the war with Poland began. Speidel commanded troops in the French campaign of 1940, becoming chief of staff of the military command there under General Carl-Heinrich von Stülpnagel. He was sent to the 5th Army Corps on the Eastern Front in 1942 as its chief of staff; then, as a major general, he was assigned as the chief of staff of Army Group South in 1943.

In April 1944 Speidel was reassigned and appointed chief of staff to Field Marshal Rommel, the commander of Army Group B, dispensed to defend the French Atlantic coast (Stockhorst 368). By this time, Speidel had already been involved in one plan to do away with Hitler in February 1943. Speidel, along with General der Gebirgstruppen Hubert Lanz and Oberst Hyazinth Graf Strachwitz, had intended to arrest Hitler when he came to visit the troops near Poltava. However, that visit never happened because Army Group B and Field Marshal von Weichs had moved to Saporozhe (Hoffmann, *The History*, 280).

Speidel continued as chief of staff to Field Marshal von Kluge (after Rommel was wounded in an air attack on July 17, 1944) and attempted to involve him in the conspiracy, but von Kluge refused to commit. Speidel was particularly opposed to Hitler's racial laws; however, he did support Germany's expansionist plans. He was suspected of being involved in the events of July 20, though there was little evidence against him. He had not been informed of the planned assassination, but when the coup attempt began to unfold, he tried to persuade von Kluge, at the last minute, to get involved. Speidel was detained by the Gestapo on September 7, 1944, and questioned. He was subsequently ordered to appear before a Court of Honor, which acquitted him of all charges, thus allowing him to avoid an appearance at the People's Court (Wistrich 239). Freisler would likely have sentenced him to death on general principles. However, Speidel was not released but held indefinitely at Gestapo headquarters even though Rommel asked Hitler to have him freed. He was actually released for a short period at the end of the year, only to be re-arrested later with no new charges being brought against him. Speidel was able to escape to southwest Germany a few days before the war ended.

After the war Speidel became a professor of modern history at Tübingen University and in 1950 published a book on Rommel (*Invasion*). He later became involved in creating the new German army (the Bundeswehr) and was made a general in NATO. Had he been expelled from the Wehrmacht by the Court of Honor in 1944, he probably would not have been considered for such a position. He was the commander in chief of all allied ground forces in Central Europe for six years, from 1957 to 1963. Speidel died at Bad Honnef on November 28, 1984 (Wistrich 239). His brother-in-law, Dr. Max Horst, survived the war and also settled in Tübingen, becoming president of the Deutsches Rot Kreuz (the German Red Cross), and was honored with the Verdienstkreuz (German Cross of Merit) for his service to the country. Dr. Hans Speidel has had his detractors, however, and there are politically biased versions of his biography, with a claim that he denounced Rommel to the Gestapo (National Council 205–6).

Dr. Andreas Anton Hubert Hermes was born July 18, 1878, in Cologne. After his Arbitur he studied philosophy and agriculture at the Bonn, Berlin, and Jena universities and taught agriculture for a time. He earned a doctorate in agriculture at Jena University in 1906 and became a respected consultant in the field, being named to the German Ministry of Economics after the First World War. A year later he was appointed minister of food and agriculture. He married Anna Schaller in 1920 and the couple would have three sons and a daughter. (Two of his sons would later be killed in the Second World War.) Hermes served as the chief of the Ministry of Finance from 1921 to 1923; in addition, from 1924 to 1928 he was a member of the Prussian parliament. From 1928 until the Nazi takeover, he was a member of the Reichstag as a representative of the Center Party (*Allgemeine Deutsche Biographie*; Jacobsen 2: 706–7).

Hermes was temporarily imprisoned soon after the Nazis came to power for speaking openly against the new government and he eventually left Germany and his family for Colombia, South America, in 1935. He became an agricultural advisor for that country but returned to Germany when Poland was invaded, immediately joining Goerdeler and other members of the Kreisau Circle in planning for a post–Hitler government. Hermes would likely have become minister of agriculture had the coup succeeded (Zeller 250). By 1943 Hermes was the recognized leader of the conspiracy in the Rhineland and was ultimately arrested by the Gestapo and sent to Moabit Lehrter Strasse Prison, being brought before the VGH on January 11, 1945 (Koch 221). Hermes was sentenced to death, but his wife succeeded in getting his execution postponed and the war ended before the sentence could be carried out. He was among those released from Lehrter Strasse on April 25. Two weeks later the Russians asked him to be in charge of food supplies for Greater Berlin. He agreed but insisted that they provide him with a bicycle (Kuby 303).

Hermes was a founding member of the CDU party in Russian-occupied East Berlin after the war, but he was harassed as much by the Communists as he had been by the Nazis. He eventually left East Berlin for Bad Godesberg and joined the West CDU, becoming a member of the West German Economic Council in 1947 and president of the German Farmers Union. He served that group from 1948 to 1955, and then he retired from politics altogether. Hermes died January 4, 1964, at age eighty-five (German Resistance Memorial Center; *Allgemeine Deutsche Biographie*).

Father Frederick Erxleben was born the son of a baker on January 29, 1883, in Koblenz. There he was educated at the Kaiserin-Augusta Gymnasium and, after graduating, studied music, theology, and philosophy in Trier, Heidelberg, Innsbruck, Vienna, and Rome. After being ordained a priest, he became the pastor of a church in Trier. In the First World War Erxleben served as a chaplain in the Wehrmacht and was twice wounded. After the war, he moved to Berlin and later became a professor of ancient languages at the Jesuit College in Rome and a lecturer in religion at the universities of Vienna and Prague. His association with diplomats and the German upper class led him to the

Solf Circle, and he was present at the Solf tea party (Benz 139; Wheeler-Bennett 594). Paul Reckzeh, the Gestapo spy at the party, described Erxleben to his superiors as a major force behind the resistance in the Solf Circle. Erxleben was arrested in May 1944, along with other members of the circle, and sent to Sachsenhausen, Ravensbrück, and finally Gestapo detention on Berlin's Lehrter Strasse. He was scheduled to be tried in the VGH several times, but the war ended before the trial could take place. He and other prisoners were released on April 25, when the Russians were already inside the city limits (Hoffmann, *The History*, 533). Erxleben had been badly treated by the Gestapo and, when freed, was in no condition to work. After recovering, he became a priest in Müden, where he lived until retiring in 1951. He later moved to Linz and died there on February 9, 1955 (www.arenberg-info.de/htm/Erxleben.htm).

Jakob Kaiser was born February 8, 1888, into a Catholic family in Hammelburg and learned the trade of bookbinding early in his youth. His parents were Johann and Elisabeth (née Zwecker), and he married Therese Mohr in 1918. Kaiser was to be just under Leuschner (who was to be vice chancellor) in the post–Hitler cabinet, which meant his name was no doubt on several lists (Wheeler-Bennett 623).

Kaiser joined the Catholic Trade Union and the Catholic Center Party, where he became active in politics for the first time and grew to be an important union leader during the Weimar Republic. He was repeatedly elected to the governing body of the politically powerful Christian Trade Union for almost ten years, beginning in 1924, until the National Socialists were installed (*Allgemeine Deutsche Biographie*). Soon after that, Kaiser joined the resistance. He was already being watched by the Gestapo for his union activities and was arrested for a short time in 1938. His first contact with organized resistance came when Leuschner was released from the Börgermoor (Emslandlager) concentration camp in 1934. They joined forces with Max Habermann, who was the leader of the German White Collar Workers Union and envisioned the formation of a united trade union in opposition to Hitler. The group wrote multiple petitions to General von Fritsch regarding the treatment of German workers and Jews (Wheeler-Bennett 33). It was about this time that Kaiser met Goerdeler, who led him to the larger resistance groups. Within these groups, Kaiser expounded a monarchy-socialist type government to replace the Nazis. With those views, he and Josef Wirmer soon became Goerdeler's closest political advisors (Fest, *Plotting*, 389).

After July 20, a warrant was issued for Kaiser's arrest, but he evaded the Gestapo by going into hiding. Several of his relatives were arrested and sent to concentration camps, but they survived the war (his wife, his daughter Elisabeth and his wife's brother Josef Mohr and wife, Käthe, among them).

Kaiser became involved in politics again after the war and organized the CDU of East Berlin and the Free German Trade Union Federation in 1946. He was later elected president of the combined East and West Berlin CDU, being popular with the Allies and tolerated for the time being by the Soviets (MacDonogh, *After the Reich*, 265). Within the CDU he was a recognized socialist, but he strongly opposed the German Communist Party and the organizations it supported (Hoffmann, *The History*, 363). Kaiser's socialist ideas were formally made a part of the CDU's platform in 1947. As a reward, his resignation as party chairman was called for by the dominant Communists who had Soviet backing. Nevertheless, his stature was such that he persevered as a member of the party, even serving on its executive committee.

The Communists finally drove Kaiser out of East Berlin altogether in 1948. He moved to West Berlin and joined the West German CDU, along with Dr. Andreas Hermes, where he continued to campaign for the nationalization of major industries. This directly opposed Konrad Adenauer's economic plans, but in spite of that, in 1950 Hermes was elected chairman of the West German CDU and became a member of Adenauer's cabinet, where he served until 1957.

Jakob Kaiser was honored with a state funeral in Berlin after his death on May 7, 1961. His gravesite is among the historic "graves of honor" of that city.

Karl Seitz was born September 4, 1869, into a poor family in Vienna. His father worked in the coal business and died when Karl was only six years old. This event forced the family into poverty, and Karl ultimately grew up in an orphanage. He was a bright student, however, and earned scholarships that funded his educational goal of becoming a teacher. He graduated from the Teachers College of Sankt Pölten (Saint Pölten) and became an elementary school teacher in Vienna in 1888 and a leading Austrian Social Democrat. In 1900 he married Emilie Heindl (*Wiener Zeitung*, February 3, 2000). However, Karl Seitz's unpopular political leanings caused him to be removed from his teaching position in 1897. He turned to politics even more aggressively after that, becoming the Social Democrats' expert on education, and he was soon elected to serve in the Imperial Council and in the Lower Austrian provincial parliament.

After the First World War, as Austria was falling apart, Seitz became the president of the Austrian National Assembly and was a member of the Austrian National Council. On October 30, 1918, Seitz became acting head of state and, after the abdication of Emperor Karl, became acting president. In 1919 he emerged from the political wreckage as president of Austria, a position he held until Austria adopted a formal constitution on October 1, 1920. Seitz then stepped down and was elected mayor of Vienna in 1923. He was an extremely popular mayor and held this position for eleven years. The Nazis arrested Seitz after the Anschluss in 1938 in the general sweep of all Austrian political and union figures. As a warning, he was held for several weeks before being released.

Seitz was to be political advisor to the military Wehrkreis commander in Wehrkreis XVII (Vienna) in a post–Hitler Germany (Zeller 249). Both he and Josef Reither were recommended to Kaiser (unbeknownst to either of them) for this position, and both names appeared on the list found by the Gestapo in the Bendlerstrasse on July 20. Kaiser was arrested by the Gestapo on orders from Oberregierungsrat (Judge) Dr. Rudolf Mildner and Dr. Karl Ebner (deputy chief of the Vienna Gestapo). When he was brought to Berlin from Vienna, Seitz was deposited in the Ravensbrück concentration camp (Hoffmann, *The History*, 470). He was seventy-five years old at the time, but he survived and was released shortly before the end of the war, only to be exiled to the Thuringian town of Plaue. In a strange twist, Seitz was recruited by Kaltenbrunner immediately after the war to lend credence to his short-lived attempt to create a North Austrian government (MacDonogh, *After the Reich*, 308). Seitz's first wife died in 1943 and he married Emma Seidl in 1945. He returned to Vienna in the spring of 1946 and served as the honorary chairman of the Social Democrat Party of Austria and president of the Austrian Red Cross until his death on February 3, 1950. Karl Seitz was buried in a place of honor in Vienna's State Cemetery. His life has been the topic of several doctoral dissertations and books, notably Spitzer's *Karl Seitz: Waisenknabe, Staatsprasident, Burgermeister von Wien.*

Dr. Eugen Gerstenmaier was born August 25, 1906, in Kirchheim-Teck, Württemberg, to a Protestant family of considerable means; his father was a master toolmaker. He married Brigitte von Schmidt in 1941 and the couple would have two sons and a daughter (von Meding 41). Gerstenmaier was an early follower of Hitler and joined the SA (Reitersturm 1/29) in 1929 (National Council 344). After completing his Arbitur in Stuttgart in 1931, he studied theology, literature, and philosophy in Tübingen and Rostock, but not before learning a basic trade (textiles) and working in that field for eight years. According to him, he was an early leader of the university-centered Christian youth movement, which opposed the Nazification of the church. According to another (questionable) source, however, Gerstenmaier was "Office Head in the 'Reich Leadership of the German Student Body' within the National Socialist German Student Federation. Gerstenmaier was a vehement advocate of the 'Führerprinzip' [leader principle] and of Nazism within the Evangelical Church" (National Council 318). In any event, for being a member of the Confessing Church, he was arrested in 1934 on orders from the Nazi governor of Mecklenburg/Lübeck, Friedrich Hildebrandt, and held for a short time in Rostock before being released due to an amnesty declared by President von Hindenburg (Boehm 173). Gerstenmaier's situation was not unique; numerous religious leaders and activists were being rounded up and held for a short time as a warning to them and others that no opposition would be tolerated from any group, even religious ones.

Gerstenmaier continued his education in Rostock University, earning a doctorate in theology, and he was invited by the faculty to remain as an instructor. Unfortunately, this offer was rescinded after his trial lecture at the University of Berlin, as the National Socialist–installed observer of the lecture declared him politically unreliable. Gerstenmaier then found a position in 1936 under Bishop Theodor Heckel in Berlin, within the Division of External Affairs of the German Evangelical Church. He rose to the position of chief of the Ecumenical Office of the church, which allowed him some freedom of movement even after the invasion of Poland, and by the time war broke out, he was familiar with a number of the resistance leaders in Germany and had made additional contacts abroad. His anti–Nazi sentiments and travel opportunities attracted the attention of the Kreisau Circle and he was approached by Werner von Haeften and Adam von Trott zu Solz of the Foreign Ministry, being invited to attend two major meetings of the group (Mommsen 284). Gerstenmaier volunteered his services in communicating messages outside Germany using the church's international connections. The Gestapo, however, also knew of Gerstenmaier's extracurricular activities.

Gerstenmaier was actively involved in planning for the post-coup recovery of Germany, but he was not involved in the July 20 attempt on Hitler's life (or those leading up to it), though he made it clear that he was in favor of assassination (Hoffmann, *The History*, 371). After several publicized arrests in early 1944, including those of von Moltke and Wilhelm Bachmann (secretary of the Evangelical Welfare Association), Gerstenmaier knew that he was in danger himself and disappeared into the province of Carinthia in Austria. He was aware of the von Stauffenberg plan and its delays; yet, despite the risks, he chose to return to Berlin with his wife, arriving at 3:00 a.m. on July 20 at Peter Yorck von Wartenburg's house, where he learned that Reichwein and Leber had already been arrested and that there was a new warrant issued for his arrest as well (Boehm 184). Von Wartenburg left a few hours later for the War Ministry on Bendlerstrasse, leaving Gerstenmaier at his house. Shortly after 5:00 p.m. that day, he called Gerstenmaier and told him to come to the Bendlerblock headquarters. Gerstenmaier observed the collapse of the coup first-hand and was arrested that night, barely missing being executed (Dulles 194).

Gerstenmaier, von Moltke, Father Delp, Haubach, and Steltzer were tried by the

VGH on January 11, 1945, with Judge Freisler presiding. All were charged with treason. The others were sentenced to death, but Gerstenmaier succeeded in defending himself and was sentenced to seven years in prison, in spite of the Gestapo recommendation of death. Gerstenmaier was sent to Bayreuth Prison, which was liberated by American troops a few weeks later. Immediately after the war he became head of the Protestant Church Aid Center in Stuttgart and later a leader of the CDU. He was elected president of the West German Parliament (Bundestag) and served from 1954 to 1969 (Fest, *Plotting*, 385). Gerstenmaier died March 13, 1986, in Bonn.

General Georg R. Thomas was born February 20, 1890, the son of a factory owner in Forst Brandenburg, and he joined the military as soon as he was of age, becoming an ensign in Infantry Regiment 63 in 1908. As a young officer, Thomas served in World War I and was promoted and decorated for his bravery and proficiency (German Resistance Memorial Center). After the war he remained in the Reichswehr, intending to make the military his career. He was posted to the Armaments Office of the OKH in Berlin in 1928, which was his first exposure to the inner workings of the military. This job was primarily technical, but it also involved working with other branches of the military on common weapons used by all the services. Thomas was regularly promoted, and in 1939 he became chief of the Defence Economy and Armament Office in the OKW (Deutsch, *The Conspiracy*, 26). Along the way, Thomas had also gained membership on the boards of directors of Continental Oil and the Reichswerke Hermann Göring (iron and steel works).

Thomas was promoted to general of the infantry in 1940. One historian makes the following observation regarding the general officers and their division of loyalty to the regime and to God: "A few, a very few, of the senior officers saw this division of loyalties clearly from 1938 onwards. Ludwig Beck, Kurt von Hammerstein-Equord, Erwin von Witzleben, Carl-Heinrich von Stülpnagel, Erich Hoepner, Georg Thomas and Wilhelm Adam—these names may be remembered" (Wheeler-Bennett 395). Conversely, there are historians who believe that Thomas should be better remembered for his deeply held belief in plundering Russia with no regard for the hardships civilians would endure (Tooze 479).

Thomas recognized early on that military strength depended on economic strength, and he believed Hitler was in the process of destroying both. After the defeat of Poland, he recorded his economic concerns in a memo to Wilhelm Keitel, but it's not likely that Hitler ever saw it (Hoffmann, *The History*, 110). Thomas still maintained contact with his former chief, Colonel General Beck, who made certain as early as 1938 that Thomas was kept informed by Goerdeler and Popitz regarding any plans for a coup. Thomas, however, was not in favor of an assassination, arguing that killing Hitler would make him a martyr in the eyes of many Germans. This would, he believed, be worse than total defeat (Dulles 68). Thomas tried on several occasions to arrange a meeting between Keitel and Goerdeler before the war began, but each time Keitel refused, saying that Hitler was a genius and that there would be no war (Goerlitz 345).

By late 1942 Speer's Armament Ministry had taken over most of the duties that Thomas had been responsible for, so he resigned from the Defence Economy and Armament Office. After July 20, the 1938–1940 papers of Goerdeler and Popitz were found and Thomas' name appeared in many of them. He was arrested on October 11, 1944, and sent to the Flossenbürg and Dachau concentration camps. In late April 1945, when the Allies were getting close to the camps, he was moved to Tyrol as one of the 139 "prominent prisoners" (MacDonogh, *After the Reich*, 82). Thomas was interrogated after the war by the American Captain Nordon at the Reservelazarette (reserve hospital) Falkenhaus in Taunus on November 9, 1945 and died of unnamed causes in Allied custody (at a Frankfurt hospital) on December 29, 1946 (Mitcham, "Hitler's Commanders," 20). Another source gives the date as October 29, 1946 (Peter 255).

Ewald Oskar Ludwig Loeser was born April 11, 1888, in Storkow, Brandenburg, and was educated as a lawyer, receiving a doctorate from Göttingen University in 1911. He was married to Ilse Thies and served as deputy mayor and treasurer of Leipzig under Carl Goerdeler from 1930 to 1934. Undoubtedly it was Goerdeler who initially turned Loeser toward the resistance.

Loeser was not drafted into the military during World War II, but he served as a representative for German businesses owned by the Dutch conglomerate Philips (German Resistance Memorial Center). He was later also on the board of directors of Krupp Steel from 1934 (thanks to Goerdeler's recommendation) and the Dresdner Bank from 1939. By 1943 Loeser was heavily involved in Goerdeler's resistance group and was to become the minister of either finance or economics in post–Hitler Germany (Dulles 181; Hoffmann, *The History*, 369). Soon after the failed attempt of July 20, he was arrested by the Gestapo, though he was not tried in the People's Court until January 17, 1945. Loeser's amnesia act in court was skillful enough to get him sent to a sanatorium in Wittenau for treatment, where he remained until the end of the war.

Loeser found himself in court again after the war, positioned on the wrong side of the table in the postwar trial of German industrialists because of his seat on the Krupp board of directors. The trial ran from late 1947 through mid–1948 and involved German firms that had aided the war effort—and profited considerably from it. Alfred Krupp von Bohlen und Halbach, the son of Gustav von Bohlen und Halbach, was sentenced to twelve years and relieved of all his personal property (MacDonogh, *After the Reich*, 454). Loeser was sentenced to seven years and served all of them, being released in 1955. He died December 23, 1970.

General Franz Halder was born June 30, 1884, in Würzburg into a Catholic military family. His father was General Max Halder. At eighteen, he joined the 3rd Royal Bavarian Field Artillery Regiment in Munich and was promoted to lieutenant in 1904. He graduated from military training schools in Munich: the Artillery School in 1907 and the Bavarian Staff College in 1914. General Halder is included in this account of those who survived the aftermath of the July 20 attempt because he was suspected of being involved, even though he was not. However, Halder was involved with several of the early attempts and was arrested by the Gestapo soon after July 20 during the general roundup of suspects. He was never tried for any crime against the Reich (World War II Database).

In World War I, Halder became an ordnance officer in the Bavarian 3rd Army Corps, and in August 1915 he was promoted to Hauptmann (captain) on the General Staff of Bavaria's 6th Infantry Division. He served as a General Staff officer of the 2nd Army Headquarters in 1917 and was finally transferred to the 4th Army, where he served until the end of the war (Wistrich 95).

After the war, Halder volunteered for the Reichswehr and served in the War Ministry Training Office until 1920. For the next two years he was a military instructor in Munich, being promoted to major in 1926 and becoming the Oberquartiermeister (chief quartermaster) of operations on the General Staff of Wehrkreis VII in Munich. In February 1929 he was promoted to Oberstleutnant and from October of that year through 1931 he served on the training staff of the Reichswehr Ministry. He was promoted to colonel in December

1931 and became chief of staff of Wehrkreis VI in Westphalia. Other promotions came soon, and by mid–1936 Halder had become a Generalleutnant (lieutenant general); the next year he became the quartermaster of training on the General Staff of the army in Berlin. As a traditional German officer, Halder was not impressed with Hitler's SA and frequently found reasons to report their lack of respect for the customary military chain of command (Goerlitz 284).

Halder was made General der Artillerie on February 1, 1938, during the time that General Keitel was being tasked by Hitler with restructuring the leadership of the entire German army. As a result, Keitel asked Halder to become the chief of the General Staff, reporting directly to General Walther von Reichenau. This would have been an excellent opportunity for Halder, but he did not get along well with von Reichenau and did not care to be his subordinate. The problem was solved when Keitel convinced Hitler to appoint General Walther von Brauchitsch as commander in chief of the army. Halder then accepted Keitel's offer to become chief of the General Staff of the army, replacing General Ludwig Beck on September 1, 1938 (Goerlitz 330).

Early in this assignment, Halder created plans for invading Czechoslovakia, with Hitler modifying the plans to add von Reichenau as the general to take the lead into Prague, but these proposals were all abandoned following the Munich Agreement between Hitler and Chamberlain. Previously, Halder discussed with several other generals how Hitler could be removed, but the agreement made him drop the idea for the time being. Halder later worked on the plans for invading Poland and, after the invasion began, wrote in his diary that Heydrich was beginning to cleanse Poland of all Jews. This note, indicating that he knew of Hitler's plans for the Jews, would haunt Halder in postwar inquiries, but it never led to war crimes charges.

In November 1939 Halder approached von Brauchitsch, declaring that he would have his support if he acted against Hitler's expansion of the war, but von Brauchitsch promised nothing. "A department for 'special employment' headed by Lieutenant Colonel [Helmuth] Groscurth was entrusted by Halder and Canaris in the winter of 1939 with working up the existing plan for a coup" (quoted in Rothfels 72). Halder strongly opposed expanding the war, but he, like the rest, had sworn an oath and could not take action against the legally elected leader of the country, although it is reported that he often carried a loaded pistol with him with the intention of shooting Hitler himself (Frieser and Greenwood 58).

In late 1939 Halder supervised the development of Hitler's invasion plan for France, the Low Countries and the Balkans. The success of the invasion led to Halder's promotion to Generaloberst (colonel general) on July 19, 1940. Halder was rapidly becoming Germany's best-known general and popular in unlikely places, even appearing on the cover of the June 29, 1942, issue of *Time* magazine. His popularity and strategic planning skills both pleased and worried Hitler, who was always looking over his shoulder for intrigue. Perhaps Halder was bolstered by his newfound success and popularity, because in the summer of 1942, after the invasion of Russia, he told Hitler plainly that he was underestimating the new enemy and went on to denigrate the attack on Leningrad and the incursions into the Caucasus. This was enough for Hitler, who decided that Halder no longer had the personal ambition required to lead. Halder was forced into retirement (into the Führer Reserve) on September 24, 1942. "Half my exhaustion is due to you," Hitler said to him. "It is not worthwhile going on" (quoted in Hughes and Mann 128).

On June 21, 1944, Halder was arrested by the Gestapo even though he was not involved in the coup attempt of July 20 and there was no hard evidence against him. It was a good excuse in any case for Hitler to get rid of someone he thought capable of replacing him. Halder was held at both the Flossenbürg and the Dachau concentration camps, and on January 31, 1945, he was dismissed from the Wehrmacht, perhaps with the expectation of hauling him before the People's Court later. Eventually Halder was transferred to Tyrol, where he was liberated by U.S. 5th Army troops on May 5 as one of the 139 "prominent prisoners" (historywarsweapons.com/franz-halder/). He would spend the next two years in a prisoner-of-war camp, but he was alive and Hitler was not. He was awarded the U.S. Meritorious Civilian Service Award in 1961 for his accomplishments while working with the U.S. Army Historical Division. General Halder died at age eighty-seven on April 2, 1972, in Aschau, Germany.

Over the years Halder has had his detractors—and he is not universally praised today. "As Chief of the German General Staff, Halder had played a delicate and dangerous balancing game. Although his cautious nature probably saved his life, the accumulation of disobedience and deceit was fatal to German strategy and the conduct of the war" (Komar).

Gustav Dahrendorf was born February 8, 1901, in Hamburg and was one of the Social Democrats elected to the Reichstag in 1932 (Mommsen 296). He was married to Lina Maria Sörnsen, and the couple would have two sons, Ralf and Franz. When the Nazis came to power, Dahrendorf, like many of his fellow Social Democrats in leadership positions, was arrested multiple times on fabricated charges. Dahrendorf was a businessman involved in the wholesale trade and transportation of diesel fuel and gasoline—critical materiél for the growing military. His business travels allowed him to maintain contact with fellow Social Democrats like Julius Leber, Carlo Mierendorff, and Wilhelm Leuschner. Dahrendorf would go on to publish Leber's papers after the war (Ritter 200). Dahrendorf maintained contact with those close to Ludwig Beck and Carl Goerdeler and contributed to their coup plans by passing on information to other resistance groups. Leber proposed him as political representative for Wehrkreis X (Hamburg), and his name was on the list found by the Gestapo. However, the investigators weren't convinced that those named on the list always knew of their appointment—which probably saved Dahrendorf's life (Hoffmann, *The History*, 357). Nevertheless, after July 20, he was arrested by the Gestapo and tried on October 20 by the VGH. His co-defendants were Julius Leber, Adolf Reichwein, and Hermann Maaß, who were all found guilty and sentenced to death.

Dahrendorf was sentenced to seven years' imprisonment and was an inmate in the Brandenburg-Görden Prison until it was liberated by the Russians. After the war he once again became politically active, speaking out against the forced merger of the Social Democratic Party and the Communist Party in the Russian zone (MacDonogh, *After the Reich*, 266). He soon discovered the Communists were no more open to conciliation than the Nazis had been. He escaped to Hamburg and never looked back. Dahrendorf died October 30, 1954 in Braunlage.

Cavalry Captain Eberhard von Breitenbuch was born July 20, 1910, in Dietzhausen, Thuringia. He was a reserve cavalry captain in Army Group Center and an aide to field marshals Erwin von Witzleben, Ernst Busch, and Günther von Kluge (Hoffmann, *The History*, 266). Von Tresckow arranged the von Kluge appointment in August 1943 so that von Breitenbuch could attempt to strengthen von Kluge's leanings toward the resistance.

Von Breitenbuch became an aide to Busch after von Kluge was seriously injured in an automobile accident on October 27, 1943. His single assassination attempt on March 9, 1944, has already been mentioned. Even at this late date, there were a few opportunities for members of the resistance to get close enough to Hitler with a pistol to simply shoot him, which was von Breitenbuch's plan (Hoffmann, *The History*, 331). He had nothing else to do with coups, and his role in that one was never discovered, nor was he implicated during the investigations after July 20. After the war he worked in forestry management and died on September 21, 1980, in Göttingen.

Father Augustinus Rösch was born May 11, 1893, to Catholic parents, Philipp and Franziska (née Auböck), in Schwandorf, Upper Franconia. He joined the Jesuit order, the Novitiate of the Society of Jesus, in Tisis, Austria, in 1912 after completing his Arbitur. He was drafted into the military in 1914 after finishing his novitiate and served in World War I (*Allgemeine Deutsche Biographie*). Rösch earned the Iron Cross First Class, the Bavarian Military Service Order, and the Silver Wound Badge. After the war he studied theology in Valkenburg (near the Dutch border) and was ordained a priest in 1925. In 1928 he accepted a position at Stella Matutina, the Jesuit school in Feldkirch, Austria (where Father Delp would be in residence), later becoming its rector. From 1935 to 1944 he was provincial of the Jesuits' Upper German Province in Munich (Rothfels 110).

When the Nazis began their persecution of the Jesuits, soon after taking control of the government, Rösch became a visible antagonist. He was an outspoken proponent of religious independence and was regularly dragged in for questioning by the Gestapo. He met von Moltke in 1941 and introduced Father Delp to Kreisau Circle members shortly afterward (Steinbach and Tuchel 164). Von Moltke sought the aid of these two Catholic priests leading the circle's effort to advocate for a post–Hitler German government based on fundamental Christian values. Rösch and Delp agreed to help and acted as contacts for Catholic opposition groups throughout Germany. Rösch also advised members of the Kreisau Circle on how to survive arrest and interrogation (Fest, *Plotting*, 158). He managed to evade the Gestapo after July 20, but when Father Delp was arrested, he knew that he would eventually be caught. After his arrest on January 11, 1945, Rösch was held first at Dachau and then interrogated at the Moabit Lehrter Strasse Prison in Berlin. By April 25, more than a million Russians were advancing toward the city center, which likely influenced the decision to release him on that date. Rösch made his way to Munich two months later. Having survived the war, he became the permanent director of the Bavarian Caritas (the Catholic Social Justice Agency) and died in Munich on November 7, 1961 (German Resistance Memorial Center).

Father Dr. Lothar König was born January 3, 1906, in Stuttgart and attended the Friedrich-Eugen secondary school there, graduating in 1924. His parents were Paul and Elisabeth König, small business owners in Stuttgart (www.kreisau.de/en/kreisau/kreisauer-kreis/mitglieder/lothar-koenig/). Paul König would be killed early in World War I. At the secondary school, Lothar joined the Catholic Youth Movement in 1919, and in 1924 he became a Jesuit novice. After his novitiate in Tisis in Vorarlberg from 1926 to 1929, he studied philosophy at Berchman Jesuit College in Pullach. In 1929 he enrolled in Ludwig-Maximilian University in Munich and studied physics, graduating in 1933. He studied theology in Valkenburg, as well as philosophy and theology at Saint George University in Frankfurt, ultimately graduating with a doctorate from Ludwig-Maximilian in 1938. He took his vows as a priest in 1939, and Father Rösch made König his representative at Berchman, where he was later made a professor of cosmology (German Resistance Memorial Center; Steinbach and Tuchel 117).

König was a founding member of the Ausschuss für Ordensangelegenheiten (Committee of Religious Affairs) in 1941, along with Fathers Odilo Braun, Rösch, and Laurentius Siemer, and he attended the Fulda Bishops Conference led by Konrad Graf von Preysing and Johann Baptist Dietz. The committee was created after the Nazi opposition to the church was authorized in a decree from Reichsleiter Martin Bormann on January 13, 1941. König grew to be an outspoken campaigner within civilian and political circles in defending Catholic institutions and holy orders against the Nazis (Burleigh 728).

In 1942 Rösch introduced König to members of the Kreisau Circle. König then began meeting regularly with the bishops of Berlin and Freiburg to keep them informed of the circle's plans. This he did with the encouragement and consent of Peter Yorck von Wartenburg in an effort to include as many religious organizations within the resistance as possible. König was one of few members of the Kreisau Circle who favored action over endless planning and he often disagreed with von Moltke. However, he had persuasive allies in von Wartenburg, Gerstenmaier, and Father Delp (Mommsen 139). They warned the Kreisau Circle in 1942 that if the Nazis remained in power for much longer, there would be little left with which to reconstruct a German civilization. These views were clearly expressed in a paper written by Father Georg Angermaier with help from König and Delp, which was presented at the second Kreisau conference (Mommsen 144).

A warrant for König's arrest was issued two months after the July 20 coup attempt, based on his known involvement with the Kreisau Circle. He knew of the warrant and narrowly missed being arrested. After the Gestapo arrested Rösch, König went into hiding, sometimes living in the coal cellar of Berchman College. During this time, the stomach cancer he had been suffering from since 1941 (for which he refused treatment, saying that "the fight comes first") only got worse (Riebling 122). Father Lothar König died on May 5, 1946, in Munich, having outlived the Third Reich by a year. His and other stories of the undercover roles played by Catholic clergy in the resistance are well documented (Riebling).

Justus Delbrück was born in Berlin on November 25, 1902. His father was Hans Delbrück, a professor of history at the University of Berlin and a former member of the Reichstag, and his mother, Carolina Thiersch, was a granddaughter of Justus von Liebig, considered by many to be the father of organic chemistry (*Allgemeine Deutsche Biographie*). Justus' sister Emmi was married to Klaus Bonhoeffer, whose brother, Max, would become an American Nobel prize winning biophysicist in 1969. After moving to the United States in 1937. Justus was a student at the Grunewald Gymnasium, with Klaus and Dietrich Bonhoeffer and Hans von Dohnanyi, and after completing his Arbitur in 1928, he went on to study law at the Berlin and Heidelberg universities. After graduation he did an internship at the Reichsverband der Deutschen Industrie (Federation of German Industry) and took a position there as a civil servant (Stockhorst 101). In 1930 he became an assessor in the city government of Schleswig and later held similar positions in Stade and Luneburg. Because of his membership in the German Democratic Party, he was refused membership in the Nazi party in 1933 when Hitler was made chancellor. In 1935 Delbrück joined Bonhoeffer's Confessing Church and in 1936 he resigned all his civil service positions and went to work in the Sommerfeld textile factory. He became a member of the board there and made every effort to safeguard Jewish ownership of the business.

Delbrück was drafted into the Wehrmacht in 1940 and on October 10, 1941, he was transferred to the Abwehr at the request of his long-time friend, Hans von Dohnanyi, who had grown up in the Delbrück house as a child (Fest, *Plotting*, 123). Delbrück was among the group that met with Louis Lochner, the head of the Berlin Associated Press Bureau, in November 1941 to deliver a message to him for President Roosevelt from Popitz, Beck, Oster, von Dohnanyi, and Canaris, with a cover letter from Prince Louis Ferdinand of Hohenzollern. The aim was to clearly state the group's desire to end the war immediately and reveal their plans for overthrowing the Nazis. The letter asked for Roosevelt's assistance and a promise from him not to take military advantage of the coming coup (von Klemperer 233).

After Canaris was dismissed as Abwehr chief, Delbrück was transferred (in early 1944) to the 3rd Rifle Battalion; after July 20, his involvement in the resistance was soon discovered by the Gestapo. He was arrested on August 17; eventually tried by the VGH on February 2, 1945; and sentenced to death, but he managed to survive (von Meding 2). He was among the group of prisoners released from the Moabit Lehrter Strasse Prison on April 25. However, on May 20 the Soviet secret police (the NKVD) arrested Delbrück and charged him with, of all things, collaboration with the Nazis. He was first sent to the Russian Special Camp 6 in Frankfurt on June 19; then, in September, he was moved to the Russian Special Camp Jamlitz. Justus Delbrück may have survived the war, but he died of diphtheria in Russian imprisonment on October 29, 1945, in Jamlitz (German Resistance Memorial Center).

Otto John, the brother of Hans John, was born March 19, 1909, in Marburg. His strange story is perhaps best told through excerpts from *Time* magazine and his obituary. According to some accounts, "Otto John had been warned not to return to Berlin for the putsch, but he found it impossible to stay away. On the twentieth, a solar eclipse turned the sky murky and the atmosphere oppressive. It seemed to him an ugly omen and he suggested to his brother that it was 'no weather for a revolution'" (quoted in von Hassell and MacRae 237; John 146–68). There was indeed an annular solar eclipse on July 20; however, it would not have been visible at all from anywhere north of Greece, so at least that part of John's story is verifiably made up (eclipse.gsfc.nasa.gov/SEgoogle/SEgoogle 1901/SE1944Jul20Agoogle.html).

There were actually two *Time* magazine articles about Otto John, with the first appearing in the August 2, 1954, issue. No one quite knew what to do with him or what to make of his wild stories that would not be confirmed (and in some cases were outright denied) by either the British or the Russians. He would probably have gone unnoticed by both groups had he quietly lived out the rest of his life, but that was not Otto John's style. He enjoyed the publicity and made several very public appearances and statements, building himself up to be a secret agent of some sort—but no one was quite certain who he had been (or was) a spy for. Eventually the British, Russian, and German governments had to speak up, and he was officially (or unofficially) labeled a traitor by all three.

The following information is taken from the *Time* article "Foreign News: The Case of Otto John," published on August 23, 1954:

> Chancellor Konrad Adenauer, riding so high as the year began, was now deep in trouble. Labor unrest was increasing. France was threatening to upset his cherished EDC and, worst of all, the strange case of Otto John was haunting and hurting the old Chancellor.
>
> Last week, after 22 days under Communist wraps, Otto John faced a press conference in East Berlin that was open to Western correspondents. No more nervous than usual, Adenauer's former security chief read a six-page statement into a battery of microphones, then freely answered

questions from 300 correspondents for an hour. Gist of his statement: he had defected to the Communists because "the Nazis and the militarists in West Germany are again in power" and "the Bonn-Paris axis is only a tool of the Americans." Americans, he said he had learned on his recent visit to Washington, are "downright hysterically mad in fear of Communism."

Later, accompanied by four Communist officials but seemingly not intimidated by them, he drank beer and talked for 45 minutes with three old acquaintances: *New York Herald Tribune* Correspondent Gaston Coblentz and two British newspapermen. He was neither a Communist nor a traitor, he insisted, and he certainly had not been lured across the line. "My decision [to stay in East Germany] was only finally made after my talks with the Communist authorities," he said. "I would have been free to return if I had wanted to."

After this performance, the West German government did an about-face. Gerhard Schröder, Adenauer's Minister of Interior, an ex-Nazi who is John's old boss, had stoutly defended him and offered $119,000 reward for information about John's "abduction." Now he flatly called him a traitor. Schröder also did his best to free the Adenauer government of any blame: the British, he said, had forced John's appointment as West Germany's security chief after rejecting Bonn's own candidates, and the West German government had suspected him for a long time.

From Adenauer's opposition, the Social Democrats, came demands for Schröder's dismissal and a special session of Parliament to discuss the John case. At week's end Chancellor Adenauer, facing what may be a fight for his political life, reluctantly agreed to Socialist demands and ordered Parliament to meet early in September.

Excerpt from Otto John's obituary:

It was something of an international sensation when Otto John turned up on 11 August 1954 in East Berlin.

He had gone missing on 20 July while attending a commemoration of the anti-Hitler July plot of 1944. Good-looking, well-built, smartly tailored, charming and blond, John, then 45 years old, looked like a 1930's film actor. He was in fact the head of West Germany's internal security organ, the Federal Office for the Protection of the Constitution (Bundesamt fur Verfassungsschutz or BfV). At a press conference held in East Berlin John attacked West Germany, warning that the Nazis were again in the ascendancy.

His outpourings were a bitter blow to Konrad Adenauer's government in Bonn, at a time when many abroad were still suspicious of the rapidly developing West German state. However, they were very useful to the Soviets, less sure of themselves after the death of Stalin in 1953 and hoping to gather together anti-Adenauer "national" conservatives to opt for a more pro-Soviet solution to the division of Germany. In December 1955, John reappeared in the West claiming he had escaped. He also claimed he had been drugged by the West Berlin medical practitioner Wolfgang Wohlgemuth and taken to East Berlin against his will. He had spoken at the press conference because he feared for his safety. John's version of events was not believed and he was tried for treason and sentenced, in December 1956, to four years' imprisonment.

Although a ladies' man, John did not marry until 1949, when he married a singer seven years his senior. Thus he was free in the Nazi era to pursue his risky political interests. John and his brother Hans John, also a lawyer, who worked in the Air Ministry, were involved in the anti-Nazi military resistance before the Second World War. Otto used his position at Lufthansa to fly to neutral Spain and Portugal to sound out the Western Allies on their attitude to an anti-Hitler government. He was certainly a brave man who risked his life on any number of occasions relaying the messages from the plotters to the Western powers. When the putsch against Hitler finally took place, on 20 July 1944, Otto John managed to leave the headquarters of the plotters in Bendlerstrasse, Berlin, just before the revolt collapsed. Four days later he got to neutral Spain on a Lufthansa flight—his brother was not so lucky....

John helped the British interrogating German officers at the Bridgend Prison camp. In 1949, he assisted the British in the controversial prosecution of Field Marshal Erich von Manstein. This placed him on the blacklist of the surviving Wehrmacht officers, including General Reinhard Gehlen. In the same year the new President of the Federal Republic (West Germany), Professor Theodor Heuss, urged John to help in rebuilding his shattered country by working for the new state....

John soon had a reputation for being a dilettante and a drunk. It could not have been easy for him—Adenauer turned a blind eye to dossiers on many former Nazis who were recruited to construct the new state and its economy. Many in Germany at that time regarded the July plotters as traitors who had stabbed the fighting troops in the back, although later they were to be regarded as heroes who had saved the honour of Germany.

After his release from prison, John chose to live in Austria for the remaining years of his life, all the time protesting his innocence. On five occasions he sought to get German courts to clear his name. His last attempt was in 1995. He failed and, officially at any rate, died a traitor. The full truth we are never likely to know. Neither the statements of former KGB officers nor the opening of the East German archives have revealed the full story.

Otto John, secret agent: born Marburg an der Lahn, Germany 1909; married 1949; died Innsbruck, Austria 26 March 1997 [*The Independent* (London), April 1, 1997].

Dr. Karl Blessing was born February 5, 1900, in Württemberg and was married to Ida Harden; the couple would go on to have two sons and three daughters. Later Goerdeler would propose naming Blessing as the new Reichsbank president, price commissioner, or minister of economics in a post–Hitler government (Hoffmann, *The History*, 369).

As a young man of twenty, Blessing was employed by the Reichsbank, but he was able to continue his education at the Handelshochschule in Berlin, graduating in 1925 with a degree in business. In 1929 he became an assistant to Hjalmar Schacht (the Reichsbank president) and was appointed to the Reich Ministry of Economics in 1934 while continuing his position at the Reichsbank. He also became a member of the "Circle of Friends of the Reichsführer SS," according to one decidedly subjective source (National Council 51). This was a group of established German industrialists working toward a closer relationship between the Nazi party and commerce. When Schacht was removed by Hitler as Reichsbank president in February 1939, Blessing and other principal Reichsbank officials were also dismissed. Soon Blessing was attending meetings of the Kreisau Circle at the invitation of Hermann Abs and Peter Yorck von Wartenburg, becoming one of the circle's chief economic advisors (Mommsen 74).

Blessing was appointed director of the German division of the Unilever Corporation in 1939 and served until 1941, when he became the director of Continental Oil and supervised German oil exploration in the Caucasus region after Operation Barbarossa (German Resistance Memorial Center). Blessing's name no doubt appeared on lists of proposed cabinet members assembled by the principal actors in the resistance, but, inexplicably, he was not arrested after July 20, survived the war, and rose to become president of the Deutsches Bundesbank from 1958 to 1969 (Mommsen 287). Blessing died April 25, 1971, in Rasteau, France.

Captain Dr. Paulus van Husen was born February 26, 1891, into a traditional Westphalian conservative Catholic family. He completed his Arbitur in Münster, eventually receiving a doctorate in political science and law after studying at several major universities, including Oxford. He also served in the military during World War I until the surrender. In 1920 he became a probationary government officer in Upper Silesia and then deputy district councilor under Hans Lukaschek, Oberpräsident of Upper Silesia. Later, as a high-ranking civil servant in Oppeln, van Husen witnessed first-hand the growing tension between Poles and Germans (German Resistance Memorial Center). Between 1934 and 1940 he was a member of the "Mixed Commission" in Upper Silesia and the Supreme Administrative Court, but he was denied a promotion because he refused to join the National Socialist Party (Rothfels 111).

Van Husen was drafted into the Wehrmacht, or rather reactivated, in 1940 and became a cavalry captain assigned to the Operations Staff of the OKW in Berlin. He soon joined von Moltke and von Wartenburg in meetings of the Kreisau Circle, a fact uncovered by Gestapo investigations after July 20 (Jacobsen 1: 299). Van Husen's task in the circle was establishing trustworthy connections with Catholic Church resistance circles. He soon became one of Kreisau's legal experts while helping to keep the Communist resistance groups at arm's length because he was sure they had been infiltrated by the Gestapo (Fest, *Plotting*, 234). Van Husen was responsible for writing several of the Kreisau Circle's legal opinions, including the "Principles for the Punishment of Violators of Law and Justice" (Ritter 255). Von Wartenburg convinced him to accept the position of state secretary in the Interior Ministry of the post–Hitler government (Large 111). This position, however, would have been under Leber and the two men rarely agreed on crucial political issues.

Van Husen was arrested by the Gestapo in August 1944 and held at Moabit Lehrter Strasse Prison for trial. (Leber had already been arrested a month before the attempt.) On April 19, 1945, the VGH, with Judge Harold Haffner presiding over the very last trial, sentenced van Husen and Lukaschek to three years' imprisonment, although one source states that van Husen was sentenced to death (Hoffmann, *The History*, 532). In any case, a week later, on April 25, Soviet troops liberated him from Berlin-Plötzensee Prison, where he had been transferred. Immediately after the war, van Husen became one of the founders of the Christian Democratic Party (CDU) in Berlin. Between 1949 and 1959 he was president of the Higher Administrative Court and the Constitutional Court of North Rhine-Westphalia, and he never approved of the forced multi-party democracy instituted by the Allies after the war (Mommsen 39). Paulus van Husen died September 1, 1971.

Dr. Horst von Einsiedel was born June 7, 1905, in Dresden to an aristocratic Protestant Meissen family headed by his father, Gotthard von Einsiedel, the chief medical officer of the Landwehr (regional militia). Young Horst attended Breslau University, where he studied administrative science and law, graduating with a degree in law in 1930. He soon joined the SPD and continued his studies at the University of Kiel, completing his doctorate in 1933 under Professor Adolf Löwe after spending two years in the United States studying Roosevelt's New Deal. His first position after graduation was in the Reich Statistics Office in Berlin, but refusing to join the Nazi party led to his dismissal in 1934 (German Resistance Memorial Center). Von Einsiedel put his administrative skills to work, however, and found a position in the Reich Technical Planning Office for the chemical industry, where his political views were of little interest to anyone (Wheeler-Bennett 546). He soon became acquainted with Otto Heinrich von der Gablentz, who was a prominent member of the CDU and worked in the same office. They both became participants in the Kreisau Circle in 1940.

Von der Gablentz was superficially involved with July 20 but never questioned by the Gestapo and, after the war, was taken prisoner by the Russians and sent east. For some undocumented reason, he was eventually released and became a professor of political science at the Free University of Berlin. He died April 27, 1972 (MacDonogh, *After the Reich*, 109; German Resistance Memorial Center).

Before joining the Kreisau Circle, von Einsiedel was a member of the Löwenberg Working Group, a loosely organized political roundtable for young adults. He was a political theorist among many other political theorists in Kreisau, and he and Carl Dietrich von Trotha became the group's specialists on political economy, which was a very real notion under Hitler. Von Einsiedel was an able speaker and writer, and (with von Moltke and von Wartenburg) he wrote endlessly for the circle. In 1942, however, a different topic attracted his interest, and he began researching agricultural methods. He preached the merits of community and work camps (for the common Volk, anyway) while at the same time promoting the need for keeping large agricultural estates intact (Mommsen 67). He, Reichwein, and von Moltke had all worked as volunteers in one of these camps in the 1920s (Fest, *Plotting*, 157). Von Einsiedel also, unlike some of the other Kreisau members, had no objections to working with the Communists, and in 1943 he was in touch with his former university schoolmate Arvid von Harnack of the Red Orchestra (Hoffmann, *The History*, 363). Von Einsiedel was also a distant relative of Lieutenant Graf Heinrich von Einsiedel, who was a great-grandson of Otto von Bismarck and a relative of the von Tresckows. Heinrich was a prisoner of war in Russia by this time and a member of the Russian propaganda front, "Free German Movement," based in Moscow; at a meeting on July 12, 1943, he was elected one of the group's vice presidents (Wheeler-Bennett 614).

Von Einsiedel was not involved with the assassination attempt of July 20, but he was certainly involved with planning for a post–Hitler government. His name appeared on many of the documents of the Kreisau Circle, but the Gestapo had better-known suspects in Kreisau, so von Einsiedel was not arrested even though he remained in Berlin through the end of the war. Immediately after the war's conclusion, he found a position in the Berlin Municipal Council as an economics advisor, and then, in August 1945, he took a position with the Department of Industrial Planning in the Russian zone of Berlin, rising to an administrative position on the Berlin City Council. He worked with von Trotha to formulate a plan for postwar economic development in cooperation with American authorities. The Russian NKVD arrested him in October 1945 as a suspected spy for the Americans. Horst von Einsiedel died under mysterious circumstances on February 25, 1947, while in Soviet custody at Special Camp 7 at Sachsenhausen. He was never married (German Resistance Memorial Center).

General Alexander Ernst Alfred Hermann von Falkenhausen was born October 29, 1878, in Gut Blumenthal (Province of Silesia) and is known for being the head of the Nazi military government of Belgium and northern France from 1940 to 1944. Oddly enough, a cousin of his, Ludwig von Falkenhausen, was also the head of the military government there during part of the First World War (Fest, *Plotting*, 383).

Von Falkenhausen was commissioned a second lieutenant in the German army at the age of nineteen and became a military attaché in Japan just prior to World War I. He served in the Reichswehr after the war and eventually became the director of the Dresden Infantry School, where he was Rommel's superior. Rommel quickly grew to respect this decidedly intellectual German officer. Von Falkenhausen retired from military service in 1930 and moved to China, becoming a military advisor to Chiang Kai-shek (Weiß 116). This surely put him in an awkward position in 1937, when Hitler aligned Germany with Japan, which was at war with China at the time (a conflict known as the Second Sino-Japanese War). Von Falkenhausen accomplished a great deal in China, helping the Chinese modernize their arms industry during his tenure, and he was well treated by the Chinese government. He had to leave China when he was recalled by Hitler to active duty in 1939 and initially served as an infantry general on the Western Front (Wistrich 57).

In May 1940 von Falkenhausen was appointed military governor of Belgium. He was ordered in 1942 to deport his Jews to the east or to various labor camps in northern France. "In the face of incredible difficulties, he succeeded in counteracting Hitler's orders in Belgium and Northern France, and governed this area as a gentleman. Belgium's recovery after the war is evidence of his good administration" (Speidel 66). There were also large numbers of non–Jewish Belgians ordered deported to concentration camps located throughout the general government, but von Falkenhausen successfully circumvented a number of those orders as well. His creative sidestepping of directives from Berlin got him replaced by Gauleiter Josef Grohe as military governor of Belgium on July 15, 1944.

By this time von Falkenhausen had become well acquainted with two of the major leaders of the conspiracy: Carl Goerdeler and Erwin von Witzleben. His experience in facilitating (or evading) the orders of the Nazi regime had long since turned him against Hitler. He offered his support to the conspiracy; however, he was never asked to actively participate in any coup attempts, perhaps because of his age. Nevertheless, von Falkenhausen was once recommended by Goerdeler for a cabinet position in the post–Hitler government. After July 20, his association with Goerdeler and von Witzleben (and a tryst with a certain aristocratic Belgian woman) was enough to land him in a collection of concentration camps (Hoffmann, *The History*, 352). He was not, however, expelled from the Wehrmacht and was never tried in a Court of Honor or the VGH. In April 1945 he was among the group of prisoners transferred to Tyrol from Dachau and eventually freed by the Americans on May 5. Von Falkenhausen was brought to trial in Belgium in 1948 and sentenced to twelve years' imprisonment for his treatment of Jews while military governor there. He was justifiably acquitted three weeks later after evidence was presented showing that he had tried to slow the deportations and persecutions (Fest, *Plotting*, 383). Von Falkenhausen died a free man on July 31, 1966, in Nassau, Rhineland Palatinate.

First Lieutenant Dr. Randolph Freiherr von Breidbach-Bürresheim was born into an aristocratic military family on August 10, 1912, in Bonn. He spent much of his childhood living with his grandparents in Satzvey Castle in Eifel and at Fronberg Castle in Schwandorf. He attended the prestigious Humanistische der Benediktiner Abtei in Neiderbayern and completed his Arbitur in 1931. He then studied at the law school of Ludwig Maximilian University in Munich (the same university attended by Eduard Hamm and Father Lothar König) and at the Friedrich Alexander University in Erlangen, completing a doctorate in 1938. He took a position as a junior member of the Josef Müller law firm and defended many who found themselves in trouble with the Nazi regime. By that time Müller was already closely associated with several members of the resistance, including Canaris, von Dohnanyi, and Oster (Rauch 36 and 42).

In November 1939 von Breidbach-Bürresheim was drafted as a lieutenant in the Wehrmacht and stationed in Munich. A year later he was transferred to the Western Front and then, in 1941, to the Eastern Front, where he contracted yellow fever and was hospitalized. During his time on the Eastern Front, von Breidbach-Bürresheim sent regular reports of the atrocities he observed back to his law office; those reports were shared with other members of the resistance. After Dietrich Bonhoeffer was arrested, the Gestapo found some of those reports, which led to von Breidbach-Bürresheim also being arrested. He was tried and acquitted, though not released, instead being held at the RSHA. In the spring of 1944, his mother contacted Claus von Stauffenberg, asking him to help free her son and he promised to do what he could. After July 20, however, the connection between von Breidbach-Bürresheim and von Stauffenberg was discovered by the Gestapo and he was subsequently imprisoned at Moabit Lehrter Strasse Prison, being transferred to Sachsenhausen near the end of the war because of the advancing Allies (Steinbach and Tuchel 143). The camp was liberated on April 22, 1945, but von Breidbach-Bürresheim was already suffering from advanced tuberculosis. He died in Sachsenhausen on June 13 and was buried in a mass grave at the camp (Rauch 72; Moll 295–98). A book on his life was published in 2007 by Andreas M. Rauch.

Lieutenant Philipp von Boeselager was involved in the March 1943 attempt on Hitler's life (Operation Spark), but he was not implicated and managed to stay alive through the end of the war. He was one of the last survivors among those directly involved in the July 20 plot, dying at age 90 on May 1, 2008. The last survivor, as mentioned earlier, was Ewald Heinrich von Kleist-Schmenzin (died 2013), regardless of the following *Telegraph* article's contention. Von Boeselager's brother was Georg von Boeselager, who was killed in action August 27, 1944, not hanged (as claimed in one account) or otherwise executed (as claimed in another) (Wheeler-Bennett 744; von Schlabrendorff, *They Almost Killed*, 53; Moorhouse 271). A book has also been written on the life of Georg von Boeselager (von Hobe and Görlitz). The following excerpt from Philipp von Boeselager's obituary tells his life story, though some of the details do not agree with other accounts (Havas 47).

> Philipp Von Boeselager, who died on Thursday aged 90, was the last surviving conspirator in two failed attempts to assassinate Hitler during the Second World War, including the July 20 plot for which most of his co-conspirators were executed....
>
> Claus Schenk von Stauffenberg and other officers involved in the plot were rounded up and shot the same day, while others, including thousands of their relatives, were tortured and executed; but Boeselager, who had obtained the explosives, escaped detection....
>
> Philipp Freiherr von Boeselager was born on September 6, 1917 at Burg Heimerzheim, near Bonn, into a distinguished Rhenish Roman Catholic family that could trace its origins to the Archbishopric of Magdeburg in 1363....
>
> In 1942, as a 24-year-old field lieutenant in the 41st Cavalry, Boeselager turned against the Nazi government after hearing how five Romany gypsies had been shot in cold blood purely on the ground of their ethnicity.
>
> With his commanding officer, Field Marshal Gunther von Kluge, Boeselager joined a plot to assassinate the Führer. The first attempt was in March 1943, when both Hitler and Heinrich Himmler were expected at the Eastern Front for a strategy meeting with Kluge.
>
> Once Hitler was dead, Boeselager was to order his troops (who were ignorant of the plot) to commandeer horses and return to Berlin to seize key parts of the city and to round up senior Nazis in a full-scale coup d'état....
>
> In the spring of 1944 the conspirators planned a second attempt on Hitler's life, Boeselager helping to supply Stauffenberg with explosives; a job with an explosives research team provided von Boeselager with cover....
>
> While most of the other conspirators were executed by firing squad, Boeselager's part in the plot remained undetected, as was that of his brother Georg—who was later killed in action on the Eastern Front.
>
> It was only after the war that Boeselager's role in the failed assassination attempts was revealed. He was hailed as a hero in both Germany and France, and awarded the highest military honours both countries could bestow [*The Telegraph* (London), May 2, 2008].

General Günther Blumentritt was born February 10, 1892, in Munich and served on the Eastern Front in Prussia during World War I. After the war, he remained in the Reichswehr under Field Marshal von Leeb with his close friend, Erich von Manstein. He and von Manstein were two of the major planners of the invasion of Poland in 1939 (Shirer, *The Rise and Fall*, 488). Blumentritt was then a colonel and chief of operations, and von Manstein was chief of staff, both serving under General Gerd von Rundstedt in Army Group South in Silesia. Blumentritt was involved in the 1940 invasion of France and later was made chief of staff of the 4th Army under von Kluge and promoted to general of the infantry (spartacus-educational.com/GERblumentritt.htm). Neither he nor von Kluge approved of Operation Barbarossa in 1941, but both followed Hitler's orders. However, the next year Blumentritt recommended withdrawing from Stalingrad before the operation had turned decidedly against them. "General Blumentritt paid a visit of inspection to some of the Italian and Hungarian contingents and was particularly adversely impressed by the quality of the Italian troops" (that is, General Italo Gariboldi's Italian 8th Army) (quoted in Goerlitz 416).

Blumentritt was chief of staff to von Rundstedt in June 1944 when Normandy was invaded by the Allies; soon afterward, he was assigned to von Kluge in the same capacity, which made him a suspect by association in the events of July 20 (Goerlitz 473). He was on the side of the conspirators, but he had not been informed of the coup plans and received most of his information on July 20 from Colonel Eberhard Finckh (Zeller 322). When von Stülpnagel's role in the coup was discovered, Blumentritt was made temporary military governor of France, but he did not order any arrests so as to give the conspirators time to escape or otherwise cover their tracks. He was dismissed from this position in mid–August but not summoned to a Court of Honor because of Hitler's direct orders to the contrary. Hitler did not believe that Blumentritt could have been involved in the plot and personally recommended him for the Knight's Cross, which he was awarded on September 13, 1944 (Das-Ritterkreuz; spartacus-educational.com/GERblumentritt.htm). Blumentritt was then assigned as commander of the SS XII Corps, which was thrown into the battle of the Roer Triangle (called Operation Blackcock by the British). After the German defeat in this series of town-to-town encounters, Blumentritt was appointed commander of the 25th Army. In March 1945 he briefly assumed command of the 1st Fallschirmjäger (Parachute) Army and finally commanded "Army Group Blumentritt" until being captured by the British on June 1, 1945, in Schleswig-Holstein. After interrogation, he was held in a British POW camp and eventually moved to the Island Farm POW camp in South Wales. On November 6, 1947, he was moved to a U.S. camp, where he remained until January 1, 1948 (http://www.specialcamp11.co.uk/General_der_Infan terie_Gunther_Blumentritt.htm).

While in prison camp Blumentritt wrote, "Rather a third world war than a repetition of the weeks after July 20. But an outsider cannot possibly understand that" (quoted in Zeller 376). Blumentritt wrote extensively after the war, adding considerably to the American evaluation of tactics on both sides. He was also called as a witness at the Nürnberg trials, but he was never asked to testify, nor was he ever implicated in war crimes. General Günther Blumentritt died in Munich on October 12, 1967.

Major General Otto-Ernst Remer was born August 18, 1912, in Neubrandenburg and volunteered for the Wehrmacht in 1932. He was married twice, perhaps three times: first to Marga von Blaes, with whom he had two sons and a daughter; later to Anneliese Heipke; and, according to the *New York Times* (October 9, 1997), finally to Marie Agustin. Remer received regular promotions and by the beginning of the war with Poland he was an Oberleutnant in a motorized infantry company and was sent to the Balkans, and then to Russia when Barbarossa began. In 1942 he joined the Großdeutschland Infantry Regiment and led the 4th Battalion. A year later he was made commander of the 1st Armored Battalion of Grenadier Regiment Großdeutschland. Remer was subsequently awarded the Knight's Cross for his bravery and leadership during the battle of Kharkov. Hitler personally awarded the Oakleaves to Remer's Knight's Cross in November 1943 (Wistrich 200). Soon afterward, he was promoted to major. Remer was made commander of the

Berlin-based Infantry Regiment Großdeutschland in March 1944 after being wounded in battle. Though not a party member, he was nonetheless a zealous Nazi, as conspirator Wolf-Heinrich von Helldorf had warned his fellow travelers (Dulles 188).

On July 20 Remer was ordered to arrest Goebbels, but after speaking to Hitler by phone, he lost no time in ordering his troops to put down the coup. His report on the events of the day, written on July 22, survived the war (Zimmermann and Jacobsen 144). His life after July 20 was anything but placid. He commanded brigades in East Prussia and in the Ardennes, being promoted to major general in 1945 before being captured by the Americans. He spent the next two years in a POW camp.

After his release, Remer became politically active, cofounding the Socialist Reich Party in 1950. The party was banned in 1952 when it seemed to be gathering strength, having won sixteen seats in the Lower Saxony State Parliament and eight in the Bremen State Parliament. Apparently Konrad Adenauer and others in the post–Hitler government (as well as the Allies) were wary of a possible resurgence in nationalistic sentiments. Remer was sentenced to three months' imprisonment in 1952 for libeling the resistance movement (a crime even then), but he escaped Germany and went into exile in Egypt instead (Wistrich 200). The threat of imprisonment did little to silence Remer, who was always willing to retell his story while injecting his opinions on the then current state of German politics and the presence of foreigners in the country. He published one book, *Verschwörung und Verrat um Hitler* (*Conspiracy and Betrayal around Hitler*, released in 1981) (*Allgemeine Deutsche Biographie*).

In 1985 the West German Bundestag passed legislation that is interpreted by the courts even today to mean that the denial of any aspect of the Nazis' ill treatment of the Jews is a crime in itself. In 1992 Remer was sentenced to twenty-two months in prison for publishing articles in his paper, the *Remer Depesche*, that were interpreted as being violations of this law. Remer appealed the ruling and eventually escaped to Spain in 1994 (www.independent.co.uk/news/obituaries/obituary-otto-ernst-remer-1234799.html). The Supreme Court of Spain ruled against legal attempts made by the German government to extradite him. Remer died in Marbella, Spain, on October 4, 1997, at the age of eighty-five.

A great deal has been made by hindsight historians of Remer's missed opportunity—namely, that he could have turned the tide in favor of the conspirators by ignoring Hitler's orders during their phone conversation, which could perhaps have ended the war earlier. In reality, a personal phone call with Stalin, Mussolini, or Roosevelt would have had exactly the same effect on any mid-rank officer being commanded by them. Sometimes it is fear and sometimes it is loyalty that causes men to act—Remer no doubt experienced both emotions at that critical moment.

Major Wilhelm Georg Joachim Kuhn was born August 2, 1913, in Berlin into a family with military and engineering history. His father, Arthur Julius Kuhn, was an engineer and a patent attorney. His mother was Maria Clara Kuster, a descendant of cavalry general Graf von Klinckowstroem (Hoffmann, *Stauffenbergs Freund*, 10). Kuhn completed his Arbitur in 1931 at the Friedrichs Realgymnasium in Berlin, and then enrolled in the Technischen Hochschule (technical university) in Karlsruhe, but he came to choose the military as a vocation. In 1932 he left school, joined the Reichswehr, and was posted to a Pioneer Battalion in Ulm. Kuhn nevertheless continued his formal education at the war colleges of Dresden and Munich. In the Polish campaign, he became a regimental adjutant, and then a company chief in 1940 during the invasion of France (Hoffmann,

Stauffenberg, 189). In the Russian war, he was an ordnance officer in the 111th Infantry for a short time before being admitted for advanced training to the War Academy in Berlin. In 1942 he was assigned to the OKH General Staff and served in this capacity until March 1944, having been promoted to major in 1943. Kuhn was a close friend of Claus von Stauffenberg, and in 1943 he became engaged to von Stauffenberg's cousin, Marie Gabriele Gräfin von Stauffenberg (Jacobsen 1: 435; Hoffmann, *Stauffenberg*, 52).

Kuhn and Albrecht von Hagen obtained and buried explosives in November 1943 for the aborted von dem Bussche-Streithorst "uniform display" attempt on Hitler's life. In May 1944 Kuhn and von Hagen (then working as General Hellmuth Stieff's aides) again procured explosives and delivered them to Stieff, who gave them to von Stauffenberg (Zimmermann and Jacobsen 120). In June 1944 Kuhn was transferred to the 28th Jägerdivision under Lieutenant General Gustav Heisterman von Ziehlberg, who helped him avoid arrest after July 20 by sending him to the front; for this action, von Ziehlberg was eventually shot on Hitler's orders (Zeller 380). He was arrested in September for disobeying orders to detain Kuhn immediately after the coup attempt but was subsequently freed, only to be re-arrested a month later and shot four months after that, on February 2, 1945, when Hitler refused to support a recommendation of mercy (Reitlinger 144). On July 21 Kuhn met up with von Tresckow near the front at Białystok and was given details of the failed coup. He was only a hundred meters away that day when von Tresckow blew himself up with a hand grenade, and it was he who first reported that von Tresckow had been killed by partisans.

Kuhn was captured in Bialystok on July 27, 1944, by troops of the Soviet Belorussian Front. He was then brutally tourtured during interrogation. Some believe that Kuhn deserted rather than being captured, but they offer no proof for this assertion (Zeller 445). On August 4 he was dismissed from the German military by a Court of Honor for his role in the coup attempt (Zimmermann and Jacobsen 196), and on February 6, 1945, he was sentenced to death in absentia by the VGH for desertion and treason. Kuhn's father was arrested and held as one of the 139 "prominent prisoners" until being liberated by German troops near the end of the war. Kuhn himself was held by the Russian Intelligence Division (SMERSCH) in Moscow until 1951, having been sentenced by the Russians to twenty-five years' imprisonment as a war criminal. The charge was that the members of the resistance, while they certainly intended to get rid of Hitler, were also planning a continuation of the war (with the Allies' help) against Russia. Kuhn was held from 1951 to 1955 in the Alexandrowski Central Prison in Irkutsk, where he was starved to the point of insanity, eventually claiming that he was not Joachim Kuhn at all. Severe episodes of schizophrenia would debilitate him throughout the rest of his life (www.h-net.org/reviews/showrev.php?id=14222).

On September 28, 1955, Kuhn was released from prison by order of the Presidium of the Supreme Soviet of the USSR. He was handed over to the German federal government in Göttingen on January 16, 1956 (Hoffmann, *Stauffenbergs Freund*, 135). When he applied for government assistance, owing to his service in the Wehrmacht, he was told that he was not eligible because he had been expelled from the military. He then applied for assistance as a victim of National Socialism but was again rejected. He tried several other routes, even attempting to have his death sentence (imposed by the VGH) rescinded. Instead of getting assistance, he was labeled a deserter and a spy for the Russians.

After the deaths of his parents, Kuhn lived alone in Bad Bocklet, refusing to see or speak to other members of the resistance. He died of a stroke on March 5, 1994, in Römershag bei Brüchenau. On November 13, 1998, the Military Prosecutor's Office in Moscow declared that Kuhn had been wrongly prosecuted. On December 23 of that year, a Soviet military court declared that the charges against Kuhn were unfounded and that the verdict against him was therefore rescinded—four years after his death. In 2007, Peter Hoffmann, the well-known historian and author of several standard texts on Nazi Germany, published a book on Kuhn's tragic life (*Stauffenbergs Freund*). Newly released Russian documents on Kuhn have also clarified history considerably (Chavkin and Kalganov).

Professor Rudolf Fahrner was born December 30, 1903, in Arnau (today, Hostinné, Czech Republic). As a young adult he studied history at Heidelberg University, beginning in 1921, and then at the University of Marburg. In 1925 he completed a doctorate on the study of Goethe and Schiller at Marburg under the advisement of Friedrich Wolters (König et al. 1421). After graduating, Fahrner became a lecturer at Marburg, where one of his students was Eberhard Zeller. The two formed a friendship that would last until Fahrner's death.

As an early supporter of the National Socialists, Fahrner joined the SA on February 5, 1933 (Hoffmann, *Stauffenberg*, 63; Hamerow 93). A year later, he was appointed to a university lecturer position at Heidelberg University, but he requested a sabbatical in the fall of 1935 and began his leave the following spring. Fahrner had lost his enthusiasm for the Nazis by then and began writing a biography of August von Gniesenau. It was about this time that he came to know the von Stauffenberg brothers and developed a close friendship with both. In 1939 he was appointed director of the German Research Institute in Athens, which gave him the opportunity to travel and learn the rest of the world's opinion of the National Socialists (Hausmann 238). By 1943 Fahrner was a committed member of the resistance and one of Claus von Stauffenberg's closest collaborators on constitutional matters. Fahrner and Zeller both survived their arrests after July 20 (Zeller 203).

Fahrner was not directly involved with the military planning of July 20, but von Stauffenberg did speak openly with him: "On the evening of 4 July [1944] as he [von Stauffenberg] walked with his friend Rudolf Fahrner through the villa district of Wannsee on the outskirts of Berlin, the two came to agree that what mattered was 'internal purification' and the question of honour" (quoted in von Klemperer 384).

After the war, Fahrner was held as a prisoner of war by the Americans for a short time before coming to live (with other former followers of Stephan George) in Uberlingen at Lake Constance (Bodensee). It is largely through Fahrner's writings that Claus von Stauffenberg's true character is known (Zeller 422). In 1950 he gained an appointment at Ankara University; then, in 1958, he became a lecturer at the Techniche Hochschule in Karlsruhe and remained there until he retired in 1972. Rudolf Fahrner died February 29, 1988, in Landeck, Tyrol.

And finally, some mention should be made of the best-known Nazi judge to survive the war and a lesser-known SS prosecutor of July 20 suspects. Dr. Otto Thorbeck was born August 26, 1912, in Brieg, Silesia, into a wealthy and influential family, which gave him the opportunity to study classical literature (especially European Renaissance literature) and law. After graduating, he entered the legal system and dedicated himself to becoming an expert in the laws created by the National Socialists after they came to power. He advanced quickly and (just as important for his career) was considered politically reliable by those above him. He was appointed chief judge of the SS and police court in Munich and given the rank of Sturmbannführer in the Allgemeine (general) SS. The court's prosecutor was SS Standartenführer Walter Huppenkothen, and the two worked together from 1941 to the end of the war. Judge Thorbeck would hear hundreds of cases, but the ones that would get him into the history books (and later put him on trial for war crimes) were the five cases he was assigned at the very end of the war.

Judge Thorbeck was ordered by Kaltenbrunner to try Hans von Dohnanyi at Sachsenhausen and Pastor Dietrich Bonhoeffer, General Hans Oster, Judge Karl Sack, Captain Ludwig Gehre and Admiral Wilhelm Canaris at Flossenbürg. The trial at Sachsenhausen on April 6 (presided over by Thorbeck, with Standartenführer Huppenkothen prosecuting) was quick, with Dohnanyi only semi-conscious, and, as expected, the sentence was death. The next day Thorbeck left by train for the Flossenbürg concentration camp near Weiden. It was a long ride in the final days of the war, and the train ran out of fuel several miles from the camp, forcing Thorbeck to commandeer a bicycle for the final leg of the trip (Hoffmann, *The History*, 530). He was dedicated to his purpose—and just as fearful of Kaltenbrunner. At this late date any hesitation on his part could have been interpreted as treason. It would have been a simple matter for all the prisoners to have been executed on the orders of Kaltenbrunner, Himmler, or Hitler, but these particular executions needed to be legal, and time was running out. Perhaps Hitler did not imagine a future after the war, but others did, and they did not want to be saddled with the outright murder of such well-known Germans, so there would have to be a trial with a judge present.

Like Thorbeck himself, Oster, Bonhoeffer, Sack, and Canaris were all well educated, intellectual men, but the judge knew what was expected of him at their trials, which began at Flossenbürg on the afternoon of April 8, with Huppenkothen prosecuting. There were no witnesses called and no defense representation for the accused. There were also no records kept of the proceedings. The four men were found guilty of treason, sentenced to death and hanged the next day. Two weeks later the camp was liberated by U.S. forces. This would have been the end of the story except that, after the war, Thorbeck continued to practice law—in Nürnberg, of all places—and there were many unanswered questions about what had happened to Canaris and the others.

Thorbeck was indicted by a Munich court in 1952 and finally, on October 15, 1955, was tried in Augsburg and convicted of assisting in the murder of the four conspirators, for which he was sentenced to four years in prison (Reitlinger 342). Thorbeck had testified in Huppenkothen's trial in 1951 that the trials of the four conspirators had lasted three hours and that he had permitted a brief defense before the death sentences were imposed ("Hitler's Advocate," *Time*, February 26, 1951). Then, on June 19, 1956, Thorbeck's verdict was overturned by the German Federal Constitutional Court (Karlsruhe) on the grounds that the executions had been legal under the existing law, which classified treason as a capital crime. Otto Thorbeck died October 10, 1976, in Nürnberg. However, that did not prevent the Berlin State Court (Landgericht) from rescinding the previous ruling in 1996, twenty years after his death, and reinstituting the original sentence of 1955 (Ueberschär 308).

Standartenführer Walter Huppenkothen was an only child, born December 31, 1907, in Haan (Rhineland). He was educated at Opladen Gymnasium and studied political science and law at the universities of Düsseldorf and Cologne. He and his wife Erika, whom he married in 1942, had one son. Huppenkothen passed the required examinations to be qualified as a lawyer and joined the National Socialist Party on May 1, 1933. He joined the Allgemeine SS at the same time and soon found a permanent position in the SD in Düsseldorf. After the defeat of Poland, Huppenkothen was named chief of the SD in Krakow, and in early 1940 he was transferred to Lublin as the Gestapo chief there. In July

1941 he was again transferred (with a promotion to Sturmbannführer) to the RSHA in Berlin (Wistrich 95). He was assigned to replace Walter Schellenberg in the office dealing with counter-espionage. The "unification" of all intelligence services under the SD after Canaris was dismissed in 1944 was an opportunity for Huppenkothen and he advanced quickly in the organization. He left Berlin later that year with a promotion to Standartenführer (colonel) and became the chief prosecutor in the SS and police court of Munich, presided over by Judge Thorbeck. Near the end of the war he was involved in several infamous trials, beginning with the prosecution of the semi-conscious Hans von Dohnanyi on April 6, 1945, at Sachsenhausen and ending with the prosecutions of the four conspirators at Flossenbürg. In all of these cases, Huppenkothen requested the death penalty. Thorbeck sentenced all of the accused to death and the sentences were duly carried out.

Huppenkothen was captured by American troops on April 26, 1945, in Gmünden, along with fragments of the SS Liebstandarte Adolf Hitler, and he worked for the U.S. Army Counterintelligence Corps (CIC) until 1949—mostly to keep himself out of the hands of the Russians, and for his knowledge of Russian intelligence operations (Breitman 300). His cooperation with the Americans likely saved him from being indicted at the Nürnberg trials, though he was ultimately tried a total of five times after the war. He was first tried in Munich in 1951 for being an accessory to the five executions detailed above, but the charges were dismissed. He was, however, sentenced to three and a half years for extorting evidence and causing bodily harm, and a second trial was ordered (with Thorbeck as an additional defendant). Nonetheless, in November 1952 the Munich court upheld the original sentence. A third trial was ordered by the West German Supreme Court at Karlsruhe. This trial took place in Augsburg on October 15, 1955, with Huppenkothen being sentenced to seven years and Thorbeck to four, but they were acquitted of the murder charges (Reitlinger 342). The prison sentences were subsequently suspended by the West German high court (Bundesgerichtshof) on the grounds that the actions of Huppenkothen and Thorbeck had to be judged by the Nazi standard of legality. Finally, in 1961 Huppenkothen was sentenced to six years' imprisonment, although an admittedly unreliable book published in 1965 states that he was at that time living "unmolested in Mannheim as an insurance agent" (quoted in National Council 95). His co-interrogator, Franz Sonderegger, also survived the war and testified against Huppenkothen in his 1951 trial, but, in Huppenkothen's defense, he did state that he had actually seen confirmation from Hitler of the sentences for Canaris and the others (Deutsch, *The Conspiracy*, 200; Reitlinger 341). Huppenkothen provided written statements used in the 1961 Eichmann trial, and in 1969 he testified at one of the trials of Dr. Werner Best.

Walter Huppenkothen died in 1979 in Lübeck. His 1951 trial made national news, as reported in *Time* magazine.

> A British-made acid bomb hidden in a briefcase exploded on July 20, 1944 in Adolf Hitler's headquarters, "Wolfsschanze," deep in an East Prussian pine forest. Four men were killed, but Hitler staggered out slightly burned and bruised, though his hearing was affected. Within a few hours, an implacable hunt for the conspirators was unleashed. Before it was over, thousands of Germany's anti–Nazis were exterminated.
>
> The man in charge of tracking down the conspirators was veteran SS Agent Walter Huppenkothen. Last week, Huppenkothen, 44, tight-lipped and cold-eyed, stood trial in a Munich court. The charges against him: torture and murder of Admiral Wilhelm Canaris and five other July 20 conspirators.
>
> To show how Huppenkothen made a farce out of a legal proceeding, the prosecution produced

a surprise witness, Otto Thorbeck, who presided at Canaris' trial and since the war has been conducting a quiet, respectable law practice in Nürnberg. Said Thorbeck: "I submitted to the law in force at that time." He testified that under Huppenkothen's direction, conspiracy trials took three hours. Defendants were allowed no lawyers, got no bill of charges. Instead, Huppenkothen shouted the accusation at them, permitted a brief answer period. Then the death sentence was imposed, and next day the prisoners were executed.

Huppenkothen coolly asserted his innocence, insisted he had never seen atrocities or torture chambers. It was Hitler's fault; he had decreed both the manner of trial and execution.

Munich judges and jury agreed that within the limits of Hitlerian law then governing Germany, the trials of Canaris and fellow conspirators were legal. Huppenkothen was acquitted of murder. But he was found guilty of using torture and sentenced to three and a half years in prison ["Hitler's Advocate," *Time*, February 26, 1951].

8

The Beginning: A Germany Without Hitler or an Officer Corps

Twelve years of rule by Hitler and the National Socialists could have made Germany a third world country after the end of the war—and, according to some highly placed Allied officials of the time, that would not have been such a bad idea. By the end of the war, there was as much hatred of the Germans as there was fear of yet another war with them sometime in the near future. Germany surrendered unconditionally on May 7, 1945, repeating the surrender on May 8 for the Russians. This gave the Allies complete control of the country and the Russians temporary control of Berlin.

New political parties sprang up immediately after the surrender, with some familiar names and characters, and they were mostly tolerated by the Allies as long as they did not express nationalistic goals. The Democratic Union of Germany, which later changed its name to the Christian Democratic Union of Germany (CDU), led by Andreas Hermes, issued a policy statement written by Hermes on June 26, 1945, calling for laws to again become "the basis of all public life…. The independence of the judicature and due process of law must be restored…. We demand a public life free of lies … and a responsible press…. We demand freedom of conscience and of religion…. Science and art must be allowed to flourish without fetters." Hermes also demanded some decidedly socialist laws: "It is essential that all mineral resources should become state property. Mining and other key industries enjoying a monopoly must clearly be controlled by the state." Thirty-four leading citizens signed this statement, including Jakob Kaiser, Otto Nuschke, Rudolf Pechel, and Theodor Steltzer (quoted in Kuby 350).

The CDU soon became the party of Konrad Adenauer; by that time, the "of Germany" part of the name had already been deleted. On June 15 the competing Social Democratic Party of Germany (the SDP) called for the nationalization of even more German businesses, including banks, insurance companies, natural resources, and the mining and power industries. This platform had the support of Max Fechner, Gustav Dahrendorf, Bernhard Göring (no relation to the Nazi Reichsminister), and Karl Litke, and by September the party had 70,000 members in Berlin alone. The German Communist Party (KDP) was not to be outdone, and its platform of June 11 proposed "the complete liquidation of all vestiges of the Hitler regime and Hitler Party, the struggle against hunger, unemployment and lack of housing, the restoration of popular democratic rights and liberties, the building up of a democratic German administration, the expropriation of all Nazi leaders and war criminals, the liquidation of large landed estates, and the transfer of all enterprises supplying vital public needs to the local, provincial or land authorities" (quoted in Kuby 356). The Liberal Democratic Party (LDP) platform of July 5 called for "the physical and spiritual cleansing of the German people from the shame of National Socialism, the creation of a true sense of community, the public control of all enterprises in which such control is clearly in the common interest... agricultural holdings of excessive size, restoration of the educational system, popular representation on the basis of universal, equal and secret suffrage, and the collaboration with other anti–Fascist parties" (quoted in Kuby 357). All of these new or resurrected political parties shared basic socialist traits and stayed away from any statements regarding national defense and specific individual rights. Germany would be socialist, regardless of what the party gaining control was called.

The official communiqué on the Potsdam conference (July 16–August 2, 1945), attended by Harry S Truman, Clement Attlee, and Josef Stalin (along with Winston Churchill, who had just been replaced by Attlee as British prime minister), declared:

> It is not the intention of the Allies to destroy or enslave the German people. It is the intention of the Allies that the German people be given the opportunity to prepare for the eventual reconstruction of their life on a democratic and peaceful basis. If their own efforts are steadily directed to this end, it will be possible for them in due course to take their place among the free and peaceful peoples of the world [quoted in Shirer, *End*, 95].

The conference attendees also decreed that roughly a quarter of Germany's *pre-war* territory would be given to Poland and Russia and that the German population in these areas would be removed—by force if necessary. This eviction also applied to the Germans of the Sudetenland and any other groups of Germans scattered throughout Eastern Europe. It is difficult today to accept that Truman and Churchill comprehended the loss in civilian lives that this displacement would entail.

Germany was soon divided into four zones: American, British, French, and Russian. Berlin itself was also divided into four zones. Germany east of the Oder and Neisse rivers was transferred to Poland and Russia. The German population in these areas and other European countries that had been occupied by Germany was expelled and forcibly moved to Germany. This displacement involved almost 12 million people in what was supposed to be an orderly movement, but more than two million Germans died during the "relocation" (Burleigh 799). This is approximately the contemporary population of Houston or Paris. However, there was little notice taken in the world press regarding these losses. The quote (incorrectly attributed to Stalin) that "A single death is a tragedy; a million deaths is a statistic" seems appropriate. Another quote (correctly attributed to Stalin) that "Death is the solution to all problems—no man, no problem," is perhaps even better (quoted in Moorhouse 157).

> The Soviet authorities were severe when it came to Pgs. [Parteigenossen, Nazi party members]. Before the Western Allies arrived, they closed 1,400 shops owned by Party members and sacked nearly 12,000 functionaries. "Nacht und Nebel" [night and fog] kidnappings also removed nearly 5,500 Berliners, many of them members of the press and the police [MacDonogh, *After the Reich*, 109].

The division of Germany after the war fell roughly along lines corresponding to the territory seized and occupied by each of the major powers, with France being given a zone as an afterthought to pacify Charles de Gaulle. Stalin realized that this division would likely be the plan and pushed for rapid advancement toward Berlin at the end of the war, while telling the American and British that his aims were purely military. They believed him and halted their advance toward Berlin in favor of capturing more strategic military targets. With the ruse established, Stalin proceeded to direct all Russian forces toward taking the capital.

> Even before the war with Nazi Germany was over, Stalin had already accepted the possibility of a future conflict of ideologies with the west. In April 1945 he told Yugoslav communist Milovan Djilas: "This is not a war as in the past: Whoever occupies a territory will also determine its societal system. Everyone introduces his own system as far as his own army can advance. It can't be any other way."
>
> Documents discovered in former East German archives (following the fall of the Wall) have confirmed Djilas's account. Stalin's plan for postwar Europe was simple: to hold on to what the Red Army had conquered in Eastern Europe. That included the Soviet Zone of Occupation, and Stalin assumed that the west would do the same. Following a meeting in the Kremlin on June 4, 1945, the day before the Allies assumed governmental powers in Germany, East German Communist Party Chief Wilhelm Pieck recorded in his diary Stalin's decision: "There will be two Germanys—despite all solidarity of the Allies" [Selig].

Long before the end of the war, books were being written that advocated harsh treatment of the Germans, and it is known that at least one of those books was read and praised by then senator Harry S Truman. In a quote for the dust jacket he had this to say: "Louis Nizer's book, *What to do with Germany*, is one of the most fascinating and informative books I have ever read. Everyone in this country should read it" (Nizer). And the vice president at the time, Henry A. Wallace, had his own contribution to the dust jacket:

> A timely book for those who are doing serious thinking about the post-war period; several chapters deal in a succinct and a clear way with the problems that followed immediately after the signing of the armistice in 1918, many of which are bound to present themselves again at the end of this war [Nizer].

Another book, published in 1943—*Is Germany Incurable?* by Richard M. Brickner—had a few comments about the brainwashing of Germany's youth:

> If a subversive psychiatrist had set out to devise the optimum system for impregnating the malleable young mind with a paranoid set of values, he could have done no better than to follow the typical curriculum of the German Gymnasium. That this should culminate in the Nazi Weltanschauung [worldview] is no more astonishing than that a vigorous apple tree should bear fruit in due season [quoted in Nizer 163].

Whatever treatment the victors had in mind for the Germans could not be much worse than the conditions already in existence for them just before and immediately after the end of the war. The German economy and infrastructure was a wreck, and the inflation continued after the surrender, with prices of essentials (if they could be bought) rising to double and triple those of 1943. Only the war industry continued to function reasonably well right up until the surrender. Parts of the intelligence-gathering segment of the German military continued to function even after the war through the capture of Major General Reinhard Gehlen and a substantial portion of his command. In August 1945 they were transferred to "Box 1142" at Fort Hunt, Virginia, along with Gehlen's vast microfilmed records. "Only gradually did American intelligence come to the conclusion that Gehlen's gloomy predictions of aggressive Soviet ambitions were not so far off the mark after all. The Soviet occupation of northern Iran in early 1946 marked a critical shift in American perception and cleared the way for Gehlen's future efforts to establish a spy network in Germany against the U.S.'s new enemy" (von Hassell and MacRae 279).

A year after the surrender, the situation for German citizens, particularly those in large cities, was not much improved. However, the denazification of Germany had already begun, with anyone wishing to maintain a position of responsibility, such as teachers and policemen, being required to undergo the process immediately in order to resume their jobs. The denazification orders were not popular with the Americans who had to implement them or with the Germans, many of whom resented this treatment, as few of them were willing members of the Nazi party or had any particular political affiliation. A significant number of those who were members of the party had joined under duress. "Already what the Germans had done was being rapidly forgotten. A new enemy and a new war was beginning to be talked about. Russia! The Bolsheviks! Gotta fight them bastards next" (Shirer, *End*, 356). Citizens of major cities were forced to clear debris from roadways, with the majority of the work falling on the women. In exchange for work, they and their children were fed. The return of German POWs took an inordinate amount of time, with the Russians holding some until the mid-1950s. Relatives often had no word on whether their men were even alive.

> What the German people regret, you soon find, is not that they made this war, but that they lost it. If only Hitler had listened to his generals during the Russian campaign; if only he hadn't declared war on the United States; if only the whole world hadn't ganged up on poor Germany, they whimper, Germany would have won and been spared the present sufferings. There is no sense of guilt or even remorse. Most Germans you talk to merely think they have been unlucky [Shirer, *End*, 131].

The German poet Johannes Becher, in conversation with Shirer, revealed, "With few exceptions, there is no feeling of guilt in the entire people" (quoted in Shirer, *End*, 174).

The Nürnberg trials began on November 20, 1945, with most Germans initially seeing the event as a stunt by the victors for the news media. There was considerable discussion of the actual credibility of such a trial, not only in Germany but also in the United States, with the *U.S. Army and Navy Journal* stating that Justice Robert Jackson was trying to discredit the profession of arms. This story was picked up by *Stars and Stripes*, which was available all over Allied-occupied Europe, and also available to the Nazi defendants in the dock at Nürnberg (Shirer, *End*, 325). This publicity did not affect the progress of the trial, which took almost a year and resulted in mostly predictable verdicts. By the end of the trials of the major defendants, the evidence produced had changed the minds of some in Germany, especially the upper class, who had initially supported Hitler and had not known of his behind-the-scenes plans (made as early as 1938) for war on a global scale. Evidence of Russian involvement in Hitler's early plans was not presented in open court, but the documents were all there and available to those interested—generally, ordinary Germans on the street or in the fields were not.

The Morgenthau Plan—named for its author, Roosevelt's treasury secretary Henry Morgenthau—was a retributive plan designed to convert Germany into two non-industrial, agricultural states with little or no manufacturing capability. These and similar words are universally used by historians to describe the plan; however, after actually reading Morgenthau's book and imagining the world at the time, that impression of the intent is not justifiable.

> In September 1944, President Franklin D. Roosevelt asked me to outline for him a program for the treatment of Germany after her defeat. He wished to take such a document to the Quebec Conference, which was to be held in a few days, and he knew that I had devoted a good deal of thought and study to the subject. As Secretary of the Treasury, I had been led into the whole problem by questions of reparations, currency and financial controls. I had seen that these could not be divorced from the broader aspects of what to do with Germany. The President, with whom I had been privileged to work on terms of intimacy and confidence for many years, knew of my interest and my research….
>
> The elimination of German heavy industry is no hate campaign. The world has seen enough of hatred, and the United Nations have no need to adopt the policy of their enemies. Nor is the program a panacea for peace. It is, however, an essential preliminary to peace, to realization of the ideals for which the United States has fought, to the security of all nations (even including Germany), and to that better world which the sacrifices of all peoples have entitled them to expect [Morgenthau xi and 28].

The suggested "Post-Surrender Program for Germany" (Original Memorandum of 1944, signed by Morgenthau) is provided in Appendix D of this book. The memo to Roosevelt, written by Morgenthau, had the somewhat histrionic title (for the ears of modern readers) "Program to Prevent Germany from Starting a World War III" (Morgenthau 1).

The intent was not to punish the Germans—at least not any more than necessary—but to quickly remove their war-making capabilities and convince them of their complete loss of the war. The victors, with only a little hindsight, were acutely aware of the short time Germany had needed to recover its armaments after World War I. Churchill was initially opposed to the plan, but at the Second Quebec Conference on September 16, 1944, Roosevelt and Morgenthau convinced him to go along with it after he was given the opportunity to rewrite portions of the document. (The additional $6 billion in promised U.S. Lend-Lease money may also have had something to do with Churchill's conversion.) "Both statesmen later dissociated themselves from this plan; Churchill called it an act of madness, and Roosevelt told his Secretary of war that he 'did not know how he had initialled that particular language in the Quebec Agreement. It must have been done without much thought'" (Zeller 447). "Morgenthau would, with some justification, point to [Dwight D.] Eisenhower as the father of his famous plan" (Irving 17). Regardless of how the plan came into existence and came to be signed, it grew into the guiding principle for dealing with the Germans.

It wasn't long before reporters got wind of the agreement's existence and learned the gist of the plan. An article in *Time* (October 2, 1944) spelled out the basic details and reported on the split in the U.S. cabinet over Roosevelt's proposal (www.time.com/time/magazine/article/0,9171,933072-1,00.html). Roosevelt denied, a week later, that there had been a split and declared that "every story that had come out was basically untrue." He quickly stopped leaks to the press with orders to the principal players not to talk to reporters or to give interviews (*Time*, October 9, 1944). However, the Nazi propaganda minister, Dr. Goebbels, was not constrained by Roosevelt's wishes and made political hay out of the plan with blistering articles in the party-controlled press detailing what the Allies would do to a defeated Germany—with the world news outlets supplying him with the details. "The Morgenthau Plan was made to order for Hitler and the Party, insofar as they could point to it for proof that defeat would finally seal the fate of all Germans" (Speer 549). It has been said that this publicity over the Morgenthau Plan extended the war, and it probably did, but it was the Allies' repeated demand for unconditional surrender that really drove the Germans to fight long after the end result was already a certainty.

> After long, close experience with the German people, I know this: unless the British, the Russians and the Americans offer, with deep sincerity, to the German people another way out besides life or death with Nazism, this war is going to last for an unnecessarily long time, and the Germans, to avoid their horrible fate, are going to fight it with the reckless spirit of men who have absolutely nothing to lose but their lives! [quoted in H. Smith 332].

The "on the ground" implementation of the Churchill-modified Morgenthau Plan came after Roosevelt's death, through the JCS (Joint Chiefs of Staff) Directive 1067, signed by President Truman on May 10, 1945. Truman even remarked that he hoped no one would recognize the directive as essentially the Morgenthau Plan (Beschloss 233). This order went far beyond the suggestions in Morgenthau's document, however, and was the real "punitive plan to convert Germany into two non-industrial, agricultural states." JCS Directive 1067 prohibited U.S. occupation forces and organizations from providing any form of economic or reconstruction assistance to the German people. U.S. personnel (who were much more interested in getting out of Germany and back home) were to concentrate exclusively on denazification and the destruction of anything that could loosely be called war industry, extending even to areas like plumbing, furniture, and household electronics manufacturing. The results were predictably disastrous. For a hundred years, technology, industry and trade had supported Germany's economy. The country would literally starve to death before that national philosophy could be changed by force.

Morgenthau's ideas were not a secret; his book was on the U.S. market in 1945 so that anyone who was interested could read it, though few people actually did (probably even fewer within the government). Roosevelt had given Morgenthau permission to write his book before he died, although he was not really supportive of the idea of a treasury secretary (and a Jew) having so much to say about how Germany would be dealt with.

While these plans were being implemented, the German population (including what was left of the historic officer corps and the nobility), particularly in the larger cities, began to starve in earnest. The German Red Cross was dissolved immediately after the end of the war, and relief agencies like the International Red Cross were prohibited from aiding the Germans with food and supplies. Even the Vatican was told not to interfere when an attempt was made by Catholic relief organizations to help starving German children. Predictably, juvenile death rates rose to ten times those of pre-war Germany. The effects of the U.S.-enforced starvation could not be kept quiet for long, and in early 1946 Truman was forced by the public and its elected senators and representatives to allow relief organizations into Germany. By this time, the entire population was on the edge of starvation, not receiving the bare minimum just to stay alive.

Extremely creative bookkeeping techniques were devised by all the occupiers of Germany to avoid providing aid while forcing returning military servicemen into what amounted to slavery. Probably the most imaginative measure was General Eisenhower's declaration that defeated German soldiers were "Disarmed Enemy Forces" (DEFs) instead of prisoners of war (thus circumventing Geneva Convention rules). More than four million former POWs were used for years after the war as slave labor outside Germany as well. Conditions for POWs (or rather DEFs) under Allied guard in Germany were at times even worse. At one prison, Schwaebisch Hall, near Stuttgart, which was set up for

Germans suspected of major war crimes (among them Jochen Peiper and Sepp Dietrich),

> the Americans had used methods similar to those employed by the SS in Dachau.... Worse still were the mock executions, where the men were led off in hoods, while their guards told them they were approaching the gallows. Prisoners were actually lifted bodily off the ground to convince them they were about to swing. More conventional methods of torture included kicks to the groin, deprivation of sleep and food and savage beatings. When the Americans set up a commission of inquiry into the methods used by their investigators, they found that, of the 139 cases examined, 137 had "had their testicles permanently destroyed by kicks received from the American War Crimes Investigation team" [quoted in MacDonogh, *After the Reich*, 406].

This treatment was exposed as part of the U.S. investigation into the Malmedy Massacre (www.loc.gov/rr/frd/Military_Law/pdf/Malmedy_report.pdf).

The Soviets had their own directives after the war and became adroit in disassembling German manufacturing facilities and shipping them back to Russia. To their credit, the Russians assumed full responsibility for feeding the citizens of Berlin, employing a decidedly non–Communist approach: the rations given out were proportional to the amount of work done.

> One might have thought that the Russians would have found it exceedingly difficult to get Berliners back to work. The exact opposite was the case. The Russians were greatly impressed by the way people rolled up their sleeves and buckled to. The speed with which the Germans achieved the dismantling of industrial plants in Berlin exceeded anything the Russians might have been able to manage by themselves....
>
> The cost of all this food, which was mainly produced in Germany, was debited to the account of the municipal administration, on the grounds that it should really have gone to the Army of Occupation. The Russians charged 41.5 million Reichsmarks for it, and they were paid in industrial goods delivered to the Soviet Union from 1946 onwards [Kuby 290 and 293].

So the Russians distributed food produced in Germany to those in Berlin, and then they charged the Germans for it. This system may seem horribly unfair today, but it was better than starving (and certainly better than how the Germans had treated the Russians in cities they overran earlier in the war). What could not be moved by the Russians was often burned to the ground, usually with the forced help of former German POWs.

The Allies, particularly the Americans and British, wanted the reconstruction of Germany to be a long, drawn-out effort so that they would have ample opportunity to denazify the country. There was plenty of reconstruction to do. The almost unimpeded bombing during the last year of the war had devastated the major German cities, and the country was not able to produce enough to feed its own citizens. More than 10 percent of the total population had been killed during the war, and agricultural output was barely a third of what it had been. While Russia was busy dismantling German industry (and occupying northern Iran in early 1946), the other Allies were busy absconding with German technology. A draconian ruling issued soon after the end of the war invalidated all German patents and copyrights, giving free reign to the victors in claiming ownership of German science and technology (as well as the scientists themselves in many cases). At the Moscow meeting of the Council of Foreign Ministers in 1947, Russian foreign minister Vyacheslav Molotov, quoting unidentified press reports (probably the *New York Times*), concluded that the value of the intellectual property seized by the United States and Great Britain amounted to close to $10 billion (in 1946 dollars) (Gimbel 134; *New York Times*, February 10 and 16, 1947). However, this oft-quoted story always ends with what Molotov said. What is usually not mentioned is that during that conversation, George C. Marshall immediately and vehemently disagreed with Molotov's figures and further reminded him that the Soviet Union was by far the largest buyer of patent and technology information pamphlets—sold to them by the U.S. government for printing costs alone (Gimbel 134). The $10 billion figure may or may not be right, but quoting Molotov alone for this information certainly is not sufficient.

The end of the war in 1945 and the occupation of their country by the Allies led German citizens and ex-regular military to adopt different methods for coping with the reality of defeat. The Allies did not generally identify these two classes of Germans as war criminals; however, Germany as a whole, from the nobility to the vagabonds (in the three Western occupation zones, anyway), would be forced to participate in some form of denazification. The SS was officially labeled a criminal organization, and its members were subject to arrest and detention for indefinite periods without being charged. They were not often forced to undergo denazification because they were considered beyond rehabilitation.

The official purpose of the denazification program was to *inform* the Germans about what their country had done. However, many believed that the true intent was to instill collective guilt in citizens and former soldiers for what their country had done. For those who went through the process, there was no other reasonable explanation for why so many were forced to view films of the concentration camps and depictions of the atrocities committed against Jews and others. Even children as young as fourteen were often required to attend the programs, but many Germans had witnessed Allied and German atrocities themselves during the war and saw denazification as simple Allied propaganda. Some believed the films and other evidence had been faked. In the end, the real effect of the program was to "collectively silence" all discussion of anything that happened during the war (Wyden 271–72). Parents would not allow their children to even mention the war or the names of the military heroes they had learned about in school for years. The result was that the children, not the parents, grew to believe that there was something about the war they should feel guilty about—and that guilt was passed on to their children, the present generation of middle-aged Germans who make up the majority of the electorate.

The response of the returning military was quite different. There was a sort of collective adaptation to the world as it was being run by the Allies for the present, and just waiting them out. The former soldiers went along with the proclamations and laws made by the occupiers and experienced the denazification process, but they did not absorb the guilt they saw the Allies trying to instill in them. By this time they were experts at recognizing propaganda, so they either did not believe what they were being shown or attached little importance to the fate of the Jews and others at the time. Many could argue from personal experience that the Jews were not the only ones who had suffered during the war (Heck 238). "Das war nicht unter Hitler gefallen" was a phrase heard often after the Allied occupation of Germany, and it's still heard occasionally today. Its translation is "that would not happen under Hitler." Many ordinary Germans preferred life under Hitler after experiencing a few years of occupation by the Allies, particularly the Russians.

An incidental use of the term "collective adaptation" to describe a social-psychological response comes from the book *Voices from the Third Reich*, which is a collection of war stories by soldiers and civilians written after the war. One story is by Pater Basilius Heinrich Bartius Streithofen, who was born in 1922 and served in the Luftwaffe's Hermann Göring Division. He became a Dominican priest after the war and, at the time the book was published in 1989, lived in a monastery in Walberberg, Rhineland. His short story is reproduced here with only minor grammatical editing:

> Heroes and saints make up only a very small portion of humanity. Most people are opportunists who simply adapt themselves to circumstances. For this reason, I don't believe in collective guilt. There may be such a thing as "collective adaptation." That was certainly my experience during the war. Initially, my friends and I signed up for the Waffen SS. I was only 17 and hadn't started to shave—political considerations had nothing to do with my choice. We were troublemakers, tough kids, and we wanted experience and adventure. Instead, a friend of my mother's pulled some strings and I wound up in the Hermann Göring Division as a radioman.
>
> I was sent to Holland for training. Next to our barracks was a large concentration camp, and Jews were always being moved in and out. One day we were asked if any of us wished to volunteer for a firing squad. In my room there were 16 or 17 of us, from everywhere in the Reich, and not one of us signed up, even though that would have meant extra rations.
>
> After this, I went to Italy and participated in the retreat from Calabria to Abruzzo, on the Mediterranean coast. Since we were fighting against the Americans, we had no qualms about being taken captive. In 1944, we were sent to Poland, and there we felt completely different. We did not want to fall into Russian hands. It was a hard war, and the Hermann Göring Division was a tough outfit. During the Warsaw uprising, we were shot at from a row of houses. In the evening we got together a detachment and early the next morning we made short work of the snipers. These are the sorts of things you can't forget. But we were soldiers, not butchers. In East Prussia, some Russians deserted to us. Our commander ordered us to shoot them. We told him, "Lieutenant, shoot them yourself!" And he said, "I insist that you obey my order." We let them go ... collective adaptation [quoted in Steinhoff et al. 279].

With the realization after the war that Stalin's idea of democracy was to allow everyone to vote Communist, the United States backed away from the notion of inflicting hardline punishment on all of Germany and repealed JCS Directive 1067 in July 1947. This action was provoked by speeches from Secretary of State James F. Byrnes and former president Herbert Hoover calling for the establishment of a new government in Germany. JCS Directive 1779 in July 1947 was 1067's replacement, proclaiming, "An orderly, prosperous Europe requires the economic contributions of a stable and productive Germany" (*Time* review, October 5, 1983). This development led to the "European Recovery Program," more widely known today as the Marshall Plan. The Harvard University speech outlining the plan was given by U.S. Secretary of State George C. Marshall on June 5, 1947 (Newell 225). A transcript of that speech is given in Appendix E.

This was the first shot fired in what would become the Cold War. The Allies had come to realize that only Germany could lead Europe's industrial recovery and stop the country-by-country advancement of Communism. The first concrete step taken was the introduction of a new German currency in 1948 to replace the occupation currency, which had been the only legal money since the end of the war. This development served to connect the Western zone's economy to that of the rest of the world and stop the runaway inflation. The Russians did not recognize the new currency, and its use was prohibited in their zone, which led most Germans to realize that their country (and perhaps even their capital) would soon be split. The traditional leadership provided by the officer class and the nobility was gone, and there was little respect for the new German government (such as it was).

> It is hard for most people under 40 to remember that Germany—both Germanies—was occupied by "foreign" troops for decades after the war. On both sides of the iron curtain Germans' indepen-

dence was circumscribed. The Soviets knew what they wanted in their eastern zone: they created a state in Stalin's image, reliant on the Stasi to retain power [www.theguardian.com/books/2011/apr/24/exorcising-hitler-germany-frederick-taylor].

On June 12, 1948, the Soviet Union declared that the Autobahn, the highway leading into Berlin from West Germany, would be closed. The excuse given was that repairs had to be made because of bomb damage. All traffic between the sectors ceased completely three days later, and on June 21 all shipping traffic into the city was stopped by the Russians. All rail traffic into and out of Berlin was halted on June 24, with another obviously contrived reason provided for this action. The next day, the Soviet government announced that the Soviet sector would not supply food to Berlin's western (United States, British, and French) sectors, nor could food be brought through the Soviet sector to West Berlin. The Russians were supposed to supply food for Berlin, although the Western Allies had been supplying flour (MacDonogh, *After the Reich*, 525). The real aim of this blockade was to force West Berlin to become completely dependent on the Soviet government for food and fuel. There was no written agreement among the Allied victors regarding transportation through sectors governed by others, and the Soviets were not persuaded by (factual) rejoinders, which pointed out that the routes had been open for the previous three years. This was a blatant attempt by the Soviets to bring West Berlin to its knees through starvation and eventually make its residents more vulnerable to Communist influence. There was talk in Washington about using force to supply the encircled Germans, but it was felt that the American people would not support action that could lead to a military conflict with the Russians so soon after the end of the war. Diplomatic solutions were proposed and promptly rejected by the Soviets. There was nothing in the joint agreements reached before the end of the war that covered this sort of unilateral action by one of the Allied nations. This was the first major conflict with the Soviets after the war, and it would not be the last.

West Berlin had enough food for just thirty-five days and maybe enough coal for a little longer. Something would definitely have to be resolved before winter, or there would be wholesale starvation and deaths due to the cold. Thousands of tons of fuel and food would have to be delivered every day just to keep the population fed and warm. The Americans and British were seriously outnumbered militarily due to the postwar reduction of their armies, and manpower was not available elsewhere. The Russians had not appreciably reduced the size of their standing army, mostly because Stalin was not at all certain there would be long-term peace. In hindsight, it is likely that if a military conflict had started over Berlin, the city would have been overrun by the Soviets before the other nations could have agreed on a response. General Lucius Clay, the military commander of Germany's American zone, was not optimistic about being able to defend West Berlin in the event of a Russian offensive, and his opinion was shared by most high-ranking officers who had been on the ground in Berlin immediately after the end of the war (J. Smith 542). Berlin would be lost right away if it came to a shooting war with the Russians. Clay went on to say that Berlin had become a symbol of the American intent to preserve and protect Europe from future Communist threats and the city was essential to America's prestige in the eyes of the rest of the world. "All my recent intelligence reports point to a rapid penetration of communism" (quoted in J. Smith 337).

General Clay also knew that the Soviets would not want to be the identifiable cause of another world war, and he proposed testing them by sending an armored convoy along the Autobahn from West Germany to West Berlin—just to see how far it could go (J.

Smith 735). President Truman, supported by Congress, vetoed this idea; neither wanted to risk war with the Russians over Berlin if it could be avoided without losing face. Everyone felt there had to be another way, and, indeed, a loophole was found in the pre- and postwar agreements: the rail and ground access had not been negotiated, but the air access had. The Soviets could not claim that aircraft loaded with food was any sort of military threat, but would they nonetheless shoot down an unarmed aircraft that refused to change course away from Berlin?

The Russians were placed in the awkward position of either violating their own negotiated agreement regarding airspace or backing down and allowing flights into and out of West Berlin. In the end, the Soviets backed down and did not attack Allied aircraft bringing supplies into the city. The Berlin airlift was wholly successful, and by the spring of 1949 it was providing more cargo than had previously been delivered by rail or truck—and winning the hearts and minds of Germans throughout the country. Eventually more supplies were delivered than were needed. All of this was humiliating to the Soviets, who had claimed (after the airlift started) that it would be impossible to supply Berlin by air with enough food and fuel to survive. The Soviets had no choice but to lift the blockade in May 1949. It was evident even to them that the Allies could and would keep the airlift going indefinitely if need be.

The Marshall Plan pumped some 150 billion U.S. dollars (in today's dollars) into Western Europe, with the United States contributing most of the funds. There was no corresponding Eastern European recovery plan funded by the Russians. An equivalent amount of funding in the way of loans was allocated specifically to the newly created West Germany in the years 1949–1952. Western Europe (specifically, West Germany) began immediately to export products, which led to increased employment and food production. By 1950, Great Britain and France had been convinced to stop looting German heavy industry, whereas East Germany was still being picked clean by the Russians. As a result, the standards of living between the two Germanies grew widely divergent and would stay that way for decades. Finally, in 1951, the restriction on coal and steel production was relaxed, which allowed West Germany to once again compete in the world energy marketplace, and soon the country was accepted as a member of the common market.

For a good ten years after the end of the war there was genuine concern that Nazism would reappear in Germany, but every new party with a nationalistic bent was soon made illegal and there was no longer an officer class that might support them. Apparently those in power and their Allied overseers had learned a lesson or two from Hitler in how to deal with opposition parties. A good example is Otto Ernst Remer's Socialist Reich Party, which won 300,000 votes in Lower Saxony in 1951 before being declared unconstitutional in October 1952 (Wyden 109; Russell 23).

Scores of memoirs were written by high-ranking military leaders blaming the loss of the war on Hitler as a military strategist, not on his fundamental politics. Many of those books were banned, but not before they were published, distributed, and bought by a public anxious for answers. A few "tell all" books were published soon after the end of the war, but they were largely written by members of the July 20 conspiracy and ignored by the ordinary, non-academic German citizens, who were much more interested in knowing what had gone wrong militarily. The conspirators remained relatively unknown in early postwar Germany except for the von Stauffenberg "clique of ambitious, irresponsible and, at the same time, senseless and stupid officers" (as Hitler had described them). The Nürnberg trials had exposed a few more conspirators through witness testimonies against those charged with war crimes. In addition, when former officers involved in the coup attempt who were subsequently discharged from the military by Courts of Honor tried to rejoin the postwar Bundeswehr or collect on war pensions, their roles were exposed. Slowly, over the span of five decades, those who had been witness to July 20 died off along with what had been the officer class, and the next generation was left with history books and movie scripts glorifying the conspirators as heroes. Today in Germany they cannot legally be thought of as anything else. The "rehabilitation" of those men (many of whom actually called themselves traitors) is complete. The task left by Helmuth James von Moltke to "fabricate a legend" has been fulfilled.

9

Epilogue and an Outsider's Observations

This is necessarily an incomplete account of the events and people associated with post–July 20, 1944, Germany, with little mention of the long-term influence each had on the country's collective soul—which would fill another book. While it is undoubtedly tempting for the average German citizen today to jump on one bandwagon and say (quietly) that the assassination attempt of July 20 was all the doing of the nobility and the officer corps, and declare that they got what they deserved, it must be just as tempting to jump on the other bandwagon and proclaim (loudly) that they were all heroes and deserve their current recognition. The truth is, there were both heroes and villains in the resistance, and the coup *was* primarily the doing of the nobility and the officer class. The common German citizen or soldier had little to do with it beyond following orders. The German nobles were the best educated and had the political, industrial, and military influence to be *able* to do something, whereas, at that time, the rest of the country not in uniform typically saw no farther than the edges of their respective communities. The nobility was cultured and worldly, had connections outside Germany, and could see a much bigger picture.

A subset of the elite and the officer corps felt responsible for allowing the Nazis to get hold of the government in the first place. After all, for generations they had been in a position to shape the character of the country. Without their eventual backing, or at least their passivity, the National Socialist Party would have been just another regional faction that would have soon disappeared, and Hitler would probably not even be a footnote in history books today. Of course, there were notable exceptions to the compliance of the nobles, as Fabian von Schlabrendorff points out:

> One of the most widespread and persistent myths about the German anti–Hitler resistance is that this opposition was born out of the disillusionment following the defeats of the German Army in the latter years of the Second World War. This idea is bolstered by such books as *Eichmann in Jerusalem*, by Hannah Arendt, which was published in the U.S. in 1963. What is ignored is that many of the central figures of what later became the German resistance movement were declared adversaries of National Socialism even before Hitler's rise to power, and that they did their best to warn the German people of the dangers inherent in National Socialism [von Schlabrendorff, *The Secret War*, 357].

In the last sentence, von Schlabrendorff might have been referring to the pamphlet titled *National Socialism—a Danger*, written by Ewald von Kleist-Schmenzin, which was printed and distributed in 1932. By 1932 it was late, but not too late to derail Hitler's plans. The politicians after 1940, with a few prominent exceptions, were all National Socialist politicians, so the legal route of eliminating Hitler would have been fruitless. At that point, it was up to a clutch of influential nobles, a few renegade ex-politicians, labor leaders, clergy, and the resistance in the military—and often they were the same people.

In German schools, for years after the war, history basically stopped at the end of 1932, and it did not begin again until mid–1945, as this report from May 1959 illustrates.

> A television crew took the camera and microphone into scores of West German classrooms.... They found that nine out of every ten students between fifteen and seventeen years of age knew nothing about Hitler or believed that on the whole he had done more good than harm.... The students were asked, "What do you know about Hitler?" It was found that one in ten gave what was considered an intelligent reply, namely that Nazism was a "concoction of the anti–Semitic Nationalist and Socialist belief latent in the German people at the time." But for every one such reply the television encountered nine others, which set German educators' hair on end. "Hitler revived Germany. He cured unemployment and built the Autobahn" was one of the most general [Russell 130].

It seems no one could quite figure out how to tell the story of the Nazi era, let alone the events of July 20. The officer corps had essentially disappeared, and immediately after the surrender the surviving nobility enjoyed little of their former status; they starved alongside the common Bürgers. The only history books available at the time were those written during Hitler's reign, and those of that era that had managed to survive were banned. German education was not helped in this respect by the Allies (particularly the Americans), who seemed more interested in indoctrination and punishment than recent historical facts, or by German writers who wanted to inflate (or obscure) their involvement in the Reich or the resistance. In Russian-occupied Berlin, "History and geography—subjects that have been particularly imbued with the Nazi spirit ... were struck off the curriculum until further notice ... the teaching of these subjects will be replaced by the study of German literature, Heine, Goethe, and others" (quoted in Kuby 318–19). However, the Russians did value traditional education and set about reconstituting the school system in Berlin immediately after the end of the war. According to at least one source, they did not subject citizens under their control to "superficial denazification" (Kuby 319). That is technically a true statement, but it doesn't mean the Soviets did not denazify—according to their own definition of the word. "Denazification was most radically pursued in the Soviet zone, where it was simultaneously used as an instrument of socio-economic restructuring, to consolidate a Marxist-Leninist-Stalinist dictatorship. Nazis were those who had enjoyed power, wealth and influence in the preceding twelve years, a blanket category joined by anyone politically opposed to a Marxist-Leninist society" (Burleigh 806). In fact, the Soviets' denazification process was anything but superficial.

Psychiatrists and sociologists have discovered a gold mine in probing the psyche of Germans since the end of the war. A husband-and-wife team of psychiatrists produced what has been called the standard work on the topic. *The Inability to Mourn* investigates the inability of postwar Germans to feel pity for the victims of the Nazis and blames that loss on Hitler having taken over or removed that part of their collective conscience. An explanation is given, in distinctly psychological language, of the observed reluctance of parents to talk to their children about the war. In any event, few would have included a reference to the July 20 conspirators.

> The inability to mourn the loss of the Führer is the result of an intensive defense against guilt, shame, and anxiety, a defense which was achieved by the withdrawal of previously powerful libidinal cathexis. The Nazi past was de-realized, i.e., emptied of reality. The occasion for mourning was not only the death of Adolf Hitler as a *real* person, but above all his disappearance as the representation of the *collective ego-ideal* [Mitscherlich and Mitscherlich 23].

This was far from the first attempt to analyze the Germans under Hitler. More than forty years before *The Inability to Mourn* was published, Dr. Richard M. Brickner wrote of the country and its people from an anthropological and sociological standpoint: "The combination of paranoid ideals and the ruthlessness necessary to attain them led the Germans into a striking glorification of hatred and cruelty. In the last fifty years, one finds in Germany a wallowing in ideas of blood and horror that, even to the uninitiated, must seem to call for psychiatric attention" (Brickner 211).

The collective adaptation after the war that allowed citizens and former soldiers to tolerate the occupation and control of their country continues today in the older generation of Germans, who might yet perceive their fatherland as being occupied by foreigners. A visit to Germany may well convince the astute observer that these seasoned Germans are right. A sizeable portion of Germany's population and workforce on any given day is foreign, as there are no enforced borders with any of its nearest neighbors. "Das war nicht unter Hitler gefallen" might be said about the border problem, but it can't be used regarding foreign workers, given that there were millions of them in Germany during the war.

Today Germany is often called a model socialist country, even though the Germans do not refer to their government as such. They are socialist, however—perhaps more so than at any time during the Third Reich, as the word "socialist" substantially lost its meaning for the National Socialists soon after they took control (H. Smith 171 and 246). There are elections held in Germany now, but the outcome typically results in a forced coalition between opposing parties that guarantees a certain amount of dysfunction. There is also a modern German military, the Bundeswehr; nevertheless, it is largely without recognized tradition. Even before reunification, "West German security policy became essentially dependent upon, and was made to be a function of, East-West relations in general, and Soviet-U.S. relations in particular" (Verheyen 142). The thousand-year-old Prussian officer class became completely extinct less than half a century after the war. The country now depends on alliances with the West for defense. Germans do not pretend to be able to defend themselves in the event of a major conflict, and coalition governments guarantee that funding for the military is kept to a token level compared to major world powers. Germany has, however, assigned non-fighting representative military support to Western anti-terrorist operations for specified periods of time. The Allies' goal of removing Germany's war-making capabilities after the war was successful, but it has also resulted, it seems, in removing that part of the country's collective consciousness providing the instinct for self-defense.

On the Allies' side, it is apparent that only Henry Morgenthau really understood the role of reparations as punishment. In the few pages devoted to the topic in his book, he succinctly describes how this idea had played out in the past—including some surprises for those unfamiliar with the history.

> By the time France had finished paying off Germany after the Franco-Prussian War, French industry and trade had grown so strong that Bismarck is said to have remarked ruefully that the next time he beat the French he would insist Germany pay the indemnity. The exaggerations serve to emphasize the dangers concealed behind the alluring façade of reparations [Morgenthau 76–88].

It is true that by the time France had paid its reparations (in cash) to Germany in 1873, ahead of the deadline, the country had become a major European industrial center, which it certainly had not been before the Franco-Prussian War. Morgenthau goes on to say, "Cash indemnities no longer have any place in practical negotiations.... Unless the items to be taken by the Allies are carefully selected, the payment of reparations, especially over any protracted period, will build up German industry."

Morgenthau's advice was certainly not taken by the Allies, who seemingly allowed anything to be taken if an argument could be made for its use (Gimbel 94). After the First World War, Germany obtained generous loans from the victors to build up its industrial base so that reparations could be made; those facilities were subsequently turned into war armament–producing plants in preparation for the Second World War. It can be argued that the Allies, particularly the United States, repeated the same mistakes after World War II; so what was different this time? It is important to recall that when Morgenthau wrote his book, the State of Israel did not yet exist, so he could not have imagined the influence of this country and its individual citizens seeking reparations from Germany on an astronomical scale—with the blessing of the rest of the world. Unlike the victors in previous wars (and even this one), the Israelis desperately needed the influx of heavy infrastructural hardware and cash. They made excellent use of both in building a country and buying armaments to defend it.

Trying to follow reparation payments after the end of the war results in as tangled a web as that spun by the members of the resistance—and, like that history, some of the tangle has to be intentional. Sources do not even agree on how much has already been paid in reparations. An Associated Press report dated November 22, 2007, quotes $25 billion as the amount paid to Holocaust survivors and "more than $700 million in goods and services to the Israeli government," while another source says a total of $89 billion has been paid since 1952 (*The Times of Israel*, November 16, 2012; Jewish Virtual Library).

The 1952 Luxembourg Agreement required Germany to pay $3 billion (in 1952 dollars, which is about $24 billion today) in money and goods to Israel between the years of 1953 and 1965, but that would turn out to be just the beginning of the beginning of reparation payments for Germany. An additional $107 million was also sent to the Conference on Jewish Material Claims, which administered a fund set up to compensate Jewish survivors and businesses (Greiff 399 and 886). Most of Israel's infrastructure was built with German reparations, in the form of either cash payments or heavy equipment and industry. The world viewed this form of funding as justifiable, as did many Germans, as part of their retribution for the role their country had played in persecuting Jews during the war. This would not be the end of the story, however.

> Before the books are closed on the reparation effort, West Germany will have paid out 10 billion dollars—a voluntary "conscience fund" unique in history ... claims have been filed by 1.3 million people. Payments already exceed 6 billion dollars [*U.S. News and World Reports*, August 10, 1964, 57].

The $10 billion figure quoted in 1964 to "close the books" was exceeded before the end of the decade. By June 30, 1965, there were more than three million individual claims submitted by Jews against the West German government claiming physical or psychological abuse during the Nazi regime. That number rose to more than four million by 1988. It is not known how many claims were made against and collected from the Communist East German government; a generally reliable source says that the answer is none (Jewish Virtual Library). "By December 2001, the West German government had paid approximately 21.8 billion dollars (24.7 billion DM) in health related claims to individual Jews. In 2001, the average pension under this category was approximately $450 per month (510 DM)." Other categories, such as wrongful death claims, had been compensated $3.5 billion (3.9 billion DM) at an average pension of $697 per month (792 DM), and $8.8 billion (9.9 billion DM) had been paid for damage to careers or economic advancement (Doxtader and Villa-Vicencio 327). The total paid by the year 2000 was "more than DM 100 billion" (www.jewishvirtuallibrary.org/jsource/judaica/ejud_0002_0005_0_04564.html). These were cash payments to individuals, not reparations to the state of Israel. A revised total was calculated five years later.

> An Israeli government report that claims to be the first of its kind has set material damage to the Jewish people during the Holocaust at some $240 billion to $330 billion. Although previous studies have estimated the value of looted Jewish property, the Israeli government calculation includes lost income and wages, as well as unpaid wages from forced Jewish labor.... But this represents just a small fraction of the Jewish material damage during the Holocaust, and "there is much to be done in order to achieve a measure of justice" for survivors and their heirs, the report said [*New York Times*, April 21, 2005].

Creative ways have also been found to extend reparation payments to those previously denied. The Yiddish website *Vos Iz Neias* reported on June 3, 2009, that the German Federal Social Affairs Court in Kassel had decreed that two Jews who were forced to work in the ghettos during the Nazi era have the right to a government pension, not just payment for the work done. They are now being classified as government employees during the war; even though they were not officially paid, they were given food, which the court interpreted as payment, thus making them technically employees of the state at the time. This ruling opens the door for perhaps 70,000 Jews (and descendants) who could claim an amount that will likely reach $1.4 billion, which will come from Germany's federal pension program (www.vosizneias.com/date/2009/6/3/). If history is any indication, neither the facts nor the dollar amount will be seriously disputed in Germany. The Conference on Jewish Material Claims (which still exists today) applauded the court's decision. "The verdict of the Federal Social Affairs Court speaks to the spirit of the law, and provides many Holocaust survivors whose claims for pensions have been refused a little justice," said Georg Heuberger, a spokesman for the conference (*Seattle Times*, June 3, 2009). The Jews' demand for reparations has not exclusively been directed at Germany. The U.S. government lost a case in Miami in December 2004 filed by a group of Jews and their heirs claiming that American soldiers looted a captured German train in early 1945, which contained the stolen property of Jews. The $25.5 million settlement was to be distributed by Jewish social service agencies (Jewish Virtual Library).

Demands for additional reparation payments since Germany's reunification have come from some unexpected places. Italy's highest court demanded reparation payments from Germany for the killing of 203 men, women, and children in Civitella, in the central province of Tuscany, on June 29, 1944, but the German government did not agree on this one: "The German government has stated that seeking compensation for World War Two crimes was 'morally understandable, but it is, in judicial terms, the wrong way to address this injustice, and so this ruling is not acceptable for us.'" Italy's claims were eventually dismissed by the International Court of Justice in The Hague (*Bloomberg News*, February 3, 2012). Germany paid millions in Italian claims before a treaty between the two countries was supposed to end all reparation payments in 1961. Germany has also paid $625 billion to victims or their relatives in the former Soviet Union (*Washington Post*, Associated Press, April 17, 1993). This is in addition to the billions in reparations taken from Germany by the Russians in goods, machinery and slave labor over a period of several years after the war. The latest claims from Greece totaling 278.7 billion Euros in World War II reparations from Germany are not being taken seriously by anyone, least of all the Germans (*Reuters*, April 7, 2015).

And what does this discussion have to do with the events of July 20? Even before the end of the war, dialogues were being held among the conspirators regarding reparations.

> The Freiburg Circle, for instance, with whom Bonhoeffer met several times, issued a memorandum that "sketched the contours of a post–Nazi government" and included "the first acknowledgement that the German people owed reparations to the Jews." These scions of the German nobility were joined by the trade unionists Wilhelm Leuschner and Julius Leber as well as by leaders of the Social Democrats [quoted in Marsh 375].

By the time formal reparations became a serious issue in Germany, the surviving nobility, labor leaders, and Ally-approved politicians were attempting to recover their previous standing before the war. A fragile coalition with occupying forces developed, which distanced this group of Germany's former elite from the opinions of ordinary citizens, who cared little for talks of reparations. Discussions began, however, and demands were made that the country pay restitution to those wronged by the Nazis. Unknown to the planners of the attempt on Hitler's life, the seeds of future reparation payments were sown by them, and those seeds grew into perpetual payments that, seventy years later, are rarely contested.

In present-day Germany, free speech effectively ends when any discussion of the war begins. The exception to this rule is glorifying the July 20 conspirators or condemning the Nazi persecution of Jews. As stated before, the "rehabilitation" of the traitors of July 20 is now complete. It is illegal in Germany to express opinions contrary to the government's regarding any aspect of the Nazi regime, which certainly includes the July 20 assassination attempt; many have tested those laws and have gone to jail. The swastika is a constitutionally banned symbol and a raised stiff right arm can land the perpetrator in jail if it can be interpreted as the Nazi salute. Even the use of a swastika in *anti*-Nazi propaganda can lead to severe fines, although the movie industry seems to get a pass in this area (*Deutsche Welle*, October 3, 2006). Perhaps the quote of von Moltke is even more appropriate now: "We are being executed for thinking together."

The German government has become serious about trying to control what its citizens can think, which has a familiar Nazi-era ring to it. The average German appears to accept this situation as part of the eternal punishment they must endure for twelve years of belligerence that began more than eighty years ago. In recent history, a label has been invented to describe those who question the accepted record of the Nazis' treatment of the Jews, and indeed anything related to Nazi Germany, and that label often gets extended to those who criticize the conspirators of July 20 and the broader politically correct history of the Third Reich. Being a vocal "Holocaust denier" or even a serious Holocaust questioner in the United States might attract harassment in some parts of the country, to the point of not being able to earn a living, but in Europe that same behavior could lead to an extended vacation in a jail cell. In Germany and throughout much of Europe, courts have liberally interpreted ill-defined laws against "defaming the dead," "condoning a crime," and "incitement" to successfully prosecute neo–Nazi activists and Holocaust deniers. The "Holocaust denier" label in Europe is somewhat akin to being labeled a racist in the United States, except racists in the United States are not typically jailed just for being racists or using racist language. Modern historians for the most part have tried to be objective, while learning to write very carefully when it comes to dealing with the Nazi period so as to avoid the career-ending "Holocaust denier" or "neo–Nazi" label.

Current stories illustrating the zeal of German courts in prosecuting those labeled Holocaust deniers, more than seventy years after the end of the war, are not hard to find. One recent case involves eighty-seven-year-old Ursula Haverbeck, a German grandmother sentenced to ten months in jail for saying that Auschwitz was not historically proven to be a death camp and declaring on television that "the Holocaust is the biggest and most sustainable lie in history" (*Deutsche Welle*, November 13, 2015). Another case involves Horst Mahler, seventy-plus years old at the time, a formerly convicted German neo–Nazi sentenced in a Munich court to six years in prison for denying the Holocaust. The sentence was appealed but upheld in federal court. Horst had earlier been convicted of "condoning a crime" in 2003 for saying that the September 11, 2001, terrorist attacks on the United States were justified. He was fined several thousand dollars for that offense (*Die Welt* [online], February 26, 2009; *San Diego Union Tribune*, Associated Press, August 11, 2009). No doubt, this man is a bad seed, but charging an American citizen with such crimes is unthinkable. Nor has the pursuit of former Nazis and neo–Nazis been an exclusively German/Jewish undertaking. In Austria there were 28,000 trials against former Nazis and 13,000 convictions between the years 1945 and 2000, and there were 232 charges of "extreme-right, foreigner-hostile, and anti–Semitic" crimes in the first six months of 2000 (Wyden 257). In France it can be expensive to express a "politically incorrect" opinion on any Nazi-related topic, as Jean-Marie Le Pen, a former French far-right leader, discovered. He was fined 30,000 Euros in 2016 for "contesting crimes against humanity" after being fined earlier, in 2012, for saying that the Nazi occupation of France had been "not particularly inhumane" (www.bbc.com/news/world-europe-35979522).

Books have been (and will be) written on the case of John Demjanjuk, who came to the United States in 1951 as a "displaced person" (Sheftel; Teicholz; and Rashke). A new office within the Department of Justice (the Office of Special Investigations) was created in 1979 essentially to handle his case. He was extradited to Israel in 1986 from the United States after living in this country for decades because of thin evidence that he was the notorious "Ivan the Terrible," a concentration camp guard at Treblinka. Demjanjuk had been a U.S. citizen since 1958 and worked for the Ford Motor Company until his retirement. The claim against him was finally disproven in an Israeli court, and Demjanjuk returned to the United States after spending seven years in an Israeli prison. He was then indicted for being a concentration camp guard at Sobibor for a few months during the war, and a new trial began on November 30, 2009, in Munich. He was eventually found guilty and sentenced to five years' imprisonment, pending appeal (*New York

Times, May 12, 2011). Demjanjuk admitted to having served at other concentration camps as a guard, but not at Sobibor. He died a free man on March 17, 2012, before a final verdict could be handed down by the German appellate court.

The media frenzy in Germany over the highly publicized July 2011 disinterment and destruction of the body of Hitler's deputy, Rudolf Hess, prompted a former member of the Hitler Youth who has lived in the United States for some fifty years to put things into perspective:

> It is typical for the European media to blow things out of proportion. Thousands have peacefully visited the grave every year without incident. I stopped in Wunsiedel a few years ago on a Saturday afternoon to see the grave for myself. Our car was the only one in the huge parking lot; not a soul to be seen inside the cemetery except two wardens. So where were the thousands of rioting Neo-Nazi supporters of Hess?
>
> Nobody complains when parades are held each year on January 15 past the graves of the communists Rosa Luxemburg and Karl Liebknecht in Berlin. What is the real difference I ask? Communism is VERBOTEN in Germany, same as Nazism. The real extremists are those who oppose free expression—whether it comes from Nazis or Communists—and enact silly laws that allow any government official to do what he or she pleases.
>
> I remember in the summer of 1945 when school started again after the war. The first day back there were no more "Heil Hitler" greetings, instead it was a prayer. Soon we were introduced to the recently adopted United Nations charter, something that most Germans never had heard of, and a word was added to our vocabulary: "Democracy," but soon after that, "Verboten" appeared again and it has been the substitute for Democracy in Germany ever since. A thousand years of indoctrination by the Junkers, Prussians, and Ritters who gorged themselves on rules and regulations could not be eradicated by a stroke of the pen. Germany today has a higher percentage of its population working for the government—or at least getting a check from the government, than any other country in the world. France is supposed to be Germany's big ally and Russia a good friend, but the average man on the street would rather travel to France or Russia on a tracked vehicle with an 88 mm cannon than go there in his car.
>
> The history of the Third Reich is taboo in German education. The war will only be mentioned in terms like "Hitler was a villain," but they seem to forget that the road network they travel on today was created by that villain and they forget that several thousand square miles of German swamp was made into agriculture land during that time so those idiots can eat their cake nowadays. Germany has the most stringent laws in the world protecting wildlife and requiring nature conservation—all introduced by a villain in 1936. The list is endless. Every prominent German cemetery is under lock and key after dark and in the daytime every cemetery is patrolled by a warden. It seems that they are as afraid of long dead Nazis today as we were of Stalin in 1945 [Private communication, Wilhelm R. Gehlen, nephew of Major General Reinhard Gehlen].

European courts, and particularly German courts, have certainly become activists in interpreting existing laws to deal with Holocaust deniers and anything that can be labeled pro-Nazi, to the point of trying to control not only what is said and written in traditional media but also what appears on websites, even if those websites are not of German origin, as the following excerpt from an article by Steve Kettmann illustrates: "If this week's border-transcending ruling by Germany's highest court proves anything, it's that an enormous distance remains between advocates of a free Internet and watchdogs against racism and hate-mongering" (*Süddeutsche Zeitung*, December 12, 2000). However, the courts did back down a bit when news of the decision reached Germany's highly technical communities, giving rise to protests at the idea that the government might seek to hack unacceptable websites (archive.wired.com/politics/law/news/2001/04/42961). It is generally accepted today that the internet is something that not even the German courts can completely control, but that does not keep them from trying. Communist

China has been marginally more successful in this area—but there, as in Germany (and indeed the rest of the world), the best and the brightest do not work for the government and ways are routinely found to get around repressive regulations against free speech. "Criticism is a blasphemy no paranoid can endure" (Brickner 215).

"Collective guilt" is a phrase often used to describe the aim of the denazification program instituted by the Western Allies after the war, and, by and large, it was successful. Most Germans born after the war have been convinced that they are all somehow directly responsible for the deaths of millions, particularly Jews, and that this is a debt they can never repay—although dollar values are eventually determined and paid, and then paid again when more evidence is discovered. This evidence cannot be objectively questioned by individual citizens in Europe without fear of legal action, which could easily land the questioner in jail. Rather than deal with the problem, Germany just keeps paying, and there is no end in sight. In more recent history the world has witnessed other government-sponsored mass murders (though not on the scale of the Nazis), and in some cases the guilty have been discovered and rightfully punished, but the entire country was not subjected to indefinite reparations. The people directly responsible were punished, and the world felt pretty good about it, but for the Germans, somehow the sins of the fathers have indeed been passed on to future generations. Certainly the reparation payments have been passed down. "Russia however has never made reparation payments for the Jews, Poles, etc. they murdered outright or worked to death in their own concentration camps, and they probably never will" (Moorhouse 155–57).

The youngest generation of Germans, with little first-hand information about the war, just accepts things like reparation payments as a fact of life—a sort of tax, if you will, not unlike the other repressive taxes of that country. A few decades ago German reparation payments were expected to exceed $50 billion by the year 2020. That number had in fact more than doubled in actual payments made by the year 2000, and in the grand scheme of things, that can be marginally justified, but can a country be given a life sentence? Certainly by the year 2020 all the direct victims of the Nazi era and those responsible will be long dead, and most of their children will be dead as well. History books and legislation will have also convinced the middle-aged adults of 2020 and their children that the conspirators of July 20 were all martyrs for the honor of Germany. Any other expressed opinion will be unthinkable—and certainly illegal. Hitler's pronouncement at the Nürnberg Rally of 1934 that "the German form of life is definitely determined for the next thousand years" might prove to be correct.

In a strange (viewed from this side of the Atlantic, anyway) attempt to rehabilitate history, the German parliament ruled on September 8, 2009, to overturn all Nazi-era convictions of treason, confirming and extending the 1985 Bundestag ruling (mentioned in chapter 4) that nullified all decisions made specifically by the VGH. It is not known how many people were convicted of treason during World War II, or how many of those cases would be upheld today, so just to be certain, in typical German fashion, the ruling nullifies *all* treason convictions between 1933 and 1945.

> Treason convictions carried the death penalty and were handed down in Nazi Germany for any act deemed harmful to the nation or helpful to the enemy. Under that umbrella, people were convicted of treason for political resistance, aiding Jews, helping prisoners of war, selling products on the black market and scores of other acts.

> "The people who were convicted of treason are dead, that is true, but it is important that they will be rehabilitated and remembered," said Christine Lambrecht, a lawmaker from the Social Democratic Party who supported the measure.
>
> Some members of Chancellor Angela Merkel's conservative Christian Democrats and the Bavarian-only sister Christian Social Union had initially been against a blanket measure overturning the convictions, arguing some of those sentenced may have harmed comrades in arms.
>
> But after a study concluded it was impossible to determine whether the acts for which people were sentenced "harmed a third party," they supported the legislation.
>
> "Even if not all of those who were sentenced to death as war traitors were political resistance fighters, they definitely all were victims of a criminal justice system that killed in order to maintain the Nazi regime," Zypries said [Grieshaber].

Revisionist writers in Europe wasted no time in subtly changing history to fit the new government ruling. No longer are any of those condemned by the VGH or any Nazi-era court referred to as "executed"; they were "murdered." A 2002 ruling also "rehabilitated" deserters and homosexuals prosecuted during the Nazi regime (*San Diego Tribune*, July 22, 2009). Judge Freisler surely turned in his grave—again. Rehabilitating the history of World War II is not an exclusively German undertaking though, as Stalin's grandson is attempting to rehabilitate the memory of his grandfather as well (*BBC News*, October 8, 2009).

The goal of a classless society, as professed by Hitler (and also Stalin), never came to be under National Socialism, but the conspirators of July 20 were treated and tried as classless individuals with no consideration given to status. That certainly is not to say that justice was done by today's standards, but by the standards of the time, there could have been no other result. If Judge Roland Freisler had never been born, there would have been another judge who would have interpreted the laws of Germany at the time regarding the attempted assassination of Hitler just as he did—although perhaps with less color and enthusiasm.

After the war, the German civilian leadership recovered (albeit fitfully) and, to some degree, so did the nobility. The officer class simply disappeared, along with its traditions, into a history that ordinary Germans living today are compelled to forget.

Appendix A: German Titles and Military Ranks

Freiherr—Baron
Graf—Count
Gräfin—Countess (wife of Graf)
Freifrau—Baroness (wife of Freiherr)
Freiin—Baroness (unmarried daughter of Freifrau and Freiherr)
Schenk—an honorary title (roughly a high court official) as well as a once-common German name (literally translated: a wine server)

German Army	*British Army*	*U.S. Army*	*SS*	*SA*
Generalfeldmarshal	Field Marshal	None	Reichsführer	SS Stabchef
Generaloberst	None	General (4 stars)	Oberstgruppenführer	Oberstgruppenführer
General der (Waffengattung)	General Lieutenant	Lieutenant General (3 stars)	Obergruppenführer	Obergruppenführer
Generalleutnant	Lieutenant General	Major General (2 stars)	Gruppenführer	Gruppenführer
Generalmajor	Major General	Brigadier General (1 stars)	Brigadeführer	Brigadeführer
Oberst	Colonel	Colonel	Standartenführer	Standartenführer
Oberstleutant	Lieutenant Colonel	Lieutenant Colonel	Obersturmbannführer	Obersturmbannführer
Major	Major	Major	Sturmbannführer	Sturmbannführer
Hauptmann/ Rittmeister	Captain	Captain	Hauptsturmführer	Hauptsturmführer
Oberleutnant	First Lieutenant	First Lieutenant	Obersturmführer	Obersturmführer
Leutnant	Second Lieutenant	Second Lieutenant	Untersturmführer	Untersturmführer
Feldwebel	Sergeant	Sergeant	Oberscharführer	Truppführer
Gefreiter	Corporal	Corporal	Rottenführer	Rottenführer

Appendix B: Prisoners Transferred from Dachau

On April 24, 1945, 139 high profile prisoners that had been rounded up from various concentration camps were moved to Tyrol Prison in the west Austrian Alps. These detainees were to be used by the SS as pawns in their own negotiations with the Allies. Obergruppenführer Ernst Kaltenbrunner gave the order for the transfer, but it no doubt originated with Himmler, who had for some time been planning an exit strategy. The prisoners had been concentrated at Dachau before this final move to Niederdorf/Hochpustertal 70 km northeast of Bozen. Enroute, the hostages were guarded by SS and SD men who were not anxious to be part of an operation that could be called a war crime in the very near future. Their prisoners, which included close family members of some of the July 20 conspirators, could not simply disappear without questions being asked later. The SS officers in charge of the transport were Obersturmführer Stiller and Untersturmführer Bader and they had orders to kill all the prisoners if things did not go according to plan.

When the transport arrived in Innsbruck at a detention center that had been turned into a work training camp overseen by the Gestapo (Arbeitserziehungslager Reichenau), Stiller and Bader were told their prisoners could not be accommodated, or rather, "Stiller did not consider filthy camp Reichenau a suitable place for the prisoners entrusted to him": www.go2war2.nl/artikel/4807/VIP-prisoners-of-the-SS.htm?page=3. In either case, quite possibly some of the prisoners were recognized by camp authorities who wanted nothing to do with them. The 139 prisoners were then moved to a hotel in Niederdorf, arriving on April 28. This destination, unbeknown to Stiller and Bader, was the temporary billet of three uncooperative Wehrmacht generals.

Wehrmacht Colonel Bogislaw von Bonin, who was himself among the prisoners being transported, made clandestine contact with senior Wehrmacht officers at the Niederdorf hotel, identified some of his fellow prisoners and expressed his concern that they would all be executed if U.S. troops closing in on the area attempted to liberate them. The Wehrmacht generals wanted no part of this SS supervised operation and a message describing the situation was sent from the hotel to a Wehrmacht command at Bozen. A subsequent message was sent from there to Captain Wichard von Alvensleben in Sexten, some 17 km east of Niederdorf. With orders following from Colonel General Heinrich von Vietinghoff, Commander in Chief of the Southwest, Alvensleben and his men arrived in Niederdorf to protect the prisoners. Knowing that U.S. forces were on the horizon and with Alvensleben's men having surrounded the village, Stiller and Bader made the strategic choice on April 30 to abandon their charges and get away with their SS and SD men. The Wehrmacht liberated prisoners were then quartered at the Pragser Wildsee Hotel until U.S. troops arrived in Niederdorf on May 5 (May 4 according to Richardi 158 as qtd. https://archive.is/20120910072003/ http://www.raetia.com/index.php?id=338). A complete list of the prisoners is given below and further details on individual detainees can be found at: www.mythoselser.de/niederdorf.htm.

Austria

- Konrad Praxmarer, author
- Richard Schmitz, former mayor of Vienna
- Kurt Schuschnigg, Austrian chancellor

Czech Republic

- Josef Burda, merchant
- Josef Rozsevac-Rys, journalist
- Jàn Stanek, major

Denmark

- Hans Frederik Hansen, engineer
- Adolf T. Larsen, farmer
- Hans Lunding, head of the Danish Intelligence Service
- Max J. Mikkelsen, captain
- Jörgen Lönborg Friis Mogensen, vice consul
- Knud E. Pedersen, captain

France

- Jeanne Leon Blum, wife of Leon Blum
- Leon Blum, former prime minister of France
- Prince Xavier de Bourbon
- Armand Mottet
- Gabriel Piguet, bishop of Clermont-Ferrand
- Ray N. Van Wymeersch, captain of the Free French Air Force

Germany

- Bogislaw von Bonin, colonel
- Baron Fritz Cerrini, private secretary of Prince Friedrich Leopold of Prussia
- Friedrich Engelke, merchant
- Alexander von Falkenhausen, general (former military commander of Belgium and France)
- Wilhelm von Flügge, director of I. G. Farben
- Friedrich Leopold, prince of Prussia
- Franz Halder, general
- Gertrud Halder, wife of Franz Halder
- Anton Hamm, Kaplan
- Erich Heberlein, diplomat
- Margot Heberlein, wife of Dr. Erich Heberlein
- Horst Hoepner, merchant, brother of General Erich Hoepner
- Joseph Joos, journalist and politician (Zentrum, Central Party)
- Karl Kunkel, Kaplan
- Franz Maria Liedig, navy officer (Abwehr)
- Josef Müller, officer (Abwehr)
- Johann Neuhäusler, Domkapitular (Canon)
- Martin Niemöller, pastor
- Heidel Nowakowski
- Horst von Petersdorff, colonel
- Prince Philipp of Hesse, diplomat
- Hermann Pünder, officer
- Hjalmar Schacht
- Fabian von Schlabrendorff, officer (adjutant of Major General Henning von Tresckow)
- Georg Thomas, general
- Amelie Thyssen, wife of Fritz Thyssen
- Fritz Thyssen, businessman

Great Britain

- Sigismund Payne Best, captain
- Jack Churchill, lieutenant colonel
- Peter Churchill, captain (special operations executive)
- Thomas J. Cushing, staff sergeant
- Harry M. A. Day, wing commander
- Sydney H. Dowse, squadron leader
- Hugh M. Falconer, squadron leader
- Wadim Greenewich, Foreign Office, London
- Bertram James, flight lieutenant
- John McGrath, lieutenant colonel
- Patrick O'Brien, soldier
- John Spence, farmer
- Richard H. Stevens, lieutenant colonel
- Andrew Walsh, soldier (aircraft fitter)

Greece

- Constantin Bakopoulos, general
- Panajotis Dedes, general
- Vassilis Dimitrion, soldier
- Nikolaos Grivas, caporal (corporal)
- Georges Kosmas, general
- Alexandros Papagos, general (commander in chief of the Greek army)
- Jean D. Pitsikas, general

Hungary

- Aleksander Ginzery, colonel
- Josef Hatz, major
- Samuel Hatz, teacher (father of Josef Hatz)
- Andreas Hlatky, Hungarian secretary of state
- Miklos Horthy, Jr., diplomat (son of Miklos Horthy)
- Geza Igmandy-Hegyessy, general
- Miklos Kallay, former prime minister of Hungary
- Julius Kiraly, colonel
- Desiderius Onody, secretary of Miklos Horthy, Jr.
- Peter Baron Schell, Hungarian minister of interior

Italy

- Eugenio Apollonio, vice-capo della polizia (deputy chief of the police) of the Italian Social Republic in Salò
- Mario Badoglio, son of Marshal Pietro Badoglio
- Davide Ferrero, colonel
- Sante Garibaldi, general
- Tullio Tamburini, chief of the police of the Italian Social Republic in Salò

Latvia

- Gustavs Celmins, captain of the Latvian army

Netherlands

- Johannes J. C. van Dijk, minister of defense

Norway

- Arne Daehli, captain

Poland

- Jan Izycki, pilot officer, RAF
- Stanislaw Jensen, pilot officer, RAF
- Count Aleksander Zamoyski, major

Russia

- Ivan Bessonov, general
- Victor Brodnicov, lieutenant colonel
- Fyodor Ceredilin, soldier
- Vassily Kokorin, lieutenant
- Pyotr Privalov, general
- Nikolay Ruchenko, officer

Slovakia

- Imrich Karvas, professor

Sweden

- Carl S. Edquist, director

Yugoslavia

- Hinko Dragic, lieutenant colonel
- Novak D. Popovic, head of the post administration
- Dimitrije Tomalevsky, journalist

The Kin Prisoners

- Fey von Hassell Pirzio Biroli, daughter of Ulrich von Hassell
- Annelise Gisevius, sister of Hans Bernd Gisevius
- Anneliese Goerdeler, wife of Carl Goerdeler
- Benigna Goerdeler, daughter of Anneliese and Carl Goerdeler
- Gustav Goerdeler, brother of Carl Goerdeler
- Marianne Goerdeler, daughter of Anneliese and Carl Goerdeler
- Irma Goerdeler, wife of Ulrich Goerdeler/daughter-in-law of Anneliese and Carl Goerdeler
- Jutta Goerdeler, cousin of Benigna Goerdeler
- Reinhard Goerdeler, son of Anneliese and Carl Goerdeler (not at the Pragser Wildsee Hotel)
- Ulrich Goerdeler, son of Anneliese and Carl Goerdeler
- Käte Gudzent
- Franz von Hammerstein, son of Maria and Kurt von Hammerstein-Equord (not at the Pragser Wildsee Hotel)
- Hildur von Hammerstein, daughter of Maria and Kurt von Hammerstein-Equord
- Maria von Hammerstein-Equord, wife of Kurt von Hammerstein-Equord
- Anna-Luise von Hofacker, daughter of Ilse and Cäsar von Hofacker
- Eberhard von Hofacker, son of Ilse and Cäsar von Hofacker
- Ilse Lotte von Hofacker, wife of Cäsar von Hofacker
- Peter A. Jehle (not at the Pragser Wildsee Hotel)
- Elisabeth Kaiser, daughter of Therese Kaiser
- Therese Kaiser
- Arthur Kuhn, lawyer
- Anni von Lerchenfeld, mother-in-law of Claus Schenk Graf von Stauffenberg (died in the SS camp in Matzkau)
- Lini Lindemann, wife of General Fritz Lindemann
- Josef Mohr, brother of Therese Kaiser
- Käthe Mohr, wife of Josef Mohr
- Gisela Gräfin von Plettenberg-Lenhausen, daughter of Walther Graf von Plettenberg-Lenhausen
- Walther Graf von Plettenberg-Lenhausen, merchant
- Dietrich Schatz, major (not at the Pragser Wildsee Hotel)
- Hans-Dietrich Schröder, son of Ingeborg Schröder
- Harring Schröder, son of Ingeborg Schröder
- Ingeborg Schröder
- Sybille-Maria Schröder, daughter of Ingeborg Schröder
- Alexander Schenk Graf von Stauffenberg, brother of Claus Schenk Graf von Stauffenberg.
- Alexandra Schenk Gräfin von Stauffenberg, daughter of Markwart Schenk Graf von Stauffenberg
- Clemens Schenk Graf von Stauffenberg, son of Markwart Schenk Graf von Stauffenberg

- Elisabeth Schenk Gräfin von Stauffenberg, wife of Clemens Schenk Graf von Stauffenberg
- Inèz Schenk Gräfin von Stauffenberg, daughter of Markwart Schenk Graf von Stauffenberg
- Maria Schenk Gräfin von Stauffenberg, wife of Berthold Schenk Graf von Stauffenberg
- Marie-Gabriele Schenk Gräfin von Stauffenberg, daughter of Elisabeth Schenk Gräfin von Stauffenberg and Clemens Schenk Graf von Stauffenberg
- Markwart Schenk Graf von Stauffenberg (Senior), colonel
- Markwart Schenk Graf von Stauffenberg (Junior), son of Elisabeth Schenk Gräfin von Stauffenberg and Clemens Schenk Graf von Stauffenberg (not at the Pragser Wildsee Hotel)
- Otto Philipp Schenk Graf von Stauffenberg, son of Elisabeth Schenk Gräfin von Stauffenberg and Clemens Schenk Graf von Stauffenberg
- Isa Vermehren, comedian, sister of Erich Vermehren

In addition to these prominent prisoners, two inmates of the Dachau concentration camp—the cook (or circus clown, or both [Manvell and Fraenkel, *The Men Who Tried*, 248]) Wilhelm Visintainer and the barber Paul Wauer—were also in the transport.

Appendix C: Erika Canaris' Letter to General William Donovan

library2.lawschool.cornell.edu/donovan/pdf/Batch_7/Vol_XVII_53_010_01.pdf
(with minor grammatical and language corrections)

Translation

Erika Canaris Riederau, 15 November 1945

Dear General Donovan,

First permit me to thank you for the human sympathy you have shown me. You were kind enough to send me Captain Nordon to help in some personal difficulties. This proof of your kind willingness to help has done me a lot of good and I shall never forget it.

Dr. Mueller and Captain Nordon told me that it might be of use if I made some notes concerning the life and character of my husband. I would like to comply with this request, but I would ask you to consider this letter to be written for you only, for the purpose of giving a clear picture of my husband, and not for the purpose of having any of it published.

My husband was born in Westphalia on January 1, 1887. His father was a mining director. In 1905, he entered the Navy and went first to the Baltic, then the Mediterranean and Mexico. When war broke out in 1914, he was on the cruiser *Dresden*. The *Dresden* took part in the battle of Coronel and in the battle of the Falklands, and was later sunk by English ships near the coast of Chile. My husband was interned, but escaped however and returned to Germany after an adventurous flight. He was then used in the German Secret Service. From the fall of 1917 to the end of the war he was a submarine commander in the Mediterranean. After his return he became active in an anti-Bolshevist sense. Later he was the adjutant of the Reich Defense Minister Noske. In the summer of 1920, he was transferred to Kiel as an Admiralty Staff Officer and from 1922 to 1924, he was first officer of the cruiser *Berlin*. From May to October in 1924, he went on a professional teaching trip to Japan, and then he had a command post in the Navy Head Office in Berlin for four years. Following this he spent 6 years in Wilhelmshafen as First Officer of the *Schlesien*, as Chief of the staff of the North Sea station, and as later as Commanding Officer of the *Schlesien*. On October 1, 1934, he was appointed Commander of the "Fortress of Swinemeunde," but in December 1934, he was transferred to Berlin as Chief of the Abwehr. He held this post until February 1944 when he was deposed by Hitler and the whole Abwehr was put under the jurisdiction of Himmler and the SS. Officially my husband was sent "on leave," but on July 1, 1944 he received a command as Admiral and Chief of the Special Staff for Trade and War Industry. On July 23, 1944, he was arrested because of his participation in the attempted assassination of Hitler. After having been imprisoned for eight and a half months, he died for a just cause on April 9, 1945, in the concentration camp at Flossenbuerg.

Concerning his activity as Chief of the Abwehr, and especially the details of its structure, I can say little or nothing, since as a woman I was never much interested in these things. For two years I was away from Berlin because of the air attacks and spent most of this time on the Ammersee. Before that I lived at home as his wife and the mother of our two children and never interfered in official business. My husband did not want women to know of official affairs. He sometimes did tell me things and sometimes gave me things to read, such as the Allied War Communiqués and the speeches made in Parliament, as well as those made by President Roosevelt, all of which he received in their original form. I was also informed somewhat about the preparations for July 20 and similar plans. My knowledge of this is much too general to be of any interest to you.

It might be of interest to you to know of the human side of my husband since that will explain to you the true motives of his actions. Such a description is not easy. I think that a good term to describe him would be "Christ of Action"; a friend of humanity in the truest and most beautiful sense of the word, a person for whom there was no difference among human beings as far as profession, rank, race, or confession was concerned. Many of those he helped will bear witness to this. He was very religious and believed in the supernatural. He had a high feeling of responsibility for the unexpressed duties of life. He was extremely active, did not spare himself, and yet was extremely tender in his emotions. In the office, he asked everything of himself, of his collaborators, and the people under him. He had sympathy and human understanding for them and was always ready to help.

It is impossible to say how much he suffered from developments. He used his powers to oppose as much as possible the growing lawlessness. This was known. Many people who were persecuted by the Gestapo came to him, such as Jews, pastors, members of Christian organizations, etc. Often meetings took place in our house with people or their representatives. Often he handled these cases directly in his office in spite of the dangers involved. He was supported in this respect by Dr. von Dohnanyi, who was arrested in 1933 and later died; also by General Oster who died with him. I am attaching a list of such acts of assistance but know that these are only a small percentage of all that he did for others. Miss Hanna Reichmuth who worked with the pastor in Berlin-Schlachtensee will be able to give you cases in which he saved Protestant pastors from arrest and concentration camps.

He helped everyone, be it a tubercular beggar, or the last Greek Minister Rangabe whose daughter was very sick in a Berlin sanatorium and who asked him to take her to Switzerland. He helped where help was needed. He had innumerable friends. He loved animals, particularly his small Dachshunds, which always accompanied him.

He did everything in his power for his family and words cannot describe it. He never thought of himself. He never took a vacation from January 1939 until his dismissal, because he realized that his absence would be used by his opponents and would take away from him the possibility to help. He was very modest and frugal and always declined to move into an official apartment with beautiful rooms. Up to the end we lived in our small six room house in Schlachtensee in spite of the social obligations we had.

My husband immediately recognized the dangers of National Socialism. He hoped that the danger could be mastered. To his sorrow, the first and best chance to get rid of the system was not utilized—June 30, 1934, when the Army should have struck. That same year he took over the leadership of the Abwehr. During the following years, many plans of overthrowing the regime were doomed to failure because of the mass psychosis of the people, nourished by the treatment foreign nations accorded Hitler. My husband's chief aim was to get good intelligence from abroad in order to try to convince the powers that be. He became extremely unpopular because of his continual warnings and made many enemies in the armed forces leadership staff, the Foreign Office, Gestapo, and other places. Himmler, Jodl, Schmundt, Sperrly, Richthofen, Kesselring, Rader, Doenitz, Ribbentrop, and Hitler were among his enemies.

I shall always remember the days before the outbreak of war. My husband always prophesied the disastrous end of the mad adventure and never changed his mind even in the face of the victories of the first years. He hated nothing more than the "special reports" he saw and through them, the death march of his people. After the first bombardment of Warsaw by the German Luftwaffe, he returned home deeply shaken and said: "If there is justice, and I believe there is, we will go through the same thing, and then, God save us." He also said, "We are *all* guilty, *all*, and we will all have to pay." He and his friend suffered so terribly because they had to fight on the German side and they loved their Fatherland, yet their sympathies were not on that side and could not be because their philosophical attitude was so different.

He kept on because of the hope for an overthrow of the regime, the hope to be able to help reconstruct a new better and decent Germany. "I wanted so much to help them," he once said, meaning the "other" side. Only because of his desire to help in a political and human sense, did he defend and keep his position in spite of all opponents. He stuck to his post until he was deposed by Hitler in the most undignified manner. A short time after his dismissal he showed me a bunch of letters from people who had asked him to help them and he said sadly, "There is nothing I can do for these people any more."

I shall never be able to understand why fate decreed as it did—why he had to suffer so much, he who had helped others so much. It is our task to go on living the way he would have wanted us to.

If I have told you all this, I have done it only for the sake of my husband; in order to show him to you in the proper light and also perhaps in order to convince you, General Donovan, that my husband, together with those who thought and lived as he did, represented the decent Germany, which always exists and which will always exist.

With kindest regards and renewed thanks, I am

(signed) Erika Canaris

Appendix D: The Morgenthau Plan

In September 1944, President Franklin D. Roosevelt asked me to outline for him a program for the treatment of Germany after her defeat. He wished to take such a document to the Quebec Conference, which was to be held in a few days, and he knew that I had devoted a good deal of thought and study to the subject. As Secretary of the Treasury, I had been led into the whole problem by questions of reparations, currency and financial controls. I had seen that these could not be divorced from the broader aspects of what to do with Germany. The President, with whom I had been privileged to work on terms of intimacy and confidence for many years, knew of my interest and my research.—Henry Morgenthau (xi)

This is the suggested "Post-Surrender Program for Germany" (Original Memorandum of 1944, signed by Morgenthau): Roosevelt Library, www.fdrlibrary.marist.edu/psf/box31/t297a01.html. The memo to Roosevelt, written by Morgenthau, actually had the title "Program to Prevent Germany from Starting a World War III" (1).

1. Demilitarization of Germany.
   It should be the aim of the Allied Forces to accomplish the complete demilitarization of Germany in the shortest possible period of time after surrender. This means completely disarming the German Army and people (including the removal or destruction of all war material), the total destruction of the whole German armament industry, and the removal or destruction of other key industries which are basic to military strength.
2. Partitioning of Germany.
   (a) Poland should get that part of East Prussia which doesn't go to the U.S.S.R. and the southern portion of Silesia as indicated on the attached map (Appendix A).
   (b) France should get the Saar and the adjacent territories bounded by the Rhine and the Moselle Rivers.
   (c) As indicated in part 3 an International Zone should be created containing the Ruhr and the surrounding industrial areas.
   (d) The remaining portion of Germany should be divided into two autonomous, independent states:
      (1) a South German state comprising Bavaria, Wuerttemberg, Baden and some smaller areas
      (2) a North German state comprising a large part of the old state of Prussia, Saxony, Thuringia and several smaller states.
   There shall be a custom union between the new South German state and Austria, which will be restored to her pre–1938 political borders.
3. The Ruhr Area.

(The Ruhr, surrounding industrial areas, as shown on the attached map, including the Rhineland, the Keil Canal, and all German territory north of the Keil Canal.)

Here lies the heart of German industrial power, the cauldron of wars. This area should not only be stripped of all presently existing industries but so weakened and controlled that it can not in the fore-seeable future become an industrial area. The following steps will accomplish this:

- (a) Within a short period, if possible not longer than 6 months after the cessation of hostilities, all industrial plants and equipment not destroyed by military action shall either be completely dismantled and removed from the area or completely destroyed. All equipment shall be removed from the mines and the mines shall be thoroughly wrecked.

It is anticipated that the stripping of this area would be accomplished in three stages:
- (i) The military forces immediately upon entry into the area shall destroy all plants and equipment which cannot be removed.
- (ii) Removal of plants and equipment by members of the United Nations as restitution and reparation (Paragraph 4).
- (iii) All plants and equipment not removed within a stated period of time, say 6 months, will be completely destroyed or reduced to scrap and allocated to the United Nations.
- (b) All people within the area should be made to understand that this area will not again be allowed to become an industrial area. Accordingly, all people and their families within the area having special skills or technical training should be encouraged to migrate permanently from the area and should be as widely dispersed as possible.
- (c) The area should be made an international zone to be governed by an international security organization to be established by the United Nations. In governing the area, the international organization should be guided by policies designed to further the above stated objectives.

4. Restitution and Reparation.

Reparations, in the form of recurrent payments and deliveries, should not be demanded. Restitution and reparation shall be effected by the transfer of existing German resources and territories, e.g.,
- (a) by restitution of property looted by the Germans in territories occupied by them;
- (b) by transfer of German territory and German private rights in industrial property situated in such territory to invaded countries and the international organization under the program of partition;
- (c) by the removal and distribution among devastated countries of industrial plants and equipment situated within the International Zone and the North and South German states delimited in the section on partition;
- (d) by forced German labor outside Germany; and
- (e) by confiscation of all German assets of any character whatsoever outside of Germany.

5. Education and Propaganda.
- (a) All schools and universities will be closed until an Allied Commission of Education has formulated an effective reorganization program. It is contemplated that it may require a considerable period of time before any institutions of higher education are reopened. Meanwhile the education of German students in foreign universities will not be prohibited. Elementary schools will be reopened as quickly as appropriate teachers and textbooks are available.
- (b) All German radio stations and newspapers, magazines, weeklies, etc. shall be discontinued until adequate controls are established and an appropriate program formulated.

6. Political Decentralization.

The military administration in Germany in the initial period should be carried out with a view toward the eventual partitioning of Germany into three states. To facilitate partitioning and to assure its permanence the military authorities should be guided by the following principles:

(a) Dismiss all policy-making officials of the Reich government and deal primarily with local governments.
(b) Encourage the reestablishment of state governments in each of the states (Lander) corresponding to 18 states into which Germany is presently divided and in addition make the Prussian provinces separate states.
(c) Upon the partition of Germany, the various state governments should be encouraged to organize a federal government for each of the newly partitioned areas. Such new governments should be in the form of a confederation of states, with emphasis on states' rights and a large degree of local autonomy.

7. Responsibility of Military for Local German Economy.
The sole purpose of the military in control of the German economy shall be to facilitate military operations and military occupation. The Allied Military Government shall not assume responsibility for such economic problems as price controls, rationing, unemployment, production, reconstruction, distribution, consumption, housing, or transportation, or take any measures designed to maintain or strengthen operations. The responsibility for sustaining the German economy and people rests with the German people with such facilities as may be available under the circumstances.

8. Controls over Development of German Economy.
During a period of at least twenty years after surrender adequate controls, including controls over foreign trade and tight restrictions on capital imports, shall be maintained by the United Nations designed to prevent in the newly established states the establishment or expansion of key industries basic to the German military potential and to control other key industries.

9. Punishment of War Crimes and Treatment of Special Groups.
There is attached (Appendix B) a program for the punishment of certain war crimes and for the treatment of Nazi organizations and other special groups.

10. Wearing of Insignia and Uniforms.
    (a) No person in Germany (except members of the United Nations and neutral countries) shall be permitted to wear any military insignia of rank or branch of service, service ribbons or military medals.
    (b) No such persons shall be permitted to wear, after 6 months from the cessation of hostilities any military uniform or any uniform of any quasi military organizations.

11. Prohibition on Parades.
No military parades shall be permitted anywhere in Germany and all military bands shall be disbanded.

12. Aircraft.
All aircraft (including gliders), whether military or commercial, will be confiscated for later disposition. No German shall be permitted to operate or to help operate such aircraft, including those owned by foreign interests.

13. United States Responsibility.
    (a) The responsibility for the execution of the post-surrender program for Germany set forth in this memorandum is the joint responsibility of the United Nations. The execution of the joint policy agreed upon shall therefore eventually be entrusted to the international body that emerges from United Nations discussions.
    Consideration of the specific measures to be taken in carrying out the joint program suggests the desirability of separating the task to be performed during the initial period of military occupation from those that will require a much longer period of execution. While the U.S., U.K., and U.S.S.R. will, for practical reasons, play the major role (of course aided by the military forces of the United Nations) in demilitarizing Germany (point 1) the detailed execution of other parts of the program can best be handled by Germany's continental neighbors.
    (b) When Germany has been completely demilitarized, there would be the following distribution of duties in carrying out the German program:

(i) The U.S. would have military and civilian representation on whatever international commission or commissions may be established for the execution of the whole German program and such representatives should have adequate U.S. staffs.

(ii) The primary responsibility for the policing of Germany and for Civil administration in Germany would be assumed by the military forces of Germany's continental neighbors. Specifically, these should include Russian, French, Polish, Czech, Greek, Yugoslav, Norwegian, Dutch and Belgian soldiers.

(c) Under this program, United States troops could be withdrawn within a relatively short time. Actual withdrawal of United States troops should not precede agreement with the U.S.S.R. and the U.K. on the principles set forth in this memorandum.

14. Appointment of an American High Commissioner

An American High Commissioner for Germany should be appointed as soon as possible, so that he can sit in on the development of the American views on this problem.

Appendix E: The Marshall Speech

Text of the commencement address given by United States Secretary of State George C. Marshall at Harvard University on June 5, 1947. This speech initiated the postwar European Aid Program, commonly known as the "Marshall Plan": www.usaid.gov/multimedia/video/Marshall/Marshallspeech.html.

I need not tell you, gentlemen, that the world situation is very serious. That must be apparent to all intelligent people. I think one difficulty is that the problem is one of such enormous complexity that the very mass of facts presented to the public by press and radio make it exceedingly difficult for the man in the street to reach a clear appraisement of the situation. Furthermore, the people of this country are distant from the troubled areas of the earth and it is hard for them to comprehend the plight and consequent reactions of the long-suffering peoples, and the effect of those reactions on their governments in connection with our efforts to promote peace in the world.

In considering the requirements for the rehabilitation of Europe, the physical loss of life, the visible destruction of cities, factories, mines and railroads was correctly estimated but it has become obvious during recent months that this visible destruction was probably less serious than the dislocation of the entire fabric of European economy. For the past 10 years conditions have been highly abnormal. The feverish preparation for war and the more feverish maintenance of the war effort engulfed all aspects of national economies. Machinery has fallen into disrepair or is entirely obsolete. Under the arbitrary and destructive Nazi rule, virtually every possible enterprise was geared into the German war machine. Long-standing commercial ties, private institutions, banks, insurance companies, and shipping companies disappeared, through loss of capital, absorption through nationalization, or by simple destruction. In many countries, confidence in the local currency has been severely shaken. The breakdown of the business structure of Europe during the war was complete. Recovery has been seriously retarded by the fact that two years after the close of hostilities a peace settlement with Germany and Austria has not been agreed upon. But even given a more prompt solution of these difficult problems the rehabilitation of the economic structure of Europe quite evidently will require a much longer time and greater effort than had been foreseen.

There is a phase of this matter which is both interesting and serious. The farmer has always produced the foodstuffs to exchange with the city dweller for the other necessities of life. This division of labor is the basis of modern civilization. At the present time it is threatened with breakdown. The town and city industries are not producing adequate goods to exchange with the food producing farmer. Raw materials and fuel are in short supply. Machinery is lacking or worn out. The farmer or the peasant cannot find the goods for sale which he desires to purchase. So the sale of his farm produce for money which he cannot use seems to him an unprofitable transaction. He, therefore, has withdrawn many fields from crop cultivation and is using them for grazing. He feeds more grain to stock and finds for himself and his family an ample supply of food, however short he may be on clothing and the other ordinary gadgets of civilization. Meanwhile people in the cities are short of food and fuel. So the governments are forced to use their foreign money and credits to procure these necessities abroad. This process exhausts funds which are urgently needed for reconstruction. Thus a very serious situation is rapidly developing which bodes no good for the world. The modern system of the division of labor upon which the exchange of products is based is in danger of breaking down.

The truth of the matter is that Europe's requirements for the next three or four years of foreign food and other essential products—principally from America—are so much greater than her present ability to pay that she must have substantial additional help or face economic, social, and political deterioration of a very grave character.

The remedy lies in breaking the vicious circle and restoring the confidence of the European people in the economic future of their own countries and of Europe as a whole. The manufacturer and the farmer throughout wide areas must be able and willing to exchange their products for currencies the continuing value of which is not open to question.

Aside from the demoralizing effect on the world at large and the possibilities of disturbances arising as a result of the desperation of the people concerned, the consequences to the economy of the United States should be apparent to all. It is logical that the United States should do whatever it is able to do to assist in the return of normal economic health in the world, without which there can be no political stability and no assured peace. Our policy is directed not against any country or doctrine but against hunger, poverty, desperation and chaos. Its purpose should be the revival of a working economy in the world so as to permit the emergence of political and social conditions in which free institutions can exist. Such assistance, I am convinced, must not be on a piecemeal basis as various crises develop. Any assistance that this Government may render in the future should provide a cure rather than a mere palliative. Any government that is willing to assist in the task of recovery will find full co-operation I am sure, on the part of the United States Government. Any government which maneuvers to block the recovery of other countries cannot expect help from us. Furthermore, governments, political parties, or groups which seek to perpetuate human misery in order to profit therefrom politically or otherwise will encounter the opposition of the United States.

It is already evident that, before the United States Government can proceed much further in its efforts to alleviate the situation and help start the European world on its way to recovery, there must be some agreement among the countries of Europe as to the requirements of the situation and the part those countries themselves will take in order to give proper effect to whatever action might be undertaken by this Government. It would be neither fitting nor efficacious for this Government to undertake to draw up unilaterally a program designed to place Europe on its feet economically. This is the business of the Europeans. The initiative, I think, must come from Europe. The role of this country should consist of friendly aid in the drafting of a European program and of later support of such a program so far as it may be practical for us to do so. The program should be a joint one, agreed to by a number, if not all European nations.

An essential part of any successful action on the part of the United States is an understanding on the part of the people of America of the character of the problem and the remedies to be applied. Political passion and prejudice should have no part. With foresight, and a willingness on the part of our people to face up to the vast responsibility which history has clearly placed upon our country, the difficulties I have outlined can and will be overcome.

Bibliography

Ailsby, Christopher. *The Third Reich, Day by Day*. Zenith Press, 2005.

Albrecht, Dagmar. *Mit Meinem Schicksal Kann Ich Nicht Hadern...: Sippenhaft in der Familie Albrecht von Hagen*. Dietz, 2001.

Allgemeine Deutsche Biographie & Neue Deutsche Biographie. www.ndb.badwmuenchen.de/.

Band, Adelslexikob XIII. *Genealogisches Handbuch des Adels*. Band 128 der Gesamtreihe. C. A. Starke, 2002.

Benz, Wolfgang. *Überleben im Dritten Reich: Juden im Untergrund und ihre Helfer*. DTV Deutscher Taschenbuch, 2006.

Beschloss, Michael R. *The Conquerors: Roosevelt, Truman, and the Destruction of Hitler's Germany, 1941–1945*. Simon & Schuster, 2002.

Blanke, Richard. *Orphans of Versailles: The Germans in Western Poland, 1918–1939*. University Press of Kentucky, 1992.

Bloxham, Donald. *Genocide on Trial: The Formation of Holocaust History and Memory*. Oxford University Press, 2003.

Boehm, Eric. *We Survived*. ABC-CLIO Information Services, 1985. Originally published in 1949 by Yale University Press.

Bonhoeffer, Dietrich. *The Cost of Discipleship*. SCM Canterbury Press, 2001.

———. *Dietrich Bonhoeffer Works*. Vol. 16: *Conspiracy and Imprisonment, 1940–1945*. Edited by Mark S. Brocker. Translated by Lisa E. Dahill. Fortress Press, 2006.

———. *Letters and Papers from Prison* (Enlarged Edition). Edited by Eberhard Bethge. Simon & Schuster (Touchstone Books), 1997.

Bonhoeffer, Klaus, Dietrich Bonhoeffer, and Eberhard Bethge. *Auf dem Wege zur Freiheit*. Verlag Haus und Schule, 1947.

Brakelmann, Günter. *Helmuth James Moltke: Zeitgenosse für Ein Anderes Deutschland*. LIT Verlag, 2009.

Breitman, Richard. *U.S. Intelligence and the Nazis*. Cambridge University Press, 2005.

Brickner, Richard M. *Is Germany Incurable?* J.B. Lippincott Co., 1943.

Broderskeil, Lars, and Antje Vollmer. *Stauffenberg Companions: The Fate of the Unknown Conspirators*. Hanser, 2013.

Budde, Eugene, and Peter Lütscher. *Der 20 Juli*. H. Raven, 1952.

Burchard, Christoph. "The Nürnberg Trial and Its Impact on Germany." *Journal of International Criminal Justice* 4, no. 4 (2006).

Burleigh, Michael. *The Third Reich: A New History*. Hill & Wang, 2000.

Chavkin, Boris, and Aleksandr Kalganov. "Neue Quellen zur Geschichte des 20. Juli 1944 aus dem Archiv des Föderalen Sicherheitsdienstes der Russischen Föderation (FSB) 'Eigenhändige Aussagen' von Major iG. Joachim Kuhn." *Forum für Osteuropäische Ideen und Zeitgeschichte*, Heft 2, 5. s. 378 (2001).

Churchill, Winston. *Churchill by Himself*. Edited by Richard Langworth. Public Affairs (Perseus Books), 2008.

Clifford, Angela, ed. and trans. *The Moabit Sonnets*. Athol Books, 2001.

Cook, Bernard. *Women and War: A Historical Encyclopedia from Antiquity to the Present*. Vol. 1. ABC-CLIO Information Services, 2006.

Das-Ritterkreuz. www.das-ritterkreuz.de.

Dear, I. C. B., ed., and M. R. D. Foot, consulting ed. *The Oxford Companion to the Second World War*. Oxford University Press, 2000.

Delp, Alfred. *Alfred Delp, Kämpfer, Beter, Zeuge: Letzte Briefe, Beiträge von Freunden*. Herder, 1962.

Demetz, Peter. *Prague in Danger*. Farrar, Straus, and Giroux, 2008.

Deutsch, Harold C. *The Conspiracy Against Hitler in the Twilight War*. University of Minnesota Press, 1968.

———. *Hitler and His Generals*. University of Minnesota Press, 1974.

Deutsches Historisches Museum. www.dhm.de/.

Douglas-Hamilton, James. *The Truth About Rudolf Hess*. Frontline Books, 2016.

Doxtader, Erik, and Charles Villa-Vicencio, eds. *To Repair the Irreparable: Reparation and Reconstruction in South Africa*. David Philip, 2004.

Duffy, James P., and Vincent L. Ricci. *Target Hitler*. Praeger, 1992.

Dulles, Allen Welsh. *Germany's Underground*. Macmillan, 1947.

Eberle, Henrik, and Matthias Uhl, eds. *The Hitler Book: The Secret Dossier Prepared for Stalin*. Public Affairs, 2005.

Fest, Joachim. *Hitler*. Mariner Books (a division of Houghton, Mifflin, and Harcourt), 2002.

———. *Hitler: Eine Biographie*. Propyläen, 2004.

———. *Plotting Hitler's Death*. Metropolitan Books, 1994.

Fikentscher, Rüdiger, Boje Schmuhl, and Konrad Breitenborn. *Die Bodenreform in Sachsen-Anhalt: Durchführung, Zeitzeugen, Folgen: Tagung in Stendal am 21. und 22. November, 1997*. Stekovics, 1999.

Friedlander, Saul. *The Years of Extermination*. HarperCollins, 2008.

Frieser, Karl Heinz, and John T. Greenwood. *The Blitzkrieg Legend: The 1940 Campaign in the West*. U.S. Naval Institute Press, 2005.

Galante, Pierre, and Eugene Silianoff. *Operation Valkyrie*. Dell Books, 1981.

German Resistance Memorial Center. www.gdw-berlin.de/.

Gersdorff, Rudolf-Christoph Freiherr von. *Soldat im Untergang*. Ullstein Publishers, 1977.

Gilbert, Felix. *Hitler Directs His War*. Oxford University Press, 1950.

Gilbert, Martin. *The Second World War: A Complete History*. Holt Paperbacks, 2004.

Gimbel, John. *Science, Technology, and Reparations*. Stanford University Press, 1990.

Gisevius, Hans Bernd. *To the Bitter End*. Riverside Press, 1947.

———. *Valkyrie: An Insider's Account of the Plot to Kill Hitler*. DaCapo Press, 2009. (A condensed version of Gisevius, *To the Bitter End*).

Goda, Norman J. W. "Black Marks: Hitler's Bribery of His Senior Officers during World War II." *Journal of Modern History* 72, no. 2 (June 2000).

Goebbels, Joseph. *Final Entries, 1945: The Diaries of Josef Goebbels*. Edited by Hugh Trevor-Roper. G.P. Putnam, 1978.

Goerlitz, Walter. *The History of the German General Staff*. Praeger, 1954.

Gregory, Don, and Wilhelm Gehlen. *Two Soldiers, Two Lost Fronts*. Casemate, 2009.

Greiff, Pablo. *The Handbook of Reparations*. Oxford University Press, 2006.

Grieshaber, Kirsten. "65 Years after WWII, German Parliament Overturns All Nazi-era Treason Convictions." *Baltimore Sun*, September 8, 2009.

Groeben, Klaus von der. *Nikolaus Christoph von Halem: Im Widerstand gegen das Dritte Reich*. Böhlau, 1991.

Grzesinski, Albert. *Im Kampf um die Deutsche Republik*. Oldenbourg, 2001.

Gun, Nerin. *Eva Braun, Hitler's Mistress*. Meredith Press, 1968.

Hamerow, Theodore S. *On the Road to the Wolf's Lair*. Belknap Press/Harvard University Press, 1999.

Hart, Basil Henry Liddell. *The German Generals Talk*. HarperCollins, 1948.

———, ed. *The Rommel Papers*. Da Capo Press, 1982.

Hassell, Angostino von, and Sigrid MacRae. *Alliance of Enemies: The Untold Story of the Secret American and German Collaborations to End World War II*. Thomas Dunne Books, 2006.

Hassell, Ulrich von. *The von Hassell Diaries*. Doubleday, 1947.

Hausmann, Frank-Rutger. *Auch im Krieg Schweigen die Musen Nicht: die Deutschen Wissenschaftlichen*. Vandenhoeck & Ruprecht, 2002.

Havas, Laslo. *Hitler's Plot to Kill the Big Three*. Bantam Books, 1971.

Heck, Alfons. *The Burden of Hitler's Legacy*. Renaissance House, 1988.

Heer, H., and K. Naumann, eds. *War of Extermination: The German Military in World War II*. Berghahn Books, 2000.

Henke, Klaus-Dieter. *Die Amerikanische Besetzung Deutschlands*. R. Oldenbourg, 1995.

Herzog, Rudolf. *Dead Funny: Humor in Hitler's Germany*. Melville House, 2011.

Hill, Roland. *Time Out of Joint*. I. B. Tauris, 2007.

Hitler, Adolf. *Hitler's Table Talk*. Translated by Norman Cameron and R. H. Stevens. Enigma Books, 2000.

———. *Speeches and Proclamations, 1932-1945: The Chronicle of a Dictatorship*. Vol. 4: *The Years 1941-1945*. Edited by Max Domarus. Bolchazy-Carducci, 2004.

Hobe, Cord von, and Walter Görlitz. *Georg von Boeselager: A Rider's Life*. Vantage Press, 1998.

Hoffmann, Peter. *The History of the German Resistance*. Macdonald and Jane's Publishers, 1969.

———. *Hitler's Personal Security*. Da Capo Press, 2000.

———. *Stauffenberg: A Family History*. McGill-Queen's University Press, 2003.

———. *Stauffenbergs Freund: Die tragische Geschichte des Widerstandskämpfers Joachim Kuhn*. C. H. Beck, 2007.

Hollister, Paul and Strunsky, Robert, eds. *From D-Day through Victory in Europe*. Columbia Broadcasting System, 1945.

Hughes, Matthew, and Chris Mann. *Inside Hitler's Germany: Life Under the Third Reich*. Potomac Books, 2002.

Irving, David. *Nürnberg: The Last Battle*. Focal Point, 1996.

Jacobsen, Hans-Adolph, ed. "*Spiegelbild einer Verschwörung.*" 2 vols. Seewald, 1984. (Also referred to as the "Kaltenbrunner Papers.")

Jewish Virtual Library. www.jewishvirtuallibrary.org/.

John, Otto. *Twice Through the Lines*. Harper & Row, 1972.

Jörgensen, Christer. *Hitler's Espionage Machine*. Lyons Press, 2004.

Joseph, Detlef. *Nazis in the DDR*. Edition Ost, 2002.

Kershaw, Ian. *Hitler*. W. W. Norton, 2008.

Kiel, Lars-Broder, ed. *Hans Ulrich von Oertzen, Offizier und Widerstandskämpfer: ein Lebensbild in Brief und Erinnerungen*. Lukas Verlag, 2005.

Klee, Ernst. *Das Personenlexikon zum Dritten Reich*. Fischer Taschenbuch, 2003.

Klemperer, Klemens von. *German Resistance Against Hitler: The Search for Allies Abroad, 1938-1945*. Clarendon Press, 1994.

Knopp, Guido. *Hitler's Hitmen*. Sutton Publishing, 2002.

Koch, H. W. *In the Name of the Volk*. Barnes & Noble Books, 1989.

Komar, Gary. "Generaloberst Franz Halder, Chief of the General Staff—Patriot or Traitor?" *Axis History Factbook*. www.axishistory.com/index.php?id=3597.

König, Christoph, Birgit Wägenbaur, Andrea Frindt, Hanne Knickmann, and Volker Michel. *Internationales Germanistenlexikon, 1800-1950*. Walter de Gruyter, 2003.

Korda, Michael. *Ike: An American Hero*. HarperCollins, 2007.

Kuby, Erich. *The Russians and Berlin 1945*. Ballantine Books, 1969.

Lambert, Angela. *The Lost Life of Eva Braun*. St. Martin's Griffin, 2008.

Large, David Clay. *Contending with Hitler: Varieties of German Resistance in the Third Reich*. Cambridge University Press, 1994.

Leber, Annedore. *Conscience in Revolt*. Valentine & Mitchell, 1957.

Lees, Andrew. *Cities Perceived: Urban Society in European and American Thought, 1820-1940*. Manchester University Press, 1991.

Lemons, Everette. *The Third Reich: A Revolution of Ideological Inhumanity*. Vol. 2: *Death Mask of Inhumanity*. Lulu, 2006.

Lifton, Robert Jay. *The Nazi Doctors*. Basic Books, 1986.

Liss, Ulrich. *Westfront, 1939-1940*. Kurt Vowinckel, 1959.

Loeben, Elizabeth von. *Graf Marogna-Redwitz: Opfergang einer bayerischen Familie.* Tuduv-Verlagsgesellschaft, 1984.
Loeffel, Robert. *Family Punishment in Nazi Germany: Sippenhaft, Terror and Myth.* Palgrave Macmillan, 2012.
MacDonogh, Giles. *After the Reich.* Basic Books, 2007.
_____. *The Good German: Adam von Trott zu Solz.* Quartet Books, 1989.
Majdalany, Fred. *The Fall of Fortress Europe.* Modern Literary Editions, 1968.
Manvell, Roger. *The Conspirators: 20th July 1944.* Ballantine Books, 1971.
Manvell, Roger, and Heinrich Fraenkel. *The Canaris Conspiracy.* David McKay Company, 1969.
_____ and _____. *The Men Who Tried to Kill Hitler.* Frontline Books (an imprint of Pen and Sword Books), 2008.
Marsh, Charles. *Strange Glory.* Alfred A. Knopf, 2014.
Marshall, Charles F. *Discovering the Rommel Murder: The Life and Death of the Desert Fox.* Stackpole Books, 1994.
Mazower, Mark. *Inside Hitler's Greece: The Experience of Occupation, 1941–44.* Yale University Press, 1995.
Meding, Dorothee von. *Courageous Hearts: Women and the Anti-Hitler Plot of 1944.* Berghahn Books, 1997.
Meehan, Patricia. *The Unnecessary War.* Sinclair-Stevenson, 1995.
Megargee, Geoffrey. *War of Annihilation.* Rowman & Littlefield, 2007.
Metaxas, Eric. *Bonhoeffer: Pastor, Martyr, Prophet, Spy.* Thomas Nelson, 2011.
Meyer, Winfried. *Verschwörer im KZ.* Hentrich, 1999.
Mitcham, Samuel W., Jr. *Retreat to the Reich.* Stackpole Books, 2007.
_____. *Rommel's Desert Commanders.* Praeger, 2007.
Mitscherlich, Alexander, and Margarete Mitscherlich. *The Inability to Mourn.* Grove/Atlantic, 1984.
Moll, Helmut. *Zeugen für Christus: das Deutsche Martyrologium des 20. Jahrhunderts.* Vol. 1. Schöningh, 2006.
Moltke, Freya von. *Memories of Kreisau and the German Resistance.* University of Nebraska Press, 2003.
Moltke, Helmuth James von. *A German of the Resistance: The Last Letters of Count Helmuth James von Moltke.* Oxford University Press, second impression, 1948.
_____. *Letters to Freya.* Translated by Beata Ruhm von Oppen. Alfred A. Knopf, 1990.
Mommsen, Hans. *Alternatives to Hitler.* I. B. Tauris, 2003.
Moorhouse, Roger. *Killing Hitler.* Bantam Books, 2006.
Morgan, J. H. *Assize of Arms.* Oxford University Press, 1946.
Morgenthau, H. R. *Germany Is Our Problem.* Harper & Brothers, 1945.
Mueller, Michael. *Canaris: The Life and Death of Hitler's Spymaster.* U.S. Naval Institute Press, 2007.
Müller, Ingo. *Hitler's Justice.* Harvard University Press, 1991.
Müller, Josef. *Bis zur Letzten Konsequenz.* Suddeutscher, 1967.
National Council of the National Front of Democratic Germany, Documentation Center of the State Archives Administration of the German Democratic Republic. *Brown Book: War and Nazi Criminals in West Germany.* Zeit im Bild, 1965.
Newell, Terry. *Statesmanship, Character, and Leadership in America.* Palgrave Macmillan, 2012.

Nizer, Louis. *What to Do with Germany.* Ziff Davis Publishing Co., 1944.
Oberling, Ines. *Ernst Perels (1882–1945).* Verlag für Regionalgeschichte, 2005.
Olbrich, Hubert. *Carl Wentzel-Tutschenthal (1876–1944): Zum Schicksal eines Grossen Lebenswerkes im Wandel der Spezifisch Deutschen Geschichte.* Technische Universität, 1981.
Oleschinski, Brigitte. *Plötzensee Memorial Center.* German Resistance Memorial Center, 2002.
Orth, Barbara. *Gestapo im OP: Bericht der Krankenhausärztin Charlotte Pommer.* Lukas Verlag, 2012.
Osterroth, Franz. *Biographisches Lexikon des Sozialismus.* Vol. 1. Dietz, 1960.
Parssinen, Terry. *The Oster Conspiracy of 1938.* Harper Perennial, 2003.
Pechel, Rudolf. *Deutscher Widerstand.* E. Rentsch, 1947.
Pejsa, Jane. *Matriarch of Conspiracy: Ruth von Kleist, 1867–1945.* Kenwood, 1991.
Perk, Willy, and Willi Deutsch. *Ehrenbuch der Opfer von Berlin-Plötzensee.* Verlag das Europ. Buch-Westberlin, 1974.
Persico, Joseph E. *Nürnberg: Infamy on Trial.* Viking Penguin, 1994.
Peterson, Edward Norman. *Hjalmar Schacht: For and Against Hitler.* Christopher Publishing House, 1954.
Posner, Gerald L. *Hitler's Children.* Random House, 1991.
Rashke, Richard. *Useful Enemies: John Demjanjuk and America's Open-Door Policy for Nazi War Criminals.* Delphinium, 2013.
Rauch, Andreas M. *Ein Offizier gegen Hitler: Oberleutnant Dr. Randolph von Breidbach-Bürresheim (1912–1945).* Nomos, 2007.
Reitlinger, Gerald. *The SS: Alibi of a Nation.* Arms and Armour Press, 1981.
Richardi, Hans-Günter, Caroline Heiss, and Hans Heiss. *SS Geiseln in der Alpenfestung.* Edition Raetia, 2005.
Riebling, Mark. *Church of Spies: The Pope's Secret War Against Hitler.* Basic Books, 2015.
Ritter, Gerhard. *The German Resistance.* Frederick A. Praeger, 1958.
Das-Ritterkreuz. www.das-ritterkreuz.de.
Robertson, E. M. "Hitler's Planning for War and the Response of the Great Powers (1938–early 1939)." In *Aspects of the Third Reich*, edited by H. W. Koch. Macmillan, 1985.
Rothfels, Hans. *The German Opposition to Hitler.* Oswald Wolf Publishers, 1961.
Russell, Edward Frederick Langley. *Return of the Swastika?* David McKay Company, 1969.
Salewski, Michael, and Guntram Schulze-Wegener. *Kriegsjahr 1944: im Großen und im Kleinen.* Franz Steiner, 1995.
Scheurig, Bodo. *Henning von Tresc-kow.* Propyläen, 2004.
Schlabrendorff, Fabian von. *Revolt Against Hitler.* Eyre and Spottiswoode, 1948.
Schmidt, Eberhard. *The Hitler Conspirator: The Story of Kurt Baron von Plettenberg and Stauffenberg's Valkyrie Plot to Kill the Fuhrer.* Frontline Books/Pen and Sword, 2017.
Schlingensiepen, Ferdinand. *Dietrich Bonhoeffer 1906-1945: Martyr, Thinker, Man of Resistance.* A&C Black, 2010.
Schwerin, Detlef. *"Dann sind's die besten Köpfe, die man Henkt": Die junge Generation im Deutschen Widerstand.* Piper, 1991.
_____. *Die Jungen des 20. Juli 1944: Brucklmeier, Kessel,*

Schulenburg, Schwerin, Wussow, Yorck. Verlag der Nation, 1991.

Selig, Robert A. "America's Long Road to the Federal Republic of Germany." *German Life*, June/July 1998.

Sheftel, Yoram. *Defending Ivan the Terrible: The Justice Department's Conspiracy to Convict John Demjanjuk*. Regnery, 1996.

Shirer, William L. *End of a Berlin Diary*. Alfred A. Knopf, 1947.

_____. *The Rise and Fall of the Third Reich*. Simon & Schuster, 1960.

Smith, Howard K. *Last Train from Berlin*. Alfred A. Knopf, 1942.

Smith, Jean Edward, ed. *The Papers of General Lucius Clay*. Indiana University Press, 1974.

Speer, Albert. *Inside the Third Reich*. Avon Books, 1970.

Speidel, Hans. *Invasion 1944*. Paperback Library, 1950.

Spitzer, Rudolf. *Karl Seitz: Waisenknabe, Staatsprasident, Burgermeister von Wien*. F. Deuticke, 1994.

Steinbach, Peter, and Johannes Tuchel. *Lexikon des Widerstandes, 1933–1945*. C. H. Beck, 1998.

Steinhoff, Johannes, Peter Pechel, and Dennis Showalter. *Voices from the Third Reich*. Da Capo Press, 1994.

Stockhorst, Erich. *5000 Köpfe*. Arndt, 1985.

Teicholz, Tom. *The Trial of Ivan the Terrible: State of Israel vs. John Demjanjuk*. St. Martin's Press, 1990.

Thomas, Hugh. *The Murder of Adolf Hitler*. St. Martin's Press, 1995.

Thompson, Dorothy. *Listen, Hans*. Houghton Mifflin, 1942.

Thompson, Laurence. *The Greatest Treason*. William Morrow, 1968.

Toland, John. *Adolf Hitler*. Anchor Books, 1976.

Tooze, Adam. *Wages of Destruction: The Making and Breaking of the Nazi Economy*. Penguin Books, 2008.

Ueberschär, Gerd. *Für ein Anderes Deutschland*. Fischer Taschenbuch, 2006.

Van Roon, Ger. *German Resistance to Hitler: Count von Moltke and the Kreisau Circle*. Van Nostrand Reinhold, 1971.

Vassiltchikov, Marie. *The Berlin Diaries of Marie Vassiltchikov, 1940–1945*. Chatto & Windus, 1985.

Verheyen, Dirk. *The German Question*. Westview Press, 1999.

Vierhaus, Rudolf. *Deutsche Biographische Enzyklopäedie*. K.G. Saur, 2008.

_____. *The Secret War Against Hitler*. Pitman Publishing, 1965.

_____. *They Almost Killed Hitler*. Macmillan, 1947.

Wachsmann, Nikolaus. *Hitler's Prisons*. Yale University Press, 2004.

Wallechinsky, David, and Irving Wallace. *The People's Almanac, #3*. William Morrow, 1981.

Watson, Bruce. *Exit Rommel*. Stackpole Books, 2006.

Weigelt, Andreas. *Umschulungslager Existieren Nicht*. Brandenburgische Landeszentrale für Politische Bildung, 2001.

Weinberg, Gerhard. *The Foreign Policy of Hitler's Germany*. Vol. 2: *Starting World War II*. University of Chicago Press, 1980.

Weiß, Hermann. *Biographisches Lexikon zum Dritten Reich*. Fischer Taschenbuch, 2002.

West, Paul. *The Very Rich Hours of Count von Stauffenberg*. Harper & Row, 1980.

West, Nigel. *Historical Dictionary of Sexspionage*. Scarecrow Press, 2009.

Westermeyer, H. E. *The Fall of the German Gods*. Pacific Press, 1950.

Wheeler-Bennett, John. *The Nemesis of Power*. St. Martin's Press, 1954; Viking Press, 1967.

Wieland, Günther. *Das war der Volksgerichtshof*. Pfaffenweiler Presse, 1989.

Williamson, Gordon, and Ramiro Bujeiro. *Knight's Cross Oak-Leaves Recipients, 1941–1945*. Osprey, 2005.

Wistrich, Robert S. *Who's Who in Nazi Germany*. Routledge, 1995.

World Heritage Encyclopedia. worldheritage.org.

World War II Database. ww2db.com.

Wyden, Peter. *The Hitler Virus*. Arcade Publishing, 2002.

Zeller, Eberhard. *The Flame of Freedom*. University of Miami Press, 1969.

Zimmermann, Erich, and Hans-Adolf Jacobsen, eds. *Germans Against Hitler, July 20, 1944*. Press and Information Office, Federal Government of Germany, 1964.

Index

Numbers in *bold italics* indicate pages with illustrations

Abwehr 21, 34, 42, 44, 46, 50, 52–61, 90–92, 95, 98, 102–105, 114, 131, 138, 144–151, 157, 166, 170, 173–174, 177, 189, 227, 231–232
Adam, Wilhelm 183
Adenauer, Konrad 10, 52, 178, 181, 189–191, 197, 203
Alvensleben, Ludolf von 128
Alvensleben, Wichard von 32, 226
American press 47
Angermaier, Georg 188
Armed Forces of the State 13
Armster, Otto 167
Arosa Memorandum 119
assassination plots 23, 38
Attlee, Clement 204

Barth, Karl 149
Becher, Johannes 206
Beck, Ludwig 16, 23–24, 27–28, 35, 38–39, 45, 47, 50–52, 54–56, 65, 77, 81, 84, 87, 95, 98, 102, 105, 108–109, 113–114, 116, 118–119, 130, 142, 152, 154, 157, 161–162, 169, 183, 185–186, 189
Becker, Carl Heinrich 127
Bell, George, Bishop of Chichester 40, 56, 154
Below, Nikolaus von 27
Below, Otto von 27, 112
Bendlerblock 27, 34, 36, 84–86, 89–90, 98, 100, 105, 170, 182
Bendlerstraße 13–14, 26, 35, 39, 51, 92, 97, 161, 174, 181–182
Bentivegni, Egbert von 157
Berlin airlift 213
Bernardis, Robert 77, 79–80, 86, 92
Bernstorff, Albrecht von 41–42, 75, 136, 143

Bernstorff, Andres von 143–144
Bethge, Eberhard 137, 150, 167–168, 170–171
Black Orchestra 39
Blessing, Karl 191
Blomberg, Werner von 93, 95
Blumenthal, Albrecht von 89, 102, 149
Blumenthal, Hans-Jürgen von 79, 89, 101–102, 106
Blumentritt, Günther 99, 159, 195–196
Bock, Fedor von 101, 158, 162
Boehmer, Hasso von 16
Boeselager, Philipp von 24, 195
Bohlen und Halbach, Alfred Krupp von 184
Böhm, Franz 40
Böhme, Franz Friedrich 172
Böhmer, Hasso von 16, 142–143
Bolz, Eugen 38, 44, 121, 134
Bonhoeffer, Dietrich 18, *33*, 40, 44, 52, 56, 58, 60, 84, 134–138, 143, 148–150, 153–154, 168, 170–173, 188, 194, 200, 220
Bonhoeffer, Karl 22, 60, 136–138, 149
Bonhoeffer, Klaus 22, 135–139, 145, 188
Bonin, Bogislaw von 32, 226–227
Bormann, Martin 1, 48–49, 60, 74, 107, 188
Borsig, August Ernst von 157
Bosch, Robert 113
Bose, Chandra 94
Brandenburg-Görden Prison 41, 73–74, 105, 107, 139, 168, 173, 186
Brandt, Heinz 24, 26–27, 169
Brauchitsch, Walther von 30, 36, 61, 94, 114, 152, 158, 185
Braun, Eva 22, 26

Bredow, Ferdinand von 81, 146
Bredow, Hannah von 41
Breidbach-Bürresheim, Randolph von 194
Breitenbuch, Eberhard von 25, 31, 186–187
Brickner, Richard M. 205, 217
Brinkmann, Rudolf 114
British intelligence 53, 57
Brücklmeier, Eduard Wolfgang 124–125, 143
Bruner, Wilhelm 68
Brüning, Heinrich 108, 112, 120
Buchholz, Heinz 27
Buchholz, Peter 71, 124
Buhle, Walther 27, 61
Bumke, Erwin 145
Busch, Ernst 25, 186–187
Bussche-Streithorst, Axel von dem 16, 25, 31–32, 61, 167, 175–176, 198
Byrnes, James F. 211

Canaris, Erika 53, 231–233
Canaris, Wilhelm 18, 21–22, 34, 41, 47, 50, 52–61, 81, 84, 90, 104–105, 114, 131, 137, 140, 143, 147–148, 150, 154, 157, 166, 168–169, 172, 185, 189, 194, 200–202; diary 52, 58, 60–61
Case Green 113
Catholic Workers Movement 46, 108
Chamberlain, Neville 22, 54–55, 114, 185
Christian Democratic Union of Germany (CDU) 172, 179–181, 183, 192, 203
Churchill, Winston 2, 54, 56–57, 63, 114, 140, 168, 204, 207–208
Civilian Conspiracy Leaders Trial 111–120

245

Index

Clay, Lucius 212
collective guilt 210–211, 223
Cologne Circle 45–46, 108, 135
Cords, Helmuth 167
Cramer, Wilhelm Bernardo Walter 123–124
Criminal Police (KriPo) 49, 64–65
Crohne, Wilhelm 68–69, 75–76, 139–140, 169
Curtis, Lionel 131

Dahrendorf, Gustav 125–126, 186, 203
Dahrendorf, Ralf 125
Delbrück, Hans 136
Delbrück, Justus 136, 167, 188–189
Delbrück, Max 136
Delius, Kurt 86
Delp, Alfred 44, 46, 130, 132–134, 182, 187–188
denazification 206, 208, 210, 216, 223
deserters and homosexuals 224
Dietrich, Sepp 209
Dietze, Constantin von 40, 167
Disarmed Enemy Forces (DEF) 208
Djilas, Milovan 205
Dohna-Schlobitten, Heinrich Graf zu 44
Dohnanyi, Hans von 18, 22, 56, 58, 60–61, 102, 113, 136, 138–139, 145–151, 154, 170, 173, 188–189, 194, 200–201, 232
Dollfuss, Engelbert 49
Dönitz, Karl 10, 71, 90
Donovan, William 57–58, 231–233
Drechsel-Deuffenstein, Max-Ulrich Graf von 79
Dulles, Allen 42, 122, 148, 174
Dutch War Scare 55

Ebner, Karl 181
Eden, Anthony 40
Eichmann, Adolf 49, 201, 215
Einsiedel, Horst von 192–193
Eisenhower, Dwight D. 207–208
Elser, Johann Georg 22, 65
Enabling Acts 66
Engelhorn, Karl-Heinz 79, 104–105
Enterprise Seven 138, 146–147
Erdmann, Hans Otto 79
Ernst, Friedrich 167
Ersatzheer 31, 33, 35, 50, 92, 161–162
Erxleben, Friedrich 41, 167, 179–180
Eucken, Walter 40

European Recovery Program 211, 213, 238–239

Fahrner, Rudolf 199
Falkenhausen, Alexander Ernst von 169, 193–194, 227
Fellgiebel, Erich 27, 77, 87–88, 91
Finckh, Eberhard 79, 95, 99, 159, 196
First Conspiracy Trial 80–87
Flossenbürg concentration camp 58, 138, 143, 147–148, 150–151, 153–154, 169, 173, 183, 186, 200–201
Franco, Francisco 54
Frank, Hans 75, 85, 175
Frank, Reinhold 134
Frank-Schultz, Ehrengard 74
Freiburg Circle 40, 44, 135, 220
Freiburg University 40, 125
Freisler, Roland *17*, 42, 62, 67–75, *78*, 79–91, 93, 95, 97–99, 101, 103–104, 106, 109, 111, 116–121, 124–126, 128–130, 132–140, 144, 169, 173, 178, 183, 224
Freyend, Ernst John von 27
Fritsch, Werner von 23, 34, 64, 81, 93, 95, 113, 147, 154, 179
Fritzsche, Hans *17*, 167
Fromm, Friedrich 13–16, 26–27, 34–36, *37*, 50–52, 62, 84, 86, 92, 109, 139, 169

Gablentz, Otto Heinrich von der 172, 192
Gehlen, Reinhard 103, 205–206, 222
Gehre, Ludwig 58, 138, 143, 148, 150–151, 154, 200
German Communist Party (KDP) 18, 180, 203
German National People's Party (DNVP) 112, 118, 120, 124, 140
German resistance movement 1, 32, 39, 42, 56, 69, 119, 126, 154–155, 215
Gersdorff, Rudolf-Christoph von 24–25, 31, 154, 162, 167, 176–178
Gerstenmaier, Eugen 44, 86, 130, 133–134, 167, 181–183, 188
Gestapo interrogations 105, 155–156
Gisevius, Hans Bernd 16, 27, 36, 59, 64, 146, 148, 167, 173–175, 229
Gloeden, Elizbeth 110, 129
Gloeden, Erich 110, 128
Goebbels, Josef 8, 19, 26–28, 51, 71–72, 75, 92, 113, 197, 207
Goerdeler, Carl *11*, 14, 16, *17*, 18,

26, 35, 38, 40, 44–46, 51, 56, 62, 74–75, 83, 89, 102, 108–109, 111–119, 121, 123–129, 135, 140–141, 144, 148, 151–152, 159–160, 162, 169, 172, 179–180, 183–184, 186, 191, 194, 229
Goerdeler, Fritz 112
Goerdeler Circle 45–46, 113–118
Göring, Hermann 8–9, 26, 28–29, 45, 49, 57, 64, 85, 127, 130, 174, 183, 211
Gostomski, Viktor von 80
Gottberg, Helmuth von *17*
Graf, Willi 39, 73
Groscurth, Helmuth 55, 59, 185
Groß, Nikolaus 44, 46, 108, 130, 134–135
Groß Denkte 60
Großdeutschland Guard Battalion 34–35
Guderian, Heinz 9, 51, 77, 83, 109, 152
Guttenberg, Karl Ludwig von und zu 136, 151

Habermann, Max 118, 120, 159, 180
Haeften, Hans Bernd von 33–34, 36, *78*, 91, 94, 100
Haeften, Werner von 27, 33–36, 51, 77, 91, 94–95, 100, 182
Haffner, Harold 68, 75–76, 139, 192; see also Hartmann, Heinrich
Hagen, Albrecht von 61, 77, 79–80, 86–87, 91, 198
Hagen, Maximilian von 41, 167
Hahn, Kurt 79
Halder, Franz 22–23, 41, 52, 55, 83–84, 115, 146, 152, 163–164, 184–186, 227
Halem, Nikolaus-Christoph von 41, 148
Hamm, Eduard 160, 194
Hammerstein, Ludwig von *17*, 167
Hammerstein-Equord, Kurt von 23, 46, 81, 95, 183, 229
Hanke, Karl 104
Hansen, Georg-Alexander 61, 77, 87, 90–91, 104
Hardenberg, Carl-Hans Graf von *17*, 79, 101, 161
Harnack, Arvid von 136, 140, 193
Harnack, Ernst von 125, 136, 139
Harnack, Fritz von 140
Hartmann, Heinrich 76; see also Haffner, Harold
Hase, Paul von *17*, 26, 77, 79–80, 84, 92, 107
Hassel, Kurt 167
Hassell, Ulrich von 16, 38, 45,

74, 111, 114, 118–120, 130, 132, 151, 161, 169, 229
Haubach, Theodor 38, 44, 109, 130, 134, 182
Haushofer, Albrecht 136, 143–145
Haushofer, Karl 144–145
Hayessen, Egbert 77, *78*, 91–92, 98
Heck, Alfons 18–19
Heisenberg, Werner 45
Helldorf, Wolf-Heinrich von 23, 52, *78*, 88, 91–93, 95, 197
Herfurth, Otto 107
Hermes, Andreas 38, 167, 179, 181, 203
Hess, Rudolf 8, 21, 144–145, 222
Heusinger, Adolf 27–28
Heydrich, Reinhard 48–49, 55–59, 64, 72, 107, 125, 144, 175, 185
Himmler, Heinrich 7–10, 14, 22–23, 26–28, 34, 41–42, 48–49, 53–59, 64–65, 70, 79, 85, 105, 115, 121–122, 135, 143, 148, 152, 158, 164, 172, 174, 200, 226, 231–232
Hindenburg, Paul von 29, 34, 66, 112, 164, 182
Hitler Youth 18–19, 68, 85, 111, 126, 132, 171, 222
Hochverrat 18, 32
Hoepner, Erich 14, 29–30, 38, 52, 79–84, 95, 142, 183, 227
Hofacker, Cäsar von 62, 91, 96–97, 99, 158, 229
Hoffman, Heinrich 23
Hoover, Herbert 211
Horst, Max 158, 179
Hößlin, Roland-Heinrich von 102–103, 106–107
Huber, Kurt 39, 73
Huppenkothen, Walter 48–49, 58–59, 143, 146, 154, 199–202
Husen, Paulus van 191–192
Husserl, Edmund 40

Infantry Regiment 9 16, 85, 89, 142, 161, 163, 175–176

Jaenecke, Erwin 152
JCS Directive 1067 208, 211
JCS Directive 1779 211
Jennewein, Max 136
Jessen, Jens-Peter 16, 79, 107–108
Jessen, Sydney 167
Jodl, Alfred 27–28, 159, 232
John, Hans 135–138, 167, 189–191
John, Otto 136–139, 150, 167, 189–191

Kaiser, Hermann 3, 44, 77, 97, 100, 108–110, 120, 134, 148, 167

Kaiser, Jakob 38, 44, 110, 118, 141, 159, 167, 180–181, 203
Kaltenbrunner, Ernst 10, 28, 42, 48–50, 59–60, 86, 90, 97, 107, 147, 162, 166, 174–175, 181, 200, 226; papers 86, 119, 122, 142
Kapp Putsch 54, 92, 125, 141
Katyn Massacre 177
Keitel, Bodewin 142
Keitel, Wilhelm 26–28, 51, 56, 59, 63, 77, 130–131, 148, 158, 174, 183, 185
Kempner, Franz 136
Kiep, Otto 41–42, 144
Kißling, Georg Conrad 160
Klamroth, Bernhard 77, *78*, 91–92
Klamroth, Johannes 77, 91–92
Klausing, Friedrich Karl *17*, 26, 28, 77, 79–80, 85–86, 92, 176
Kleist-Schmenzin, Ewald Heinrich von *17*, 25, 31, 167, 170, 195
Kleist-Schmenzin, Ewald von 16, 25, 54, 139–140, 169–170, 215
Kleist, Bernd von 101
Kluge, Günther von 24–25, 83, 85, 95–97, 100, 109, 115, 158–159, 178, 186–187, 195–196
Knaak, Gerhard 79
König, Lothar 44, 187–188, 194
Kordt, Erich 167
Kordt, Theodor 167
Kortzfleisch, Joachim von 106, 123, 161
Kosney, Herbert 136–137
Kracke, Franz 60
Kranke, Theodor 96
Kranzfelder, Alfred 87, 90
Kreisau Circle 30, 41–46, 82, 89, 93–94, 98, 117–119, 125–127, 130–135, 144, 157, 172, 179, 182, 187–188, 191–193
Kress, Hans von 130
Kristallnacht 30, 40, 88, 93, 105, 114, 121, 162
Krosigk, Ludwig von 165
Kuebart, Wilhelm 105
Kuhn, Joachim 61, 77, 87, 91, 167, 197–199
Künzer, Richard 41–42, 136
Kurstenhan, Kurt 58, 61
Kuznitzky, Elisabeth 128–129

Lampe, Adolf 40, 167
Lancken, Fritz von der 107
Landesverrat 18
Langbehn, Carl 121–122, 143–144, 169
Lanz, Hubert 24, 178
Lautz, Ernst 76, 122
Leber, Annedore 126

Leber, Julius 16, 18, 30–31, 38, 89, 120, 125–127, 159, 182, 186, 192, 220
Leeb, Wilhelm Ritter von 81, 158, 195
Lehndorff-Steinort, Heinrich von 100–101
Lejeune-Jung, Paul 16, 38, 111, 119–120
Leon, Friedrich 167–168
Leonrod, Ludwig von 77, 107, 111
Letterhaus, Bernhard 38, 79, 108, 135
Leuninger, Franz 136, 139, 141–142
Leuschner, Wilhelm 38, 44, 74–75, 82, 111, 115–117, 120, 125–126, 134, 139, 141–142, 151, 159, 180, 186, 220
Ley, Robert 1, 20, 117
Liberal Democratic Party (LDP) 204
Liedig, Franz Maria 22, 227
Lindemann, Fritz 77, 91, 109–111, 128–129, 229
Lindemann, Max 111, 129
Linstow, Hans Otfried von *17*, 79, 95–96, 99–100
List, Wilhelm von 158
Lochner, Louis 47, 189
Loeser, Ewald Oskar 38, 184
Loringhoven, Bernd Freytag von 166
Loringhoven, Wessel Freytag von 60–61, 77, 166, 177
Lübecker Volksboten (newspaper) 125
Lukaschek, Hans 141, 191–192
Lünick, Ferdinand Freiherr von *17*
Lutter, Kurt 21
Luxembourg Agreement 218
Lynar, Wilhelm-Friedrich Graf zu 77, 107

Maaß, Hermann 115, 117, 125–127, 186
Majnemer, Fiszel 168
Malmedy Massacre 209
Manstein, Erich von 24, 81, 106, 109, 190, 195
Marcks, Karl *see* Marks, Carl
Marks, Carl 129, 136
Marogna-Redwitz, Rudolf Graf von 52, 79, 105, 107
Marshall, George C. 210–211, 238
Marshall Plan *see* European Recovery Program
Marx, Wilhelm 160
Matuschka, Michael von 103–104, 142
Meichßner, Joachim 77, 107

Menzies, Stuart 57
Meyer, Herbert *17*
MI6 42, 53–54, 56–57
Mierendorff, Carlo 134, 186
Mildner, Rudolf 181
Moabit Lehrter Stasse Prison 42, *43*, 79, 120, 124, 133, 135, 142, 144–145, 167, 172–173, 179, 187, 189, 192, 194
Model, Walther 159
Moll, Carlos 136
Molotov, Vyacheslav 209–210
Moltke, Freya von 132
Moltke, Helmuth James von 12, 18, 41–44, 74, 82, 94, 118, 130–134, 148, 150, 162, 172, 182, 187–188, 192–193, 214, 220
Mordregister *see* Murder Register
Morgenthau, Henry 206–208, 217–218, 234–237; Morgenthau Plan 206–208, 234–237
Müller, Heinrich 122, 135, 153, 155
Müller, Josef 52, 56, 58, 60, 172–173, 194, 227
Müller, Otto 46–47, 108
Munich Agreement 29, 54–55, 81, 83, 96, 114, 185
Munzinger, Ernst 136
Murder Register 79, 90
Mussolini, Benito 21, 197

National Socialist Freedom Party (NSFP) 92
National Socialist German Worker's Party (NSDAP) 3, 14, 67, 72
National Socialist Motor Corps (NSKK) 68
Nebe, Artur 22, 61, 64–65, 139, 174
Nieden, Wilhelm zur 136
Niemöller, Martin 138, 149, 168, 227
Night of the Long Knives 34, 81, 120, 130, 139, 145–146, 166, 170; *see also* Operation Hummingbird; Operation Kolibri
Noske, Gustav 168, 231
Nürnberg trials 12, 59, 71, 76, 167, 174, 196, 201, 206, 214

Oberkommando der Wehrmacht (OKW) 14, 28, 34, 41, 52, 56–57, 86–87, 98, 100, 105, 108, 130–131, 138, 147, 152, 165, 183, 192
Oberkommando des Herres, German Army ground forces high command (OKH) 27, 30, 34, 55, 61, 81, 84–85, 87, 91, 103, 109–110, 160, 162, 166, 183, 185, 198

Oertzen, Hans Ulrich von 77, 106, 160–161
Office of Strategic Services (OSS) 20, 57, 59, 122, 132, 148, 174
Olbricht, Friedrich 13–14, 26–27, 31, 34–38, 51, 77, 84, 91, 97, 105–106, 110, 115, 119, 147, 164, 167, 169
Operation Barbarossa 33, 57, 65, 81–85, 95–96, 99, 102, 152, 191, 196
Operation Blackcock 196
Operation Foxley 25
Operation Hummingbird 10; *see also* Night of the Long Knives; Operation Kolibri
Operation Kolibri *see* Night of the Long Knives; Operation Hummingbird
Operation Overlord 103
Operation Spark 16, 24, 195
Operation Thunderstorm 10, 48
Oppen, Georg-Sigismund von *17*
Oster, Hans 16, 18, 21–22, 34, 39, 52, 55–56, 58, 60, 64–65, 81, 84, 90, 95, 98, 102, 113, 138, 143, 146–151, 154, 167, 169, 173–174, 189, 194, 200, 232

Papen, Franz von 94, 112, 130, 139, 145
Peiper, Jochen 209
People's Court *17*, 28, 41–42, 50–51, 62–63, 65–70, 73–77, 81–82, 84–94, 96, 99–100, 105–106, 108, 111–112, 116–125, 128–130, 133, 137–140, 143, 172, 178, 184, 186; *see also* VGH; Volksgerichtshof
Perels, Ernst 138
Perels, Friedrich 135–136, 138
Petersdorff, Horst von 129, 227
Pilati, Oskar von 168
Plaas, Helmuth 150
Planck, Erwin 108, 114, 129–130, 134
Plettenberg, Elisabeth von 42
Plettenberg, Kurt von *17*, 161–162
Plettenberg-Lenhausen, Gisela von 229
Plettenberg-Lenhausen, Walther von 162, 229
Plötzensee Prison 34, 42, 44, 65, 69, 71, 73, 79–110, 116–135, 140–143, 167, 192
Poelchau, Harald 71, 132
Popitz, Johannes 16, 18, 45, 108, 113, 119–122, 130, 161, 169, 183, 189

Post-Hitler cabinet 38, 48, 150, 180
Potsdam conference 204
Preysing, Konrad von 133, 188
Prinz Albrecht Straße 27, 42, 58, 116, 135, 151, 162, 169
Probst, Christoph 39, 73
Puttkamer-Nippoglense, Jesco von 27, 168

Quirnheim, Albrecht von 26–27, 34, *35*, 36, *37*, 51, 77, 91, 99, 102

Rabenau, Friedrich von 143, 152–153
Rahtgens, Karl Ernst 77, 95, 100
Ravensbrück 42, 128, 140, 144, 170, 180–181
Reckzeh, Paul 41, 150, 165, 180
Reclam-Schlee, Hans Joachim von 168
Red Orchestra 39, 58, 136, 140, 193
Rehn, Fritz 68
Reich Ministry of Justice 67, 72, 75, 79, 145
Reich Security Main Office (RSHA) 42, 49–50, 56, 90, 104, 129, 135, 194, 201
Reichenau, Walther von 158, 185
Reichwein, Adolf 18, 94, 126–127, 134, 182, 186, 193
Remer, Otto Ernst 26–27, 100, 107, 196–197, 213
Reparations 165, 207, 217–220, 223, 234–235
Ribbentrop, Joachim von 22, 42, 114, 124, 143–144, 232
Riesen, Horst von 38
Ritter, Gerhard 40, 168
Roeder, Manfred 57
Röhm, Ernst 145
Rommel, Erwin 24, 31, 46, 62–64, 91, 94, 96–97, 99, 103, 157–158, 178–179, 193
Rönne, Alexis von *17*, 79, 103–105
Roosevelt, Franklin D. 20, 57, 189, 192, 197, 206–208, 232, 234
Rösch, Augustinus 44, 132–133, 168, 187–188
Royse, Ervin 153–155
Rundstedt, Gerd von 61–63, 77, 81, 109, 158, 162, 168, 195–196
Russian Intelligence Division (SMERSCH) 198
Russian Special Camp Jamlitz 189
Russian Special Camp 6 189

Index

Sachsenhausen Concentration Camp 22, 146, 152, 154, 165–166, 168–169, 180, 195, 200–201
Sack, Alfons 148
Sack, Karl 58, 64, 109, 143, 146–148, 150, 154, 200
Sadrozinski, Joachim 77, 107
Salviati, Hans Victor von 136
Sasse, Hermann 149
Sauerbruch, Ferdinand 45
Sauerbruch, Peter 103
Sayn-Wittgenstein, Heinrich von 25
Schacht, Hjalmar 112, 114, 130, 167, 169, 174–175, 191, 227
Schack, Adolf von 84, 92, 105, 107
Schellenberg, Walter 50, 58, 157, 201
Schlabrendorff, Fabian von 13–14, 16, 23–24, 32, 36, 46, 59, 64–65, 75, 106, 110, 147, 150–151, 161–163, 167–170, 177, 215, 227
Schleicher, Kurt von 81, 110, 112, 121, 130
Schleicher, Renate 137, 170–172
Schleicher, Rüdiger 135–137, 149, 168
Schmorell, Alex 39, 73
Schneppenhorst, Ernst 136, 151–152
Scholl, Hans 39, 73
Scholl, Sophie 39, 73
Scholz-Babisch, Friedrich 79, 104, 106
Schönfeld, Hans 40
Schrader, Werner 55, 58–62, 77, 157
Schulenburg-Lieberose, Albrecht Frederick von der 161
Schulenburg-Tessow, Ehrengard Martha von der 123
Schulenburg-Tessow, Friedrich-Werner von der 38, 88–89, 120, 122–123, 125
Schulenburg-Tessow, Fritz-Dietlof von der *17*, 23, 77, 82, 85–89, 91, 98, 103, 120, 122–123, 141–142, 175
Schulze-Büttger, Georg 79, 105–106
Schumacher, Kurt 10
Schumann, Georg 129
Schwamb, Ludwig 125, 134
Schwanenfeld, Ulrich Schwerin von 30, 38–39, 77, 82, 86, 98, 125
Schwarz Rot Gold 134
Schwarzenstein, Herbert Mumm von 143
Second Conspiracy Trial 87–91

Second Quebec Conference 207
Security Police (SiPo) 49, 64
Seitz, Karl 105, 181
Settle, Edwin 155
Shirer, William L. 22, 47, 55, 206
Sicherheitsdienst (SD-Security Division) 19, 56
Sierks, Hans Ludwig 128–129, 136
SiPo *see* Security Police
Smend, Günther 77, 100
Social Democrat Party (SDP) 116, 128 141–142, 181, 186, 203, 224
Social Democrats 30, 46–47, 66, 89, 115, 118, 181, 186, 190, 220
Socialist Reich Party 197, 213
Solf, Hanna 40–43, 144
Solf, Lagi 41, 43
Solf, Wilhelm 40
Solf Circle 40–43, 144, 165, 180
Solf Tea Party 138, 150, 180
Sonderegger, Franz 58, 61, 201
Sonnleithner, Franz von 27
Sossimov, Sergi 136
Special Indian Bureau 93
Special Operations Executive (SOE) 25
Speer, Albert 21, 48, 51, 144, 183
Speidel, Hans 24, 46, 62, 158, 178–179
Sperr, Franz 44, 130, 132–134, 160
SS and Gestapo trials 50, 143–155
Staehle, Wilhelm 136
Stalin, Josef 123, 164, 177, 190, 197, 204–205, 211–212, 222, 224
Stalingrad, Battle of 115
Stauffenberg, Alexander von 29, 229
Stauffenberg, Berthold von 18, 26, 30, 82, 86–87, 89–90
Stauffenberg, Claus von 2, 7–10, *11*, 13, 16, 18, 21, 24–27, 29–34, *35*, 36, 38–39, 51, 60–62, 77, 84–87, 89–91, 94–99, 101–106, 110, 116, 121, 125–126, 132–134, 140, 160–162, 164, 166, 170, 175–177, 182, 194–195, 198–199, 214, 229
Stauffenberg, Hans von 176
Stauffenberg, Marie Gabriele von 198, 230
Steinäcker, Hans-Joachim von 168
Stella Matutina College 133, 187
Steltzer, Theodor 130, 168, 172 182, 203
Stieff, Hellmuth 24, 60, 77, 79–80, 84–85, 87, 91, 110, 198

Stimmen der Zeit (Voices of the Time) 133
Strachwitz, Hyazinth von 24, 178
Streicher, Julius 127
Streithofen, Basilius Heinrich 211
Strünck, Elisabeth 148, 230
Strünck, Theodor 79, 143, 148, 150, 154
Stülpnagel, Carl-Heinrich von 77, 81, 87, 95–97, 99, 158–159, 178, 183, 196
Stülpnagel, Joachim von 163
Sturmabteilung (SA; Brownshirts) 1

Tegel Prison 47, 71, 107, 124, 132–133, 150, 154
Thadden, Elisabeth von 41–42
Thiele, Fritz 77
Thierack, Otto 51, 68, 70–71, 73–74
Third Conspiracy Trial 91–95
Thoma, Busso 79, 100, 134
Thomas, Georg 34, 61, 130, 169, 183, 227
Thompson, Dorothy 131
Thompson, Leslie A. 153
Thorbeck, Otto 58–59, 143, 146–148, 199–202
Thüngen, Karl von 106–107, 161
Todt Organization 13, 128
treason convictions 223–224
Tresckow, Gerd von *17*, 79, 163
Tresckow, Henning von 16, *17*, 23–24, 31–32, 35–36, 61, 77, 79, 85, 101, 106, 110, 142, 146, 150, 154, 158–164, 169, 177, 186, 193, 198, 227
Trotha, Carl Dietrich von 192–193
Trott, Adam zu Solz von 44, **78**, 82, 91–95, 144, 163, 182
Truman, Harry S 204–205, 208, 213
Tyrol Prison 84, 97, 169, 173, 183, 186, 194, 199, 226

Üxküll-Gyllenband, Nikolaus von 104

Vansittart, Robert 113, 140
Vassiltchikov, George 19, 91, 93
Vassiltchikov, Marie 19, 25, 49, 91, 94
Vermehren, Erich 42, 230
VGH 28, 50, 67–70, 73–76, 79, 84–85, 91, 95, 97–98, 101–108, 111, 122–123; 127–129, 132, 134–136, 139–144, 148, 169, 179–180, 183, 186, 189, 192, 194, 198, 223–224; *see also*

People's Court; Volksgerichtshof
Vietinghoff, Heinrich von 32, 226
Voigt, Friedrich 139–142
Volksgerichtshof 28, 50, 67; *see also* People's Court; VGH
Voß, Hans-Alexander von *17*, 106, 163–164

Waffen SS 14, 176, 211
Wagner, Eduard 26, 61, 77, 100, 108, 164
Wagner, Siegfried 79, 100, 102, 165
Waldheim, Kurt 52
Wallace, Henry A. 205
Wartenburg, Peter Yorck von 18, 30, 38, 43–44, 77, 79–80, 82–83, 86, 89–92, 98, 182, 188, 191
Wednesday Society 44–45, 108, 121
Wehrle, Hermann 104, 111
Weizsäcker, Ernst von 55, 124, 167
Weizsäcker, Richard von 176
Wentzel-Teutschenthal, Carl 127–128
Wheeler-Bennett, John 13, 20, 36, 113
White Rose 39, 73
Wiegand, Willi 168
Wiersich, Oswald 139, 142
Willisen, Achim Freiherr von *17*
Winterfeldt, Hans Dietlof von 168
Wirmer, Josef 38, 74, 111, 117–118, 120, 148, 159, 180
Wirth, Josef 41, 143
Witzleben, Erwin von 14, 22–23, 25, 28, 34, 38, 74, 77, 79–82, 84, 90–91, 95, 98, 146, 158, 163, 183, 186, 194
Wolf, Erich 40
Wolf, Karl 144
Wolf's Lair 26–27, 33, 85, 88, 166

X-Report 58–60, 173

Zarden, Arthur 41, 165–166
Zastrow, Berengar von 168
Zeller, Eberhard 14, 116, 119, 124, 127, 199
Zeughaus attempt 177
Ziegler, Delia 167
Ziehlberg, Gustav Heisterman von 198
Zitzewitz-Muttrin, Friedrich-Carl von 168

www.ingramcontent.com/pod-product-compliance
Lightning Source LLC
Chambersburg PA
CBHW081548300426
44116CB00015B/2799